Remembering the Covenants in Song

Remembering the Covenants in Song

An Intertextual Study of the Abrahamic
and Mosaic Covenants in Psalm 105

YOUNG-SAM WON

WIPF & STOCK · Eugene, Oregon

REMEMBERING THE COVENANTS IN SONG
An Intertextual Study of the Abrahamic and Mosaic Covenants in Psalm 105

Copyright © 2019 Young-Sam Won. All rights reserved. Except for brief quotations in critical publications or reviews, no part of this book may be reproduced in any manner without prior written permission from the publisher. Write: Permissions, Wipf and Stock Publishers, 199 W. 8th Ave., Suite 3, Eugene, OR 97401.

Wipf & Stock
An Imprint of Wipf and Stock Publishers
199 W. 8th Ave., Suite 3
Eugene, OR 97401

www.wipfandstock.com

PAPERBACK ISBN: 978-1-5326-8118-9
HARDCOVER ISBN: 978-1-5326-8119-6
EBOOK ISBN: 978-1-5326-8120-2

Manufactured in the U.S.A.   08/20/19

Biblia Hebraica Stuttgartensia, edited by Karl Elliger and Wilhelm Rudolph, Fifth Revised Edition, edited by Adrian Schenker, © 1977 and 1997 Deutsche Bibelgesellschaft, Stuttgart. Used by permission.

Scripture quotations marked (NIV) are taken from the Holy Bible, New International Version®, NIV®. Copyright © 1973, 1978, 1984, 2011 by Biblica, Inc.™ Used by permission of Zondervan. All rights reserved worldwide. www.zondervan.com The "NIV" and "New International Version" are trademarks registered in the United States Patent and Trademark Office by Biblica, Inc.™

Thank you, Hanna, for your constant love and support, and thank you to my wonderful kids Rachel, Caleb, and Christopher for your boundless encouragement. Each of you has painted a lovely picture of *hesed* for me.

Thank you, Mom and Dad, for modeling a lifelong love for God's word.
I hope this love shows in every aspect of this work.

Contents

Preface | ix
Acknowledgments | xiii
Abbreviations | xv
Introduction | xix

1 Studying the Covenants: Then and Now | 1
2 An Overview of Intertextuality: A Many-Splendored Thing | 45
3 A Novel Approach to Biblical Intertextuality | 78
4 A Song of Covenants: An Exegetical Study of Psalm 105 | 90
5 A Rhetorical Reading of Psalm 105: Text and Subtext | 125
6 The Abrahamic Covenant: Patriarchal Promises | 139
7 The Mosaic Covenant: From Covenant People to Chosen Nation | 153
8 An Analysis of the Covenant Intertextualities in Psalm 105 | 186
9 Conclusion: Covenant Insights from a Song | 218

Appendix A: Author's Translation of Psalm 105 [MT] | 227
Appendix B: Covenant-Related Formulas | 235

Bibliography | 237
Scripture Index | 251

Preface

A VOICE FROM THE PAST

IN THE PROCESS OF searching for a viable dissertation topic, I found myself drawn to the complexities of the relationship between the Abrahamic promises and the Mosaic law. I observed that contemporary discussion is often shaped by modern Christian interests such as the conditionality of biblical covenants and the significance of the Mosaic law in light of the New Testament. What seemed to be missing were discussions of the Abrahamic and Mosaic covenants that were framed in terms of the ancient Israelite context in which these covenant traditions were situated. I whimsically mused that it would be enlightening if one could interview an Old Testament figure representing Israel's covenant community. Who better to consult than someone who had a lived perspective on Israel's history combined with an insider's understanding of the two covenant traditions?

In seeking such a voice, a promising text was found in an unexpected place: Book IV of the Psalter. Psalm 105 is postexilic song that recalls Israel's history in terms of the Abrahamic and Mosaic covenants. Within the psalm's historical narration are multiple intertextual references to the Abrahamic promise of land as well as the laws and statutes that define the Mosaic covenant. This unique confluence of historical narration that addresses both covenants only occurs in one other text, Nehemiah 9–10. This exploration of Psalm 105 was undertaken in the hopes that the psalmist's understanding of the Abrahamic promises and the Mosaic covenant obligations might yield fresh insights on the relationship between these two defining covenants.

The confluence of both covenants in the historical narration of Psalm 105 presented a promising opportunity to discern the psalmist's understanding of the two covenants and perhaps gain some insight into the covenant-theology of the postexilic remnant. Since the psalmist refers back to the Abrahamic promise of land and the Mosaic law, it seemed fitting to undertake an intertextual study of this postexilic song in light of the seminal covenant-making narratives and covenant texts in the Pentateuch. I looked forward to gleaning fresh insights on the Abrahamic and Mosaic covenant relationship by listening to a voice from a fascinating time period in Israel's history.

THE METHODOLOGICAL CHALLENGE OF INTERTEXTUALITY

This work is a revision of my doctoral dissertation which features two historical surveys of scholarship. The first historical overview understandably entails the study of biblical covenants with an emphasis on the intercovenantal relationship between the Abrahamic and Mosaic covenants. A second historical survey is unorthodox, but the complicated origin and evolution of the concept of intertextuality seemed worthy of a dedicated discussion.

Though the term intertextuality was coined in the 1960s by Julia Kristeva, the history of the concept precedes poststructuralist philosophy and involves various perspectives spanning the fields of philosophy, literary criticism, and biblical studies. The way literary critics and linguists approach intertextuality, literary sources, and influence informs the study of intertexts—allusions, quotations, echoes, and references—in the field of biblical studies. Understanding the way intertextual studies have evolved has proven invaluable in developing the present approach to the intertextual covenant references in Psalm 105.

In the history of intertextual studies done by biblical scholars, there is no consensus regarding the definition, identification, and rhetorical analysis of intertextual devices. In developing the present method for this work, relevance theory has proven to be a valuable means of understanding referential activity in communication. Since relevance theory is not commonly used in biblical studies, I have included a discussion of how this theory informs the method used to identify allusions and literary references for the purpose of assessing rhetorical function and effect.

Though the two chapters of historical survey and methodological discussion are rather hefty, my aim is to provide the reader with a fuller sense of the scholarship that precedes and informs this work. These discussions of backgrounds and method are designed to serve as a useful introduction and bibliographic resource regarding the study of biblical covenants and intertextuality in biblical writings. While these introductory chapters provide useful context for this study, the introductory chapters and the investigation at the core of this work can be read and engaged as distinct units. The reader should find it equally fruitful to work through the historical and methodological discussions or proceed directly to the intertextual study of the covenant references in Psalm 105.

Acknowledgments

THIS WORK WAS ORIGINALLY my doctoral dissertation at Dallas Theological Seminary. As such, I am indebted to my mentors Gordon Johnston and Robert Chisholm Jr. Their influence goes all the way back to my days as a ThM student at Dallas Seminary. It was then that both of these teachers convinced me to switch from New Testament to Old Testament studies. They did so, not by any heavy-handed persuasion, but by teaching biblical Hebrew and the Old Testament with such expertise and enthusiasm that I was drawn into the study of the Old Testament. Their encouragement and guidance planted me firmly in this wonderful field of study.

It was the opportunity to work with both of these mentors that brought me back to Dallas to pursue a PhD in Old Testament studies. Their steady and generous guidance has been a great help both in the classroom and in the writing of this work. I especially appreciate Gordon who has not only been a wonderful supervisor, but a good friend. Gordon has been a steadying influence as I wrestled with this research from conception to publication.

In addition to my mentors, I am grateful to Dr. Richard Averbeck for his oversight as my outside reader. I am especially thankful for his enlightening insights regarding the nature and function of biblical covenants. His influence played no small part in helping me develop key ideas regarding the inter-covenantal dynamic of the Abrahamic and Mosaic covenants. Thank you also to Dr. David Klingler for his crucial insights on the validation of literary allusions. Dr. Klingler's dissertation presented an innovative way of assessing biblical intertextuality in terms of referential activity in human communication and rhetorical function in literary works.

Finally, this work reflects the influence of many excellent teachers and fellow students at Dallas Theological Seminary. I have had the privilege of growing in a community that has nurtured me from my earliest days as a master's student to the conclusion of my doctoral studies.

Soli Deo Gloria,
Sam Won
April 23, 2019

Abbreviations

AB	Anchor Bible
AC	Abrahamic covenant
ANE	ancient Near Eastern or ancient Near East
AOTC	Apollos Old Testament Commentary
AYBRL	Anchor Yale Bible Reference Library
BA	*Biblical Archaeologist*
BCOTWP	Baker Commentary on the Old Testament Wisdom and Psalms
Bib	*Biblica*
BTCB	Brazos Theological Commentary on the Bible
BibOr	Biblica et Orientalia
BZ	*Biblische Zeitschrift*
BZAW	Beihefte zur Zeitschrift für die alttestamentliche Wissenschaft
CBQ	*Catholic Biblical Quarterly*
CBSC	The Cambridge Bible for Schools and Colleges
CC	Continental Commentaries
D	The Deuteronomist
E	The Elohist
FOTL	The Forms of the Old Testament Literature
GKC	Gesenius, Wilhelm. *Gesenius' Hebrew Grammar*. Edited by E. Kautzsch. Translated by A. E. Cowley. 2nd ed. Oxford: Clarendon, 1910.
HALOT	Koehler, L., W. Baumgartner, and J. J. Stamm. *The Hebrew and Aramaic Lexicon of the Old Testament*. 2 vols. Translated

	and edited under the supervision of M. E. J. Richardson. Leiden: Brill, 2001.
HTR	*Harvard Theological Review*
IBE	Inner-biblical exegesis
ICC	International Critical Commentary
Int	*Interpretation*
J	The Yahwist
JAOS	*Journal of the American Oriental Society*
JBL	*Journal of Biblical Literature*
JETS	*Journal of the Evangelical Theological Society*
JNES	*Journal of Near Eastern Studies*
JNSL	*Journal of Northwest Semitic Languages*
Joüon	Joüon, P. *A Grammar of Biblical Hebrew*. Translated and Revised by T. Muraoka. 2 vols. Subsidia biblica 14/1–2. Rome: Editrice Pontificio Istituto Biblico-Rome, 1991.
JPS	Jewish Publication Society
JSOT	*Journal for the Study of the Old Testament*
JSOTSup	Journal for the Study of the Old Testament: Supplement Series
JSS	Journal of Semitic Studies
JTS	*Journal of Theological Studies*
MC	Mosaic covenant
MSJ	*The Master's Seminary Journal*
NAC	New American Commentary
NCBC	New Cambridge Bible Commentary
NIB	*The New Interpreter's Bible*. 12 vols. Edited by Leander E. Keck. Nashville: Abingdon, 2006–2009.
NIBCOT	New International Bible Commentary on the Old Testament
NICOT	New International Commentary on the Old Testament
NIDOTTE	*New International Dictionary of Old Testament Theology and Exegesis*. 5 vols. Edited by Willem A. VanGemeren. Grand Rapids: Zondervan, 1997.
NT	New Testament
OT	Old Testament
OTE	*Old Testament Essays*
OTL	Old Testament Library

OTS	Old Testament Studies
P	The Priestly source
PMLA	Publications of the Modern Language Association
PTL	A Journal for Descriptive Poetics and Theory of Literature
RTR	Reformed Theological Review
RevQ	Revue de Qumran
SJOT	Scandinavian Journal of the Old Testament
SBL	Society of Biblical Literature
SC	Sinai/Sinaitic covenant
SubBi	Subsidia biblica
TDOT	Theological Dictionary of the Old Testament. 14 vols. Edited by G. Johannes Botterweck and Helmer Ringgren. Translated by Geoffrey W. Bromiley et al. Grand Rapids: Eerdmans, 1974–2004.
THAT	Theologisches Handwörterbuch zum Alten Testament. 2 vols. Edited by Ernst Jenni, with assistance from Claus Westermann. Munich: Chr. Kaiser Verlag, Zürich: Theologischer Verlag, 1971–1976.
TNCBC	New Century Bible Commentary
TOTC	Tyndale Old Testament Commentaries
TWOT	Theological Wordbook of the Old Testament
TynBul	Tyndale Bulletin
TZ	Theologische Zeitschrift
VT	Vetus Testamentum
VTSup	Supplements to Vetus Testamentum
WBC	Word Biblical Commentary
WTJ	Westminster Theological Journal
ZAW	Zeitschrift für die altetestamentliche Wissenschaft

Introduction

RENEWED INTEREST IN THE OLD TESTAMENT COVENANTS

THERE WAS A MOMENT in biblical studies when it seemed that the study of covenant in the OT had peaked.[1] In the wake of Wellhausen's epoch-making contributions, mainstream biblical scholars spent most of the twentieth century seeking to unearth and understand the world behind the text via historical-critical approaches, such as source, form, tradition history, and redaction criticism. This resulted in a shift in focus from the theology of the OT toward the history of Israelite religion. By the end of the 1970s, mainstream scholars reached a consensus view of the covenant as a Deuteronomic invention from the time of Josiah's reforms (2 Kgs 22–23; 2 Chr 34–35; ca. seventh century BCE) that was then developed by the Priestly school during the exilic and postexilic periods. The study of the OT covenants closely followed the larger aims of mainstream scholarship, which were to describe and understand the world behind the covenant concept found in the text. Meanwhile, evangelical OT scholars spent a good portion of the last century focusing on historical-grammatical exegesis of the text with the aim of doing biblical theology that informs the practice of systematic theology. One of the arenas in which this was taking place was in the intramural debate between Dispensationalism and Covenant Theology. Though evangelical scholars in both camps shared much in common in terms of worldviews, presuppositions, and approaches, the core issues dividing Dispensationalism and Covenant Theology centered around the understanding of biblical covenants and their attendant interrelationships. As in mainstream circles,

---

1. See statements in recent works on covenant. Weeks, *Admonition and Curse*, 1–6; Nicholson, *God and His People*, v–viii; Gentry and Wellum, *Kingdom through Covenant*, 21–37; Hahn, *Kinship by Covenant*, 1–22.

the theological understanding of covenant in the OT had become fairly standardized in modern evangelical scholarship. Dispensationalist and Reformed scholars held to their respective conceptions of covenant with a distinct sense that the differing views were settled.

Fortunately, this status quo did not hold for long in either stream of OT scholarship. Toward the end of the twentieth century, there was a new wave of covenant research informed by the contributions of ancient Near Eastern specialists and promising developments in the fields of biblical and theological studies. In mainstream scholarship, the growing use of canonical approaches and the innovative use of literary criticism resulted in a renewed interest in the synchronic study of the text as opposed to a diachronic understanding of the world behind the text.[2] In the evangelical arena, scholars sought a *via media* between Dispensationalism and Covenant Theology resulting in new approaches to a biblical covenant-theology.

As for the Abrahamic and Mosaic covenants, this contemporary wave of covenant studies included fresh investigations into these two seminal covenants. Within mainstream scholarship, the study of the relationship between the Abrahamic and Mosaic covenants centers around two basic approaches. Some follow the higher-critical approach of the past by analyzing the two covenant traditions via the strata of literary sources and traditions in the world behind the text. This type of study tends toward reconstructions of the way the patriarchal and Sinai covenant traditions were combined by the tradents of various religious schools in the later periods of Israel's history. Others have embraced a synchronic approach based on the final canonical form of the text in which approaches informed by literary criticism are used to develop a coherent reading of the covenant narratives. In evangelical scholarship, the primary approach to studying the relationship between the Abrahamic and Mosaic covenants remains the historical-grammatical analysis of pertinent OT texts, comparative studies involving ancient Near Eastern treaty forms, and theological studies of covenant form and function.

---

2. Anderson discusses a new period of uncertainty and openness toward different methods, which opens the door for canonical criticism and synchronic approaches. Anderson, *Contours*, 28–31. For additional discussions of a synchronic approach, see Williamson, *Abraham, Israel, and the Nations*, 22–25; Childs, *Old Testament Theology*, 15–16; Rendtorff, *Covenant Formula*, 6–10.

A VOICE FROM THE PAST, AN INSIDER'S PERSPECTIVE

While the modern resurgence in the study of biblical covenants has been fruitful, the conversation surrounding the Abrahamic and Mosaic covenants continues to be shaped by two ongoing discussions. First, the modern study of ancient Near Eastern treaty forms continues to categorize biblical covenants as either unconditional grants or conditional suzerainty treaties. Second, the post-Reformation focus on the theological relationship between law and Gospel as well as the Old and New Testaments continues to shape the study of the Abrahamic and Mosaic covenants.

Since the Abrahamic and Mosaic covenants are different covenant types and differ in theological function, there has been a tendency to minimize the continuity and complementarity of these two covenants. The study of the relationship between these two covenants has generally been located in the pentateuchal covenant-making narratives and their respective covenant terms and stipulations. A perspective that is underrepresented in these studies is the perspective of the biblical writers outside of the Pentateuch. In this respect Psalm 105 presents a unique and promising opportunity for inter-covenantal study.

There are very few texts where the Abrahamic and Mosaic covenants are referenced together and the fact that Psalm 105 is a postexilic historical psalm adds to the value of this biblical witness. Being a member of the postexilic covenant community, the psalmist is a unique biblical voice with valuable historical perspective. The psalmist's historical narration offers an untapped insider's perspective on the way the Abrahamic promises were understood in relation to the nation-defining Mosaic covenant.

This study entails an intertextual study of Psalm 105 and the psalmist's understanding of the Abrahamic and Mosaic covenants in light of the foundational covenant texts in the Pentateuch. As such, it represents an attempt to bring the psalmist into a conversation with the writers of the Pentateuch regarding the relationship between these covenants. As it turns out, the psalmist is an especially clever and insightful composer of songs. The psalm features a sophisticated rhetorical structure that juxtaposes the unfailing covenant faithfulness of Yahweh with the covenant failure of his people which resulted in the exile. In doing so, the psalmist addresses a major theological question troubling his community: why has the postexilic return to the land not been accompanied by the unprecedented blessing anticipated in the Mosaic writings?

Psalm 105 weaves a historical narrative that attributes possession of the land to the unfailing Abrahamic covenant while reminding the reader that blessing in the land only comes in accordance with the Mosaic covenant.

This intertextual study of the psalmist's Abrahamic covenant references and Mosaic covenant allusions reveals a brilliant rhetorical strategy in which a text emphasizing Yahweh's covenant faithfulness is intertwined with a subtext that highlights Israel's covenant failures. This rhetorical interplay brings the reader to the conclusion that the postexilic remnant must renew and keep the Mosaic covenant. By rehearsing this covenant-shaped history, the psalmist uses the past as prelude. Just as the conquest generation had to keep the Mosaic covenant to experience blessing in the land, the postexilic generation must now renew and observe this same covenant to experience God's blessings anew.

The psalmist's skillful retelling of history reminds the postexilic remnant that Yahweh's covenant faithfulness to Abraham and his descendants need not be questioned. However, Psalm 105 also argues that blessing and flourishing depends on the restoration of the Mosaic covenant relationship. The psalmist's song of covenants provides the modern reader with a unique perspective on the covenant-theology of Israel. This biblical voice from the past manifests a wholistic view of the Abrahamic and Mosaic covenants as cohesive, complementary, and continuous. This perspective has the potential to serve as a helpful corrective against the modern tendency to overemphasize the differences between the form and function of these covenants.

1

Studying the Covenants
Then and Now

A HISTORICAL SURVEY OF COVENANT STUDIES: FOLLOWING TWO STREAMS

THE HISTORY OF COVENANT scholarship is not linear but complex. In broad strokes, the analogy of a river comes to mind—a river that splits into major tributaries that run in parallel at times and occasionally intersect as they meander independently through their respective fields. While the biblical covenants have long been a subject of scholarly interest in theological and biblical studies, the manner in which scholars have approached this topic has varied depending on which "stream" of scholarship they followed and at which point in history they produced their work. One can view the river as the main movement of biblical scholarship that followed the Reformation. This tradition of OT studies eventually bifurcates into two major tributaries of scholarly tradition. In the modern era, the epoch-making influence of higher criticism and a shift in focus toward the history of Israelite religion would define the major branch that forms mainstream OT scholarship and the evangelical stream of scholarship can be considered the tributary. This survey, while not exhaustive, highlights the major developments, movements, and trends that have come to characterize the modern study of OT covenants.[1]

---

1. Nicholson's historical survey is an excellent introduction to the history of

Wellhausen and the Modern Era

In many ways, the modern approach to biblical scholarship came of age in the wake of Wellhausen's epoch-making work *Prolegomena to the History of Israelite Religion*.[2] The prominence of Wellhausen's approach marked the point at which mainstream OT scholarship went from a theological endeavor to an emphasis on modern historicism. With the wide acceptance of Wellhausen's work, the source-critical approach to OT texts would affect every aspect of biblical studies, including the modern approach to the biblical covenants.

According to Wellhausen's view of Israelite religion, the earliest period of development reflected a primitive naturalistic religion that later evolved into the ethical religion of the prophets and finally culminated in the legalistic religion overseen by the Deuteronomic and Priestly schools.[3] In the framework of Wellhausen's history of Israelite religion, the covenants are literary fictions produced by the Deuteronomic and Priestly schools to support a particular narrative of Israel's ancient history.[4]

In concert with the ascendance of source criticism was an emphasis on historicism in studying the OT, which seemed to better accommodate the Hebrew writings in their existential and historical setting.[5] During this time, scholars gravitated toward four issues with regard to covenant in the OT:[6] (1) the historicity of the journey to Sinai; (2) the meaning of the term *berit*; (3) the nature of early Israelite religion; amd (4) the silence of the eighth-century prophets regarding *berit*.[7] The question of historicity in OT narratives and the dearth of covenant references in the eighth-century prophets bolstered the late dating of the covenant concept to the time of Josianic reform.[8]

---

covenant studies. Nicholson, *God and His People*, 3–117. See Oden for a discussion of the broad scholarly shifts that took place in mainstream scholarship during the modern period. Oden, "Place of Covenant," 429–47. For a survey of scholarship on the history of Israelite religion, see Zimmerli, "History of Israelite Religion," 351–84.

2. Wellhausen's work was first published in 1878 under the title *Geschichte Israels, Band 1: Prolegomena*. Wellhausen, *Prolegomena*.

3. Wellhausen, *Prolegomena*, 318–410. See also Nicholson, *God and His People*, 4–7.

4. Wellhausen, *Prolegomena*, 338–40, 417–19.

5. Naylor, "Language of Covenant," 13.

6. Nicholson, *God and His People*, 7.

7. Wellhausen denies that Hosea knew of the covenant concept since he was writing during the ethical period of Israelite religion that preceded the Deuteronomic and Priestly schools. Wellhausen, *Prolegomena*, 418.

8. This is a defining datum for the classical source-critical reconstruction of the textual history behind the Pentateuch. Wellhausen, *Prolegomena*, 402–9.

According to Nicholson, this period from Wellhausen to the end of the nineteenth century is characterized by a general scholarly consensus regarding the late date of the covenants in the last stage of Israel's religious development.[9] Thus, the covenants were seen as juridical, legalistic documents reflective of Deuteronomic and Priestly concerns. Mainstream OT scholarship became less interested in the individual biblical covenants and more interested in the concept of covenant. The view that the biblical covenant texts were late examples of historical fiction meant the covenants were mainly of value as a means of understanding the various religious schools and tradents who were active in the exilic and postexilic periods. The theological significance of the covenants was no longer of importance as scholars began to study covenant from an evolutionary and rationalistic perspective.[10]

Beyond Wellhausen: Finding Consensus

In the early part of the twentieth century, mainstream OT scholarship experienced a noticeable shift from historical-critical emphases toward sociological and phenomenological approaches. During this period, Wellhausen's view of covenant fell out of favor as several simultaneous developments brought the biblical covenant traditions back to the earliest period of Israel's history. Max Weber's *Ancient Judaism*, a seminal sociological study of ancient Israel's religion and society, contributed to this major shift in thinking regarding covenant in Israel.[11] Though it was Weber who first suggested that there were "amphictyonic" tendencies in Israel's early rituals, Martin Noth ultimately popularized the view that the pre-monarchic tribes of Israel formed a confederation according to the analogy of Greek "amphictyonies."[12]

Weber viewed the covenant between Yahweh and Israel as a distinctive feature of Israelite religion since it was a religious pact with political and sociological significance.[13] According to Weber, the covenant uniquely brought Yahweh into a sociological bond that was sufficient to unite disparate tribes

---

9. Nicholson, *God and His People*, 26–27.

10. Nicholson, *God and His People*, 26–27.

11. Weber, *Ancient Judaism*. For a helpful discussion of Weber's impact, see Eisenstadt, "Format of Jewish History," 54–73.

12. Noth, *Das System*. Noth's work on the Israelite amphictyony was influenced by Weber's observation of occasional ritual acts that seemed "amphictyonic." Weber, *Ancient Judaism*, 90.

13. Weber, *Ancient Judaism*, 75–77, 118, 120.

and significantly shape the amphictyony's early social structure.[14] Unlike Wellhausen, Weber's sociological analysis led him to view the covenant concept, not as a theoretical construction but as the functional basis for tribal cohesion and social order.[15] Weber traced this Israelite covenant tradition back to concrete, pre-monarchic era events that led to the unification of these confederate tribes.[16]

Sigmund Mowinckel's phenomenological study of Israel's religion and cult came to light around the same time and further contributed to the increasing challenge of Wellhausen's views. In particular, Mowinckel's study of the Psalms introduced his influential conception of enthronement ceremonies and covenant renewal.[17] This line of research continued to bolster the idea of the covenant concept as an ancient tradition with its roots in the earliest stage of Israelite history.[18] Scott Hahn notes that Mowinckel's work was prescient in foreshadowing later studies that focus on the social dimensions of *berit* leading to a kinship-based concept of covenant.[19] Mowinckel's work on cultic backgrounds also set the stage for Gerhard von Rad who reevaluated the religion of the OT by examining the history of various traditions that coalesced into the canonical form of the text.[20] Von Rad's study of cultic backgrounds and covenant renewal led him to see the roots of biblical covenant traditions in ancient streams of tradition that underwent theological development over time.[21]

The sociological study of Israelite religion and a new focus on Israel's cult and religious traditions brought an end to the earlier consensus regarding Wellhausen's view of the covenant concept. Per Nicholson, the end of controversy meant that there was general agreement that covenant traditions in the OT had their roots in events related to the national inception of

---

14. Weber, *Ancient Judaism*, 75–89.

15. Weber, *Ancient Judaism*, 79. See also Nicholson, *God and His People*, 39.

16. Weber, *Ancient Judaism*, 118.

17. Mowinckel, *Psalm Studies*.

18. Mowinckel's reimagination of Israel's cult is developed further in these works: *Religion und Kultus* and *Tetrateuch, Pentateuch, Hexateuch*.

19. Mowinckel's rooting of the covenant concept in kinship/tribal bonds is an early precursor to Cross's later work on kinship terms as a key to ANE covenants. Hahn, *Kinship by Covenant*, 1.

20. Von Rad's form-critical study of the "little credo" in Deuteronomy inspired a new wave of form-critical and tradition historical studies resulting in revised views on religious development in Israel. Von Rad, "Form Critical Problem," 1–78.

21. Von Rad's two-volume work on OT theology incorporates and develops a full-fledged study of tradition history in Israel and how these traditions coalesced to shape Israel's religion. Von Rad, *Old Testament Theology*.

Israel.²² This view that Israel's covenant awareness goes back to the beginning of Israel's history coheres with developments in the field of OT theology and in the impending boom in form-critical studies of ANE treaty and law documents.

Treaty and Covenant: The Golden Age of Comparative Studies

Arguably, the most significant development that contributed to the shifting view of the history of covenant had to do with the early twentieth century flourishing of the study of ANE treaty and law texts. By the turn of the century, archaeological finds resulted in a growing corpus of ANE treaty and law texts from various cultures and historical periods.²³ Victor Korošec, studying law forms in the ancient Near East, was one of the first to identify a distinct second millennium Hittite diplomatic treaty form.²⁴ Building on this work, George Mendenhall produced the seminal form-critical study comparing biblical covenants to the Hittite suzerainty treaty form.²⁵ In Germany, Klaus Baltzer's study independently reached similar conclusions around the same time.²⁶ Both Mendenhall and Baltzer discerned a basic Hittite treaty form consisting of a preamble, historical prologue, stipulations, document clause regarding deposition of the law documents, witnesses, and curses/blessings.²⁷ Meredith Kline's work on the suzerain-vassal treaty form in Deuteronomy followed the research found in Baltzer's work and helped give these ideas wider exposure.²⁸ Mendenhall's work influenced a spate of similar research that would solidify the consensus that Deuteronomy was based on second-millennium Hittite suzerain-vassal treaties.

---

22. Nicholson, *God and His People*, 28–55.

23. Amnon Altman's overview of ANE legal practices and concepts is an excellent introduction. Altman, *Tracing the Earliest*. An indispensable resource for the study of ANE texts is Kitchen and Lawrence, *Treaty, Law, and Covenant*. For Hittite treaty texts, see Beckman, *Hittite Diplomatic Texts* and Altman, *Historical Prologue*. For a collection of diplomatic texts from Alalakh see Wiseman, *Alalakh Tablets*. For the Mari texts, see Malamat, *Mari and the Bible*. For the Sefire treaty texts, see Fitzmyer, *Aramaic Inscriptions*. For Neo-Assyrian treaties, see Parpola and Watanabe, *Neo-Assyrian Treaties*. These works provide access to non-specialists through annotated translations and expert commentary.

24. Korošec, *Hethitische Staatsverträge*, 18–58.

25. Mendenhall, "Covenant Forms," 57–60.

26. Baltzer, *Covenant Formulary*, 9–18, 31–38.

27. Mendenhall, "Covenant Forms," 57–60; Baltzer, *Covenant Formulary*, 9–18, 31–38.

28. Kline, *Structure of Biblical Authority*.

The connection between Deuteronomy and the Hittite suzerain-vassal treaty would become a defining moment in the study of biblical covenants. In both mainstream and evangelical scholarship, the characterization of the Sinaitic/Mosaic[29] covenant tradition as a suzerain-vassal relationship between Yahweh and Israel continues to influence biblical scholarship to this day. In the midst of these form-critical studies, Nelson Glueck's monograph placed ḥesed at the heart of the covenant concept, prompting Glueck to suggest "covenant loyalty" as a proper translation for ḥesed.[30]

In 1970, Moshe Weinfeld's seminal work on grant-type treaty forms posited an alternative treaty type that was promissory in nature.[31] The ANE documentary evidence for a promissory grant gave important grounding to the understanding of unconditionality and promise in certain biblical covenants, such as the Noachian, Abrahamic, and Davidic covenants. A scholarly consensus was quick to form regarding Weinfeld's category of a grant-type treaty. The association of suzerainty-type treaties with conditional obligation and the association of grant-type treaties with unconditional grants became a defining dual-type paradigm for biblical covenants that still controls much of the conversation in both biblical and theological studies.

One of the most important works in this area of scholarship is D. J. McCarthy's *Treaty and Covenant*.[32] This comprehensive study of ANE treaty forms addressed the available treaty and law corpus, including the Sefire treaties from Syria and the vassal treaties of Esarhaddon, which were released subsequent to Mendenhall's work.[33] McCarthy is credited with a study of both considerable scope and depth resulting in a mediating approach to the form-critical study of OT covenants.[34] McCarthy later released a second

---

29. For the purposes of this study, the terms Sinaitic or Sinai covenant refer specifically to the covenant events at Sinai. Mosaic covenant refers to the entire covenant complex mediated by Moses, including the Sinaitic/Sinai covenant, the various law collections, and the covenant materials from Moab (Deuteronomy). Sinai and Moab are understood to be different iterations of the same covenant.

30. Glueck, *Ḥesed*, 77. Per Oden, Glueck's monograph is an influential factor that contributed to the new consensus regarding the centrality of covenant early in ancient Israel's religious development. Oden, "Place of Covenant," 431.

31. Weinfeld, "Covenant of Grant," 184–203. For additional development of Weinfeld's view of grant treaties, see Weinfeld, *Deuteronomy and the Deuteronomic School*.

32. McCarthy, *Treaty and Covenant*.

33. The Sefire treaties from Syria and the vassal treaties of Esarhaddon are key additions to the study of the ANE corpus. Nicholson, *God and His People*, 59n8. For the Sefire texts see Fitzmyer, *Aramaic Inscriptions* and for the Esarhaddon texts see Parpola and Watanabe, *Neo-Assyrian Treaties*.

34. McCarthy represents a mediating position between Mendenhall's extreme

edition of *Treaty and Covenant* that accounts for later research and perspectives that had developed since the release of the first edition. Departing from Mendenhall's conclusions, McCarthy notably denied the presence of a defined treaty structure in the Sinai covenant texts.[35] McCarthy did see treaty structure at work in Deuteronomy but he also posited that Deuteronomy was a late composition that began with *Urdeuteronomium* around the time of the fall of Syria and culminated with the final form of Deuteronomy in the time of the Josianic reforms.[36]

McCarthy believed that there was a general ANE treaty form that developed over multiple eras, which effectively blunted attempts to date biblical covenant traditions to the second millennium based on similarities to the Hittite suzerain-vassal treaty.[37] McCarthy did concede that some earlier OT covenant texts were influenced by theological reflection on the covenant relationship between Yahweh and Israel, but he referred to these texts as "literary-reflective" texts as opposed to true suzerainty treaty analogues.[38] In this way, McCarthy is credited with correcting some of the initial comparative research found in earlier works while also tempering the Neo-Wellhausenian tendency to attribute the covenant concept exclusively to the theological imagination of the Deuteronomic school.[39] Richard Bautch later credited McCarthy with laying the groundwork for an "alternative paradigm" of the Sinaitic covenant by going beyond simple juridical concepts and drawing attention to the elements of theophany and ceremony that bind human and divine parties.[40]

Paul Kalluveettill, McCarthy's student, produced a work on covenant in which he focused on a specific process of covenant making via the use of declaration formulas.[41] Kalluveettill's focus on the process of declaring a relationship necessarily leads to a consideration of relational aspects of covenant. In examining declaration formulas in the OT, Kalluveettill details the different relationship concepts found in biblical covenants, such as vas-

---

form-critical approach and the neo-Wellhausenian positions of Kutsch and Perlitt. Hahn, *Kinship by Covenant*, 2.

35. McCarthy, *Treaty and Covenant*, 243–76. See also Nicholson, *God and His People*, 68–70.

36. McCarthy, *Treaty and Covenant*, 206–42, 291. See also Nicholson, *God and His People*, 64–65, 84–85.

37. McCarthy, *Treaty and Covenant*, 122–40.

38. McCarthy, *Treaty and Covenant*, 290. See also Nicholson, *God and His People*, 84–85.

39. Hahn, *Kinship by Covenant*, 2. See also Nicholson, *God and His People*, 64–65.

40. Bautch, *Glory and Power*, 5.

41. Kalluveettil, *Declaration and Covenant*.

salage and kinship.⁴² In addition to drawing out the importance of kinship as a covenant concept, Kalluveettill also made the helpful observation that covenant love, characterized by respect and obedience, can correlate to both sonship and servanthood, which means such love can be commanded.⁴³ This insight is helpful in elucidating Yahweh's covenantal relationship with Israel.⁴⁴

Interestingly, in Nicholson's helpful survey of the history of covenant studies he concludes that this period of intense comparative research "yielded little that is of permanent value."⁴⁵ His overview sees form-critical studies that led to the rejection of Wellhausen's views as based on limited ANE data and questionable comparative research.⁴⁶ McCarthy's work is seen as part of a counter movement that challenges the early interpretation of the extrabiblical evidence using more sources and improved research, which reestablishes the Wellhausenian premise regarding the late composition of Deuteronomy and the origin of the covenant concept in the Deuteronomic/Deuteronomistic literature.⁴⁷ Nicholson further concludes that the comparative research from McCarthy onward has proven that looking to ANE treaties for help on the functional role of the covenant in Israel's social and religious life is a dead end.⁴⁸ While these conclusions may have been reasonable in 1986, they now seem short-sighted and premature.

Since the publication of the second edition of McCarthy's work, there have been significant developments in the comparative study of ANE treaty and law texts. For example, the growing contributions of specialists—such as archaeologists, Assyriologists, and Hittitologists—have given biblical scholars the benefit of a wider range of sources and expert insight.⁴⁹ After decades in which scholars unquestioningly accepted the categories of

---

42. Kalluveettil, *Declaration and Covenant*, 196–210.

43. Kalluveettil, *Declaration and Covenant*, 132–33. See also McCarthy, "Notes on the Love of God," 144–47.

44. McCarthy, "Notes on the Love of God," 144–47. Recent scholars, such as Hahn, find this insight helpful in developing a kinship-based understanding of covenant. Hahn, *Kinship by Covenant*, 39–40.

45. Nicholson, *God and His People*, 81.

46. Nicholson, *God and His People*, 59–61, 68–82.

47. Nicholson, *God and His People*, 81–82.

48. Nicholson, *God and His People*, 81. For a rebuttal to Nicholson's view regarding the end of fruitful comparative research, see Kitchen's response in his review of Nicholson's *God and His People*. Kitchen, "Fall and Rise," 118–35.

49. Some specialists who have contributed to biblical studies include the following: Hittite studies: Amnon Altman, Gary Beckman; Assyriology: Hayim Tadmor, Simo Parpola, Kazuko Watanabe; Egyptology: Kenneth Kitchen, James Hoffmeier. This list is not exhaustive but illustrative.

suzerainty-type and grant-type treaties, Gary Knoppers published a critique of Weinfeld's seminal work based on a reexamination of Weinfeld's ANE sources.[50] Benefitting from over twenty years of intervening research, Knoppers raises concerns about the validity of Weinfeld's analysis of certain ANE texts.[51] Though Knoppers's challenge of Weinfeld's paradigmatic work has not met with universal acceptance, it did serve to illustrate the potential impact of specialists and experts in the various disciplines of ANE studies.[52] What was once a fairly settled consensus regarding the relationship between biblical covenants and ANE treaty forms is now open to fresh examination.

One important example of such research is Kenneth Kitchen and Paul Lawrence's magisterial *Treaty, Law and Covenant in the Ancient Near East*. Kitchen and Lawrence undertake an exhaustive examination of available ANE treaty, law, and covenant documents that span multiple historical periods and represent major ANE cultural sources, including Egyptian, Hittite, Neo-Assyrian, and Hebrew documents, resulting in an extensive documentary database.[53] One of Kitchen and Lawrence's innovative contributions is the identification of a distinct Hebrew public covenant form that is derived by isolating the covenant form's components from the narrative and legal "matrix" that makes up the final canonical form of the Pentateuch.[54] Having surveyed all major ANE treaty, law, and covenant texts, Kitchen and Lawrence are able to do a detailed comparison of the various ANE forms in relation to the biblical public covenant form they have "isolated" in Exodus-Leviticus, Deuteronomy, and Josh 24. Kitchen and Lawrence ultimately conclude that the closest ANE analogues to the biblical covenant between Yahweh and Israel are the late second-millennium Hittite treaty-law documents that marked the diplomatic relationship with Egypt under Ramesses II.[55]

50. Knoppers, "Royal Grants," 670–97.

51. Knoppers, "Royal Grants," 670–97. For another critique of Weinfeld's proposed grant-type covenant, see Haran, "The *Berît* 'Covenant,'" 207n8.

52. Freedman rebuts Knoppers's conclusions, noting that in every covenant, initiative is still with the Divine Suzerain, which means all covenants are unilateral. Freedman and Miano, "People of the New Covenant," 8n6.

53. Kitchen and Lawrence, *Treaty, Law, and Covenant*. Kitchen's earlier 2003 work, *On the Reliability of the Old Testament*, still stands as an accessible introduction to his extensive study of ANE treaty, law, and covenant texts. Kitchen, *Reliability of the OT*.

54. Kitchen and Lawrence speak of "detaching" and "liberating" the Hebrew covenant form from its pentateuchal "matrix," which includes separating the covenant proper from the surrounding literary context consisting of narrative and law collections. Kitchen and Lawrence discern discrete covenants in Exodus-Leviticus, Deuteronomy, and Josh 24. Kitchen and Lawrence, *Treaty, Law, Covenant*, 3:117–32.

55. Kitchen and Lawrence, *Treaty, Law, and Covenant*, 3:251–61. See also Kitchen,

In addition to Kitchen's research, Amnon Altman's expert work on Hittite treaties and ANE diplomatic texts has given today's scholars an improved understanding of the Hittite treaties that are often used for form-critical and comparative research.[56] As recently as 2011, Hittitologist Ada Taggar-Cohen revisited a comparison between the biblical *berit* and the Hittite *išḫiul* ("treaty").[57] Taggar-Cohen's study provides a helpful overview of the Hittite term for treaty (*išḫiul*) and its usage in Hittite literature.[58] Taggar-Cohen demonstrates that there are significant similarities between *berit* and *išḫiul* that go beyond matters of form suggesting that it is tenable to link Israel's covenant tradition to the Hittite treaty via a process of inherited knowledge.[59]

The work of historian and Assyriologist Hayim Tadmor also provides helpful clarification regarding the Neo-Assyrian suzerain-vassal treaties that many see as the basis for Deuteronomy. Tadmor analyzes the *adê* oath form in Assyria and clarifies some common perceptions regarding this treaty form.[60] By tracing the background of the *adê* through second millennium Syro-Anatolian and Northern Mesopotamian traditions, Tadmor demonstrates that the Neo-Assyrian treaty form is not limited to the first millennium.[61] Tadmor also posits that kings who were thought to be vassal kings of Assyrian rulers may actually have been servant kings that were not bound by a treaty.[62] Having drawn into question whether the Neo-Assyrian *adê* form best corresponds to the work of the Deuteronomists, Tadmor argues for the likelihood that second-millennium West Semitic loyalty oath traditions could very well have influenced Israel's understanding of *berit* from an earlier point in Israel's history.[63] F. H. Polak makes favorable comparisons between the Sinai covenant narrative and the practice of bi-local treaty ratification found in second-millennium Mari texts.[64] The recent trajectory of research by various ANE specialists suggests that these fields

"Fall and Rise," and Walton, *Ancient Israelite Literature*, 95–110.

56. Altman, *Historical Prologue*.
57. Taggar-Cohen, "Biblical Covenant," 461–88.
58. Taggar-Cohen, "Biblical Covenant," 461–82; 482–88.
59. Taggar-Cohen, "Biblical Covenant," 462–63, 488.
60. Tadmor, "Treaty and Oath," 127–52.
61. Tadmor, "Treaty and Oath," 129–40.
62. Tadmor, "Treaty and Oath," 149–51.
63. Tadmor, "Treaty and Oath," 151–52. For a survey of ANE treaty forms that complements Tadmor's piece, see Altman, "How Many Treaty Traditions," 17–36.
64. Polak, "Covenant at Mount Sinai," 119–34. For additional analysis of the ceremonial background of berit in the OT, see Haran, "The *Berît* 'Covenant,'" 203–19.

of study will continue to yield relevant information that will be valuable to biblical scholars.

The Renaissance of Old Testament Theology

In the years following World War I, the study of theology experienced a renaissance as theologians in both mainstream and evangelical traditions contributed to a new age of vibrant theological study. The field of OT theology was included in this period of revitalization as exemplified by Walter Eichrodt's influential two-volume *Old Testament Theology*. Eichrodt's theological masterpiece reflects an attempt to bridge the growing divide between biblical historicism and systematic theology.[65]

Eichrodt's distinctive approach was to allow the OT to provide its own "organizing principle," or *Mitte*, which he famously identified as covenant.[66] Eichrodt viewed covenant as central to Israel's religion of "election," whereas Wellhausen saw covenant as a concept that appeared only after Israel's religion had evolved along legalistic lines.[67] Eichrodt's work also coincided with the aforementioned proliferation of form-critical studies featuring ANE treaty form. This influence is reflected in Eichrodt's view that covenant relates to a juridical, bilateral relationship reflected in first millennium ANE treaty forms.[68] Eichrodt's theology had a major influence by thrusting covenant to the forefront of OT studies, prompting renewed theological, historical, and linguistic study of the concept.[69]

A fresh wave of scholarly interest in other areas of biblical studies further fueled the study of covenants in both biblical and systematic theology. In the mid-1960s, Ronald E. Clements produced a series of studies on the OT covenant traditions organized according to a history of traditions and source-critical framework.[70] Clements's overall understanding of the

---

65. Naylor, "Language of Covenant," 14; See also Eichrodt, *Theology of the Old Testmant*, 30–31.

66. Naylor, "Language of Covenant," 15. See also Eichrodt, *Theology of the Old Testament*, 31–37.

67. Eichrodt, *Theology of the Old Testament*, 42–45.

68. Eichrodt, *Theology of the Old Testament*, 7–8, 36–37, 51–52. Years later Eichrodt wrote a brief reflection on the discussions taking place in the 1960s and affirmed the views he articulated in his OT theology regarding the juridical, bilateral concept of covenant, and the antiquity of the covenant concept in Israel. Eichrodt, "Covenant and Law," 302–21.

69. Naylor, "Language of Covenant," 16.

70. Clements, *Prophecy and Covenant*; Clements, *Abraham and David*; Clements, *God's Chosen People*, 44.

covenant traditions is a revealing picture of the dominant trends that were influencing OT studies at that time. Clements viewed the three seminal covenant traditions to be the Abrahamic, Sinaitic (not including Deuteronomy), and Davidic.[71] Clements's general organization of these covenant traditions relies on both the major documentary sources, the Yahwist (J), the Deuteronomist (D), and the Priestly source (P), as well as three major pre-Deuteronomic streams of tradition, namely the patriarchal tradition, the exodus-Sinai tradition, and the great prophets of the eighth century.[72]

Within this matrix of literary sources and traditions, Clements places the Abrahamic covenant tradition in the patriarchal tradition and attributes the documentary expression to J (Gen 15). In its earliest form, the Abrahamic covenant was a local promise of land possession that was promissory in nature but not unconditional.[73] Since the Abrahamic covenant was a part of the patriarchal tradition it was related to folklore and would eventually be subsumed into the Davidic covenant tradition.[74] Meanwhile, the Sinaitic covenant tradition is located in the exodus-Sinai stream of tradition, which is also the locus of the Israelite cult. Clements posits that this is why the pre-exilic prophets focused on the Sinaitic covenant as the basis for election and not the Abrahamic covenant, which was too distant from Israel's cult during this period.[75]

A major change in Israel's understanding of the covenants would take place in the Deuteronomic period. The Deuteronomist viewed the Abrahamic covenant as the ancient forerunner to the Sinaitic covenant, and it was at this time that the Abrahamic covenant was "democratized" and viewed as a covenant of election pointing toward the Sinaitic covenant and then Deuteronomy.[76] It is also at this time that the Abrahamic covenant becomes an immutable covenant of grace that contrasts with the Mosaic covenant, which now includes the Sinaitic covenant tradition and the Mosaic covenant in Deuteronomy.[77]

---

71. Clements makes use of source-critical methods but he does not follow Wellhausen's view of the history of Israelite religion. Clements denies that covenant is a theological idea and places the covenants in the context of old traditions with real-world settings. Clements, *God's Chosen People*, 37–39.

72. For a good example of Clement's approach, see Clements, *Abraham and David*.

73. Clements, *Abraham and David*, 15–22; 33–34.

74. In Clements's view, the Davidic covenant actually influences the evolution of the Abrahamic covenant since both covenant traditions were part of the developing theology of the pre-Deuteronomic era. Clements, *Abraham and David*, 54–56, 63.

75. Clements, *Abraham and David*, 61–62.

76. Clements, *Abraham and David*, 64–66.

77. Clements, *Abraham and David*, 67–69.

In the exilic and postexilic period, the Priestly school placed a greater emphasis on the Abrahamic covenant since the Mosaic covenant appeared to be failed, thus Gen 17 and the final form of the Abrahamic covenant would ultimately become an unconditional anchor for all other covenant traditions.[78] In a profound theological reinterpretation of the covenant traditions, the Priestly school sees the Abrahamic promises as unconditional and everlasting and the Mosaic covenant is now seen as the fulfillment of the patriarchal promises.[79] Clements's study of the covenants reflects a noteworthy attempt to systematize the major covenants and understand the covenant theology of Israel from a higher-critical perspective.

In 1976, John Bright of the Baltimore school, known for his work on the history of Israel, wrote an interesting study on the eschatology of the pre-exilic prophets entitled, *Covenant and Promise*.[80] Bright's study focuses on the uniqueness of Israel's prophetic eschatology, which sees hope beyond judgment.[81] Though this is a study of prophetic eschatology, Bright's linking of prophetic hope to the centrality of promise leads him into a detailed study of covenant in the OT.

Bright adheres to the widely accepted dual covenant typology in classifying the OT covenants as either promissory, like the Abrahamic covenant or obligatory, as exemplified by the Sinaitic.[82] Bright's work includes a defense of an early date of origin for Israel's covenant traditions based on his comparison of both Hittite and Neo-Assyrian treaty forms.[83] Bright's study also addresses the relative silence of the eighth-century prophets with regard to the concept of covenant, which was one of the reasons the Wellhausen school viewed covenant as a late development. Despite the absence of explicit mentions of covenant, Bright sees appeals to covenant law and covenant ideas throughout the writings of the eighth-century prophets.[84]

In 1978, Walter Kaiser Jr. published an OT theology that featured the concept of *promise* as its canonical and theological center.[85] Kaiser attributed a "constellation" of terms and ideas to the central idea of *promise*, which include many elements related to the OT covenants.[86] The very concept of

---

78. Clements, *Abraham and David*, 68–70.
79. Clements, *Abraham and David*, 75–78.
80. Bright, *Covenant and Promise*.
81. Bright, *Covenant and Promise*, 15.
82. Bright, *Covenant and Promise*, 25–43.
83. Bright, *Covenant and Promise*, 36–41.
84. Bright, *Covenant and Promise*, 84–94.
85. Kaiser, *Toward an Old Testament Theology*, 32–40.
86. Kaiser, *Toward an Old Testament Theology*, 33.

promise is covenantal in nature, but Kaiser also traces the development of other covenantal ideas, such as the covenant formula, pledge/oath, and blessing.[87] With his focus on *promise*, it stands to reason that Kaiser would see the patriarchal promises of the Abrahamic covenant as the historical and canonical starting point for his theological study.[88] As for the tension between the promise of the Abrahamic covenant and the law in the Mosaic covenant, Kaiser points out the numerous points of continuity between the two and notes the significance of obedience in the Abrahamic covenant, which was not essential to making the covenant but a means of demonstrating efficacious faith.[89]

Kaiser summarizes the continuity between the two covenants in the following points: (1) Both promise and law were initiated by the same covenant-making God; (2) the law was a means of maintaining fellowship with God, not a means of salvation; (3) the law demanded holiness but also made provision for forgiveness and atonement; (4) the context of the law's demands is an overarching principle of grace that characterizes God's role in upholding these covenants.[90] Kaiser views the Mosaic covenant as a continuation of the Abrahamic covenant both theologically and historically.[91] Kaiser's approach to the continuity and connection between the Abrahamic and Mosaic covenants is significant, for it influences and foreshadows the emphasis evangelical scholars place on the progress of revelation and theological continuity exhibited by the biblical covenants.

While not a proper OT theology, William J. Dumbrell's *Covenant and Creation: A Theology of Old Testament Covenants* features a thorough, orderly study of each major OT covenant consisting of an exegetical analysis of key texts and theological reflection on each covenant's significance.[92] Dumbrell's aims are different from Kaiser's, but their respective works are similar in terms of their handling of the OT covenants. Like Kaiser, Dumbrell views each biblical covenant as part of a larger theological framework and discerns continuity and progress with each successive covenant. One unique feature of Dumbrell's study is his use of the covenant at creation as the defining theological theme that organizes all of the OT covenants.[93] In his study

---

87. Kaiser, *Toward an Old Testament Theology*, 33–35.

88. Kaiser, *Toward an Old Testament Theology*, 84–99.

89. Kaiser, *Toward an Old Testament Theology*, 59–62.

90. Kaiser, *Toward an Old Testament Theology*, 62–63. For more detail on the relationship between the Mosaic law and the Abrahamic promise see Kaiser, *Toward an Old Testament Theology*, 110–13.

91. Kaiser, *Toward an Old Testament Theology*, 94, 101.

92. Dumbrell, *Covenant and Creation*.

93. Dumbrell follows Covenant Theology in his view of a covenant with creation.

of the Abrahamic covenant, Dumbrell finds connections to the creation theme via "new creation" language.[94] He sees the Abrahamic covenant as the "framework" for all subsequent concepts of relationships, including the Sinai covenant, which is a partial fulfillment of the Abrahamic covenant.[95]

Dumbrell's preference for the term "Sinai covenant" is due to his understanding of the relationship between the covenant at Sinai in Exodus and the covenant material in Deuteronomy. Dumbrell identifies the covenant at Sinai as the core covenant and then views Deuteronomy as a renewal of this covenant.[96] A distinctive feature of this view is his suggestion that the theology of the Sinai covenant undergoes significant development in Deuteronomy. Per Dumbrell, Deuteronomy introduces the connection of *berit* to the concept of *ḥesed*, which he specifically views as loyalty to an existing relationship.[97] Thus, *ḥesed*, i.e. covenant loyalty, results in obedience that reflects an established relationship rather than constituting a new one.[98]

Like Kaiser, Dumbrell sees significant continuity between the Abrahamic and Sinai covenants. Dumbrell sees progression in the way the Sinai covenant fulfills the patriarchal promises but also advances the global program by establishing Israel's distinct role in history.[99] With regard to the tension between promise and law, Dumbrell affirms that the law's function is not constitutive but rather an appropriate response of gratitude in light of the blessings of redemption.[100] In this sense, Dumbrell's logic is akin to Kaiser's in maintaining a clear distinction between the unconditional certainty of the promises and the functional conditionality of the law.

Bernhard Anderson's *Contours of Old Testament Theology* is a mainstream work of biblical theology that examines the OT covenants within a canonical context.[101] Coming at the end of the 1990s, Anderson considered his work to be an "experimental approach" since he saw the field of

---

He argues that Gen 1–3 implicitly reveals a foundational covenant that was made when God's act of creation placed him in a covenant relationship with humanity and the created world. Dumbrell, *Covenant and Creation*, 33–43.

94. Dumbrell, *Covenant and Creation*, 58, 61.

95. Interestingly, Dumbrell postulates that the Sinaitic covenant overshadowed the Abrahamic covenant for a time, but national crises in the postexilic period brought the Abrahamic covenant back to the forefront of OT thought. Dumbrell, *Covenant and Creation*, 78.

96. Dumbrell, *Covenant and Creation*, 80–126.

97. Dumbrell, *Covenant and Creation*, 106–7.

98. Dumbrell, *Covenant and Creation*, 106.

99. Dumbrell, *Covenant and Creation*, 87.

100. Dumbrell, *Covenant and Creation*, 98–99.

101. Anderson, *Contours*.

biblical theology as being in a period of flux and uncertainty.[102] Anderson's canonical approach reflects the influence of Brevard Childs, who critiqued the modern practice of basing biblical theology upon objective, historical events (the Albright school) or upon the historical reconstruction of traditions (Noth, von Rad, et al.).[103]

Another novel aspect of Anderson's work is how he addresses major OT subjects, such as election, promise, covenant, law, and cult, by organizing these topics according to the major covenants, the Abrahamic, the Mosaic, and the Davidic.[104] Anderson views the OT covenants as metaphorical in the sense that they were literary and theological constructs of the Deuteronomic and Priestly schools based on the forms of ANE treaties.[105] In this sense, Anderson's perspective coheres with McCarthy's view of covenant as "literary-reflective" products.[106]

Anderson accepts Weinfeld's analogy of a royal-grant-type treaty for the Abrahamic covenant, which he summarizes as an everlasting promissory covenant based on God's grace and unilateral initiative.[107] Anderson's general view of covenants as vehicles for "patterns of symbolization" means various elements of the Abrahamic covenant, such as God's election of Israel and divine presence in a holy land reflect Priestly theology.[108] It then stands to reason that the "pattern of symbols" found in Deuteronomy differs from the Priestly pattern.[109] Anderson's canonical reading of the Mosaic covenant subordinates the Mosaic covenant to the Abrahamic covenant.[110] In fact, Anderson concludes that the final editors of the canon intended the Abrahamic and Mosaic covenants to be understood as inseparable with

---

102. Anderson, *Contours*, 28.

103. Anderson, *Contours*, 28. Anderson affirms Childs's dissatisfaction with the use of historical data as well as a "history of traditions" in doing biblical theology. Childs, *Biblical Theology in Crisis*. Childs produced his own OT theology using the canonical approach around the same time as Dumbrell's work. Childs, *Old Testament Theology*.

104. Anderson, *Contours*, 33.

105. Anderson, *Contours*, 143. Here Anderson quotes Nicholson who saw covenant in the OT as " . . . a metaphor drawn from the world of treaties rather than an institution which formed the principle of cohesion among the twelve tribes of earliest Israel." From Nicholson, *God and His People*, 82.

106. McCarthy, *Treaty and Covenant*, 290. See also Nicholson, *God and His People*, 84–85.

107. Anderson, *Contours*, 102–4.

108. Anderson, *Contours*, 137.

109. Anderson, *Contours*, 137.

110. Anderson, *Contours*, 137.

the Mosaic covenant subsumed under the programmatic perspective and historical narrative of the Abrahamic covenant.[111]

Within the Mosaic covenant Anderson addresses the striking command to *love* the LORD. He assesses that this concept of *love* is within the context of a suzerain-vassal relationship, but this command is also set against the backdrop of God's love for his people, which suggests a relationship that may transcend political ties and reflect a genuine sense of kinship.[112] Since the Mosaic covenant is not a parity covenant, Anderson recognizes a tension between human freedom and divine sovereignty, which he calls the "paradox of grace."[113] Though Anderson sees the obligatory elements of the Mosaic covenant as genuinely conditional, he affirms that the relational nature of the covenant overshadows this conditionality in that the "constancy of God's loyalty" ultimately upholds the covenant relationship.[114]

As for the particular tension between the unconditional Abrahamic covenant and the conditional Mosaic, Anderson interestingly leaves this problem in the realm of the Deuteronomic theologians who were able to merge the promise of land with contingent possession so that temporary failures could never prevent God from graciously restoring the relationship.[115] In this way, Anderson sees the two covenants as complementary with the unconditional promise of the Abrahamic covenant defining the relationship into perpetuity.[116] In many ways, Anderson's work is enlightening, for he works out of a higher critical perspective on the literary and theological development of the covenants; yet, when it comes to the practical explanation of the relationship between the two covenants, some of his thinking is consistent with the way evangelical theologians handle these same issues.

Paul R. Williamson's *Sealed with an Oath* is similar to Anderson's *Contours of Old Testament Theology* in that both are characterized by a canonical approach.[117] Williamson's first work of note was his literary theological study of the Abrahamic covenant in Gen 15 and 17, which led him to conclude that there are actually two distinct covenants represented in these two pericopes.[118] *Sealed with an Oath* comes seven years later and is a

---

111. Anderson, *Contours*, 137–38.

112. Anderson, *Contours*, 137–38. See also Moran, "Ancient Near Eastern Background," 77–87.

113. Anderson, *Contours*, 148–49.

114. Anderson, *Contours*, 150.

115. Anderson, *Contours*, 152–53.

116. Anderson, *Contours*, 154.

117. Williamson, *Sealed with an Oath*.

118. Williamson, *Abraham, Israel, and the Nations*.

biblical theological work that addresses all of the major OT covenants both through exegetical and theological analysis. Williamson's research interacts effectively with mainstream positions, but his exegetical work focuses on understanding the covenantal texts within a canonical context.[119] Williamson does not see exegetical evidence for a creation covenant (*pace* Dumbrell), but he does see in the Noachian covenant a divine commitment to creation and affirms that any theological study of the covenants must place covenant within the context of creation since the restoration of creation must be a major telos of salvation history.

With regard to the relationship between the patriarchal covenants and the Sinai covenant, Williamson is clear that the patriarchal covenants are programmatic and the Mosaic covenant does not supersede the Abrahamic promise.[120] In fact, Williamson subordinates his reading and interpretation of the Sinai covenant texts to the theological agenda set forth in Genesis.[121] As for the tension between the promises to the patriarchs and the law in the Sinai covenant, it is worth noting that Williamson sees Gen 15 as an unconditional unilateral covenant while the covenant in Gen 17 is actually conditional.

Williamson sees the Sinai covenant as subordinate to the programmatic patriarchal covenants and posits that the primary purpose of the Sinai covenant is revelatory. This revelatory purpose is fulfilled in the law, which reveals the exact type of nation God wanted Abraham's descendants to become and reveals to the nations the type of God Israel served.[122] Williamson's overall work is a commendable survey of the major covenants that introduces some novel views regarding the nature of these covenants. Williamson demonstrates a good awareness of the scholarship that has come before and interacts well with both mainstream and evangelical positions.

Covenant Theology and Dispensationalism

Within evangelical circles, the ongoing intramural debate between adherents of Dispensationalism and Covenant Theology focuses on the definition of covenant as well as the interpretation of biblical texts related to covenant.

---

119. Williamson, *Sealed with an Oath*, 69–76.

120. Williamson concludes that Gen 15 and 17 describe two distinct Abrahamic covenants, hence Williamson's uses of "patriarchal covenants." As for the Sinaitic covenant, Williamson views the covenant in Deuteronomy as a renewal and modification of the Sinaitic covenant, so he purposefully uses Sinai terminology. Williamson, *Sealed with an Oath*, 94, 111–13.

121. Williamson, *Sealed with an Oath*, 94–96.

122. Williamson, *Sealed with an Oath*, 96–99.

One of the core differences between these two schools is the concept of covenant in federal theology, also known as headship theology. The basic system of federal theology describes the divine-human relationship in terms of the covenants of works (related to Adamic headship) and grace (related to Christ's headship), with the covenant of redemption usually included in modern Covenant Theology.[123] The concept of these three overarching covenants generates much discussion regarding the biblical evidence for their existence. Unlike the Noachian, Abrahamic, Mosaic, Davidic, and new covenants, which are explicitly named and described, the covenants of works, redemption, and grace are based on a theological synthesis of biblical texts spanning the Old and New Testaments.[124]

Within Covenant Theology, the specific OT covenants are seen as particular expressions of God's larger plan and subordinate to the overarching covenant of grace.[125] One of the major issues that receives scholarly attention within Reformed scholarship is the tension between the law and Gospel, which influences studies on the conditionality of the major biblical covenants. In this respect, the promissory nature of the Abrahamic, Davidic, and new covenants is often contrasted and compared to the obligatory nature of the Mosaic covenant.

Interestingly, the "golden age" of biblical archaeology and comparative ANE studies influenced the understanding of this tension in the Reformed tradition. The modern understanding of obligatory treaties and promissory grants influenced thinking about the covenant of grace since this covenant appears to be in tension with the ANE model of obligatory vassal treaties.[126] The response was an emphasis on *divine monergism* in the institution and upholding of the covenant of grace, as well as the promissory Noachian, Abrahamic, Davidic, and new covenants.[127]

The exceptional nature of the Mosaic covenant prompted Reformed theologians to describe the Mosaic covenant as subordinate to the covenant of grace in such a way that it only determines the enjoyment of stipulated

---

123. McGowan, "In Defense of Headship Theology," 179–83. For a history of federal theology see McGowan, "In Defense of Headship Theology," 178–99.

124. For a look at the development and biblical/theological basis for the covenants of works and grace, see Golding, *Covenant Theology*, 105–42. Horton surveys the history of thought regarding the biblical warrant for the covenants of works and grace. Horton, *God of Promise*, 78–110. Williamson sees no biblical warrant for an Adamic covenant. Williamson, *Sealed with an Oath*, 52–58.

125. Horton, *God of Promise*, 78.

126. Golding, *Covenant Theology*, 67, 85–88.

127. Golding, *Covenant Theology*, 89–91.

blessings without affecting the overall operation of the covenant of grace.[128] In fact, the presence of conditional elements in the Abrahamic covenant was understood to affirm the notion that law in the Mosaic covenant is consistent with the "concept of a monergistic administration of grace."[129] The priority of the covenant of grace means that the relationship between the OT covenants is characterized as complementary with a significant degree of continuity. Therefore, Covenant Theology views the promises in the Abrahamic covenant and the law in the Mosaic covenant as administering different aspects of the covenant of grace.[130]

The core difference between Dispensationalism's and Covenant Theology's concept of overarching covenants is in Dispensationalism's distinct ages or "dispensations" that are characterized by a particular means of divine governance (economy) that is effective for a finite period of time.[131] Thus, the major biblical covenants define the way Dispensationalists understand these distinct dispensations within the progressive revelation of God's plan. This approach to the biblical covenants would undergo development and revision from the classical Dispensationalism of Darby to the Revised form of Ryrie and culminating with Bock and Blaising's Progressive Dispensationalism.[132]

The defining importance of each major biblical covenant is best seen in the work of Bock and Blaising, whose concept of Dispensationalism is organized by the terms and interrelationships of the major biblical covenants. As reflected by the term "Progressive," the distinctive concept is the manner in which each covenant builds upon the preceding covenants, while also revealing an important new aspect of God's plan in history.[133]

According to Bock and Blaising, the Abrahamic covenant is programmatic and clarifies the general blessing promised in the Noachian covenant and unilaterally promises Abraham numerous descendants, territorial possessions, and blessings that are mediated through Abraham's descendants so all nations can eventually experience a peaceful relationship with God.[134] Even as a promissory covenant, Bock and Blaising recognize obligatory ele-

128. Golding, *Covenant Theology*, 93–94.
129. Golding, *Covenant Theology*, 94.
130. Golding, *Covenant Theology*, 148–58, 164–73.
131. For a summary of the way Revised and Progressive Dispensationalism organize the covenants, see Blaising and Bock, *Progressive Dispensationalism*, 37–39, 53.
132. Though Progressive Dispensationalism is the predominant version of Dispensationalism, some still hold to the framework of Revised Dispensationalism. Ryrie, *Dispensationalism Today*.
133. Blaising and Bock, *Progressive Dispensationalism*, 53, 130–39, 141–50.
134. Blaising and Bock, *Progressive Dispensationalism*, 130–31, 139.

ments, but these obligatory elements are understood to define the means and manner of blessing, not the fundamental fulfillment of the promises.[135]

The Mosaic covenant is understood to have its foundation in the Abrahamic covenant, but it is not a renewal or restatement of the Abrahamic.[136] The Mosaic covenant is a suzerain-vassal treaty with laws and stipulations that determine the physical, material, and national experience of the blessings promised to Abraham.[137] As in Covenant Theology, the tension between the promissory Abrahamic covenant and the obligatory Mosaic law is resolved by limiting the Mosaic covenant's function to temporal mediation so that covenant failure does not affect the ultimate fulfillment of the Abrahamic promises.[138] Bock and Blaising see essential continuity between the Abrahamic and Mosaic covenants as the law mediates promised blessings, but also progression in a "national religious cult" that governs the divine-human relationship via the revealed law.[139]

Recently, evangelical scholars have sought to address the divide between Covenant Theology and Dispensationalism by proposing alternative approaches to the biblical theology of covenant. John Walton's *Covenant* is not a fully-formed OT theology, but it is an attempt to reassess and develop a biblical-theological understanding of the covenants.[140] Unlike Dispensationalism's overarching purpose of kingdom or Covenant Theology's overarching goal of salvation, Walton's overarching purpose for the covenants is to progressively *reveal* God in the context of relationship.[141] Thus, Walton sees each biblical covenant as part of a unified program of revelation, which means each covenant complements and supplements what has come before without replacement, subordination, or nullification.[142]

In terms of the tension between unconditional and conditional elements, Walton's guiding principle is the irrevocability of revelation; therefore, the conditional aspects of any covenant only affect what Walton calls "covenant jeopardy."[143] Walton echoes earlier solutions to this dilemma by suggesting that violations of covenant stipulations result in *benefit* or

---

135. Blaising and Bock, *Progressive Dispensationalism*, 133–35. Chisholm posits that the promises were conditional until Abraham offered Isaac, which prompted God to make the promises an irrevocable grant. Chisholm, "Evidence from Genesis," 34–54.

136. Blaising and Bock, *Progressive Dispensationalism*, 141–42.

137. Blaising and Bock, *Progressive Dispensationalism*, 143–45.

138. Blaising and Bock, *Progressive Dispensationalism*, 143–51.

139. Blaising and Bock, *Progressive Dispensationalism*, 145–51.

140. Walton, *Covenant*.

141. Walton, *Covenant*, 24–25.

142. Walton, *Covenant*, 49–50.

143. Walton, *Covenant*, 113–14.

participation jeopardy, whereby stipulated blessings or an individual's participation in the covenant are forfeit without affecting the overall fulfillment and revelatory function of the covenants.[144] While innovative and informative, Walton's work is not a fully-formed middle gound between Covenant Theology and Dispensationalism.

A much-anticipated recent work is Peter Gentry and Stephen Wellum's *Kingdom through Covenant: A Biblical-Theological Understanding of the Covenants*.[145] This work is unique in that it contains a thorough exegetical study of major covenant texts by Peter Gentry as well as a systematic theological synthesis by Stephen Wellum. The design of the study is intended to reflect a complementary dynamic wherein biblical theology provides the data for systematic theology.[146] This work also aims to be a *via media* between Dispensationalism and Covenant Theology, which is why they refer to their approach as either "new Covenant Theology" or even "progressive covenantalism."[147]

The design and method along with the pairing of a biblical scholar and a theologian seem quite promising. Gentry and Wellum approach the study of the covenants with the aim of examining each in its respective "redemptive-historical" context and then synthesizing a systematic understanding of the way they relate to each other.[148] In terms of covenant typology, Gentry and Wellum tend to eschew traditional classifications of suzerain-vassal and grant-type covenants, opting instead to see unconditional and conditional elements in each covenant.[149] The fact that they see a covenant with creation as a biblical covenant suggests a strong biblical-theological affinity for Covenant Theology.[150]

With regard to the Abrahamic covenant, Gentry traces a developmental process from early uncertainty about Abraham's righteousness to a confirmation of the covenant relationship.[151] The presence of Mosaic law terminology in Gen 26 signals a continuity whereby the Abrahamic covenant anticipates the Mosaic covenant and national blessing is tied to obedience.[152] Gentry suggests that the Abrahamic covenant is patterned

---

144. Walton, *Covenant*, 113–34.
145. Gentry and Wellum, Kingdom through Covenant.
146. Gentry and Wellum, *Kingdom through Covenant*, 11, 21–37.
147. Gentry and Wellum, *Kingdom through Covenant*, 23–24.
148. Gentry and Wellum, *Kingdom through Covenant*, 92.
149. Gentry and Wellum, *Kingdom through Covenant*, 120, 135.
150. Gentry and Wellum, *Kingdom through Covenant*, 177–221.
151. Gentry and Wellum, *Kingdom through Covenant*, 263, 285.
152. Gentry and Wellum, *Kingdom through Covenant*, 291.

after a "general ANE treaty," except in this case it is God who takes the self-maledictory oath for both partners (Gen 15).[153] This divine self-malediction ultimately comes to fruition in the death of Christ.[154] In terms of schematic context, the Abrahamic covenant is seen as a foundational covenant for all human-divine relationships and the "backbone" to the metanarrative plot.[155]

The Book of the Covenant (Exod 19-24) is considered the center for the Mosaic covenant, whereas Deuteronomy is a supplemental but essential part of the covenant.[156] Not only is the Mosaic covenant seen as central to the OT it is also the backdrop against which the NT ought to be understood.[157] Though the Mosaic covenant is seen as a suzerain-vassal type covenant, it is still considered to be established and upheld by grace with grace serving as the motivation for obedience to the law.[158] Once again, the conditional elements of the Mosaic covenant are not determinative of the covenant's fulfillment, which coheres with Gentry and Wellum's stance that unconditional and conditional are not helpful categories for covenant typology.[159] In terms of continuity, the exodus event fulfills the Abrahamic covenant and Exod 19:5-6 means the Mosaic covenant is the means by which Israel fulfills the Adamic role assigned to Abraham.[160]

Wellum's theological synthesis is based on the central idea that creation's teleological purpose is to bring about God's kingdom.[161] The covenants are not simplistically classified as unconditional or conditional in light of unresolved theological tension in each covenant. This tension means God can graciously advance his plan while allowing fallible covenant partners to have a role requiring a genuine response of faith, and this tension is ultimately resolved when Christ fulfills the new covenant.[162] The Abrahamic

---

153. Gentry and Wellum, *Kingdom through Covenant*, 293-95.

154. Gentry and Wellum, *Kingdom through Covenant*, 294.

155. Gentry and Wellum, *Kingdom through Covenant*, 295.

156. Gentry and Wellum, *Kingdom through Covenant*, 301, 382.

157. Gentry and Wellum, *Kingdom through Covenant*, 304-9.

158. Gentry and Wellum, *Kingdom through Covenant*, 308-9, 312. Gentry views the "if-then" statement in Exod 19:5 as a *speech-act* conditional where the speech-act is performed conditionally in the apodosis making the protasis relevant. Therefore, the conditionality of the covenant is not determinative, but rather it states the "content and nature of the status" that is inherent in the "if" clause. Gentry and Wellum, *Kingdom through Covenant*, 312-13.

159. Gentry and Wellum, *Kingdom through Covenant*, 313-14.

160. Gentry and Wellum, *Kingdom through Covenant*, 388, The promises of the Abrahamic covenant are seen as coming to fulfillment in the Iron Age through the Mosaic covenant. Gentry and Wellum, *Kingdom through Covenant*, 323-27.

161. Gentry and Wellum, *Kingdom through Covenant*, 592.

162. Gentry and Wellum, *Kingdom through Covenant*, 608-10, 630-35.

covenant is seen as having unilateral/unconditional aspects as well as bilateral/conditional elements.[163] The Mosaic covenant is seen as the fulfillment of the Abrahamic covenant, therefore the election of Israel as a nation is not due to Israel's righteousness, but by the gracious election established in the Abrahamic covenant.[164] The Mosaic covenant is viewed as bilateral and conditional in nature, but its establishment and fulfillment are unilaterally enacted by God secondary to his promise.[165]

Kingdom through Covenant features robust exegetical research and innovative theological thinking. As is to be expected with an ambitious work like this, proponents of both Covenant Theology and Dispensationalism have expressed questions about its methodology and conclusions.[166] While it has not successfully solved the impasse between Dispensationalism and Covenant Theology, it is noteworthy for moving the conversation forward. Gentry and Wellum have also demonstrated that the biblical-theological study of biblical covenants is still a vibrant topic of interest.

A Return to Wellhausen

By the mid-1950s, there was a general consensus in OT scholarship regarding the role of covenant in both the formation of Israel and in Israel's social and religious life. However, this period of consensus would be followed by an interesting revival of Wellhausenian views.[167] The vanguard of this "Neo-Wellhausenian" movement consists of two German scholars, Lothar Perlitt and Ernst Kutsch. Perlitt's *Bundestheologie im Alten Testament* is a thorough treatment of the view that Israel's covenant traditions were theological constructs that originated in the late monarchic period.[168] Perlitt's work is largely predicated on his understanding of a "proto-Deuteronomic" and Deuteronomic circle that operated from around the time of the collapse of the Northern Kingdom into the exilic period.[169]

It is against the backdrop of the destruction of the Northern Kingdom and the exile that Perlitt sees a theological need to invoke the idea of the

---

163. Gentry and Wellum, *Kingdom through Covenant*, 630–35.
164. Gentry and Wellum, *Kingdom through Covenant*, 636.
165. Gentry and Wellum, *Kingdom through Covenant*, 638.
166. For a Reformed critique, see Brack and Oliphant, "Questioning the Progress," 189–217. For a Dispensational perspective, see Bock, "Critique of Gentry," 139–45 and Blaising, "Critique of Gentry," 111–27.
167. See Zimmerli, "History of Israelite Religion," 378–83.
168. Perlitt, *Bundestheologie*.
169. Nicholson, *God and His People*, 109–17.

Mosaic law within an obligatory covenant relationship. In light of the exile, the Deuteronomist provides an explanation and a glimmer of hope rooted in the unfulfilled conditions of the Mosaic covenant.[170] As for the patriarchal covenant tradition, Perlitt attributes this to a proto-Deuteronomic school and not J as widely held.[171] Perlitt also revises the interpretation of the Sinai narrative so that it is not a proper covenant-making episode but a theophany tradition into which the Decalogue and covenant concepts were added by later D and P tradents.[172] Perlitt's work revitalized a view of covenant that was similar in many ways to that of Wellhausen with differences mainly having to do with some of his source-critical analysis.

In Kutsch's *Verheissung und Gesetz,* the core position is that *berit* always means "obligation" (*Verpflichtung*), as opposed to a mutually-agreed relationship (*Bund*).[173] Kutsch's work combines analyses of various covenant texts with an etymological and semantic study of the term *berit*.[174] Per Kutsch, the idea of obligation is found in four types of uses of *berit*: (1) to take an obligation on oneself; (2) to impose an obligation on another; (3) the bilateral acceptance of obligations; and (4) an obligation imposed by a third party.[175] Kutsch's study results in an oversimplified reduction of the covenant concept that does not properly address bilateral covenant relationships.[176] Since covenant means obligation, Kutsch sets the idea in a legal setting and finds little evidence for a pre-Deuteronomic/Deuteronomistic origin of the covenant concept.[177]

As previously noted, McCarthy produced a second edition of his influential work *Treaty and Covenant* shortly after the works of Perlitt and Kutsch. In this new edition, McCarthy would move further toward the view that covenant texts in the OT originated with the Deuteronomic and Deuteronomistic schools that consciously used the analogy of suzerain-vassal

---

170. Perlitt, *Bundestheologie*, 46. See also Nicholson, *God and His People*, 109–10.

171. Perlitt, *Bundestheologie*, 7–8, 30–67. See also Nicholson, *God and His People*, 112.

172. Nicholson, *God and His People*, 116–17. Perlitt sees theophany, not covenant at Sinai. Perlitt, *Bundestheologie*, 280.

173. Kutsch defines *Bund* as a reciprocal relationship with mutual rights and obligations for both parties. Kutsch, *Verheissung und Gesetz*, 1.

174. Kutsch's semantic study of *berit* in the pre-Deuteronomic period and from the seventh century BCE on are found in chapters 4 and 5. Kutsch, *Verheissung und Gesetz*, 51–149.

175. Nicholson, *God and His People*, 90–92.

176. Nicholson notes that Kutsch's relegation of bilateral arrangements to a secondary usage of the primary "obligation" idea is insufficient. Nicholson, *God and His People*, 104–5.

177. Kutsch, *Verheissung und Gesetz*, 71–73, 146–49, 152, 162, 167–73.

treaties in a *theologically reflective* manner.[178] McCarthy's overall view of covenant in the OT now placed the lion's share of the covenant concept's development in the seventh and sixth centuries BCE with very little genuine covenant material predating the late monarchic era. A little later, Ernest W. Nicholson's *God and His People: Covenant and Theology in the Old Testament* would embrace and echo the approach of Perlitt and Kutsch from within British scholarly circles. Nicholson fully embraced the Wellhausenian revival in both his methods and conclusions.[179] Nicholson's work largely reflects Perlitt's approach with minor departures in certain source-critical details.[180]

Overall, Nicholson champions the revitalized view that a full-blown theological concept of covenant only emerges late in the monarchical era as a product of pre-Deuteronomic and Deuteronomic circles.[181] It becomes obvious that the revival of the Wellhausen school is characterized by what Zimmerli calls "Deuteronomism," which is a defining emphasis on the *berit* concept within the context of Deuteronomic theology as the key to the history of Israelite religion.[182] Paul Williamson aptly summarizes this situation:

> The historical-critical study of covenant has come full circle, and the dominant approach within mainstream Old Testament scholarship owes much more to critical reconstruction of Israel's history than to the narrative theology of the canonical biblical text.[183]

As will be discussed later, Brevard S. Childs's proposal for a canonical approach to theological study would push some in mainstream biblical studies away from diachronic studies of the world behind the text in favor of a literary-theological focus on the final form of the text. Though this shift would be significant, it was not all-encompassing and many in mainstream OT scholarship would still hold to a Wellhausenian approach.

---

178. McCarthy, *Treaty and Covenant*, 290. McCarthy also attributes the covenant concept to the Deuteronomist, but cautiously posits that the *berit* concept is present in some layers of pre-Deuteronomic tradition. McCarthy, "*Berit* in Old Testament," 110–21. See also Nicholson, *God and His People*, 84–85.

179. Hahn, *Kinship by Covenant*, 2–3.

180. Nicholson, *God and His People*, 139–50.

181. Nicholson, *God and His People*, 188. See also Whitley, "Covenant and Commandment," 37–48.

182. Zimmerli, "History of Israelite Religion," 380.

183. Williamson, *Sealed with an Oath*, 28.

The Current State of Covenant Studies

Since the "return to Wellhausen" spearheaded by Perlitt, Kutsch, and Nicholson, OT scholarship has entered a period of renewed scholarly interest in the covenants. In 1977, James Barr published his semantic study of *berit*, which features a helpful study of etymology in light of ANE linguistic data.[184] One of the more helpful insights is Barr's conclusion that the term *berit* was an "opaque word," or *brutum factum* of the Hebrew language, meaning possible etymological origins are of little use in clarifying its meaning in the OT.[185]

In the wake of Barr's piece, P. J. Naylor's dissertation provided an exhaustive and detailed structural analysis of *berit*'s semantic field in biblical Hebrew. Unlike Barr's brief treatment, Naylor sought to do a purely semantic study without the extraneous "agendas" of theological or biblical studies, which he saw as obscuring an accurate philological and semantic study of the term.[186] Naylor's work is helpful in that it conscientiously seeks to avoid "pan-covenantalism" in identifying and analyzing the various terms that ought to be part of *berit*'s semantic field.[187]

By the end of the 1980s, an important development in the field of biblical studies was a greater emphasis on synchronic studies and the canonical form of the text. The early historical-critical emphasis on the world behind the text was giving way to a focus on the text in its final form. One of the contributing factors was the increasing engagement with literary criticism as a method of reading the text. Another major development was the emergence of canonical criticism and a focus on canon as the context for textual analysis.

Though he eschewed the term "canonical criticism," Brevard Childs's canonical approach reflected his critique of the historical-critical preoccupation with historical backgrounds and the "history of traditions."[188] The influence of literary criticism and canonical criticism did not signal the end of higher-critical methods, but it did mean that there was a potentially more fruitful way to put diachronic research to use. Per Childs, the purpose of source criticism, form criticism, tradition history, and redaction criticism should not be to recover the theological meaning behind the text but to bet-

---

184. Barr, "Some Semantic Notes," 23–28.

185. Barr, "Some Semantic Notes," 26.

186. Naylor, "Language of Covenant," 21, 43–46.

187. Naylor, "Language of Covenant," 48–50.

188. Childs, *Biblical Theology in Crisis*. For additional examples of a canonical approach in covenant studies, see Anderson, *Contours*; Williamson, *Abraham, Israel, and the Nations*; Rendtorff, *Covenant Formula*; and Hahn, *Kinship by Covenant*.

ter understand the final form of the text in its canonical context.[189] Childs notes that "One can better appreciate a symphony if one has been trained to recognize the contribution of each of the various musical instruments involved."[190] Another unintended effect of these developments has been the closing of the gap between mainstream and evangelical scholarship as the canon provides common ground in which both groups operate. In this recent period of OT studies, it seems that there is less emphasis on the history behind the text and more potential for an innovative reading of the canonical text.

Gordon Hugenberger's *Marriage as Covenant* addresses marriage as a covenant in Mal 2:14; however, his research on the taxonomy of *berit* throughout the OT has proven to be a significant contribution.[191] In his chapter "'Covenant' and 'Oath' Defined," Hugenberger defines *berit* as " . . . an elected as opposed to natural, relationship of obligation established under divine sanction."[192] This definition of covenant nuances earlier extremes by balancing the ideas of relationship and obligation.[193]

Rolf Rendtorff's *The Covenant Formula* specifically addresses the *covenant formula* ("I will be your God and you will be my people") in the OT.[194] Working within a source-critical framework, Rendtorff delves into the mixing of early source traditions in later works that results in a helpful study of the developing relationship between the concept of *berit* and "election" (בחר) in late works.[195] In addition, Rendtorff expands the scope of his research to examine the covenant concept in passages where the idea seems present despite the absence of the actual term, *berit*.[196]

Williamson's aforementioned *Abraham, Israel, and the Nations: The Patriarchal Promise and Its Covenantal Development in Genesis* is a recent example of a literary theological study of the Abrahamic covenant that reflects the influence of "new literary criticism."[197] Williamson's study entails a synchronic study of literary and theological dynamics in the Abrahamic covenant pericopes of Gen 15 and 17 that leads to a novel reading of the

---

189. Childs, *Biblical Theology of the Old and New Testaments*, 104–6.
190. Childs, *Biblical Theology of the Old and New Testaments*, 105.
191. Hugenberger, *Marriage as a Covenant*.
192. Hugenberger, *Marriage as a Covenant*, 197.
193. Hahn, *Kinship by Covenant*, 6.
194. Rendtorff, *Covenant Formula*. See Appendix B for covenant-related formulas and related variants.
195. Rendtorff, *Covenant Formula*, 3–4.
196. Hahn, *Kinship by Covenant*, 6.
197. Williamson, *Abraham, Israel, and the Nations*, 22–25.

Abraham cycle.[198] One of the significant contributions of Williamson's study is a viable defense of the view that the Abraham narrative describes two distinct covenants.[199]

Another important development of this period is a focus on the ANE concept of kinship as an alternative paradigm for understanding *berit*. Many credit F. M. Cross's seminal study of kinship and covenant for popularizing this approach to *berit*.[200] Cross countered the "neo-Wellhausenian" trend by placing the original *Sitz im Leben* of the covenant concept in the kinship-based organization of Semitic tribes.[201] Following Cross's work on kinship, Scott Hahn's *Kinship by Covenant* represents a significant recent treatment of covenant featuring the kinship concept. Hahn's work is unique in that he uses kinship as the controlling concept for understanding biblical covenants, but he does so within a framework that is based on the dual typology of treaty-type and grant-type covenants.[202]

Hahn's treatment of the Sinaitic/Mosaic covenant complex is noteworthy. First, Hahn makes a technical distinction between the *vow* and the *oath* in which the *vow* is a promise made to God while the *oath* is a promise combined with the invocation of a conditional self-maledictory curse.[203] He then develops the idea of kinship in the OT and concludes that the Sinai covenant and the Mosaic covenant in Deuteronomy are two different covenants.[204] The key to this view is that the Sinai covenant is more of a familial bond characterized by kinship while the covenant in Deuteronomy is the Sinai covenant tradition reconfigured into a traditional suzerain-vassal treaty with father-son nuances.[205] The scope of Hahn's work is notable, for

---

198. Williamson, *Abraham, Israel, and the Nations*, 7–8.

199. Williamson does a detailed exegetical analysis of Gen 15 in chapter 4 and follows with a similar treatment of Gen 17 in chapter 5. In chapter 6 Williamson argues for the possibility that Gen 17 describes the making of a different covenant altogether. He then concludes by proposing a new reading that accounts for the presence of two covenants. Williamson, *Abraham, Israel, and the Nations*, 121–259.

200. Cross, "Kinship and Covenant," 15–21.

201. Cross, "Kinship and Covenant," 15–21.

202. This is reflected in the outline of his study. In chapter 3, Hahn focuses on treaty-type covenants, which he differentiates as either a *vow* or an *oath* and includes the Sinaitic and Mosaic covenants. In chapters 4–7, he examines the grant-type covenants, devoting a chapter each to the Noachian, Abrahamic, and Davidic covenants. Hahn, *Kinship by Covenant*, 49–216.

203. Hahn, *Kinship by Covenant*, 50–51.

204. Hahn, *Kinship by Covenant*, 64–65.

205. Hahn, *Kinship by Covenant*, 63–65, 82–83, 90–92.

he covers both the OT and NT, but its depth is also impressive as evidenced by his review of recent covenant scholarship.[206]

The innovative and diverse nature of current covenant scholarship is exemplified in the recent work of Richard Bautch. Bautch's monograph *Glory and Power, Ritual and Relationship: The Sinai Covenant in the Postexilic Period* remains rooted in a historical-critical approach without being subject to the older source-critical presuppositions of Wellhausen. Bautch pushes conventional views in his study of the Sinai covenant tradition by placing its origin in the Persian period toward the beginning of Second Temple Judaism.[207] This is not a total surprise when one considers that McCarthy's work set the stage for Bautch's view that the two essential elements of the Sinai covenant tradition are theophany combined with a ritual that formalizes relationship.[208]

Bautch also did a study of the Abrahamic covenant in an article entitled, "An Appraisal of Abraham's Role in Postexilic Covenants," which places the Abrahamic covenant in the context of the Persian period and the postexilic theological milieu.[209] One characteristic of Bautch's work is a rejection of the long-accepted two-typology approach, which distills all biblical covenants to either the Davidic tradition or the Mosaic/Sinaitic tradition.[210] Bautch chooses to see much more fluidity between various covenant types due to the coalescing of covenant traditions during the Persian period.[211] Bautch's influence as a proponent of the Persian period as the setting for Judaism's covenant theology is also evident in a collection of studies he and Knoppers edited, entitled *Covenant in the Persian Period*.[212] This collection of current studies provides a helpful glimpse of the *status quaestionis* in mainstream OT scholarship. The work in this volume is characterized by a departure from classical source-criticism in favor of reading the OT texts through the lens of more complex redactional layers.[213]

While innovative work goes on within biblical studies, the current state of comparative research involving ANE treaties is also far from stagnant. As noted above, an influx of research by specialists, such as Assyriologists and Hittitologists, has proven invaluable in helping biblical scholars reassess

---

206. Hahn, *Kinship by Covenant*, 1–22.
207. Bautch, *Glory and Power*, 6–9.
208. Bautch, *Glory and Power*, 4–6.
209. Bautch, "Appraisal of Abraham's Role," 42–63.
210. Bautch and Knoppers, *Covenants in the Persian Period*, 5.
211. Bautch and Knoppers, *Covenants in the Persian Period*, 5.
212. Bautch and Knoppers, *Covenants in the Persian Period*, 5.
213. Bellinger, "Psalms," 309–23.

earlier conclusions regarding the value and meaning of extrabiblical treaty and law texts.

One of the best recent examples of a fresh look at older research is a 2004 monograph by Noel Weeks. In this study, Weeks undertakes an innovative study of the treaty form as found in Mesopotamian, Hittite, and Israelite sources. Weeks recognized the need for this type of study in light of the way earlier studies of ANE treaties had been carried out. Weeks observed that the aim of much of the scholarship on treaty and covenant from the mid-1950s to the 1970s tended to serve other priorities in OT studies, such as the dating of sources and the analysis of literary strata.[214] Weeks also noted that earlier studies were often subject to the particular manner in which various schools approached the history of Israelite religion.[215] By the end of the twentieth century, Weeks felt that many fundamental assumptions regarding ANE treaty forms were going unquestioned since scholars were often preoccupied with other questions.[216] Weeks's monograph is an attempt to revisit ANE treaty forms free of the assumptions and presuppositions that affected earlier research.

Weeks's work also addresses the "Pan-Babylonian controversy," which involves the assumption that Mesopotamia is the common source for culture in the surrounding regions.[217] He questions whether it might be possible that different cultures arrived at similar forms independently since there is a human tendency to arrive at similar solutions to common problems.[218] By attempting to enter into his study without undue assumptions, Weeks produced a work characterized by fresh, detailed analysis of much of the same data McCarthy studied, but without some of the unnecessary agendas.

In Mesopotamian treaties, Weeks observes that there is no specific form since the treaty traditions cover such a long period of time. In keeping with his questioning of pan-Babylonian tendencies, Weeks gives two reasons for questioning borrowing theories that see Mesopotamia as the source: (1) The sheer variety of forms in Mesopotamia makes it difficult to ascertain if a document has been borrowed and then changed; (2) Mesopotamian documents lack distinctive features that allow for clear identification in a different cultural context.[219] Weeks also sees a similar difficulty with

---

214. Weeks, *Admonition and Curse*, 8.
215. Weeks, *Admonition and Curse*, 8.
216. Weeks, *Admonition and Curse*, 1–3.
217. Weeks, *Admonition and Curse*, 2. For more on the Pan-Babylonian controversy see Larsen, "'Babel/Bible' Controversy," 95–106.
218. Weeks, *Admonition and Curse*, 2.
219. Weeks, *Admonition and Curse*, 53–54.

Syrian sources (e.g., Mari and Alalakh) since there is no discernible treaty tradition.[220] Despite complex questions about Hatti's relationship to Mesopotamian culture, Weeks finds the Hittite corpus to be most useful due to the consistency and distinct nature of the treaty form.[221]

In Weeks's analysis of Israelite texts, he incorporates a thorough understanding of earlier scholarship, including the works of Mendenhall, Bright, and Wellhausen.[222] The highlight of Weeks's conclusions is his suggestion that Israel's covenant traditions actually originated in a common mid- to late- second-millennium ANE treaty culture that includes Mesopotamia, Hatti, and Egypt, which then resulted in the independent development of treaty and covenant forms in each respective cultural context.[223] Weeks's findings cohere with Kitchen and Lawrence's position that the late-second-millennium Hittite treaty form is the closest ANE analogue to the biblical covenant form.[224] Weeks is well aware of the difficulty his hypothesis presents in light of modern scholarship's affinity for Wellhausen's view, but he deftly addresses the underlying tendencies and presuppositions that equally affected Mendenhall's and Wellhausen's research.[225]

At this time, the question of covenant conditionality continues to elicit active discussion within the fields of biblical theology and covenant studies. Since Weinfeld's work on grant-type treaties, this issue has defied an easy consensus. Despite the continued progress being made in the study of ANE treaties, there are still discussions regarding the tension between the unconditional grant and the conditional treaty in the OT context.

David Noel Freedman's 1964 essay "Divine Commitment and Human Obligation" still stands as a thoughtful approach to this issue of covenant tension.[226] In addressing this issue, Freedman proposes an alternative way of describing and classifying unconditional and conditional covenants, i.e., the covenant of divine commitment (unconditional, unilateral) and the covenant of human obligation (conditional, bilateral).[227] Freedman's proposed classifications are based on his study of covenant types within the context of

---

220. Weeks, *Admonition and Curse*, 132.
221. Weeks, *Admonition and Curse*, 92–98.
222. Weeks, *Admonition and Curse*, 132–70.
223. Weeks, *Admonition and Curse*, 170–73, 178.
224. Kitchen and Lawrence, *Treaty, Law, and Covenant*, 3:251–61.
225. Weeks, *Admonition and Curse*, 134–73, specifically 71n97.
226. Freedman, "Divine Commitment," 419–31.
227. Freedman, "Divine Commitment," 420.

OT documentary sources.[228] Freedman concludes that the tension between divine commitment and human obligation may be a hard impasse:

> Can covenant bond be broken—and at the same time persist? Can God sever a relationship as a result of covenant violations— and nevertheless maintain it in perpetuity? The Bible seems to answer in the affirmative.[229]

Freedman goes on to posit a fluid relationship between God's unconditional commitment and the real role of human response within this relational context.

Freedman would later revisit this topic in more detail in his coauthored piece "People of the New Covenant" in which he and Miano further flesh out an examination of the grant-type and suzerainty-type covenants in the OT.[230] Of note is how Freedman now incorporates Weinfeld's view of grant-type treaties, which had not been published in 1964 at the time of his first article. In this recent article, Freedman interacts with Knoppers's critique of Weinfeld's work, noting that in divine-human covenants the divine initiative rests solely with God, which is why Weinfeld's grant-type covenant still has value.[231]

In 1983, Ronald Youngblood addressed this issue by reexamining the conditionality of the Abrahamic covenant.[232] While it had been recognized that there seem to be conditional elements in the Abrahamic covenant texts, Youngblood investigated these in more detail, especially the details of the covenant narrative that are ostensibly conditional.[233] Youngblood also explores the Abrahamic covenant's connections to the Mosaic covenant, which may imply conditionality in parts of the Abrahamic covenant.[234] Youngblood acknowledges the differences in treaty form between the Abrahamic and Mosaic covenants, but then argues that there are also many significant similarities between the two covenants from a theological perspective. He concludes that the Abrahamic covenant is best viewed as a "conditional" covenant with the crucial caveat that "condition" be understood as the

---

228. Freedman, "Divine Commitment," 421–26.
229. Freedman, "Divine Commitment," 429.
230. Freedman and Miano, "People of the New Covenant," 7–26.
231. Freedman and Miano, "People of the New Covenant," 8n6.
232. Youngblood, "Abrahamic Covenant," 31–46.
233. Youngblood, "Abrahamic Covenant," 36–41.
234. Youngblood, "Abrahamic Covenant," 40–44.

instrument of receiving grace as opposed to the meritorious means of obtaining grace.[235]

One of the more helpful contributions on this topic is Bruce K. Waltke's "The Phenomenon of Conditionality within Unconditional Covenants."[236] Waltke proposes the categories of the irrevocable grant, or *oath*, and the *law*, which is characterized by obligation. He then outlines both conditional and unconditional elements in each covenant, including the ostensibly unconditional Noachian, Abrahamic, and Davidic covenants.[237] Per Waltke, those covenants that are divine oaths, including the Noachian, Abrahamic, and Davidic, are *irrevocable* on the strength of Yahweh's unimpeachable commitment.[238] However, there are both unconditional and conditional aspects to these irrevocable covenants. On the other hand, the Mosaic covenant is clearly bilateral and conditional in nature, yet Waltke observes that there is still an ultimate safeguard insuring that failure to keep the covenant and the ensuing curses are not final.[239] In this way the dialectical tension between the irrevocable promises based on Yahweh's faithfulness and the law based in Yahweh's holiness is finally resolved by the new covenant, which perfectly fulfills the terms of the Mosaic law and ultimately fulfills the Abrahamic promises.[240] Waltke's emphasis on the distinction between irrevocable and unconditional is an elucidating bit of analysis. By separating the concepts of revocability and conditionality, Waltke provides a helpful grouping of concepts with which covenants can be described.

Waltke's treatment of the complexities and difficulties associated with the simple binary of conditional versus unconditional covenants has been helpful in identifying inadequacies in using this approach to classifying ANE and biblical covenants. While Waltke's move towards viewing covenant promises as either irrevocable or revocable does allow for greater clarity and nuance, Richard Averbeck contends that scholars ought to eschew all descriptions of covenants as unconditional or conditional.

In a helpful discussion on OT treaties and covenants, Averbeck finds the notion of unconditional versus conditional covenants to be problematic and at odds with the biblical data.[241] Averbeck further notes that the

---

235. Youngblood interacts with Freedman in developing his view, which accounts for the theological tension between unconditional grace and conditional human response in the divine human relationship. Youngblood, "Abrahamic Covenant," 43–45.

236. Waltke, "Phenomenon of Conditionality," 123–39.

237. Waltke, "Phenomenon of Conditionality," 125–34.

238. Waltke, "Phenomenon of Conditionality," 135.

239. Waltke, "Phenomenon of Conditionality," 135–36.

240. Waltke, "Phenomenon of Conditionality," 136–37.

241. Averbeck, "Old Testament Treaties," 17–18. This unpublished study by Richard

ANE analogues commonly compared to the biblical covenants are complex and do not fit neatly into an unconditional/conditional binary.[242] As for the major biblical covenants, Averbeck proposes that each covenant has two aspects: "permanent promise and ongoing obligation," which are not expressed in each covenant in equal degrees.[243] Averbeck summarizes his perspective thusly:

> Basically, the *promises* assure the *enduring nature of a covenant relationship* no matter what may happen, while the *obligations* focus on the importance of *faithfulness to God in order to experience the Lord's blessings* within the covenant relationship—as opposed to his chastisement, the curses. Like good relationships everywhere in all times, these covenants are made up of a combination of both permanent promise and ongoing obligation.[244]

In current scholarship, there is still a tendency to rely almost exclusively on the conditional/unconditional binary that became a consensus under the influence of the seminal works by Mendenhall and Weinfeld. Recent nuanced approaches to promise and obligation, like Waltke's and Averbeck's, represent a welcome move in the right direction. For the purposes of this present work, this writer opts to discuss covenant promises and stipulations according to the framework proposed by Averbeck and in line with the suggestions of Waltke.[245] Rather than classifying the biblical covenants as entirely conditional or unconditional, this writer understands the biblical covenants to entail both permanent promises and ongoing obligations according to each covenant's individual function, as well as its historical and canonical context. With regard to the Abrahamic and Mosaic covenants, this approach facilitates a nuanced understanding of the complex relationship between these covenants by addressing the promissory and obligatory aspects apart from a limited binary set of categories. It is the hope of this writer that this understanding of the two covenants will mitigate against perceiving inter-covenantal tension when this may not be warranted in light of ANE and biblical data.

Averbeck is slated to be published in a collection of Evangelical Theological Society papers from the OT Backgrounds and ANE group.

242. Averbeck, "Old Testament Treaties," 18.

243. Averbeck posits that there is flexibility as to how promise and obligation are stipulated depending on the purpose of the covenant as well as its historical and textual context. Averbeck, "Old Testament Treaties," 18.

244. Averbeck, "Old Testament Treaties," 18.

245. This writer will continue to use the terms unconditional and conditional when it is warranted in discussions that still use these categories.

As one surveys the most recent research being done in the various fields of biblical and theological studies, it should be apparent that the study of biblical covenants is far from stagnant. Scholars have revitalized this area of research and have done so in a way that sheds new light on old topics by incorporating the recent findings of outside specialists and experts. This spirit of cross-pollination and innovative study is not limited to the comparative study of ANE cultures and literature. Though there is a clear bifurcation in methods and priorities when it comes to mainstream and evangelical scholarship, there is great potential for helpful overlap when it comes to the research being done in the various areas of biblical and theological studies. It is the hope of this writer that future covenant scholarship will flourish by both looking outward to external specialties and also looking inward to the biblical and theological research going on in both streams of scholarship.

CURRENT APPROACHES TO THE RELATIONSHIP BETWEEN THE ABRAHAMIC AND MOSAIC COVENANTS

A particular complexity in summarizing the *status quaestionis* of the relationship between the Abrahamic and Mosaic covenants is that a scholar's worldview exerts considerable influence on the manner of the research being done. Mainstream scholars tend to view the two covenant traditions through the lens of religious development in Israel and assign the final development of the Abrahamic covenant (patriarchal) and Sinai/Mosaic covenant traditions to religious schools that operated late in Israel's history. They also rely on the comparative study of ANE literature, religions, and history in order to understand the context for Israel's religious development.

Evangelical scholarship, on the other hand, tends to focus on the historical-grammatical exegesis and interpretation of these two covenants within their respective canonical literary contexts. This study of the covenants often serves OT biblical theology in developing a coherent systematic theology. In these circles, the biblical covenants are instrumental to understanding and characterizing God's relationship to Israel and humanity as well as his overall plans in history. It is in this sense that the Abrahamic and Mosaic covenants are essential components of both Covenant Theology and Dispensationalism. In light of the substantial history of scholarship that has come before, the question of how the Abrahamic and Mosaic covenants are related is best addressed according to the respective approaches of mainstream and evangelical scholarship.

The Two Covenants in Mainstream Scholarship

Within mainstream OT scholarship, the relationship between the two foundational covenants can broadly be divided into two general views. The first view is characterized by the approach of the Wellhausen school, which interestingly went from being the predominant view to falling out of favor before finding a new generation of proponents. In this view, the concept of covenant is a theological construct that did not appear in Israel until the late monarchic period when the Deuteronomist developed the idea of a law covenant around the time of the Josianic reforms. The Priestly school of the exilic and postexilic periods would ultimately bring the patriarchal traditions to the fore and synthesize a coherent theology of covenants involving the patriarchal promises and the Mosaic law. Various scholars who take this general view might differ on some secondary details, but this basic outline is still a mainstay of mainstream scholarship.[246]

Various developments at the beginning of the twentieth century, including the influence of sociological (Weber) and phenomenological (Mowinckel) studies, caused a reconsideration of Wellhausen's construction of the world behind the text. Two of the most significant figures in eliciting a shift away from Wellhausen's views were Eichrodt with his work of OT theology and von Rad with his pioneering work on the history of traditions using form criticism.[247] The combination of all these concurrent trends led scholars to push covenant origins and traditions as far back as the formational period of Israel's history. Viewing the covenants as more than theological constructs, these scholars sought to identify the roots of covenant in the earliest Israelite traditions.

In this approach, the two covenant traditions are seen as developing in parallel streams going as far back as the pre-Israelite tribal period. The Abrahamic covenant was ostensibly located in patriarchal traditions that were primarily characterized as folklore. The Mosaic covenant featuring the law was rooted in the exodus-Sinai tradition, which would be closely associated with Israel's cult. During the late monarchic period, pre-Deuteronomic and Deuteronomic tradents incorporated the Abrahamic and Mosaic covenant traditions into the book of Deuteronomy, which the Priestly school would ultimately incorporate into the final form of the Pentateuch during the postexilic period.

---

246. For examples of this approach see Wellhausen, *Prolegomena*; Kutsch, *Verheissung und Gesetz*; Perlitt, *Bundestheologie*; Nicholson, *God and His People*.

247. Eichrodt, *Theology of the Old Testament*; von Rad, "Form Critical Problem," 1–78.

The exilic/postexilic milieu was defined by national catastrophe causing the Priestly school to revitalize the patriarchal promises as the foundational covenant in order to mitigate against the failure of the Mosaic covenant. This resulted in the Mosaic covenant being subordinated to the Abrahamic covenant in the final formulation of Israel's covenant theology. In his work on the history of covenants in Israel, Hillers credits P with combining the covenant traditions into a cohesive, progressive covenant history.[248]

Clements's work on the Abrahamic and Mosaic covenants is a good example of how this approach looks in practice.[249] Von Rad used the same basic approach but differed slightly in his understanding of how the covenant traditions were later combined. In von Rad's work "The Form Critical Problem of the Hexateuch," he surmised from the so-called "little credo" in Deut 26:5–9 that the patriarchal narratives and the Sinai tradition were in separate streams of tradition that were later combined by J during the exile.[250] Other examples of scholars who follow this general approach include Bernhard Anderson and Brevard Childs, who did studies of OT theology in a canonical context.[251]

In both Wellhausen's approach and the tradition-centric approach, one notable issue is the theological tension surrounding the unilateral, promissory nature of the Abrahamic promises and the bilateral, conditional nature of the Mosaic covenant. Some discern similarities between the two covenants in that both have unconditional and conditional elements, but the tension between the opposing types of covenants poses a real dilemma.[252] John Bright referred to this as a "theological collision" and credited the great prophets with finding ways to reconcile this theological tension.[253]

In his innovative OT theology, Walter Brueggemann briefly addressed this issue by emphasizing that God is a God who commands, but also noted that his commands are always in a covenant context so that they are covenantal commands operating as part of a dynamic divine human

---

248. Hillers, *Covenant*, 158–68. Childs credits P with having a significant hand in the final development of the Pentateuch. Childs, *Old Testament Theology*, 155–56.

249. Clements, *Abraham and David*, 64–78. See also Anderson, *Contours*, 239–42.

250. Von Rad, "Form Critical Problem," 1–26. See also Kaiser, *Toward an Old Testament Theology*, 61.

251. Anderson attributes most of the synthetic work to the Deuteronomists as opposed to P. Anderson, *Contours*, 152–54. See also Childs, *Old Testament Theology*, 93–94.

252. A note of interest: Hillers, writing right before Weinfeld's work on the royal-grant type of treaty was published, observes that the Abrahamic covenant is a different type of covenant even though no known example of a grant-type treaty had been proposed. Hillers, *Covenant*, 104–5.

253. Bright, *Covenant and Promise*, 165.

relationship.²⁵⁴ In fact, Brueggemann actually downplays the tension between unconditional and conditional covenants as a modern preoccupation.²⁵⁵ Brueggemann suggests that Israel did not think of the covenants in these logical terms but rather in relational terms and as a result, keeping these two covenantal ideas in tension was not the conundrum modern thinkers believe it to be.²⁵⁶ Childs also deemphasized the tension between the promissory and obligatory natures of the two covenants in his canonical approach to OT theology. Childs saw God's formation of a covenant with a chosen people as a "red thread" that joins the various parts of the OT together, so much so that the promises of the patriarchal narratives anticipate the Sinai covenant tradition.²⁵⁷

In surveying some of the ways scholars have attempted to reconcile the tension between the Abrahamic and Mosaic covenants, one finds that mainstream scholars are, by and large, well-positioned to address this issue by virtue of their presuppositions and methods. Since mainstream scholars see a substantial amount of late theological development and synthesis in the way the Deuteronomic and Priestly schools combine the Abrahamic and Mosaic covenant, it stands to reason that theological and practical tensions can be consciously resolved, or at least smoothed out in the process of producing the final canonical form of the text.

The Two Covenants in Evangelical Studies

Despite differences in some of the details and nuances, most evangelical biblical scholars and theologians hold similar views on the relationship between the Abrahamic and Mosaic covenants. The general view is that the Abrahamic covenant is a programmatic, foundational promissory covenant involving land, descendants, and universal blessing mediated by Abraham's descendants. Understandably, Dispensationalism and Covenant Theology differ on the specific terms of the Abrahamic covenant. Covenant Theology tends to link the Abrahamic covenant to the covenant of grace and views the new covenant promises (and the NT) as an extension and fulfillment of the Abrahamic promises.²⁵⁸ Even the institution of the universal church is linked to the Abrahamic covenant.²⁵⁹ In Progressive Dispensationalism,

---

254. Brueggemann, *Theology of the Old Testament*, 198.
255. Brueggemann, *Theology of the Old Testament*, 199.
256. Brueggemann, *Theology of the Old Testament*, 199.
257. Childs, *Old Testament Theology*, 94.
258. Golding, *Covenant Theology*, 153–55.
259. Golding, *Covenant Theology*, 153–55.

the land, descendants, and mediation of blessing are seen as key promissory features that have their main connection to the nation of Israel.[260]

In Progressive Dispensationalism, the Mosaic covenant is understood as a bilateral, obligatory covenant that constitutes Israel as a nation and establishes the laws and religious practices that administer blessings and curses for the nation.[261] It is also seen as a fulfillment of the patriarchal promises and continuous with the Abrahamic covenant as a subordinate covenant.[262] Across the evangelical spectrum, the Mosaic covenant is generally understood to establish the descendants of Abraham in the land of promise and function constitutively in establishing the people as the national entity, Israel. The Mosaic covenant is also defined by the law, which defines the people of God and provides rules for community life and cultic conduct. Evangelical scholars generally understand the two covenants as being in theological continuity despite perceived inter-covenantal tensions.

In Covenant Theology, there is a long history of varying views regarding the Mosaic covenant. Golding provides a helpful survey of the different views held in Reformed circles.[263] These views have ranged from the Mosaic covenant being a reissued covenant of works to a particular administration of the covenant of grace.[264] Some saw virtual unity between the Abrahamic and Mosaic covenants while others saw the Mosaic covenant as a new "dispensation."[265] The historic majority view of the Reformed tradition can be summarized thusly: (1) The covenant of grace as established in the Abrahamic covenant supersedes law, meaning the law can never void the covenant of grace; (2) the law is intended to subserve the covenant of grace and contribute to the fulfillment of the Abrahamic promises by revealing sin and providing rituals, services, and offices that foreshadow the Kingdom of Christ.[266] Within Covenant Theology, the view of the Mosaic covenant is nuanced by the awareness of an overarching covenant of grace.

For most evangelical scholars, the crux of the covenantal tension is rooted in the question of conditionality. For adherents of Covenant Theology, this understanding of covenantal tension is informed in part by the influence of the perceived law versus Gospel tension that is still addressed in

---

260. Blaising and Bock, *Progressive Dispensationalism*, 130–40, esp. 139–40.
261. Blaising and Bock, *Progressive Dispensationalism*, 140–51.
262. Blaising and Bock, *Progressive Dispensationalism*, 141–45.
263. Golding, *Covenant Theology*, see Appendix I, 164–73.
264. Golding, *Covenant Theology*, see Appendix I, 164–73.
265. Golding, *Covenant Theology*, see Appendix I, 164–73.
266. Golding, *Covenant Theology*, 169.

studies of Pauline theology, vís a vís the interpretation of Galatians.[267] In this tension, the Abrahamic covenant represents grace, i.e. the Gospel, and the Mosaic covenant represents the law. The orthodox Reformed view equates the two covenants as being virtually the same with any differences being a matter of form.[268] Though later proponents of Covenant Theology have placed a greater emphasis on the contrasts, there is still a strong sense of continuity between the two covenants since they are both subordinated to the covenant of grace.[269]

Today, Covenant Theology does not link the Mosaic covenant with the covenant of works via the law but views the Mosaic covenant as functioning administratively within the context of the redemptive covenant of grace.[270] As a result, Covenant Theology does not see obedience as a means of justification or establishment of a right relationship with God.[271] The Mosaic covenant takes the election of the Abrahamic covenant and nationalizes it in Israel and the law functions pedagogically as a means of preparing a people for Christ.[272]

In general, today's Dispensationalists tend to follow the view outlined in Progressive Dispensationalism, which is that the Mosaic covenant functions historically with regard to Israel's national blessings and curses in relation to the land but has implications for a final fulfillment in Jesus Christ.[273] In terms of the relationship with the Abrahamic covenant, the Mosaic covenant does not negate or supersede the Abrahamic promises, but only affects the manner in which the promises are experienced in Israel's history.[274] It also follows that the law is not determinative or constitutive of election or a redemptive relationship but is the expected result or natural consequence of God's gracious election.[275]

Older Dispensationalists (e.g., Scofield) perceived a much greater disconnect between the Abrahamic and Mosaic covenants with some even

---

267. Kaiser, *Toward an Old Testament Theology*, 59.

268. Golding, *Covenant Theology*, 155–56. See also Youngblood, "Abrahamic Covenant," 42–44.

269. Golding, *Covenant Theology*, 155–56.

270. Golding, *Covenant Theology*, 156–58.

271. Golding, *Covenant Theology*, 156–58.

272. Golding, *Covenant Theology*, 156–58.

273. Blaising and Bock, *Progressive Dispensationalism*, 150–51.

274. Blaising and Bock, *Progressive Dispensationalism*, 141–50.

275. Blaising and Bock, *Progressive Dispensationalism*, 130–40. Though he is not a dispensationalist, Kaiser's reasoning is illustrative of this view. Kaiser, *Toward an Old Testament Theology*, 62–63.

understanding the Mosaic covenant as an exchange of law for grace.[276] However, most Dispensationalists currently hold a view akin to that of Blaising and Bock with regard to the continuity and subordination of the Mosaic covenant to the overarching promises of the Abrahamic covenant. This also reflects the general approach of many evangelical scholars who are not proponents of either Covenant Theology or Dispensationalism.

Examples of evangelical scholarship that is not influenced by this intramural debate include the aforementioned works of Dumbrell and Williamson. The covenant studies by Dumbrell and Williamson also provide a helpful look at biblical theological studies of the covenants that are not shaped by the debate between Covenant Theology and Dispensationalism. Dumbrell affirms the programmatic and foundational nature of the Abrahamic covenant when he notes that the Abrahamic covenant "continues to be seen throughout the OT as the framework within which all other concepts of relationships which concern the people of God would arise."[277] Dumbrell also interestingly observed a tendency in later OT writings to appeal to Abrahamic promises in times of calamity since the Abrahamic covenant provides an overall sense of hope.[278]

In keeping with his theological theme of creation redemption, Dumbrell characterizes the Sinai/Mosaic covenant as serving the larger purposes of the Abrahamic covenant and he views the nation of Israel as the agent by which God achieves these larger purposes, namely the redemption of creation.[279] This is also the context for law, which provides the direction for life within the covenant relationship.[280] Dumbrell, following mainstream views, sees Deut 26 as "marrying" nation and land to theologically unite theAbrahamic and Sinai covenants and also sees possession of the land as fulfillment of the Abrahamic covenant.[281]

Williamson also views the Abrahamic covenant as programmatic, though his unique view is of two patriarchal covenants, one unconditional in Gen 15 that is specific to Israel's nationhood (people and territory) and one conditional in Gen 17, which includes an international dimension with royal lineage.[282] While Gen 15 was ratified unilaterally by God, Gen 17 is only "ratified" following the offering of Isaac, which fulfilled the obliga-

276. Golding, *Covenant Theology*, 171.
277. Dumbrell, *Covenant and Creation*, 78.
278. Dumbrell, *Covenant and Creation*, 78.
279. Dumbrell, *Covenant and Creation*, 89–90.
280. Dumbrell, *Covenant and Creation*, 126.
281. Dumbrell, *Covenant and Creation*, 117, 121.
282. Williamson, *Sealed with an Oath*, 86–91.

tory terms first revealed in Gen 17.[283] Williamson sees the Sinai covenant as subordinate to the patriarchal covenants and sees the law as part of the Sinai covenant's revelatory purpose, which is to reveal God to the nations as the king who established righteous laws for his people.[284] Williamson sees Deuteronomy as a renewal of the Sinai covenant with the addition of theological development, including the recognition of inevitable failure and the assurance of an ultimate fulfillment of the patriarchal promises.[285]

An Ongoing Conversation

This historical survey of covenant scholarship reveals that both mainstream and evangelical approaches to the Abrahamic and Mosaic covenants and the relationship between the two covenants is an ongoing conversation in which there are some fairly established positions. What is interesting to note is that the majority of the studies of these two covenants and their interrelationship has been focused on either the depiction of the world behind the text that synthesized these two covenant traditions or a biblical theological study of the covenant texts in their pentateuchal context. As noted at the outset, it would seem quite interesting to access biblical minds that could share insights and perspectives regarding the way these two seminal covenants were understood in relation to one another. It is in this sense that a search for intertextual connections outside of the Pentateuch would be a valuable source of new insights.

Fortunately, it turns out that there are references to both the Abrahamic and Mosaic covenant traditions in Ps 105. What is not clear is what the nature of these intertextual phenomena might be. Therefore, one of the aims of this study is to discern what is taking place in terms of intertextual connection when the psalmist refers to these two covenants.[286] For this analysis, this writer will appeal to methods and ideas gleaned from the field of literary criticism with special attention given to literary discussions of allusion

---

283. Williamson, *Sealed with an Oath*, 90.

284. Williamson, *Sealed with an Oath*, 96–98. Williamson sees a revelatory element in the Sinaitic covenant but disagrees with Walton's covenant-theology which is rooted in the idea of revelation. Williamson, *Sealed with an Oath*, 98. Cf. Walton, *Covenant*, 24–46.

285. Williamson, *Sealed with an Oath*, 111–12.

286. The date and authorship of the books of the Pentateuch and Ps 105 remain open to discussion with various viable views regarding chronological priority. A detailed discussion of these issues is beyond the scope of this study since a synchronic, canonical approach to intertextual analysis only requires literary priority, not definitive dates of authorship.

and the relationships between author, audience, reference, and referent. It is the hope of this writer to then find this a fruitful means of discussing what the psalmist might have thought and understood regarding these two covenants. Of course, the ultimate aim is to gain new insight by allowing a voice from the biblical world to offer commentary on the question of the inter-covenantal relationship and tensions involving the Abrahamic and Mosaic covenants.

2

An Overview of Intertextuality
A Many-Splendored Thing

NOT "BANAL": A HISTORY OF KRISTEVAN INTERTEXTUALITY

THE CONCEPT OF INTERTEXTUALITY has such a complicated history it warrants a clarifying overview that provides helpful context for the examination of intertextuality that is featured in this work. In order to provide some conceptual footing for the ensuing survey, a good starting point is Julia Kristeva's coining of the term in the 1960s. Kristeva, a post-structuralist critic and linguist, understood intertextuality as an ideological concept as opposed to a literary term.[1] To Kristeva, intertextuality was the refined term for the concept of "intersubjectivity" in which all forms of discourse are interconnected in such a way that any text can transform another text without any sense of chronological priority or regard for literary or aesthetic values.[2] Kristeva proposed that "tout texte se construit comme mosaique de citations, tout texte est absorption et transformation d'un autre texte. A la place de la notion d'intersubjectivité s'installe celle d'intertextualité."[3] The

---

1. Per Miller, "intertextuality" is not an "innocent" term in that intertextual dynamics have the potential to change other texts/systems. This reflects Kristevan thought. Miller, "Intertextual Identity," 20.

2. Miller, "Intertextual Identity," 25.

3. Kristeva, "Le mot," 146.

following overview traces the post-structuralist origin of the term intertextuality and the evolution of the concept from philosophical idea to a study of influence in the realm of literary criticism. This discussion includes the study of intertextuality in biblical studies.

The Challenge of Defining Intertextuality

The main difficulty in defining intertextuality is rooted in the fact that it is an amorphous term spanning several scholarly disciplines. Owen Miller aptly observes that even now the term is "in the process of becoming identified just as it confers on a literary work a variety of identities."[4] He further notes that it is not a unified concept even though various conceptions of intertextuality may share a "family relationship."[5] Thus, Miller observes that different definitions of intertextuality may share common features, but "... there is no constituent feature, satisfactory to all, which would allow us to define the term."[6]

The complexities of understanding and defining intertextuality are not a recent phenomenon. The concept and the term were based simultaneously upon old ideas long held in the field of literary criticism and new ideas coming out of the post-structuralist movement; thus, the meaning of the term was unstable from its very inception.[7] This partially explains why it was so quickly adopted and adapted in the field of literary criticism in a way that was at odds with Kristeva's own idea. In fact, the bifurcation between the post-structuralist ideological concept and the literary concept is not a clean one. Even within the field of literary criticism, practitioners use the term as a broad reference to any relationship between texts, but beyond this, there is little consensus as to the precise meaning of intertextuality.

The Decline of Influence: Setting the Stage

Prior to the emergence of intertextuality, certain developments in the sphere of literary criticism set the stage for the emergence of post-structuralist critics who championed the concept of intertextuality. Prior to the works of Kristeva, Roland Barthes, and Michael Riffaterre, the predominant approach to intertextuality was a diachronic, historical study of sources,

---

4. Miller, "Intertextual Identity," 19.
5. Miller, "Intertextual Identity," 19.
6. Miller, "Intertextual Identity," 19.
7. Clayton and Rothstein, "Figures," 18.

literary borrowing, and the influence earlier literary works exerted on later works. One could argue that this diachronic understanding of literary influence is how most people understand intertextuality as a literary term. Incidentally, this traditional understanding of intertextuality is compatible with the historical-critical approach to source, form, and tradition criticism that came to prominence in biblical studies under the influence of Wellhausen.

The cultural, political, economic, and social upheaval of the mid-twentieth century was characterized by an emerging resistance to the notion of cultural hegemony and elitism in both popular and academic settings.[8] In addition, the political climate of the time, especially the rise of Marxist socialism, led to suspicion regarding the importance of individual works and cultural canonicity.[9] The impulse to democratize and promote equality affected the academy as critics questioned the outsized influence afforded "canonized authors and works" in relation to "minor" works.[10] Iconoclasm and a resistance to cultural hegemony led critics to question normative judgments and focus increasingly on the author's work rather than the author, which in turn led to a decline in interest in the author's sources or influences.[11]

This trend of divorcing the text from the author proved to be a key development. One consequence was a decreasing interest in biography and influences on the author.[12] The minimization of the author was predictably accompanied by elevation of the reader to center stage in literary criticism.[13] It was in this setting that reader-response criticism gained popularity and Roland Barthes would famously conclude that "the birth of the reader must be at the cost of the author."[14] By the mid-1960s, diminishing interest in the author and a diminishing focus on the influence of classic works led to the decline of *influence* in literary criticism. Kristeva's and Barthes's concept of all texts being related in a synchronic, structural manner fit organically in the social, cultural, political, and academic setting of the mid-twentieth century.

---

8. Clayton and Rothstein provide a helpful overview of the various developments that helped shape the post-structuralist understanding of intertextuality. Clayton and Rothstein, "Figures," 14–17.

9. Clayton and Rothstein, "Figures," 16–17.

10. Clayton and Rothstein, "Figures," 16–17.

11. Clayton and Rothstein, "Figures," 13–14.

12. Clayton and Rothstein, "Figures," 15.

13. Clayton and Rothstein, "Figures," 16. For a work that shifts the focus from the author to the reader, see Wimsatt and Beardsley, "Intentional Fallacy," 468–88.

14. Barthes, "Death of the Author," 148.

Precursors and Influences

In addition to these aforementioned socio-cultural and political forces, there were also important precursors to the seminal works of Kristeva and Barthes within the field of literary criticism. One of the key influences on Kristeva's theory of intertextuality is the work of Russian literary critic and semiotician, Mikhail Bakhtin. In fact, Yuri Lotman, a formalist and structuralist semiotician, suggested that Bakhtin may have been the first to develop the literary concept of intertextuality, though not the term.[15]

In Bakhtin's criticism of traditional historical literary criticism and newer studies of "stylistics," he rejected the "monological" reading of literary works, which he characterized as incorrectly seeing the work as a "homogeneous representation of reality" and limited to the "author's personal opinions and psychology."[16] In his study of Dostoevsky's poetics, Bakhtin saw his work as "polyphonic" in embodying the "*coexistence* and interaction" of different uses of language and ways of evaluating reality.[17] Bakhtin's nascent understanding of intertextuality is best exemplified in his concept of *carnival* in a literary work. Per Bakhtin, a literal carnival is a "syncretic pageant" so a novel with a "carnivalistic" attitude allows for ideas to be held in tension via the "*jolly relativity* of every system."[18] Later Bakhtin would develop this idea in the concept of *heteroglossia*, which he defines as a space of interdiscursivity where various idiolects and sociolects interact.[19]

Kristeva affirmed the importance of Bakhtin's ideas in her formulation of the concept of intertextuality. She credited Bakhtin's work on dialogism and *carnival* as a key influence on her view of intertextuality.[20] Kristeva replaced Bakhtin's concept of voices with her concept of texts, resulting in her modification and paraphrase of Bakhtin: "each word (text) is an intersection of words (texts) where at least one other word (text) can be read."[21] Though it may seem that Kristeva's "text" is simply a synonym for "word," she was actually changing Bakhtin's ideas and moving toward her own concept of intertextuality.[22]

---

15. Morgan, "Intertext," 9.
16. Morgan, "Intertext," 10.
17. Morgan, "Intertext," 11. See also Bakhtin, *Problems*, 20–23.
18. Bakhtin, *Problems*, 102.
19. Morgan, "Intertext," 12.
20. Kristeva, "'Nous Deux,'" 8.
21. Kristeva, *Desire*, 66.
22. Clayton and Rothstein, "Figures," 18–19.

The Birth of Intertextuality

Around the same time that Kristeva was processing Bakhtin's connection of texts with cultural systems, other developing concepts, such as anthropologist Claude Lévi-Strauss's *bricolage/bricoleur* and philosopher Jacques Derrida's deconstructionism, expanded the epistemological fields in which human discourse could be connected.[23] The final piece of the puzzle in the development of Kristeva's concept of intertextuality is the work of linguist/semiotician Roland Barthes, who many view as the co-creator of intertextuality. As Kristeva's mentor, Barthes took great interest in her work and Kristeva credited Barthes's understanding of text as a key to her conception of intertextuality.[24]

One of the main things Barthes did to facilitate the concept of intertextuality was to highlight the reader's role in interacting with texts. Per Barthes, the signification of signs belongs to the individual reader such that "any set of intertexts will always be only those intertexts noticed by the individual analyst."[25] At this point, Kristeva's initial articulation of intertextuality becomes intertwined with Barthes's own thoughts. Barthes posits that there are two types of texts: first, the *lisible* ("readable") text, which is transparent, referential, ideologically innocent, only requiring a passive consumer and the *scriptible* ("writable") text, which involves the reader in the active work (*travail*) or production of the literature itself.[26] Thus, the act of interpretation depends on the reader's ability to collect various texts and connect them to a given text, prompting Barthes to state, "*I read the text*" (emphasis his).[27] Interestingly, Barthes also views the reader ("I"), not as an

---

23. Morgan, "Intertext," 18. Anthropologist Claude Lévi-Strauss posited that the "savage" mind (non-literate cultures) approached problem-solving by combining a closed set of "terms and operations" in novel and inventive ways, like a *bricoleur* piecing together various elements to build "do-it-yourself" projects. The *bricolage/bricoleur* concept describes intertextual interactions as various pieces of texts are combined into something cohesive. Lévi-Strauss, *Savage Mind*, 16–30. Jacque Derrida, known for deconstructionism, challenged Saussure's semiotics and its dependence on the determinate relationship between signifier and signified. Per Derrida, there is no determinate meaning since the text is perpetually shaped by other discourses, resulting in a permanent *deferment* of any final meaning. Derrida, *Positions*, 26. Derrida's concept of indeterminacy allows Kristeva to adapt Bakhtin's work on "heteroglossia," which roots utterances in a unique historical context and views intertexts as open to endless dissemination. Clayton and Rothstein, "Figures," 19.

24. Kristeva, "'Nous Deux,'" 8.

25. Barthes, *Mythologies*, 10. See also Morgan, "Intertext," 19.

26. Barthes, *S/Z*, 5.

27. Barthes, *S/Z*, 10.

"innocent" consumer, but as a collection of intertexts so that the reader is also plural and open—essentially, intertextual.[28]

Influenced by Kristeva's definition of intertextuality, Barthes summarizes the essence of the concept in his words:

> So the text: it can only be it in its difference (which does not mean its individuality), its reading is semireflective (this rendering illusory any inductive-deductive science of texts—no 'grammar' of the text) and nevertheless woven entirely with citations, references, echoes, cultural languages (what language is not?), antecedent or contemporary, which cuts across it through and through in a vast stereophony. The intertextual in which every text is held, it itself being the text-between of another text, is not to be confused with some origin of the text: to try to find the 'sources', the 'influences' of a work, is to fall in with the myth of filiation; the citations which go to make up a text are anonymous, untraceable, and yet *already read*: they are quotations without inverted commas.[29]

This now brings us to Kristeva's own articulation of intertextuality. To borrow Barthes's terminology, it is clear that Kristeva's earliest conceptions of intertextuality are not "innocent," meaning there is a strong ideological aspect to Kristeva's thought process. Kristeva's view of intertextuality includes the potential for social revolution motivated by the "productivity" of intertextual relations, which not only "work" the "materiality" of language but even history.[30] The potential for social revolution is based on what Kristeva sees as a special class of revolutionary texts that are characterized by dialectical transformations.[31] In this process, Kristeva rejects the usual relationship between signifier/signified as in structural linguistics and proposes the alternative concept of *signifiance*, which reorganizes the semantic and grammatical categories of discourse and language resulting in a challenge to societal norms.[32]

The key to Kristeva's concept of *signifiance* is the *genotext* and the *phenotext*. As suggested by the prefixes, the *genotext* issues from internal drives (the Freudian concept of unconscious, bio-physiological processes) and reworks the "tissue of language" as previously defined by the values

---

28. Morgan, "Intertext," 19. See also Barthes, *S/Z*, 211.
29. Barthes, "Work to Text," 159–60.
30. Kristeva, *Semeiotikè*, 9–10. See also Morgan, "Intertext," 21.
31. Morgan, "Intertext," 21.
32. Kristeva, *Semeiotikè*, 9. See also Morgan, "Intertext," 21.

and desires of others.³³ The *genotext* comes from within and represents an infinite potential for signification constrained only by the social code and cannot be reduced to language. The *phenotext* is structural and based in societal, cultural, syntactical, and grammatical constraints.³⁴ Thus, for Kristeva, intertextuality occurs at "zero-moment," which is when the internal drive to reorder the values and desires of others (*genotext*) is made manifest (*phenotext*).³⁵ In effect, the *phenotext* is the grammatical/syntactical expression of this reworking of texts.³⁶ Kristeva classifies these transformations of intertextual relations as oppositional, permutative, and indefinite and formulates logical rules that govern how the production of texts alters intertexts.³⁷

As with Barthes, Kristeva's understanding of intertextual transformation ultimately depends on the reader's cultural and literary awareness in being able to discern and "decipher" intertexts and their attendant presuppositions.³⁸ This seemingly innocuous qualification means that even Kristeva and Barthes cannot disregard the old questions of intentionality and influence.³⁹ To this point, Jonathan Culler aptly observes that in Kristeva's textual analyses involving works of poetry, her *praxis* reveals a much greater awareness and dependence on sources and influence than her theoretical approach would indicate.⁴⁰ Kristeva ironically critiques the use of the term intertextuality "dans le sens banal de <<critique des sources>> d'un texte"⁴¹ despite the fact that her concept of intertextuality cannot escape the gravitational pull of sources and influence.

33. Morgan, "Intertext," 22.

34. Roudiez, "Introduction," 5.

35. Kristeva, *La révolution*, 340. Morgan provides a helpful explanation of Kristeva's thought process. Morgan also notes that those in the camp of stylistics would mistakenly consider the *phenotext* to be the final form of the text, whereas Kristeva considers "zero-moment" to be an ongoing psychic/historic activity. Morgan, "Intertext," 22.

36. Kristeva, *La révolution*, 340.

37. Kristeva, *La révolution*, 343–57.

38. Kristeva, *La révolution*, 339. See also Morgan, "Intertext," 23.

39. Morgan, "Intertext," 23–24.

40. Culler critiques Kristeva's examples of intertextual analysis in *Semiotikè* and in *La Révolution du langage poétique* for being dependent on identifiable sources and contextual presuppositions. Culler, "Presupposition and Intertextuality," 106–7.

41. Kristeva, *La révolution*, 59–60.

A Return to "Banal" Studies of Literary Influence

Though Kristeva saw intertextuality as more than a "banal" study of influence and sources, intertextuality, as she and Barthes understood it, still had some of its roots squarely in the field of literary criticism. As Clayton and Rothstein observe, the instability of the term was due in no small part to the fact that it was closely tied to older practices of literary criticism that were in use in academic circles.[42] This interesting tension between post-structuralist conceptions of intertextuality and the more traditional study of literary influence resulted in an almost immediate adaptation of some aspects of Kristeva's and Barthes's ideas into the practice of literary criticism.

The work of Michael Riffaterre can be viewed as a bridge into the field of literary criticism. Riffaterre's works represent a more pragmatic use of post-structuralist intertextuality as a means of achieving "greater interpretive certainty."[43] Riffaterre views words and sentences as the basis for a "matrix" that eventually grows into a structure, i.e., a literary work; however, the existence of identical "matrices" does not mean that the final structures are similar.[44]

There are post-structuralist tendencies in his approach, such as a focus on the reader, but Riffaterre diverges from Kristeva and Barthes in rejecting the "dispersal of meanings through an infinite system of interlocking code."[45] The uniqueness of Riffaterre's approach is his proposed process of interpretation. Riffaterre posits that the indeterminacy ("ungrammaticalities," difficulties, obscurities) of an initial reading at the basic level of words and grammar signals the presence of an intertext and it is here that the right intertextual reading will give proper significance to the intertext and unfailingly direct the reader to the correct interpretation.[46] This process can involve repeated retroactive readings that test each ostensive intertextual reading, but the process inevitably results in the proper interpretation.[47] Despite the positivistic nature of Riffaterre's approach, he cannot avoid the question of how a reader's own culture, race, gender, and other individual contextual factors might subjectively affect the reader's interpretation.[48]

---

42. Clayton and Rothstein, "Figures," 18.
43. Clayton and Rothstein, "Figures," 23.
44. Clayton and Rothstein, "Figures," 23.
45. Clayton and Rothstein, "Figures," 24.
46. Riffaterre, "Interpretation," 227–28.
47. Riffaterre, *Semiotics*, 164–65.
48. Clayton and Rothstein, "Figures," 26.

Harold Bloom's influential work *The Anxiety of Influence* illustrates the complicated influence of Barthes and Kristeva in the field of literary criticism.[49] Bloom embraces the idea of literature as a system of interrelated texts but is not "ultimately able to shake off the metaphors of 'influence' and 'source' and the teleology that the model of literary history implies."[50] Bloom's thesis challenges traditional notions of literary influence by proposing that influence is best understood as the "misreading" or "creative correction" of past authors.[51] This understanding of literary influence as "misreading" is characterized by six stages in the development of a poet's psyche.[52] This interaction between the poet and past poets takes place in the psychological realm as opposed to the realm of "source-hunters and biographers," so that intertextual relationships do not involve the "transmission of ideas and images from earlier to later poets."[53] Culler insightfully notes that "Bloom transforms intertextuality from an endless series of anonymous codes and citations to an oedipal confrontation, one of whose effects is to preserve the integrity of his poets as agents of the poetic process."[54] In some ways, Bloom's approach represents the complicated tension between the intertextuality of Barthes and Kristeva and the traditional understanding of literary influence that has long been the staple of literary studies.

Summary: Post-Structuralist Intertextuality

Though not exhaustive, the above overview demonstrates why defining and understanding intertextuality is a fraught task. Kristeva sought to present a revolutionary approach to linguistics and philosophy that had the potential to existentially change reality through the transformative effect of one text upon another. However, a survey of the historical, cultural, and academic background behind Kristeva's and Barthes's works reveals that the post-structuralist concept of intertextuality is inextricably tied to literary

---

49. Bloom, *Anxiety of Influence*. The approach Bloom introduces in *The Anxiety of Influence* is detailed and applied in his companion piece *A Map of Misreading*. Bloom, *Map of Misreading*.

50. Morgan, "Intertext," 6.

51. Bloom, *Anxiety of Influence*, 30.

52. In Bloom's six stages the poet must consciously and unconsciously distort (*clinamen*), antithetically complete (*tessera*), repeat (*kenosis*), convert (*daemonization*), purge (*askesis*), and finally gain priority over (*aprophrades*) the earlier poet. Bloom, *Anxiety of Influence*, 10, 14–16, 30.

53. Bloom, *Anxiety of Influence*, 71.

54. Culler, "Presupposition and Intertextuality," 111.

criticism, and therein lies the difficulty in understanding what it means today as a literary term of art.

In sum, post-structuralist intertextuality is an ideological concept that was born out of a reaction to formalism and structuralism and also out of a political milieu dominated by Marxist philosophy in academic circles. This concept of intertextuality was pitted against the traditional study of literary influence, sources, and the diachronic relationship between literary works. In a similar vein, this post-structuralist intertextuality privileges the reader and the text at the expense of the author, whose biography and influences are not meaningful.

The actual *praxis* of intertextuality involves a synchronic, ahistorical approach to texts. In fact, it was understood that the nature of the discursive space meant future texts could and would influence earlier texts. Furthermore, the focus of intertextual analysis is on the *process* of signification rather than on a definitive interpretation (Riffaterre's work not withstanding). Culler's oft-quoted description is a fitting summary statement:

> Intertextuality thus becomes less a name for a work's relation to particular prior texts than a designation of its participation in the discursive space of a culture: the relationship between a text and the various languages or signifying practices of a culture and its relation to those texts which articulate for it the possibilities of that culture. The study of intertextuality is thus not the investigation of sources and influences as traditionally conceived; it casts its net wider to include anonymous discursive practices, codes whose origins are lost, that make possible the signifying practices of later texts.[55]

INTERTEXTUALITY IN LITERARY CRITICISM: A "BANAL" STUDY OF INFLUENCE

Despite the fact that intertextuality was not conceived as a means of doing literary criticism, the compatibility of various aspects of intertextuality with the literary criticism of the day led many to adapt it to the reading of literary texts. In addition to Riffaterre, who applied post-structuralist intertextuality in a pragmatic manner, others, like Bloom, would be influenced by it while maintaining core aspects of more traditional literary criticism. Over time, the concept of post-structuralist intertextuality would be diluted to such an extent that the term would essentially become a catchall word for any type

---

55. Culler, "Presupposition and Intertextuality," 103.

of relationship between different texts or literary works. It is in this transition that much lexical precision was lost with regard to the term.

Based on the current state of usage it seems that the tug-o-war for the term intertextuality was eventually won by those in the field of literary criticism. Even Kristeva seemed resigned to this reality when she acknowledged that the term was being used in the "banal" sense as a reference to a text's sources.[56] Despite the confusion that persists, intertextuality is generally understood today as a broad term for a diachronic relationship between multiple texts and it is this sense that informs the use of the term in this study.

The Persistence of Influence

One reality that emerges in the above overview of post-structuralist intertextuality is the persistence of influence. Even the post-structuralist thinkers could not fully avoid some level of dependence on literary sources and the relationships that exist between a source text and a later text. While the term intertextuality and the technical study of the concept may be a modern pursuit in literary studies, the actual phenomenon of intertextuality has existed as long as humanity has communicated through written texts.[57] Some of the earliest examples of intertextuality and literary influence include the Socratic dialogues, which Bakhtin considered an early form of heteroglossia and dialogism, as well as Plato's understanding of imitation in which every "poet" always copies an earlier work.[58] Alfaro notes that Cicero and Quintilian exhibit a developed understanding of intertextual interactions when they propose that imitation is a "consciously intertextual practice" as well as the "completion of an act of interpretation."[59]

In terms of intertextuality in literary interpretation, one of the most significant sources of influence was the church in the Middle Ages. At a time when literature was largely tied to theology, the multi-leveled interpretation of the Bible featuring intertextual practices would influence the writing and reading of literature in the secular sphere.[60] This influence is seen in the way Renaissance literature exhibited an unprecedented awareness of the "textual past" as quotations and allusions to classical authors (e.g., Bacon and Shakespeare) demonstrate that writers believed "that their possibilities

---

56. Kristeva, *La révolution*, 59–60.
57. Worton and Still, *Intertextuality*, 2.
58. Worton and Still, *Intertextuality*, 4. See also Alfaro, "Intertextuality," 269.
59. Alfaro, "Intertextuality," 269.
60. Alfaro, "Intertextuality," 269–70.

of imitation, understood as interpretation and re-writing of the *Urtext*, are limitless."[61]

As literary studies entered the modern era, the historical, diachronic study of sources and literary influences developed into technical methodologies. Though the last century of literary criticism cannot be characterized by one particular method or approach, the definition of different types of intertextual connections crystallized into a functional glossary of literary devices. The most basic type of literary intertextuality is some variation on a reference, including quotation, paraphrase, allusion, and echo.[62] Of these various types of intertextual devices, allusion has historically garnered the most scholarly attention since it is most commonly used, which also holds true in the study of biblical writings.[63]

ALLUSION AND INTERTEXTUALITY

The center of gravity in intertextual studies of literature is the allusion. In colloquial usage, allusion has become the *de facto* term for any implicit referential activity in discourse and literature. Even in modern criticism, allusion is functionally synonymous with the term intertextuality.[64] The literary allusion is a helpful starting point for the discussion of literary intertextuality and other intertextual literary devices, such as echo and quotation.

The Modern Definition of Literary Allusion

Ziva Ben-Porat's seminal dissertation "The Poetics of Allusion" is the first major technical study of literary allusion.[65] In discerning the operation of each functional component of an allusion, Ben-Porat develops a model for

---

61. Alfaro, "Intertextuality," 270.

62. Technically speaking parody, pastiche, translation, calque, and plagiarism are considered types of intertextuality, but they do not usually function as literary devices so they will not be discussed in this study.

63. There has been a discernible increase in the study of intertextuality in the Bible, which reflects the popularity of intertextuality studies in literary criticism. Notable works by Michael Fishbane, Richard Hays, and Benjamin Sommer show an awareness of contemporary approaches and discussions in the larger field of literary criticism. Fishbane, *Biblical Interpretation*; Hays, *Echoes of Scripture*; Sommer, *Prophet Reads*.

64. Machacek, "Allusion," 523.

65. Ben-Porath, "Poetics of Allusion." See also Ben-Porat, "Literary Allusion," 105–28. Ben-Porat uses the spelling "Ben-Porath" on her dissertation, but all subsequent works have the spelling "Ben-Porat." For the purposes of this study, the current spelling will be the preferred spelling.

the interactions between the alluding text and the evoked text as well as the author and reader. Ben-Porat's study is notable in presenting a functional model of an allusion and heuristic criteria that are used to detect and distinguish an allusion from other intertextual devices.

The basic form of a literary allusion is "a device by which the reader links one or more elements in a *given text* with other independent and not identical elements in an *evoked text*."[66] It is significant that Ben-Porat involves the reader so prominently in her definition, for she attributes the ultimate actualization of the allusion to the reader.[67] In privileging the reader with the recognition, linkage, and activation of the interplay between the alluding and evoked text, Ben-Porat reflects the influence of post-structuralist criticism. However, Ben-Porat asserts that this method is not subjective, nor does it give the reader unbridled freedom in creating allusive patterns.[68] Ben-Porat states, "When a pattern is established at the conclusion of the process of actualization, it is a definite pattern the 'rightness' of which can be examined and texted [*sic*]."[69]

With regard to the difference between an allusion and a reference, Ben-Porat's method accounts for this distinction at the level of the reader's activation of the intertextual element. Per Ben-Porat, the text is a "reservoir of potentialities and the reader is an active participant in the creation of the work, whose role is far more complex than a simple process of linguistic decoding of ordinary discourse."[70] Ben-Porat notes that the mode of reference does not determine whether there is an allusion or reference. In her approach, the decisive factor in identifying an allusion is when the reader recognizes the marker and the evoked text and then "actualizes potentialities, to create patterns" based on the interplay of the two texts.[71] In a reference, the marker simply points to a referent whereas the allusive marker "is telling the reader, 'This is where you have to go to look for more material

---

66. Ben-Porath, "Poetics of Allusion," 1.

67. Ben-Porat outlines the following process for actualizing an allusion: 1. Recognition of the marker; 2. Identification of the source; 3. Realization of the marked component: activation of its relevant contextual elements; 4. Linking of the marker and marked components, followed by linking relevant elements from their respective contexts; and 5. Fitting the new pattern/patterns in an alluding text. Ben-Porath, "Poetics of Allusion," 10.

68. Ben-Porath, "Poetics of Allusion," 7.

69. Ben-Porath, "Poetics of Allusion," 7.

70. Ben-Porath, "Poetics of Allusion," 29.

71. Ben-Porath, "Poetics of Allusion," 30.

about me, material which will make my appearance in this new context more meaningful."⁷²

The concept of actualization in Ben-Porat's approach is not a vague recognition of an intertextual relationship but the identification of a literary relationship that has rhetorical relevance. Thus, Ben-Porat believes her method yields results where the "rightness" of the pattern can be validated. A few years after the publication of her dissertation, Ben-Porat revised her definition of allusion in the following way:

> [An allusion is] a device for the simultaneous activation of two texts. The activation is achieved through the manipulation of a special signal: a sign (simple or complex) in a given text characterized by an additional larger 'referent.' This referent is always an independent text. The simultaneous activation of the two texts thus connected results in the formation of intertextual patterns whose nature cannot be predetermined.⁷³

Ben-Porat does not change the overall dynamic of text and reader, but the description of allusion as a device implies a degree of authorial intent. The simultaneous activation of the two texts resulting in an intertextual dynamic that cannot be predetermined means that the reader is still ultimately responsible for actualizing an allusion. The inability to predetermine the intertextual pattern of an allusion is at odds with the assumption that an allusion is a literary device that is deployed for a particular rhetorical or literary effect. Ben-Porat's revised definition still allows a reader to actualize an allusion that the author never intended. This level of reader-based subjectivity sits in tension with her assertion that the "right" reading of an allusion can be verified.

Shortly after Ben-Porat's work, Carmela Perri echoed Ben-Porat's approach, but notably incorporated a semantic and pragmatics-based aspect to her analyis.⁷⁴ Like Ben-Porat, Perri views allusion as a type of literary reference in which allusion-markers not only point to a source text, "but they also tacitly specify the property(ies) belonging to the source text's connotation relevant to the allusion's meaning."⁷⁵ In terms of semantics, Perri offers this definition of an allusion:

> Allusion in literature is a manner of signifying in which some kind of marker (simple or complex, overt or covert) not only

---

72. Ben-Porath, "Poetics of Allusion," 82.
73. Ben-Porat, "Literary Allusion," 107–8.
74. Perri, "On Alluding," 289–307.
75. Perri, "On Alluding," 291.

signifies un-allusively, within the imagined possible world of the alluding text, but through echo also denotes a source text and specifies some discrete, recoverable property(ies) in the case of self-echo); the property(ies) evoked modifies the alluding text, and possibly activates further, larger inter- and intra-textual patterns of properties with consequent further modification of the alluding text.[76]

Some notable aspects of her definition include the dynamic in which an evoked text "modifies" the alluding text and potentially activates additional intertextual (even intra-textual) patterns that modify the alluding text. According to Perri, the distinguishing characteristic of a literary allusion is in the way the alluding text is changed because of the evoked text's effect on the alluding text. Perri also adds that the marker has a double referent due to Perri's construct of an allusive text having both an immediate context (the world of the text) and an allusive context (the possible world of the alluding text). Therefore, the allusive marker refers un-allusively to something in the world of the text and allusively to a referent in the possible world of the alluding text.[77]

Perri's adaptation of the speech-act relationship between the illocutionary act and the perlocutionary effect is an innovative means of describing the process by which an author and reader interact with two texts to arrive at an intended outcome.[78] Unlike Ben-Porat, Perri sees the author as an essential part of the alluding process but still gives the reader an active role in successfully completing an allusion.[79]

Though the pragmatic approach is enlightening, Perri acknowledges that this analysis does not speak to the value of an allusion for the reader.[80] Here Perri suggests that the etymological root of the word allude, which comes from the Latin *alludere* (to joke, jest, mock, or play with), sheds some light on why an allusion is satisfying, even enjoyable for a reader.[81] Perri's thoughts on the "playful" nature of allusion may be a peripheral note, but

---

76. Perri, "On Alluding," 295.

77. Perri, "On Alluding," 295.

78. Perri adapts Searle's speech-act construct in her analysis of allusion as an illocutionary act and its perlocutionary effect on the reader. Perri, "On Alluding," 300–301. For the illocutionary/perlocutionary speech-act dynamic Perri adapts, see Searle, *Speech Acts*, 94–96.

79. Perri, "On Alluding," 300–301.

80. Perri, "On Alluding," 300–301.

81. Perri, "On Alluding," 300–301. Ben-Porat also addresses the etymology of the word allusion, suggesting that the playful element affects the literary value of an allusion. Ben-Porath, "Poetics of Allusion," iv.

it is beneficial to consider how such literary devices function evocatively. This is consistent with the idea that allusion, like other intertextual literary devices, is used to elicit a desired response from the reader.

Refining the Definition

In a work on "romantic allusiveness," James Chandler observed that Romantic poetry is characterized by an abundance of clear literary influence, but this allusiveness does not always manifest as traditional literary allusions.[82] Chandler is interested in the complex way the Romantic poets used intertextual references both consciously and unconsciously.[83] Though Chandler allows for unintentional influence as part of the phenomenon of "romantic allusiveness," he defends authorial intent affirming that poets use allusions in order to elicit a response from the reader; in other words, poetry is something the poet " . . . *does* for, and with, specific readers."[84]

Michael Leddy's article on the limits of allusion presents a novel way of validating allusions. Leddy proposes limiting the scope of the definition based on what he calls the "vocabulary of allusion" or "allusion-words," such as "allusion," "allusive," and "to allude," to test whether a reference is an allusion.[85] Leddy's starting point is the following definition of an allusion: (1) it references a kind of entity or event; (2) it is a reference that invokes one or more associations of such an entity or event and brings them to bear upon a present context; (3) it must be a local or small-scale device.[86] Just evoking another text is a reference or possibly a quotation, but an allusion evokes a text and necessarily brings various intertextual associations "to bear on a present context," resulting in rhetorical impact[87]

In a more recent work, William Irwin interacts with the works of Ben-Porat, Perri, and Leddy, and offers his own definition that emphasizes authorial intent, the indirect nature of the reference, and the ability of the

---

82. Chandler, "Romantic Allusiveness," 475–79.

83. Chandler, "Romantic Allusiveness," 475–79. Chandler's understanding of echo as an unconscious or inadvertent reference follows John Hollander's view that an echo is a type of allusion that is evoked unintentionally by a "suppressed consciousness." Hollander, *Figure of Echo*, ix.

84. Chandler, "Romantic Allusiveness," 462–65, 476. Chandler's discussion of Riffaterre's view critiques post-structuralist criticism's denial of authorial intention. Cf. Riffaterre, *Semiotics*, 5, 150, 170–71; Chandler, "Romantic Allusiveness," 464n11.

85. Leddy, "Limits of Allusion," 110.

86. Leddy, "Limits of Allusion," 110–11.

87. Leddy, "Limits of Allusion," 110–11.

audience to detect the reference to a sufficient degree.[88] Irwin presents three views regarding the author and a valid allusion: (1) The *intentionalist view* in which the allusion is defined by the author and the presence of a reference; (2) the *internalist view* in which the allusion is defined by internal properties in one text calling to mind or resembling internal properties in another; (3) the *hybrid view*, which bases an allusion on some combination of authorial intent and multiple texts with shared internal properties.[89] Irwin sees authorial intent as the basis for an allusion but nuances his definition in order to avoid two disqualifying extremes. Irwin avoids complete authorial control over an allusion because the author cannot declare a non-allusion to be an allusion by authorial fiat.[90] On the other hand, when the reader defines an allusion there is too much subjectivity and unreliability with regard to the reader's ability to recognize a genuine marker.[91] In the end, Irwin believes that only an allusion enhances the alluding text since rhetorical or literary impact depends on authorial intent.[92]

Like Perri and Ben-Porat, Irwin sees the "playful" aspect of the allusion as a helpful way to imagine the interaction between author and reader. In this sense, the reader's role is like one who plays a game and seeks to solve the puzzle of the allusion, but whereas Ben-Porat sees the reader's successful play as actualizing the allusion, Irwin does not.[93] Here Irwin makes a crucial distinction when he requires that the reader ". . . must call to mind what the author intended for him or her to call to mind."[94]

Gregory Machacek's study of allusion features the influence of poststructuralist criticism and its resistance to the prioritization of past authors and their works. Machacek repeatedly proposes new terminology for intertextual activity that "privileges the agency of the later author . . . that it might thus gently counteract the tendency of terms like *echo*, *borrowing*, or *influence* to suggest a secondary, lesser, or derivative status for the imitating author."[95] This influence is also evident in Machacek's proposal for an understanding of allusion that coordinates both diachronic and synchronic intertextual influence.[96] Machacek rejects the notion that diachronic

---

88. Irwin, "What is an Allusion?," 293–94.
89. Irwin, "What is an Allusion?," 289.
90. Irwin, "What is an Allusion?," 289–90.
91. Irwin, "What is an Allusion?," 290.
92. Irwin, "What is an Allusion?," 291.
93. Irwin, "What is an Allusion?," 293.
94. Irwin, "What is an Allusion?," 293.
95. Machacek, "Allusion," 522, 524–25, 528, 530.
96. Machacek, "Allusion," 525.

and synchronic views of influence are antithetical, proposing instead that the reader's cultural and historical circumstances, which are synchronic influences, should be considered in the reader's interpretation of an allusion.[97] Machacek attempts to find middle ground between a diachronic and synchronic view of literary influence.

Per Machacek, the defining element in an allusion is the incorporation of another work into an alluding text by way of a brief marker.[98] In this sense, one can distinguish an allusion from an echo or other type of reference by removing the referent from the reading of the evoking text. If the alluding text does not make sense without the referent then this is an echo or reference where the referent is rhetorically equivalent to the marker, but if the referent is removed and the alluding text is still comprehensible then this is an allusion for the referent brings intertextual meaning beyond the basic meaning of the marker.[99] In effect, Machacek does not deny the author's role but gives the reader considerable responsibility for interpreting the allusion. In this way, synchronic influences can impact the interpretation of the allusion via the reader. As for rhetorical function, Machacek sees the hermeneutical significance of the alluded text as "enrichment" of the alluding text.[100]

Echo and Quotation

As some of the above studies have shown the definition of a literary allusion is often contrasted with other types of literary intertextuality, such as echo, quotation, and reference. In fact, echo and reference are often characterized as any intertextual connection that is *not* an allusion. Chandler suggested that an echo is an unintentional or unconscious evoking of another text, whereas Machacek describes echo as a type of allusion that evokes a phrase through verbatim wording or phraseological adaptation.[101] Like allusion, the

---

97. Machacek traces successive translations of an allusion to Homer found in a work by Milton. These translations span several generations and Machacek notes that later translators do not perceive the allusion due to historical and cultural factors. While the reader can be influenced by historical and cultural context, the failure of later readers to perceive the allusion does not mean the allusion, as intended by Milton, is invalid or absent. Machacek, "Allusion," 531–34.

98. Like Perri and Irwin, Machacek sees brevity as a vital trait of an allusion. Machacek, "Allusion," 526–28.

99. Machacek, "Allusion," 527.

100. Machacek, "Allusion," 531.

101. Chandler, "Romantic Allusiveness," 476–80, 485 and Machacek, "Allusion," 527–28.

term echo is used ambiguously as a general term for an intertextuality that is rhetorically simpler than an allusion, less overt, or evoked unconsciously.

One of the few works dedicated to the concept of echo is John Hollander's *The Figure of Echo: A Mode of Allusion in Milton and After*.[102] Hollander classifies echo as a type of allusion so it has many of the same properties as a literary allusion.[103] Hollander thinks of intertextuality metaphorically in that literary devices refer to a representation of a relationship between texts, therefore, he loosely defines echo in relation to allusion and quotation in the following way:

> [T]here is echo, which represents or substitutes for allusion as allusion does for quotation. There seems to be a transitive figurational connection among them; it points to what we generally mean by *echo*, in intertextual terms. In contrast with literary allusion, echo is a metaphor of, and for, alluding, and does not depend on conscious intention.[104]

Hollander positions the three devices from most explicit (quotation) to least (echo). Hollander does require authorial intent in the case of allusion but allows for unconscious literary influence in the case of echo. When an intertextual echo becomes a trope, Hollander views this as a *transumptive* or *metaleptic* effect whereby repeated echoes of a trope cause the trope to become a figure that can be refigured through repeated allusions and echoes.[105] Through transumption, these tropes become figures that have their own interpretive or revisionary power, and in this way an echo can become "louder" than the original voice, even distorting the original voice through interpretation.[106]

Quotation as a literary device is easier to identify and define since it has a discrete, identifiable form. The simplicity of form, a verbatim reproduction of an evoked text, belies its complexity as a rhetorical device. Like an allusion, the quotation has a rhetorical relationship to its new literary context, but it can never be fully "absorbed" by the quoting text since it will always have a relationship to its own literary context.[107] Meir Sternberg deftly addresses the complex intertextual dynamics of a quotation, observing that "Quotation brings together at least two discourse-events: that in which things were originally expressed (said, thought, experienced) by one subject

102. Hollander, *Figure of Echo*.
103. Hollander, *Figure of Echo*, ix.
104. Hollander, *Figure of Echo*, 64.
105. Hollander, *Figure of Echo*, 114.
106. Hollander, *Figure of Echo*, 111, 114.
107. Morawski, "Basic Function," 691.

(speaker, writer, reflector), and that in which they are cited by another."[108] What is often underestimated due to the apparent simplicity of a quotation is how profoundly the recontextualization of the quoted text reframes, mediates, interferes with, and ultimately changes the very meaning of the quoted text.[109] Sternberg sums up this rhetorical shift thusly:

> Each act of quotation serves two masters. One is the original speech or thought that it represents, pulling in the direction of maximal accuracy. The other is the frame that encloses and regulates it, pulling in the direction of maximal efficacy. Reported discourse thus presents a classic case of divided allegiance, between original-oriented representation (with its face to the world) and frame-oriented communication (with its face to the reader).[110]

Sternberg's analysis highlights the importance of the author's intentions and rhetorical aims whenever a quotation is deployed. It is clear that a quotation is much more than the neutral act of reporting another's words.

The typical uses of quotations include an appeal to authority, a show of erudition, a stimulative-amplificatory function, and an ornamental function.[111] Morawski's uses of a quotation do not describe the various theories on the rhetorical function of a quotation. In his helpful study on the rhetoric of quotations, Christopher Stanley surveys several theories on the rhetorical function and operation of a written quotation.[112] For example, the *Demonstration Theory* posits that a quotation rhetorically adds vividness and drama to a discourse by distancing an author from her subject matter and by promoting solidarity between the author and the reader.[113] As Sternberg noted, the quoting writer's rhetorical intent reframes the quoted author's words in order to serve a new rhetorical purpose. Though allusion and quotation are different in terms of form and intertextual dynamics, there are commonalities when it comes to rhetorical function.

---

108. Sternberg, "Proteus," 107.
109. Stanley, "Rhetoric of Quotations," 51.
110. Sternberg, "Proteus," 152.
111. Morawski, "Function of Quotation," 692–96.
112. Stanley, "Rhetoric of Quotations," 44–58.
113. Stanley, "Rhetoric of Quotations," 44–58. Stanley cites Clark and Gerrig, "Quotations as Demonstrations," 792–93 and Wade and Clark, "Reproduction and Demonstration," 806–8.

INTERTEXTUALITY IN BIBLICAL STUDIES: ALLUSION AND BEYOND

The period from the 1960s to the 1980s was a fruitful time in the field of literary criticism as the post-structuralist camp produced influential works on intertextuality and related literary devices. Meanwhile, in biblical studies, the diachronic study of literary influence already had a long history since the earliest students of the Bible understood that biblical writings are replete with inner-biblical intertextualities. In the modern era, diachronic methods, such as source, form, and tradition criticism, have maintained a focus on diachronic intertextual relationships in biblical writings.

In the last fifty years, post-structuralist criticism and modern studies of intertextuality have gained popularity in biblical studies. Many scholars in the fields of theology and biblical studies have consciously adopted the Kristevan theory of intertextuality as the basis for studies of intertextuality in the Bible.[114] These studies are characterized by a synchronic approach and explorations of all influences that might affect the reading of a biblical text. Richard Hays observes:

> The appeal of [Kristevan] 'intertextuality' was that it provided a way of discerning literary, thematic, and theological linkages within the biblical canon without having to make any historical arguments about processes of transmission or events 'behind' the texts and without having to address issues of extratextual reference.[115]

As Hays implies, this type of approach to intertextuality affords scholars a kind of freedom in the exploration of themes and concepts that are not "found" in the text when read through a historical-grammatical lens. As a "reader-oriented enterprise," Kristevan intertextuality invites creative readings of the Bible through surprising connections and juxtapositions of biblical texts that both "affect and effect meaning."[116] In shifting the focus from literary criticism to biblical studies, it becomes apparent that biblical scholars ask and address many of the same questions with regard to intertextuality, allusion, and other types of literary reference; however, the nature of the answers is different due to the unique nature of biblical writings.

---

114. Examples of works employing a Kristevan approach include: Draisma, *Intertextuality in Biblical Writings*; Fewell, *Reading between Texts*; and Hays et al., *Reading the Bible Intertextually*.

115. Hays et al., *Reading the Bible Intertextually*, xiii.

116. Fewell, *Reading between Texts*, 17–18.

Inner-Biblical Exegesis

In 1963, Nahum Sarna studied the psalmist's use of Nathan's oracle to David concerning the Davidic covenant.[117] Past studies of Ps 89 had analyzed the presence of Nathan's oracle using diachronic methods, such as source and redaction criticism, but Sarna makes the argument that the psalmist's use of Nathan's oracle is an example of inner-biblical exegesis. Sarna begins with a comparison of the oracle as it appears in Ps 89 and in the historical books (2 Sam 7:4–17; 1 Chr 17:3–15).[118] In previous studies, noticeable textual variations in the psalmist's version were attributed to free paraphrasing, the literary priority of the poetic form, or to another textual tradition that is no longer available.[119] Sarna, however, concluded the psalmist intentionally adapted the original oracle for use in the psalmist's immediate historical situation.[120]

Sarna's study was followed by several studies that similarly examined the use of a biblical text by another biblical writer or redactor.[121] Though inner-biblical exegesis (IBE) is generally treated as a distinct form of intertextuality, Benjamin Sommer and Lyle Eslinger correctly note that inner-biblical exegesis is a particular type of allusion since an author is evoking another text in a way that draws attention to the evoked text while using it rhetorically in the author's own text.[122]

In an earlier article, Michael Fishbane first described the process by which a later writer, confronted with an unforeseen situation, adapts an earlier Scripture (*traditum*) so that it can be reapplied by exegesis (*traditio*) resulting in a new understanding.[123] In his seminal work *Biblical Interpretation in Ancient Israel*, Fishbane develops his approach to biblical *traditum* and *traditio* within four broad rubrics: (1) scribal exegesis, which entails an analysis of scribal comments and corrections on earlier texts;[124] (2)

---

117. Sarna, "Psalm 89," 29–46.
118. Sarna, "Psalm 89," 30–33.
119. Sarna, "Psalm 89," 36–37.
120. Sarna, "Psalm 89," 37–39.

121. Other studies on inner-biblical exegesis include Eslinger, "Hosea 12:5a," 91–99; Clines, "Nehemiah 10," 111–17; Kaiser, "Inner Biblical Exegesis," 33–46.

122. Sommer has a category of intertextuality called exegesis, but he views the inner-biblical exegesis of Sarna and Fishbane as a category of allusion. Sommer, *Prophet Reads Scripture*, 23–31. See also Eslinger, "Inner-Biblical Exegesis," 47–58.

123. Fishbane, "Revelation and Tradition," 343–61. Kaiser distinguishes the interpretation of the evoked text from the interpretation that takes place in the later text so that the original meaning is not "fused with" or lost in the adapted reinterpretation, which he calls reapplication. Kaiser, "Inner Biblical Exegesis," 33–34.

124. Fishbane, *Biblical Interpretation*, 23–88.

legal exegesis, which is the reinterpretation of biblical laws for later novel application;[125] (3) Aggadic exegesis, which involves any exegetical activity that draws out meaning from the text;[126] and (4) Mantological exegesis, which involves genres, such as dreams and oracles.[127]

Fishbane's work, while a notable contribution in its own right, has served to spark discussions about the nature of intertextuality in the Bible. In Eslinger's critique of Fishbane's work, he suggests that what Fishbane calls exegesis is actually allusion, which means an alternative approach might be appropriate.[128] Eslinger envisions a " . . . self-consciously literary analysis of the textual interconnections in biblical literature" and he suggests using canonical context as a way of establishing textual priority.[129]

Benjamin Sommer's response helps clarify the meaning and use of the terms intertextuality and allusion. Sommer notes that Eslinger's use of the term "allusion" conflates what literary theorists view as two separate categories.[130] When Eslinger proposes using the canonical context to establish textual priority, he is describing a synchronic, ahistorical approach, from a historical-critical standpoint. By definition, allusion requires a diachronic, historical study of influence whereas the study of intertextuality is a synchronic, ahistorical exploration of textual interplay, thus, Eslinger actually describes intertextuality, not allusion.[131] This discussion illustrates the ambiguity surrounding the inchoate understanding of intertextuality and allusion in biblical studies.

Allusion and Echo in Biblical Studies

The studies surveyed demonstrate that the terms intertextuality and allusion often function as generic terms for all types of intertextual devices.[132]

---

125. Fishbane, *Biblical Interpretation*, 91–277. Legal exegesis is the rubric in which Fishbane's concept of inner-biblical exegesis finds its best fit, evidenced by the depth of Fishbane's analysis in this section. Childs, "Biblical Interpretation," 511.

126. Fishbane, *Biblical Interpretation*, 281–440.

127. Fishbane, *Biblical Interpretation*, 443–524.

128. Eslinger, "Inner-Biblical Exegesis," 56.

129. Eslinger continues to use historical-critical constructs of textual history but sees the final canonical form of the biblical narrative and history as the context for reading inner-biblical allusions. Eslinger, "Inner-Biblical Exegesis," 56.

130. Sommer, "Exegesis," 479.

131. Sommer, "Exegesis," 486–88.

132. Sommer gives examples of scholars who use the terms "intertextuality" and "allusion" loosely without accounting for their respective technical distinctions. Sommer, *Prophet Reads*, 207n8.

Early studies of intertextuality in the Bible did not yield a consensus as to the precise definition of the major intertextual devices. Though various definitions of allusion, echo, and reference still persist, several important works have helped advance the technical understanding of intertextual literary devices in the Bible.

Refining the Study of Intertextuality in Biblical Studies

In literary criticism, discussions on the definition and poetics of allusion, echo, and reference often take place in the context of literary theory. In biblical studies, these discussions pragmatically serve the task of biblical exegesis. Scholars in the field of biblical studies rarely take on studies of poetics and literary devices in a vacuum. These treatments occur in praxis in relation to particular texts or interpretational issues. The abundance of allusions and intertextual connections in the Bible means that biblical scholars have had to develop definitions and methods that account for intertextual phenomena in the unique context of the Bible.

The book of Revelation is fertile ground for studies of allusion since it contains vivid imagery with intertextual significance. Studies of allusion in Revelation are a valuable source of insight into the poetics of biblical allusions. Gregory K. Beale's 1984 dissertation explores the use of the book of Daniel in Revelation. Beale proposes five elements that indicate a "definite and demonstrable connection between two documents": (1) theme; (2) content; (3) specific constructions of words; (4) structure; and (5) a reasonable explanation of authorial motive.[133] Beale's approach deals in probabilities based on an aggregate of evidence as well as other related factors, such as the clustering of allusive texts that are from the same source, i.e., "allusive clusters."[134] Beale notes that some Jewish apocalyptic writers may not have been conscious that they were "modeling their works on Daniel, but that the models are a result of tradition or an unconscious element in the writers' minds from their learned past."[135] Beale does not consider such examples of appropriation as allusion.

Jon Paulien's study of the trumpets in Revelation features a discussion on how to identify and validate an allusion. Paulien highlights the need for a more systematic way of detecting and validating literary allusions in Revelation. Paulien surveys the criteria posited by various scholars and notes that there is no uniformity or consensus regarding methods or even the types of

---

133. Beale, *Use of Daniel*, 308.
134. Beale, *Use of Daniel*, 307.
135. Beale, *Use of Daniel*, 317.

intertextual forms in Revelation.[136] Paulien ultimately laments that there is a "desperate" need for objective criteria to evaluate the possible allusions in Revelation.[137] In 2001 Paulien revisited this topic by reviewing newer studies on OT allusions in Revelation and again concluded that there is still a glaring need for a method that objectively and precisely evaluates allusions.[138] It is interesting that the methods Paulien surveyed in 1987 are not significantly different from those surveyed in 2001.

Richard Hays on Allusion and Echo

Richard Hays's work *Echoes of Scripture in the Letters of Paul* is an important contribution on allusion even though the titular focus of the study is echo. Hays's work is informed by the post-structuralist concept of intertextuality that is a staple of modern literary criticism. Hays believes that Paul's faith is "intertextual in character" since the "vocabulary and cadences of Scripture . . . are imprinted deeply on Paul's mind, and in the great stories of Israel that condition his perception of the world, of God's promised deliverance of his people, and of his own identity and calling."[139] Despite the potential impact of synchronic intertextuality on the mind of Paul, Hays pragmatically limits his study to "actual citations of and allusions to specific texts."[140]

Though Hays's focus is on the concept of echo, he develops a helpful definition of allusion against which he contrasts the concept of an echo. Hays's definition notes that the major functional difference between an allusion and an echo has to do with authorial intent:

> The concept of allusion depends both on the notion of authorial intention and on the assumption that the reader will share with the author the requisite 'portable library' to recognize the source of the allusion; the notion of echo, however, finesses such questions: 'echo is a metaphor of and for, allusion, and does not depend on conscious intention.'[141]

---

136. Paulien, *Decoding Revelation's Trumpets*, 103–18.
137. Paulien, *Decoding Revelation's Trumpets*, 114, 118.
138. Paulien, "Criteria," 127–29.
139. Hays, *Echoes of Scripture*, 16.
140. Hays, *Echoes of Scripture*, 15.
141. Hays quotes Hollander in his explanation of the difference between allusion and echo. Hays, *Echoes of Scripture*, 29. Cf. Hollander, *Figure of Echo*, 64.

Hays views allusion as a device that fulfills the alluding writer's desired poetic or rhetorical purposes.[142] In addition, understanding an allusion requires a sense of historical context so that the reader can " . . . know not only the tradition to which the allusion points but also the way in which the tradition was understood in the poet's time and the contemporary historical experience or situation with which the poet links tradition."[143]

It is helpful to understand that Hollander's work on echo provides the conceptual basis for Hays's understanding of echo. Like Hollander, Hays sees echo as a special type of allusion. Hays places echo on a continuum ranging from explicit ("loud") or overt to subliminal ("quiet"), thus, a quotation is the "loudest" followed by an allusion and then the echo.[144] Hays also adopts Hollander's concept of *transumption* or *metalepsis*, which is the process by which echoed texts become a diachronic trope.[145] Per Hays, transumption occurs when two texts are linked by an echo, which has a figurative effect that includes unstated or suppressed (*transumed*) "points of resonance between the two texts."[146] Hays summarizes the echo's function in this way:

> Allusive echo functions to suggest to the reader that text B should be understood in light of a broad interplay with text A, encompassing aspects of A beyond those explicitly echoed . . . Metalepsis. . .places the reader within a field of whispered or unstated correspondences.[147]

Hays sees this definition of echo to be compatible with Paul's situation since Israel was a reading community and "all significant speech is Scriptural or Scripturally-oriented speech."[148] Thus, it is reasonable to "hear" echoes of Scripture in biblical writings since all Scriptures are produced in Hollander's "cave of resonant signification."[149]

In Paul's writings, Hays discerns that Paul uses scriptural references, not as proofs, but as tropes, thus, scriptural allusions, quotations, and echoes can "generate new meanings by linking the earlier text (Scripture) to the later (Paul's discourse) in such a way as to produce unexpected correspondences,

---

142. Hays, *Echoes of Scripture*, 17–18.
143. Hays, *Echoes of Scripture*, 18.
144. Hays, *Echoes of Scripture*, 23.
145. Hays uses Hollander's terms *transumption* or *metalepsis* to describe the process by which an echo is used repeatedly becoming a trope. Hays, *Echoes of Scripture*, 20–21. Cf. Hollander, *Figure of Echo*, 113–4.
146. Hays, *Echoes of Scripture*, 20.
147. Hays, *Echoes of Scripture*, 20.
148. Fishbane, *Biblical Interpretation*, 34.
149. Hays, *Echoes of Scripture*, 21. Cf. Hollander, *Figure of Echo*, 65.

correspondences that suggest more than they assert."[150] Hays is not simply implying that the author can generate new meanings through intertextual connections, he sees intertextuality as a source of new meanings that go beyond the text and the author's intentions.[151] This Kristevan view of intertextuality creates a tension between some of Hays's own views on authorial intention and his view of unintended correspondences and meaning.

The question then is who creates the new meaning based on the interplay of texts? Hays addresses this question in terms of "where" this hermeneutical event takes place and how the creation of meaning is validated. Hays proposes the following five options: in the author's mind, in the original reader's mind, in the text, in the mind of the present reader, and in a community of interpretation.[152] Hays does not choose one particular option but chooses to hold all five options in "creative tension" yet still acknowledges that the strongest means of validating created intertextual meaning are the text's literary structure, authorial intention, and the competence of the original reader.[153] Still, he laments the way "arbitrary hermeneutical restrictions" limit the interpretation of scriptural echoes and new readings that transcend conscious authorial intentions.[154]

Having defined and contrasted allusion, quotation, and echo, Hays proposes seven "tests for hearing echoes."[155] Hays's seven criteria or tests are: (1) *Availability*; (2) *Volume* which entails the explicitness of the echo, the prominence of the source, and authorial emphasis; (3) *Recurrence*; (4) *Thematic Coherence*, or how well the echo fits its rhetorical context; (5) *Historical Plausibility* of the author's intent and the original reader's comprehension; (6) *History of Interpretation*, which asks whether other interpreters/readers discerned the echo; and (7) *Satisfaction*, which asks whether the proposed reading makes sense or is satisfying for the reader.[156]

In his dissertation on the validation of literary allusion, David Klingler's helpful critiques of Hays's tests highlight a tendency to diminish the author's role and favor the reader's subjective reading.[157] Even Hays recognizes the tension between author and reader in his approach. This tension

---

150. Hays, *Echoes of Scripture*, 24.

151. Hays, *Echoes of Scripture*, 32–33.

152. Hays, *Echoes of Scripture*, 26–27.

153. Hays, *Echoes of Scripture*, 28.

154. Hays is not advocating a wide-open, reader-response hermeneutic, but sees intertextual echoes as a form of figuration that can potentially reveal new connections and readings that Paul did not see. Hays, *Echoes of Scripture*, 32–33.

155. Hays, *Echoes of Scripture*, 32–33.

156. Hays, *Echoes of Scripture*, 30–31.

157. Klingler, "Validity," 129–32.

is evident in the way he concludes his discussion of the five locations where the hermeneutical process occurs. Refusing to choose one, Hays holds the author, the original reader, the text, the current reader, and communities of interpretation in "creative tension." It is revealing when he states:

> I am neither prepared to embrace the doctrine of any of the hermeneutical schools represented by these five options (let the reader understand) nor inclined to jettison any of the elements of interpretation to which they draw attention. The working method of this book should be understood as an attempt to hold them all together in creative tension.[158]

It is apparent that Hays understands the importance of authorial intention and rhetorical coherence but still stresses the generative power of intertextuality as tropes reshape connected texts in a way that creates new meaning. The elasticity of his definitions, especially with regard to echo, allows him great flexibility in identifying and interpreting echoes. In fact, he acknowledges as much as he concludes his section on methods:

> Despite the careful hedges that we plant around texts, meaning has a way of leaping over, like sparks. Texts are not inert; they burn and throw fragments of flame on their rising heat. Often we succeed in containing the energy, but sometimes the sparks escape and kindle new blazes, reprises of the original fire. That is a way of saying that texts can generate readings that transcend both the conscious intention of the author and all the hermeneutical strictures that we promulgate.[159]

In an even more pointed statement, Hays overtly questions the importance of authorial intent in interpreting the possible meaning of intertextual connections in Scripture:

> To limit our interpretation of Paul's scriptural echoes to what he intended by them is to impose a severe and arbitrary hermeneutical restriction. In the first place, what he intended is a matter of historical speculation; in the second place, his intertextual echoes are acts of figuration. Consequently, later readers will rightly grasp meanings of the figures that may have been veiled from Paul himself.[160]

---

158. Hays, *Echoes of Scripture*, 27.
159. Hays, *Echoes of Scripture*, 33.
160. Hays, *Echoes of Scripture*, 33.

One gets the sense that Hays uses the concept of echo as a way of "finessing" the concept of allusion, liberating it from certain "severe and arbitrary hermeneutical restrictions." Despite reasonable questions about some of Hays's assumptions, his work stands as an important study of biblical intertextuality.

Michael B. Thompson on Allusion

Shortly after Hays's work, Michael B. Thompson released his own study of Jesus tradition (dominical sayings/teachings) in the Pauline letters. Thompson's work features a detailed method for identifying intertexts and defining the nature of such texts. Thompson begins by summarizing three core characteristics of an allusion based on notable studies of intertextuality and allusion, including the works of Ben-Porat and Perri. Having surveyed the literature, Thompson accurately observes: "Little has been written about how to identify allusions in biblical literature."[161]

Per Thompson, the basic characteristics of an allusion can be summed up in this way: an allusion uses a sign marker in order to call to mind a known text for a specific purpose.[162] Thompson further distinguishes between "allusion," "allusive citation," and "allusive quotation" based on criteria such as authorial intent, degree of specificity in evoking dominical traditions, reader recognition, the recognizability of the allusion-marker, and purpose of the allusion.[163] Thompson's understanding of allusion affirms the necessity of authorial intent and a desired rhetorical effect or purpose for the allusion.

Thompson's method for identifying an allusion entails eleven detailed criteria: (1) verbal agreement; (2) conceptual agreement; (3) formal agreement; (4) place of the gospel saying in the tradition; (5) common motivation or rationale; (6) dissimilarity to Graeco-Roman and Jewish traditions; (7) dominical indicators; (8) tradition indicators; (9) other dominical echoes or word/concept clusters in the immediate context; (10) likelihood the author knew the saying; and (11) exegetical value.[164] Some of the criteria are specific to the study of the Jesus tradition, but several criteria are useful in the broader study of biblical literature.

Unlike Hays, Thompson assumes authorial intent in the alluding act. Methodologically speaking, Hays's tests include evaluations that rely on

---

161. Thompson, *Clothed with Christ*, 29–30.
162. Thompson, *Clothed with Christ*, 29.
163. Thompson, *Clothed with Christ*, 29–30.
164. Thompson, *Clothed with Christ*, 30–36.

subjective interpretation, such as volume and satisfaction, but Thompson uses criteria, such as forms, tradition markers, dissimilarity, and verbal agreement, which are better suited to objective validation. The influence of Hays's and Thompson's general approaches can be seen in more recent studies as others have used variations of these criteria in studies of other biblical texts.[165]

Benjamin D. Sommer on Allusion and Echo

In *A Prophet Reads Scripture*, Benjamin Sommer exhibits an impressive understanding of the history of the study of intertextuality in literary criticism and its impact on the study of allusion in the Bible. Sommer opens with a discussion of intertextuality in which he contrasts a synchronic, semiotic, sign-based study of texts in a discursive space versus the genetic, historic study of one text's influence on the production and interpretation of a later text.[166] Sommer's method for allusion identification is fairly simple in comparison to the many criteria proposed by Hays and Thompson, but his approach is not simplistic. Sommer adapts Ben-Porat's four stages of allusion activation to his method. Thus, an allusion is identified by the following criteria: (1) Recognition of the marker; (2) identification of the evoked text; (3) modification of the interpretation of the sign in the alluding text; and (4) reader activation of the evoked text resulting in additional intertextual correspondences that transcend the sign.[167]

Though Sommer acknowledges the role of the author in any study of literary influence, his reliance on Ben-Porat's method indicates that authorial intent is not central to his approach. Sommer is aware that Ben-Porat's method is based on the reader's activation of an allusion, but he also notes that reader activation is not necessary for a valid allusion.[168] In essence, Sommer does not deny the necessity of authorial intent in a valid allusion

---

165. An example of a similar approach is found in a recent study of inner-biblical allusion in Ps 78. Jeffery Leonard proposes the following eight principles, which are reminiscent of criteria posited by Hays and Thompson: (1) Shared language. (2) Shared language is more important than nonshared language. (3) Shared language that is rare suggests a stronger connection than does language that is widely used. (4) Shared phrases are stronger than individual terms. (5) The accumulation of shared language is stronger than a single shared term or phrase. (6) Shared language in similar contexts is stronger than shared language alone. (7) Shared language need not be accompanied by shared ideology. (8) Shared language need not be accompanied by shared form. Leonard, "Inner-Biblical Allusions," 246.

166. Sommer, *Prophet Reads*, 6–10.
167. Sommer, *Prophet Reads*, 11–12.
168. Sommer, *Prophet Reads*, 7, 12–13.

as much as he assumes it. Sommer's approach shifts the emphasis squarely on to the allusion itself as a textual phenomenon with readily identifiable components. Thus, the essential distinguishing feature of an allusion is the rhetorical effect of the referent in the literary context of the alluding text.[169]

Sommer defines an echo as an intertextual form that consists of only the sign and the recognizable text, therefore, an echo is a literary reference without a "rhetorical or strategic end."[170] Sommer explains that an echo can make a text more interesting or it can even be clever, but if the referenced text does not affect the meaning of the referring text, it is not allusive.[171] This is a conscious departure from Hays's understanding of echo, which hinged on the "volume" of the echo, not its rhetorical function. Sommer proposes exegesis as another type of intertextuality that is specific to biblical literature. He defines exegesis as any effort to "analyze, explain, or give meaning to (or uncover meaning in) a text."[172] In this type of intertextual relationship, a text "clarifies or transforms an earlier text," whereas "an allusive text utilizes an earlier text."[173] Sommer does acknowledge that the dividing line between allusion, influence, echo, and exegesis, is "permeable, and individual cases may straddle the distinction or challenge it."[174]

In terms of the *formal* use of older material, Sommer identifies three methods: *explicit citation*, *implicit citation*, and *inclusion*.[175] Implicit citation, in which the author uses a marker borrowed from the vocabulary of an earlier text, is the most common method used in inner-biblical exegesis.[176] Inclusion is the incorporation of entire sections of an earlier text into a later text, as in the Chronicler's use of Samuel-Kings.[177]

In addition to types of intertextuality, Sommer discusses the various reasons for the use of older texts. Sommer believes that *allusion* and *echo* reflect authorial reasons for evoking an older text.[178] Allusion is when a writer uses an older text to "bolster" her own argument, thus, it is crucial

169. Sommer, *Prophet Reads*, 14–15.
170. Sommer, *Prophet Reads*, 15.
171. Sommer, *Prophet Reads*, 16–17.
172. Sommer, *Prophet Reads*, 17.
173. Sommer, *Prophet Reads*, 17.
174. Sommer, *Prophet Reads*, 17.
175. Sommer, *Prophet Reads*, 21.
176. Sommer, *Prophet Reads*, 21.
177. Sommer, *Prophet Reads*, 21.
178. The other reasons are *exegesis, influence, revision,* and *polemic*. Sommer uses *exegesis* differently than Fishbane. When Sommer refers to Fishbane's use of inner-biblical exegesis, he disambiguates with the expression "inner-biblical allusion and exegesis." Sommer, *Prophet Reads*, 23.

to understand that the rhetorical effect of the allusion takes place in the alluding text and does not speak to the older text.[179] As noted earlier, an echo may resemble an allusion in form but in terms of rhetorical function, an echo does not alter the understanding of the passage in which it appears.[180]

Summary: Intertextuality in Biblical Studies

In a recent article on inner-biblical allusion, Jeffery Leonard observes that scholars continue "to wrestle with matters of classification as they determine precisely how connected texts relate to one another. The sustained debates over terminology (intertextuality, allusion, exegesis, discourse, etc.) that characterize the field highlight the challenges in this area."[181] As evidenced above, Leonard is right: there is no consensus today regarding terminology, definitions, and methodology in the study of biblical intertextuality. Though the surveyed works are important contributions to the discussion, each scholar's proposed methods tend to be specific to the particular area of interest in which he or she works, therefore, not all aspects of their work are equally applicable or adaptable to other areas in biblical studies.

Though there is no clear consensus regarding a universally accepted set of definitions or method, it is possible to piece together a working definition of intertextuality, allusion, and echo based on the research outlined above. Unless specified otherwise, intertextuality is used in the field of biblical studies as a general descriptive term referring to a literary device in which a textual marker evokes another known biblical text.

Allusion refers to a literary device that is used by the author to evoke an earlier text so that the alluded text has an intended rhetorical effect on and in the alluding text. While the reader must recognize the allusion in order for the allusion to have its full rhetorical effect, it is solely the author who crafts the allusion. An echo is a literary reference that entails a textual marker that points to a recognized text without exerting a rhetorical effect on the evoking text. While an echo can be intended by an author, it is possible to have an echo that is not consciously deployed by the author.

Despite the lack of consensus, fruitful scholarship continues to take place. Currently, scholars continue to build upon general principles that have taken root while also adapting terms and concepts to particular areas of interest. To borrow from Emanuel Tov's insightful description of good textual criticism, the study of biblical intertextuality is an "art" bringing to

---

179. Sommer, *Prophet Reads*, 29.
180. Sommer, *Prophet Reads*, 30–31.
181. Leonard, "Inner-Biblical Allusions," 242.

bear the scholar's "intuition based on wide experience" to weigh different viable approaches and arrive at the best understanding of the intertextual and rhetorical interplay in the biblical text.[182]

---

182. Tov, *Textual Criticism*, 309–10.

3

A Novel Approach to Biblical Intertextuality

IN SURVEYING THE SCHOLARSHIP that has been done on biblical intertextuality, three key issues emerge. First, does the author or reader create or evoke the intertextuality? Second, what is the rhetorical or literary purpose of the intertextuality? Third, how does the intertextuality function in the evoking text? A recent dissertation by David Klingler addresses these issues in a promising way.[1] Klingler's approach innovatively employs relevance theory, a pragmatics-based model of communication, to explain the interplay between author and reader, as well as alluding text and referent.[2] Klingler posits that all communication is governed by certain universal operating principles, which can be applied to the process by which a writer evokes another text for rhetorical effect.

THE "RELEVANCE" OF RELEVANCE THEORY

Two of the central issues in any discussion of literary allusion are authorial intent and the rhetorical function of the evoked text. The relevance theory of communication is an untapped resource in these discussions. Deirdre Wilson and Dan Sperber's relevance theory presents an alternative to code-based models of communications.[3] Relevance theory is based on a model

---

1. Klingler, "Validity," 163–96.
2. Klingler, "Validity," 149–62.
3. The first presentation of relevance theory is found in Sperber and Wilson's work, *Relevance: Communication and Cognition*. Wilson and Sperber later published

called *ostensive-inferential communication*. This model, rooted in the linguistic field of pragmatics, accounts for the fact that human communication entails "something much larger than what is encoded in the sign system."[4]

In *ostensive-inferential communication*, intentional communication is understood from the perspective of both the speaker and hearer. On the part of the speaker (or writer), communication is *ostensive*, meaning the speaker overtly signals the intention to communicate (*communicative intent*). As for the hearer (or reader), communication is *inferential* in that the communicative intent must be *inferred* from the evidence provided by the speaker. The inferential nature of the hearer's role accounts for the fact that communication is both explicit and implicit.

The *ostensive* nature of communication means that communication is intentional and involves particular signals that make the intent to communicate clear to the audience. The *communicative principle* states that, "every act of ostensive communication conveys a presumption of its own optimal relevance."[5] In every act of ostensive communication, the speaker explicitly communicates an intent to inform, which is called the *informative intention*, and this is always accompanied by the *communicative intention*, which states that every act of ostensive communication begins with the speaker informing the audience of their *informative intention*.[6]

Inference is a distinctive feature of relevance theory that accounts for communication beyond coded signs. *Explicatures* are communicated assumptions that are the logical development of a form encoded by an utterance/text or an explicitly communicated assumption.[7] Thus, an *implicature* is information that is communicated inferentially, i.e., information that is unencoded by signs. Sperber and Wilson's inferential model posits that *all* communicated assumptions are inferred, including *explicatures*.[8] An *implicature* is a "contextual assumption or implication which a speaker, intending her utterance to be manifestly relevant, manifestly intended to make manifest to the hearer."[9] In short, an implicature is all information that is not communicated explicitly.

---

a follow-up work that focuses on cognition and addresses developments in the theory. Sperber and Wilson, *Relevance*; Wilson and Sperber, *Meaning and Relevance*.

4. Green, "Relevance Theory," 78.
5. Sperber and Wilson, *Relevance*, 266–72.
6. Sperber and Wilson, *Relevance*, 57–63.
7. Sperber and Wilson, *Relevance*, 182.
8. Sperber and Wilson, *Relevance*, 182–83.
9. Sperber and Wilson, *Relevance*, 194–95.

The key to inference is processing explicatures and implicatures in the proper context, which allows the hearer to begin the heuristic process of interpretation. In terms of intertextuality this understanding of context is significant for it means that it is the literary context of the intertextual reference, more than the intertextual marker, that enables the reader to process the intertext. When implicatures are combined with adequate contextual assumptions, an utterance produces attendant *implicated assumptions* and *implicated conclusions*.[10] So when a writer communicates a text, the net product is a set of *implicated assumptions* and *implicated conclusions*. These assumptions and conclusions are what the reader will use in the process of interpretation, which is the domain of cognition.

In relevance theory, *cognition* is governed by two basic assumptions: (1) The concept of *relevance* is a trade-off between processing effort and cognitive effects, and (2) cognition always tends toward maximizing relevance (the *cognitive principle*).[11] The concept of *relevance* is a property of inputs to the cognitive system and is evaluated in terms of *cognitive effects* and *processing effort*. There are two extent conditions that describe this:

> *Extent condition 1*: an assumption is relevant to an individual to the extent that the positive cognitive effects achieved when it is optimally processed are large.
>
> *Extent condition 2*: an assumption is relevant to an individual to the extent that the effort required to achieve these positive cognitive effects is small.[12]

These conditions assume that human cognition has developed so that mental mechanisms and biases "allocate attention to inputs with the greatest expected relevance, and process them in the most relevance-enhancing way."[13] A desirable cognitive effect is more than added knowledge since this does not account for other "positive contributions to cognitive functioning, involving, for instance, the reorganisation [sic] of existing knowledge, or the elaboration of rational desires."[14] This optimized process of measuring

---

10. Sperber and Wilson, *Relevance*, 194–95, 137–38.

11. The first assumption is a basic understanding of the concept of *relevance*. Relevance is a property that is maximized by a combination of maximizing outcome and minimizing the effort needed to achieve that outcome. The second assumption is called the first principle of relevance, which posits that cognition naturally tends toward maximum relevance. Sperber and Wilson, *Relevance*, 125–32, 261–66.

12. Sperber and Wilson, *Relevance*, 265–66.

13. Wilson, "Relevance Theory," 394.

14. Sperber and Wilson, *Relevance*, 265–66.

relevance is not a conscious calculation but an intuitive process that is not quantifiable.[15]

At this point, there is communication that is both explicit and implicit that has been accompanied by the intent to inform and the communication of this intent. On the writer's side, there is a presumption that her ostensive communication is optimally relevant. This is where the *cognitive principle* moves the reader to find relevance in the writer's communication. This involves two clauses in this *presumption of optimal relevance*: (1) The ostensive stimulus (communication) is relevant enough to be worth the hearer's effort to process it, then (2) the ostensive stimulus is the most relevant one compatible with the communicator's abilities and preferences.[16] If the writer's text meets minimal levels of relevance then the reader automatically processes explicatures, pairing implicatures with appropriate contextual assumptions, and developing a set of implicated assumptions and conclusions. The final step, then, is *utterance interpretation*, a heuristic process in which the implicated assumptions and conclusions are tested against the clauses of optimal relevance. This involves determining whether the hypothetical interpretation is worth the effort and whether it coheres with the writer's abilities and preferences. This process stops either when a satisfactory interpretation is reached or if nothing optimally relevant is found with reasonable effort.

Based on relevance theory, a few important principles can be applied to biblical interpretation. First, the Bible is a collection of utterances written by humans, for humans (literature that addresses God directly notwithstanding). Therefore, it is tenable to view biblical interpretation through the lens of ostensive-inferential communication. In this model, biblical writers make manifest their intention to communicate information that is relevant to the reader, then their communication provides explicatures and implicatures for the reader to process.[17] One can further infer that biblical writers communicated in a way that maximizes relevance, and one way to do so is by using literary and rhetorical devices that minimize the effort a reader must expend to process a maximal amount of information. It is in this sense that intertextual devices enhance the efficiency and relevance of a writer's communication. In effect, a well-deployed intertextual device is like an evocative photo that is worth a thousand words.

---

15. Sperber and Wilson, *Relevance*, 132.
16. Sperber and Wilson, *Relevance*, 270.
17. Green, "Relevance Theory," 84.

USING RELEVANCE THEORY IN THE STUDY OF ALLUSIONS

Klingler's use of relevance theory is an innovative approach describing what takes place between the author and the reader when an allusion is utilized.[18] Klingler has aptly recognized that relevance theory models communication in a way that lends itself well to the description of referential thinking.[19] Since the context for biblical texts includes the immediate literary context and canonical contexts, it stands to reason that readers of biblical texts would be quite sensitive to inner-biblical intertextuality. For this reason, a literary device, like an allusion, is an attractive tool due to the potential for increased relevance. Klingler explains this dynamic thusly:

> An author chooses an allusion to something in another text because its contextual effects in his developing context are large. The point that he wishes to make in his developing context has a meaningful relationship to something in another text. While the author could take the time and effort to spell out the point in laborious detail, alluding to the thing in the other text can be more efficient and effective so long as the relationship between the author's text and the thing being alluded to can be readily accessed.[20]

Relevance theory also addresses the process by which readers interpret an allusion. The process of reading a text involves a continuous process of adding utterances to the developing text that increasingly evoke relevant situations and texts as well as people, places, ideas, and themes that are brought to the reader's mind.[21] A helpful aspect of Klingler's discussion is in recognizing *relevance* as the key to understanding how an allusion works. From a relevance-theoretical standpoint, the key to an allusion is the relevance of another text to the developing meaning of the alluding text. "As contextual meaning is narrowed, texts with related textual meaning become

---

18. Klingler provides a helpful introduction to relevance theory and then elucidates a way to incorporate principles of relevance theory into a method for validating a literary allusion. This writer is indebted to Dr. Klingler for the method developed in his dissertation. Klingler, "Validity."

19. Relevance theory describes interpretation as a process of taking implicatures and putting them in an appropriate context resulting in implicated assumptions and conclusions. Inference-based comprehension emphasizes the effect of context and authorial intention. Sperber and Wilson, *Relevance*, 194–96.

20. Klingler, "Validity," 154.

21. Klingler, "Validity," 155.

more relevant in the mind of the author and reader."[22] It is only when the alluded text has maximum relevance in the alluding text that literary markers can be used by the author to formally signal an allusion.[23] However, the literary marker does not actually bring the alluded text in proximity to the reader, rather it is the alluded text's *relevance* to the developing meaning of the alluding text that determines its "nearness."[24] Klingler's innovative adaptation of relevance theory results in a helpful model of the intertextual dynamic involving author, reader, referencing text, and evoked text.

Validating a Literary Allusion

Building upon the model of relevance theory, Klingler proposes a five-step process for the validation of a literary allusion. Klingler's method is unique in two ways. First, his emphasis on the author's communicative intentions and the reader's interpretational process gives his method a perspective that is often ignored or only given a cursory treatment by others. Second, this method brings a technical approach to the resultant rhetorical relationship involving the alluded text in the literary context of the alluding text. Attributing the allusion to the author necessarily means that this method handles intertexts diachronically in a way that aligns with traditional views of literary influence.

The proposed method entails five steps that are based on five working components of a valid literary allusion. The first component is *the developing textual meaning of the alluding text*. According to relevance theory, every utterance communicates the presumption of its own relevance (the communicative principle); therefore, every statement in the alluding text is assumed to be of maximum relevance to those that preceded it.[25] In practical terms, Klingler asserts that the reader must explain the developing meaning of the text through relevance of genre, context, and meaning; in other words, through exegesis that is contextually valid.[26] Thus, the first step is an exegetical reading of the alluding text.

The second component is *the stable meaning of the alluded text*. The next step determines the relevance of the alluded text to its new literary context. From the author's vantage point, the relevance of an outside text's stable meaning to her own developing meaning must be established prior

---

22. Klingler, "Validity," 156.
23. Klingler, "Validity," 156–57.
24. Klingler, "Validity," 157.
25. Klingler, "Validity," 172.
26. Klingler, "Validity," 173–75.

to inserting allusive textual markers. This is because relevance theory states that the author gives precedence to maximizing relevance in her text over encoding formal signs.[27] Thus, step two entails exegesis of the alluded text in its original literary context so that the stable meaning of this text can be determined.

The third step involves the *allusive textual markers*, which serve as a signal that directs the reader to the appropriate text containing the allusion. Klingler poses two additional criteria regarding the allusive marker. First, the marker must be identifiably relevant, meaning if the reader/interpreter is correctly following the developing meaning of the alluding text, the markers should be identifiable. Second, the markers must require minimal processing effort to identify.[28] The ease of identification of a familiar text is one way an allusion can make use of intertextual links to make communication more efficient. Evoking a familiar text greatly reduces the reader's processing effort.

The fourth step assesses the *rhetorical relationship*. Per Klingler, the rhetorical relationship between the alluding and alluded texts follows the rules of classical logic. The two texts will be related in one of the following ways: (1) equal, (2) greater than, (3) less than, (4) similar to, and (5) not equal or ironic opposite.[29] These rhetorical relationships can also be conceptual, for example, metaphoric (B is like A), validation (B = A), ironic (B is *not* like A, failure), climactic (B > A, this is better), and emblematic (B < A, this is worse).[30] By definition, an allusion requires a rhetorical relationship between the alluding text and the alluded text, for if there is no rhetorical relationship, then the intertextuality in question is not an allusion.[31] This is the key step, for it can be used diagnostically to identify non-allusive types of intertextuality.

The fifth step assesses the resulting *imported meaning and rhetorical function* of the allusion. The ultimate purpose of an allusion is to enhance the author's textual meaning (argument) so that the cognitive goal may be achieved, which is the reader's understanding of the intended message.[32] The meaning of the allusion is found in what the author intended to import into her text; in other words, the *imported meaning* makes the point of the

---

27. Klingler, "Validity," 175.
28. Klingler, "Validity," 178–79.
29. Klingler, "Validity," 179–80.
30. Klingler, "Validity," 179–80.
31. Klingler, "Validity," 179–80.
32. Klingler, "Validity," 181.

allusion.[33] This is the essence of the rhetorical effect and the right literary device will help the author make her argument efficiently and effectively. Determining the imported meaning of the allusion completes the reading of an allusion and validates it if all the conditions are properly met.

A strength of Klingler's approach is objectivity of method. For example, there are no cases of strong allusion, weak allusion, or possible allusion, since the author's intention determines whether an intertextuality is an allusion. Klingler does acknowledge that there is still subjectivity in the approach since readers can disagree on interpretations of alluding and alluded texts, authorial intent, and the identification of allusive textual markers.[34] This method is not the final word on identifying and validating an allusion, but it represents a promising approach to the study of biblical allusions.

Validating a Non-literary Allusion

According to relevance theory, cognition is an inferential process that relies heavily on context. Texts are brought near, not by a textual marker, but by the process of contextual narrowing that occurs as an author's developing textual meaning (rhetorical point) brings related texts closer in proximity.[35] In this way, a reader finds that non-literary referents, such as events, people, places, works of art, and concepts, can be brought to mind as she reads progressively through a text. A reasonable question then is whether an author can allude to something other than a specific literary text. The idea of a valid non-textual allusion has merit from a relevance theoretical point of view. According to relevance theory a literary device, such as an allusion, can greatly increase contextual relevance and minimize processing effort on the part of the reader. Just as a text can allusively maximize relevance, a concept with some discernible meaning can also relate logically to an alluding text resulting in enhanced rhetorical impact.

The main issue with this proposal is in the determination of an idea's meaning. Whereas exegesis is an effective way to interpret a biblical text, there is no established method for "exegeting" an idea. Nevertheless, there are biblical examples where a writer references an idea without using a specific text. For example, in Mic 6:8 when the prophet distills the law to doing justice, loving mercy, and walking humbly with God, he is not referring to a specific text but to a conception of the law's essence. Note that no specific text in the Pentateuch summarizes the law in this way. A similar

---

33. Klingler, "Validity," 182.
34. Klingler, "Validity," 186–95.
35. Klingler, "Validity," 186–95.

conceptual reduction occurs when Jesus distills the law to loving God and loving one's neighbor (The Great Commandment; Matt 22:35–40; Mark 12:28–34). Thus, in the context of this study, it is reasonable to think that a well-established biblical concept can convey the kind of meaning that is rhetorically significant in a different literary context.

This study is constructed around an intertextual study of references to the Abrahamic and Mosaic covenants found in Ps 105. Ps 105 is noteworthy because it is a rare non-Pentateuchal text where the Abrahamic and Mosaic covenants are referenced together (Neh 9 is another such text). Ps 105 recalls Israel's history from the patriarchs to the exodus and up to Israel on the verge of the conquest. The psalmist explicitly refers to the Abrahamic covenant but alludes to the Mosaic covenant in developing an argument about Israel's postexilic return to the land.

At the conclusion of the psalm, there is one allusion to the Mosaic covenant (Ps 105:45) that does not evoke a specific text. In this instance, the psalmist uses common Torah terms to import the Mosaic covenant and its covenant stipulations into the psalm's developing argument. The psalmist uses the well-known Torah terms "statute" (חק) and "law" (תורה) to make the point that a return to the land must be accompanied by renewed covenant faithfulness and obedience. While these terms do not point to an exact text in the Pentateuch, the two terms are used metonymically throughout the Law and Prophets as a reference to the Mosaic covenant and its laws (e.g., Lev 26:46; Deut 4:8; Deut 17:19; 2 Kgs 17:37; Amos 2:4; Mal 3:22 [MT]; Neh 9:13; 10:30 [MT]; 2 Chr 33:8).

Furthermore, these references to the Mosaic covenant and law often occur in relation to the question of covenant fidelity and covenant renewal. Therefore, the method for allusion validation used in this study can accommodate a non-literary allusion as long as the referent is recognizable and conveys meaning that is rhetorically discernible. In this sense, the historical narration in Ps 105 provides the literary setting in which a non-literary allusion to the well-known Mosaic covenant can function in a rhetorically meaningful manner.

OUTLINE OF THE INVESTIGATION

The primary aim of this work is to examine the references to the Abrahamic and Mosaic covenants in Ps 105. The unique nature of this intertextual convergence means Ps 105 has the potential to provide a glimpse into the postexilic covenant thinking of the Jewish remnant through this psalmist's song. The core of this study involves the identification of each intertextual covenant reference followed by an analysis of these references and allusions in relation to the psalmist's rhetorical approach and argumentation. The rhetorical function of the two defining covenants is then used to discern the psalmist's understanding of these covenants within his postexilic historical context.

The investigative portion of this work begins in earnest with a detailed study of Ps 105. As the referencing text and the location of the intertextual references, Ps 105 is a fitting starting point for this investigation. The study of the psalm begins with an overview of introductory matters, including authorship, date of composition, provenance, and canonical placement within the Psalter. Next, the study delves into the details of the psalm featuring an exegetical reading as well as a rhetorical reading. The exegetical reading focuses on lexical, syntactical, and grammatical features while the rhetorical reading delineates the psalmist's rhetorical meaning and lines of argumentation.

The following stage of the investigation turns the focus to the intertextual referents, the Abrahamic and Mosaic covenants. This portion of the work features an overview of each covenant, including a survey of each covenant's narrative, content, and stipulations within their respective Pentateuchal contexts. The aim of this portion of the investigation is to understand each covenant in its original literary context so that they can then be examined in the new literary context of Ps 105. The Abrahamic covenant is evoked through literary references to the land promise (Ps 105:8–11, 42) while the Mosaic covenant is evoked through three allusions at key structural points in the rhetorical framework of the song (Ps 105:7, 8, and 45).

The culmination of this study brings the referencing text and the referents together as the covenant references and allusions are examined via the rhetorical significance of the covenants within the psalmist's argument. The literary references to the Abrahamic covenant help the psalmist construct the historical and conceptual framework for his argument. The allusions to the Mosaic covenant undergird a vital subtext that culminates in the main point of the psalmist's argument. The Mosaic covenant allusions work in concert with the explicit Abrahamic covenant references to create a *text-subtext* dynamic that the psalmist uses to great rhetorical effect. In this way, the remembrance of the great covenants through song serves as a unique look at the postexilic covenant theology of the psalmist, and by extension the Jewish remnant.

A SYNCHRONIC STUDY USING A DIACHRONIC METHOD

The essence of this study is the reading of various biblical texts in relation to other texts. The focus is Ps 105, but the investigation of the psalmist's rhetorical use of the Abrahamic and Mosaic covenants means that numerous texts in the Pentateuch will be examined in order to develop a working understanding of the two covenants. In addition, Neh 9 will be incorporated into the discussion of the historical and theological context of Ps 105. Both Neh 9 and Ps 105 come from the same postexilic historical context. In addition, the historical content of Neh 9 uniquely parallels that of Ps 105 while also focusing on the Abrahamic covenant in relation to the postexilic renewal of the Mosaic covenant. Thus Neh 9 is a valuable source for understanding the provenance of Ps 105.

This writer is aware of the issues that continue to divide various scholarly circles with regard to the authorship and date of the books in the Pentateuch and individual psalms. Though the method employed in this investigation assumes a diachronic use of biblical references in Ps 105, the use of the final canonical placement of these various texts means a conclusive word on authorship and provenance is not necessary for the purposes of this study. The various pentateuchal texts and Ps 105 are read within their final canonical context giving literary priority to the pentateuchal texts and ideas referenced in Ps 105. In this sense, the approach is akin to that of Rendtorff in his work on the covenant formula as well as Hahn's approach in his work on the theology of the biblical covenants.[36]

Hahn characterizes his method as both narrative analysis and canonical criticism. Per Hahn, "narrative analysis treats Scripture as an integrated whole, engages in a holistic literary study of its constituent parts," while canonical criticism provides ". . . a broader interpretive perspective than any single text can provide, one that reflects the historical continuity and theological unity of God's saving plan."[37] Rendtorff adds that a synchronic approach to the OT allows each covenant to be viewed in the context of the preceding covenant(s) as revealed in the final canonical form of the OT narrative.[38] For the purposes of this study, a synchronic reading of the various covenant-related texts has great value in developing an overarching understanding of how the Abrahamic and Mosaic covenants are not only instituted but also relate to one another. The final benefit of a synchronic,

---

36. Rendtorff, *Covenant Formula*, 7–10; Hahn, *Kinship by Covenant*, 22–28.
37. Hahn, *Kinship by Covenant*, 24–25.
38. Rendtorff, *Covenant Formula*, 7–8.

canonical approach is in providing a coherent framework for the literary priority of the pentateuchal covenant texts in relation to Ps 105.

4

A Song of Covenants
An Exegetical Study of Psalm 105

IN ANY EXPLORATION OF intertextuality, the starting point is the text in which the author has referenced an earlier text or concept. This analysis consists of an exegetical and rhetorical study of Ps 105. The exegetical reading of Ps 105 analyzes the psalm in lexical, grammatical, and syntactical terms.[1] The rhetorical reading delves into the psalmist's intended argument as conveyed through the psalm's literary, poetic, and rhetorical features. It is the rhetorical reading of Ps 105 that elucidates the developing argument in which the intertextual references to the Abrahamic and Mosaic covenants function rhetorically.

INTRODUCTORY MATTERS

Psalm 105 is unique in featuring Abraham, the patriarchs, the Abrahamic covenant, and Joseph. The psalm begins with a hymnic call to praise that highlights the theme of Yahweh's universal reign (vv. 1–6). The body of the psalm then covers the covenant with the patriarchs (vv. 7–11), the patriarchal sojourn in Canaan (vv. 12–18), Joseph's bondage and Israel's fruitfulness in Egypt (vv. 19–24), Moses and the plagues (vv. 25–36), the exodus and the wilderness wanderings (vv. 37–42), and concludes on the verge of

---

1. Appendix A is this writer's working translation of Ps 105 with text critical notes.

entering the land (vv. 43–45).² The psalm concludes with a didactic, prescriptive statement on obedience to the Mosaic law (v. 45). Through this curated historical narration, the psalmist makes the case that God's sovereignty means his covenantal faithfulness to Abraham and the patriarchs is patently evident in Israel's history.

This exegetically informed reading of Ps 105 is the first level of reading in which the psalmist's message and meaning is discerned. In a sense, this reading is intended to be a summary of the psalm without the added layers of data found in its canonical context or in the editorial activity that juxtaposes Ps 105 with Ps 106 at the conclusion of Book IV. This approach keeps the focus upon the individual psalmist and his rhetorical activity.

The Date and Provenance of Psalm 105

Psalm 105 is not attributed to any particular author so any degree of specificity on a date of composition is difficult to ascertain. Several studies have attempted to investigate Ps 105 and discern a time period in which it may have been written. For the purposes of this study, the most relevant aspect of the date discussion is the chronological and literary relationship between Ps 105 and the Pentateuch as well the psalmist's historical context. The demonstration of literary priority with regard to the patriarchal narratives and the Sinai materials in the Pentateuch is a necessary starting point for any discussion of literary influence and the psalmist's referential activity.³ The historical and socio-cultural setting is an important source of background information that fleshes out the reading of the psalm.

The dates of composition for the books of the Pentateuch continue to be open to discussion. For the purposes of this study, the question of date is tied to the *terminus ante quem* for each of the books of the Pentateuch since the primary concern is to demonstrate that the covenant materials in the Pentateuch were available to the psalmist.⁴ If there is overlap in terms

---

2. Commentators outline the psalm differently, but the general outline can be discerned chronologically according to the historical events being narrated. Ceresko notes that there is a basic chronological structure to the psalm involving the sequence of events, but there are also poetic features that result in alternative ways of structuring the psalm. Ceresko, "Poetic Analysis," 20–46.

3. This study employs a synchronic, canonical methodology that accounts for narrative unity in the OT. The literary priority of the Pentateuch is assumed in this approach, but a discussion of Ps 105's provenance is a helpful means of locating the psalm in a larger historical context.

4. Conservative estimates place the earliest core of the Pentateuch between the time of Moses and the monarchic era prior to the exile. Mainstream scholars view P as

of possible dates of composition for the pentateuchal covenant texts and Ps 105 then another way to discern literary priority is to identify textual features in the psalm that point to the influence of pentateuchal texts. The use of terms, expressions, and formulas that are unique to the covenant accounts in the Pentateuch potentially indicate that the psalmist made use of pentateuchal traditions. Of course, it is possible that both the authors of the pentateuchal texts and the psalmist used common sources and traditions, so discretion must be exercised in drawing conclusions based solely on textual and lexical connections between the Pentateuch and Ps 105.

Traditional Approaches to the Date of Psalm 105

In looking at traditional approaches to the date of Ps 105, there are two pieces of textual data that are addressed in these discussions. The first such datum is the quotation of Ps 105:1–15 in 1 Chr 16:8–22 and the second is the omission of an explicit reference to the Sinai covenant history. As for the first, the Chronicler attributes the quoted portion of Ps 105 to David as a song of praise sung on the occasion of the ark's arrival in Jerusalem from the house of Obed-Edom (1 Chr 15–16). On the surface, the quotation of Ps 105:1–15 in this context seems to indicate that Ps 105 predates the Chronicler and represents a date of composition in the monarchic era, possibly as early as the Davidic period.[5]

Robertson suggests that the portion quoted by the Chronicler reflects a genuine Davidic psalm tradition that was composed on the occasion of the ark's arrival in Jerusalem and then became a part of Israel's cultic hymnody.[6] Robertson looks at the compositional unity of 1 Chr 16:8–36 and the manner in which oral traditions were transmitted as well as the way psalms and song fragments could be adapted to various worship settings, and posits that Ps 105 could be a monarchic era composition.[7] Hossfeld does not see Ps 105:1–15 as genuinely Davidic, but suggests that the quoted portion of Ps 105 represents an Asaphite tradition that likely predates 1 Chr 16.[8]

---

the last source in the composition of the Pentateuch. Some current scholars posit that P was active as late in the postexilic period (~539–330 BCE). Bautch and Knoppers, *Covenant in the Persian Period*, 1–9.

5. Dahood believes the quotation of Ps 105 in 1 Chr 16 indicates a pre-exilic date of composition. Dahood, *Psalms III*, 51.

6. Robertson, *Flow of the Psalms*, 161–64.

7. Robertson, *Flow of the Psalms*, 161–62.

8. Hossfeld and Zenger, *Psalms 3*, 68. Choi views Ps 105 as a composite work that is "composed of a collection of discrete units." Thus, the quotation of Ps 105:1–15 in 1 Chr 16 is not of much value in determining the provenance of the psalm since the

Nevertheless, most commentators see this quotation as the Chronicler's use of existing postexilic cultic material in a manner appropriate to the context of the narrative in 1 Chr 15–16.[9]

As for the second datum, those who adhere to a tradition-historical approach see the conspicuous omission of the Sinai material and the apparent subordination of the Sinaitic covenant to the Abrahamic covenant as reflecting the theology of the Priestly school.[10] Füglister's study of Ps 105 is a good example of the conventional traditio-historical approach. He detects both Deuteronomic and Priestly influences in Ps 105, which suggests a *terminus ante quem* around 300 BCE.[11] Gunkel also views Ps 105 as a composition of the exilic to postexilic period but does so based on form-critical considerations. Gunkel sees the style of the hymnic poetry in Ps 105 as a very late form of poetry, while acknowledging that the Chronicler seems to view the beginning of Ps 105 as though it were already an old hymnic fragment by the postexilic period.[12]

Despite the various attempts to discern a tradition history that accounts for the way various biblical writers recount Israel's history, it is not necessary to explain the omission of Sinai elements in terms of the Priestly source or different textual traditions. Goldingay aptly notes that the lack of emphasis on the events at Sinai may reflect the psalmist's particular agenda. According to Goldingay, the psalmist knows that the people are aware of the Sinai events but intentionally places the focus squarely on God's praiseworthy acts from the exodus to the conquest for didactic and rhetorical reasons.[13] Choi posits that the psalmist viewed the Sinai covenant as ideologically incompatible with his view of covenant, thus excluded the Sinai covenant in order to emphasize the Abrahamic covenant.[14] Though Choi operates within a tradition-historical framework, his observation regarding the psalmist's rhetorical agenda highlights the possibility that something other than textual traditions can explain the absence of an explicit reference to Sinai. From a rhetorical perspective, it stands to reason that the postexilic

---

psalmist may be appropriating an existing hymnic text. Choi, *Traditions*, 123.

9. Allen, *Psalms 101–150*, 40. See also Kraus, *Psalms 60–150*, 309.

10. Kraus questions whether Ps 105 was composed after the completion of the Pentateuch and sees the omission of the Sinai events as being related to the omission of the Sinai events in the so-called "little credo" of Deut 6:20–24; 26:5b–9. Kraus, *Psalms 60–150*, 309. See also von Rad, "Problem of the Hexateuch," 11–26.

11. Füglister, "Psalm 105," 46.

12. Gunkel and Begrich, *Introduction to Psalms*, 64.

13. Per Goldingay, the psalmist is writing to a postexilic community needing reassurance that God can act now as in the past. Goldingay, *Psalms 90–150*, 203.

14. Choi, *Traditions*, 123.

community would be buoyed by a recounting of Israel's history that focuses on God's covenantal faithfulness, the lasting nature of the patriarchal promise of land, and the great power of Israel's God.[15]

The Exile as the Key to Dating Psalm 105

In addition to discussions regarding the Chronicler and the absence of an explicit Sinai reference, there are specialized studies that have proved helpful in dating Ps 105. In surveying these studies, the exile and postexilic settings emerge as a key to the provenance of Ps 105. The following survey illustrates the variety of ways in which scholars have examined this question. In general, the body of evidence points toward a postexilic date and provenance.

Hildebrandt analyzes the poetic devices in Ps 105 as a means of locating it in the compositional history of the Psalter.[16] Hildebrandt sees the psalmist as a *bricoleur*, an artist who pieces together various texts to produce something relevant to his present setting.[17] Hildebrandt notes a significant pattern of terminology shifting in which theologically significant terms, such as "covenant," "land," "servant," and "chosen," are reapplied in a way that "binds together two sojourning communities, Abraham and the postexilic returnees, who are separated by over a millennium."[18] For example, the psalmist refers to the postexilic remnant as "chosen" (Ps 105:6, 43) and "anointed" (Ps 105:15) by virtue of their familial connection to Abraham and also represents them as recipients of the covenant promise of land that Yahweh remembers as an eternal covenant.[19] In doing so, the postexilic community finds hope in the many parallels between their own situation and that of Abraham and the patriarchs. In Hildebrandt's analysis of the poetic use of language, he sees the contextual evidence as consistent with a late-exilic or postexilic period.[20]

Another line of reasoning for a late date can be found in Holm-Nielsen's study of Exodus traditions in Ps 105.[21] Holm-Nielsen discusses linguistic and conceptual affinities between Ps 105 and Priestly sources (and

---

15. Allen, *Psalms 101–150*, 40.
16. Hildebrandt, "Song of our Father," 51–65.
17. Hildebrandt, "Song of our Father," 51–54.
18. Hildebrandt, "Song of our Father," 66.
19. Hildebrandt, "Song of our Father," 66.
20. Hildebrandt, "Song of our Father," 54–65.
21. Holm-Nielsen, "Exodus Traditions," 22–30.

Deutero-Isaiah) as evidence for an exilic to postexilic provenance.²² Holm-Nielsen's analysis indicates that whenever the psalmist uses Exodus terminology and traditions, he depicts the exile and deliverance as a repetition of the exodus.²³ The depiction of Joseph with feet in fetters and neck clasped in iron (Ps 105:18) is not found in Genesis, but could symbolize Israel's plight in exile.²⁴ For Holm-Nielsen, an exact dating of Ps 105 is elusive but linguistic and conceptual clues place the psalm against the backdrop of the exile.²⁵

Emanuel notes that signs of literary influence reflect the Pentateuch's literary priority and a late date. Emanuel sees the most extensive literary influence coming from Exodus.²⁶ Though Leviticus, Numbers, and Deuteronomy, are not quoted, Emanuel posits that Leviticus and Deuteronomy probably did not have enough narrative material of value, while the history of Israel's failures in the wilderness likely made Numbers rhetorically unsuitable for the psalmist's purposes.²⁷ Like Hildebrandt and Holm-Nielsen, Emmanuel views the thematic and linguistic affinities between the pentateuchal account of the exodus from Egypt and the exodus from Babylon as an indicator that Ps 105 comes from a postexilic setting.²⁸

Others tend to follow this general line of reasoning. For example, in a rhetorical study of Ps 105, Olbricht views the exile and the loss of the land as the most important aspect of the background for Ps 105, prompting him to place the psalm sometime in or after the exile.²⁹ Some of the language and terminology of Ps 105 also seems to indicate a late exilic or postexilic setting. For example, in the psalmist's version of the plague narrative, Gerstenberger identifies terms and phrases, such as sending "hail" instead of "their" normal "rain" (נתן גשמיהם ברד, Ps 105:32), which reflects Judean climate conditions as well as the terms "vines" and "figs" (גפנם ותאנתם, Ps 105:33), which reflect Judean vegetation more than Egyptian flora.³⁰

---

22. Holm-Nielsen posits that the primary tradition behind Ps 105 is the Exodus tradition, thus P becomes the *terminus a quo* for composition. He also sees linguistic and conceptual affinities to Isa 40–55 which he associates with an exilic provenance. Holm-Nielsen, "Exodus Traditions," 24–27.

23. Holm-Nielsen, "Exodus Traditions," 24–27.

24. Holm-Nielsen, "Exodus Traditions," 24–25.

25. Holm-Nielsen, "Exodus Traditions," 24–27.

26. Emanuel, *From Bards*, 73.

27. Emanuel, *From Bards*, 73–74.

28. Emanuel, *From Bards*, 72.

29. Olbricht, "Rhetoric," 162–63.

30. Gerstenberger, *Psalms*, 233. See also Goldingay, *Psalms 90–150*, 214.

Wallace's study on the narrative effect of Book IV of the Psalter employs a holistic reading of the Psalter in order to discern the overarching narrative as opposed to the poetic meaning of individual psalms.[31] In the narrative of Book IV, Wallace posits that there is more to the historical narrative than simply recounting Israel's movement from the time of the patriarchs to the conquest of Canaan. According to Wallace, "the narrative effect of the Psalter provides a polyvalent meaning which seems to be exilic."[32] As others have similarly observed, Wallace cites examples where the psalmist uses words, images, and ideas that have a distinctly exilic feel even though they occur in the narrative of Israel's early history.[33]

Linguistic and Textual Data

In terms of linguistic evidence, Emanuel notes that there are no examples of Archaic Biblical Hebrew (ABH) typical of early pre-pentateuchal poetry.[34] The most compelling linguistic evidence for a postexilic date is found in Ps 105:10 where the psalmist uses the verb עמד instead of the verb קום, which would have been used in the Pentateuch with regard to the covenant-making act (e.g., Gen 26:3; Lev 26:9).[35] Emanuel notes that קום means "to establish" or "confirm" in the Standard Biblical Hebrew (SBH) of the Pentateuch, but it is עמד that takes on this meaning in Late Biblical Hebrew (LBH).[36]

Brooke's study of Pss 105–106 at Qumran is worth considering due to his examination of the manuscript evidence from the Judean desert.[37] Brooke believes that most have it wrong in giving Ps 105 literary priority over 1 Chr 16, proposing that Ps 105 was actually composed after the work of the Chronicler.[38] Brooke posits that Pss 105 and 106 were composed independently from various prose and poetic elements, including an older Asaphite psalm segment that is featured in 1 Chr 16, a covenant remembrance motif from Lev 26, and general "programmatic influences" from

---

31. Wallace, *Narrative Effect*, 11.

32. Wallace, *Narrative Effect*, 78.

33. Wallace, *Narrative Effect*, 78–80. Clines sees an exilic undertone where exile and return from exile are reminiscent of the exodus from Egypt. Clines, *Theme of the Pentateuch*, 105–6.

34. Emanuel, *From Bards*, 71.

35. Emanuel, *From Bards*, 72.

36. For examples of עמד used with the meaning of "establish/confirm," see 1 Chr 17:14; 2 Chr 9.8; Dan 11:14. Emanuel, *From Bards*, 72. For a detailed survey of עמד in different periods of biblical Hebrew, see Hurvitz, *Linguistic Study*, 94–98.

37. Brooke, "Psalms 105 and 106," 267–92.

38. Brooke, "Psalms 105 and 106," 275, 283, 291.

Deuteronomy and Exod 34 (especially the teaching of the law at Moab).[39] In comparing Ps 105:1–15 with the nearly identical 1 Chr 16:8–22, Brooke argues that where Ps 105 differs from 1 Chr 16 there is a sense that Ps 105 is a later adaptation of the Chronicler's text tradition.[40]

Brooke presents several pieces of textual data to paint this picture. For example, Ps 105:6 reads "Abraham" where the Chronicler has "Israel" (cf. Ps 105:6a and 1 Chr 16:13a), but in the text, "Israel" seems the more natural parallel for Jacob (Ps 105:6b and 1 Chr 16:13b), indicating that "Abraham" is a later emendation by the psalmist, who conspicuously features Abraham.[41] In 1 Chr 16, the name Isaac is spelled with a צ (*tsade*) whereas the psalmist spells it with a שׂ (*sin*) which is a variant spelling found in later texts (e.g., Jer 33:26; Amos 7:9, 16; 11QPsᵃ Frg. E, III, 15).[42] In 1 Chr 16:15, זכר appears as a plural imperative that tells the reader to "remember" his (Yahweh's) covenantal decree, but in Ps 105:8 (and in 11QPsᵃ Frg. E, III,14), זכר is a *qal* perfect, which turns out to be a significant refrain in both Pss 105 and 106 that recalls Lev 26:42 where it is Yahweh who remembers his covenantal decree.[43]

Interestingly, Ps 105:9–10 refers to a covenant with Jacob akin to the way the Abrahamic covenant is attributed to the other patriarchs, but the Jacob narrative in Genesis never explicitly mentions the term *berit*. What is noteworthy is that a late Qumran text, 11QTᵃ XXIX 10, does make mention of a "covenant" with Jacob at Bethel.[44] This seems to favor the notion that the psalmist is working with later materials than the Chronicler. Finally, Ps 105:15 has the preposition, -ל, associated with רעע while 1 Chr 16:22 has -ב. Brooke notes that this same verb is also used with -ל in Ps 106:32, which seems to indicate that the psalmists were working with an idiomatic variant that was known in their time but different from the Chronicler's version of the same hymnic material.[45] Though this textual datum does not specify which text has literary priority, the fact that both psalmists use the same variant against the Chronicler's variant is consistent with the idea that 1 Chr 16 uses a text tradition that is older than Ps 105.[46] The overall body of

---

39. Brooke, "Psalms 105 and 106," 293.
40. Brooke, "Psalms 105 and 106," 274–77.
41. Brooke, "Psalms 105 and 106," 274–75.
42. Brooke, "Psalms 105 and 106," 275.
43. Brooke, "Psalms 105 and 106," 275.
44. Brooke, "Psalms 105 and 106," 275, 290.
45. Brooke, "Psalms 105 and 106," 275.
46. Brooke, "Psalms 105 and 106," 275–76. The postexilic date of Ps 106 is widely accepted since the historical narrative includes the exile. Thus, textual agreement between Pss 105 and 106 against Chronicles indicates a later date.

evidence presented by Brooke builds a tenable case for Ps 105 being later than 1 Chr 16 though drawing upon the same Asaphite psalm tradition as the Chronicler.[47]

McKelvey looks at the various arguments (including Brooke's) for dating Ps 105 before the Chronicler as well as arguments for dating Ps 105 after 1 Chronicles and concludes that it is impossible to definitively establish which text is earlier.[48] In light of the present studies and the various arguments, McKelvey seems correct in asserting that a definitive placement of Ps 105 before or after 1 Chronicles is not possible. However, Brooke's analysis of the data from Qumran and his conclusions do support the dating of Ps 105 at least in the exile and more likely in the postexilic period. Given the general consensus regarding the late date of the Chronicler's work, Brooke's analysis coheres with the position that Ps 105 is a postexilic composition.

A Postexilic Provenance and Pentateuchal Literary Priority

From a literary standpoint, Mascarenhas argues that Pss 104–106 cover the whole "milieu" of the Pentateuch, including creation, the patriarchal narratives, the exodus, the wilderness journey, and possession of the promised land.[49] The historical and narrative details as well as the chronological framework follow the Pentateuchal traditions, which Mascarenhas sees as an indication that the psalmist had access to the completed Pentateuch.[50] Though the apparent dependence on the Pentateuch does not yield a specific date, it does support the general position that the Pentateuch has literary priority over Ps 105.

Based on the overall evidence, it is best to place Ps 105 in the late exilic to postexilic period. The quotation of Ps 105:1–15 in 1 Chr 16 does not necessitate a preexilic date for the entire psalm since the psalmist may be using part of an older hymn, such as an Asaphite composition. In addition, the work of the Chronicler is a late work in its own right so some ambiguity as to which work has literary priority does not mitigate against an exilic to postexilic date of composition. This survey demonstrates a general consensus regarding a late date of composition based on linguistic, stylistic, lexical, and thematic affinities to the work of a late exilic or postexilic writer.

---

47. Brooke, "Psalms 105 and 106," 274–77, 290–92.

48. McKelvey, *Moses, David*, 222n1.

49. Mascarenhas, "Psalm 105," 86.

50. Mascarenhas, "Psalm 105," 86. Brooke sees indications that Pss 105 and 106 follow Deuteronomic and Priestly historical traditions from the Pentateuch. Brooke, "Psalms 105 and 106," 293.

Most importantly, a postexilic date of composition means that it is tenable to place Ps 105 after the Pentateuch, which has a compositional history that spans several periods but is generally considered no later than the Persian period. This provides a basis for proceeding under the assumption that the psalmist had access to the Pentateuch and was aware of its historical narratives and traditions.

Form and Genre Considerations

In terms of form-critical categories, Gunkel broadly classifies Ps 105 as a hymn and Westermann further labels it a descriptive psalm of praise that focuses on God as the lord of history.[51] As for the literary *Gattung* of the psalm, it is a "selective review of Israel's history ... with the accent on Yahweh's work on his people's behalf and his faithfulness to his ancient promise."[52] While the coverage is not comprehensive, Ps 105 provides a summary of Israel's national history from Genesis to Joshua. The other so-called *Geschichtspsalmen* are Pss 78, 106, 135, and 136, but the category of "historical psalm" is only based on a common use of historical narration. There are significant differences amongst the historical psalms in terms of theology, historical content, and literary features.[53] Interestingly, the historical work that is closest to Ps 105 in terms of historical content is Neh 9, which also uniquely features Abraham and the Abrahamic covenant.[54]

As for the *Sitz im Leben* of the psalm, there is no firm consensus. Mowinckel views Ps 105 as a non-cultic "learned psalmography" that simulates hymnic style.[55] Others have proposed various cultic usages and settings with most linking it in some way to a major Israelite festival.[56] The one strong indicator for cultic usage comes from 1 Chr 16 where Ps 105:1–15 is

---

51. Gunkel and Begrich, *Introduction to Psalms*, 22. Westermann further specifies hymns as descriptive psalms of praise. Westermann, *Psalms*, 85–87, 92–96.

52. Allen, *Psalms 101–150*, 40

53. Duggan does a comparison of the historical content in Neh 9 versus Pss 78, 105, 106, 135, and 136. Per Duggan, the psalms differ in terms of historical content as well as theological emphases and tenor. Duggan, *Covenant Renewal*, 226–28.

54. Duggan, *Covenant Renewal*, 227.

55. Mowinckel, "Psalms and Wisdom," 213–17. Gunkel posits that Ps 105 exhibits less original "creativity," appearing to simulate an older form. Gunkel and Begrich, *Introduction to Psalms*, 64.

56. Kraus and other later commentators see Ps 105 as a cultic hymn, as opposed to a didactic psalm (*pace* Mowinckel). Kraus, *Psalms 60–150*, 309. See Allen for a helpful summary of various views on the cultic *Sitz im Leben* of Ps 105. Allen, *Psalms 101–150*, 40.

used to celebrate the return of the ark to Jerusalem from the house of Obed-Edom (1 Chr 15–16).[57] Weiser posits that the reference to the Decalogue in Ps 105:45 indicates that Ps 105 may have been part of annual covenant renewal ceremonies and festal ritual.[58] In light of the dearth of concrete evidence, these various proposals can only be considered informed speculation. There is nothing in the superscript or within the body of the psalm that gives a clear indication of its authorship, audience, and the occasion for the psalm's composition.[59] Marttila is correct in asserting that one must be cautious about concluding too much from ancient Israelite cultic practice since actual knowledge of such practices is meager.[60]

Canonical Placement and Context

The interesting situation one faces in reading Ps 105 is that there is an exegetical and rhetorical meaning that the psalmist intended, but in the final canonical form of the psalter the editor(s) and compiler(s) of the Psalter have created a canonical reading in which Ps 105 is part of the larger narrative context of Book IV. In light of this editorial activity, it is appropriate to ask whether the editorial meaning is consistent with the original meaning or whether the editorial meaning reflects a new reading that does not contradict the psalmist's original meaning. Ideally, the canonical placement should reflect the psalm's original meaning since the editor/compiler ought to have read the psalm in a manner consistent with the psalmist's intentions. Thus, the psalm's relationship to Ps 106 and Book IV should not contradict the reading of the psalm.

In his seminal study on the editing of the Psalter, Wilson posits that Book IV of the Psalter is the editorial "center" of the Psalter, addressing the failure of the Davidic covenant and the collapse of the monarchy at the end

---

57. This writer is aware that it is not certain that the Chronicler is quoting Ps 105. This language is used descriptively to note that a segment of Ps 105 appears in 1 Chr 16 as a song of David.

58. Weiser, *Psalms*, 676. The possibility of Ps 105 being used in covenant renewal ceremonies coheres with the postexilic setting reflected in Ezra-Nehemiah (see Neh 8–10).

59. Based on comparisons of Pss 104–106 in the MT and in the LXX, Waltke posits that the superscript or incipit for Ps 105 may be the transposed postscript from Ps 104. This pattern of conflating the postscript and superscript in successive psalms seems to have taken place somewhere in the compilation and transmission history of Pss 104–106 (=Pss 105–107 LXX). Waltke, "Superscripts," 593.

60. Marttila, *Collective Reinterpretation*, 236.

of Book III (Ps 89).⁶¹ Book IV is also known as the Moses book of the Psalter since he replaces David as the central figure in this collection of psalms.⁶² Wallace notes that Moses is the "unifying character throughout Book IV" due to obvious references (Pss 90 and 95), Mosaic terms and language in the "YHWH Reigns" (יהוה מלך) psalms (Pss 93, 96, 97, 99), and Mosaic remembrances in Pss 101–106.⁶³ As the nation contends with an uncertain future, the pivot toward Moses is understandable since he is viewed as the mediator of the covenant that constituted Israel as a nation as well as the giver of the laws that define Israel's identity as God's people.

Editorial activity and rhetorical design are apparent as Book IV opens with Ps 90, an appropriate lament in light of the national tragedy in Ps 89, followed by a shift toward hope by the end of Book IV, which is where Ps 105 is paired with Ps 106 as the conclusion to the book. Psalms 105 and 106 are considered "twin psalms" (*Zwillingspsalmen*) due to their complementary historical narratives.⁶⁴ Psalm 105 is decidedly positive in its focus on Yahweh as faithful and sovereign, while Ps 106 reminds the people of Yahweh's grace in spite of their repeated failures and sinfulness.⁶⁵

In the midst of a book that prominently features Moses, Ps 105 stands out in placing Abraham and the patriarchs at the forefront of its historical narrative. The editorial placement of Ps 105 seems to address the postexilic community's uncertainty regarding its status in the land and its national future. The divine promises to the patriarchs are a fitting foundation for

---

61. Wilson views Books I–III as Davidic books, which means Book IV is a significant shift in the theme and subject matter of the Psalter's books. Wilson, *Editing of the Psalter*, 215.

62. Wallace, *Narrative Effect*, 5, 15–18, 93. For more on the "Moses dimension" in Book IV, see Zenger, "God of Israel's Reign," 165–66.

63. Wallace, *Narrative Effect*, 93.

64. Zimmerli first coined the expression "twin psalms" (*Zwillingspsalmen*) to describe pairs of psalms that were paired for rhetorical or poetic effect. Zimmerli, "Zwillingspsalmen," 109. For more on the composition of "twin psalms," see also Zenger, "Psalmenexegese," 36–37. Waltke's study of postscripts and superscripts in the Psalter sheds light on the editorial activity that placed Pss 104, 105, and 106 together in Book IV of the Masoretic Psalter. Per Waltke, the acceptance of the postscript-superscript conflations by the time of the LXX indicates that these conflations had taken place early in the process of compilation and were accepted as part of the textual tradition. Waltke further notes that this indicates that there was some time between the composition of these psalms and their final canonical compilation. Waltke, "Superscripts," 593–95.

65. Zenger views Pss 105 and 106 as an example of antithetical *parallelismus memborum* in which the psalms themselves sit in antithetical parallel. Zenger, "Psalmenexegese," 36n39. For more on the contrasting historical narratives and rhetorical purposes, see Emanuel, *From Bards*, 162; Brueggemann, *Abiding Astonishment*, 16–18; Gelston, "Editorial Arrangement," 174.

a community in search of stability and hope. Despite the importance of Moses and the Mosaic covenant, there is an awareness that the exile was the result of the nation's failure to keep the Mosaic law. Psalm 105 pushes the gaze of the people back, past the failure of the Mosaic covenant, to the patriarchs and the promises that stand as the ultimate foundation for Israel's nationhood. In essence, Abraham represents Israel's foundational roots as a nation as well as its national future.

AN EXEGETICAL STUDY OF PSALM 105

Structure and Outline

The content of the psalm lends itself to a general outline based on the historical events being narrated, but there is some variance with regard to the overall structure and delineation of specific narrative sections. The following is a representative outline of Ps 105 based on the clear divisions between the introductory section, the body of the psalm (featuring the historical narration), and the conclusion.

1. Opening call to praise (vv. 1–6)
2. Yahweh remembers his covenant with the patriarchs (vv. 7–11)
3. Yahweh guided the patriarchs to Egypt (vv. 12–15)
4. Yahweh *sent* Joseph ahead into Egypt where Israel was fruitful (vv. 16–25)
5. Yahweh *sent* Moses to afflict Egypt with plagues (vv. 26–36)
6. Yahweh delivered Israel out of Egypt (vv. 37–41)
7. Yahweh remembered the Abrahamic promise in the conquest of the land (vv. 42–44)
8. Conclusion: Show covenant loyalty by obeying the Mosaic law (v. 45)

The main body of the psalm begins after the call to praise (vv. 1–6) and includes the historical narration (vv. 7–41). The כי construction in v. 42 signals the start of the concluding section culminating with the didactic statement in v. 45 marked by the adverbial conjunction בעבור. Surrounding the main body there is an *inclusio* framed by two statements regarding Yahweh's faithfulness to the covenant he made with Abraham: "He always remembers his covenant, the word he decreed to a thousand generations"

(זכר לעולם בריתו דבר צוה לאלף דור) in v. 8 and "For he remembered the sacred word he decreed to Abraham his servant" (כי זכר את־דבר קדשו את אברהם עבדו) in v. 42a. The poetic structure of the psalm features movement from Canaan to Egypt in the first half of the narrative section followed by movement from Egypt to Canaan in the second half.

Psalm 105:1–6: Call to Praise

Ps 105:1–2 opens with a hymnic call to worship that is divided into two parallel sets of exhortations marked by imperative verb forms that call on the worshiper to give thanks or praise followed by a call to make known his praiseworthy works.[66] In v. 3b a jussive verb, "let ___ rejoice" (יִשְׂמַח), breaks up the chain of imperatives and signals the "self-understanding of the group being addressed" as those who are seekers of Yahweh.[67] The chain of imperatives resumes in vv. 4 and 5, but now the exhortation is to seek Yahweh followed by a call to remember both Yahweh's words and deeds. In v. 6 the psalmist identifies his audience with a series of terms that speak to the psalmist's perspective on his community's identity and place.[68]

Psalm 105 is unique in that it is the only psalm that features Abraham as a central figure.[69] Verse 6 clarifies the psalmist's intended audience by the use of two expressions, "seed of Abraham" and "sons of Jacob," that are both associated with the early postexilic Jewish community.[70] The significance of this verse is tied to the unusual association of two theologically significant terms, "servant" (עבד) and "chosen" (בחיר), in conjunction with the patriarchs, Abraham, and Jacob.

The term "servant" and the expression "his servant" are common designations for Moses throughout the OT (e.g., Exod 4:10; 14:31; Num 11:11; 12:7; Deut 34:5; Josh 1:7; 8:31; 9:24; 1 Kgs 8:56; 2 Kgs 18:12; Neh 1:7; Dan 9:11; Mal 4:4). For the psalmist to refer to Abraham as "his servant" (עבדו)

---

66. Jacobson opts to read הודו as "make known" rather than "give thanks," and similarly reads קראו בשמו as "cry out about" with an emphasis on making Yahweh known rather than addressing him directly. In this sense, he also reads the two ל + pronoun constructions (לו) in v. 2 as subjective, not objective, again reading the psalmist's exhortation as a call to make Yahweh known. Jacobson, "Psalm 105," 787. Goldingay also reads the two prepositional constructions in v. 2 subjectively, not objectively. Goldingay, *Psalms 90–150*, 204.

67. Hossfeld and Zenger, *Psalms 3*, 69.

68. Hildebrandt, "Song of Our Father," 54–57.

69. Abraham is only mentioned one other time in the Psalter outside of Ps 105. In Ps 47:10 [BHS] the people of Israel are associated with אלהי אברהם ("God of Abraham").

70. Gerstenberger, *Psalms*, 230.

in a psalm that also features Moses would not have gone unnoticed. When Moses asked God for mercy following the golden calf apostasy (Exod 32:13), he asked him to "remember your servants, Abraham, Isaac, and Jacob." The use of "his servant" and "his chosen ones" is also striking in that these two terms are also associated with David, which means the psalmist has enacted an additional expansion of special terminology by associating these Davidic terms with Abraham and his descendants.[71] The use of Davidic terms in this context is a rhetorical tool that speaks to national identity, not the democratization of the Davidic covenant's royal promises to the nation.

In tracing the development of the covenant formula ("I will be your God and you will be my people") in conjunction with the concept of election, Rendtorff notes that the election of Israel is described by בחר (e.g., Deut 7:6; 14:2), but only in the postexilic writing of Neh 9 is this term connected to Abraham (see Neh 9:7).[72] Since Ps 105 is also from around the same time period as Nehemiah, it is likely that the linking of Abraham's covenantal relationship and his "election" (בחר) would have been a familiar concept. The psalmist's use of the term "chosen" is a subtle way to evoke the related concepts of election and covenant in the present rhetorical context.

The identification of Mosaic and Davidic terms with Abraham is not limited to the patriarchs. Goldingay notes that the psalmist's use of the plural form בחיריו ("his chosen ones") connects the deeds God did for the patriarchs with their descendants.[73] The psalmist's identification of the people of Israel as "servants" and "his chosen ones" through their relationship to Abraham implies an additional continuity and identification involving the people and Moses and David, two of the central figures in the Hebrew Scriptures. This widened application of Davidic and Mosaic titles captures the reader's attention. Per Gosse, the postexilic community would have been struck by this enlarged application of Davidic titles to Abraham and his descendants since Ps 105 is found in Book IV, which is a response to the failure of the Davidic dynasty as addressed in Ps 89.[74] It is the very Davidic terminology found in Ps 89 at the close of Book III that is now being used in

---

71. David is called "servant" in many texts (e.g., 1 Kgs 8:24–26; 2 Kgs 8:19; 19:34; 1 Chr 17:7; Ps 18 and 36 superscripts; Ps 78:70; 89:3; Jer 33:21–22, 26; Ezek 37:24). He is also called "chosen" in a few texts (e.g., 2 Sam 22:51; 1 Kgs 11:34; Ps 18:50; 89:3). Hossfeld and Zenger, *Psalms 3*, 70.

72. Rendtorff observes that the terms ברית and בחר are positively linked via the covenant formula. This lexical connection instills the term בחר with covenantal significance. Rendtorff, *Covenant Formula*, 3–4, 9, 39.

73. Goldingay, *Psalms 90–150*, 206.

74. Gosse, "Le quatrième livre," 246.

a noticeably similar manner of Abraham in Ps 105 of Book IV.[75] To be clear, this canonical correlation is the work of the editor(s) not the psalmist, but the psalmist's rhetorical intentions in applying symbolic terms to Abraham and transitively to the nation are consistent with the editor's subsequent thought process.

Psalm 105:7–11: Yahweh Remembers his Covenant

The end of the introductory section is signaled by the shift from a series of imperatives to predicate-nominative sentences.[76] After the psalmist references Abraham and Jacob by evoking terms regularly used of Moses and David, the next section opens with the important declaration that Israel's God is יהוה אלהינו ("Yahweh our God"). Though the voicing of this declaration is shifted into the third person ("He is Yahweh our God"), this is a recitation of Yahweh's self-declaration formula, "I am Yahweh" (Exod 6:2–3, 8) and the fuller version "I am Yahweh your God" (Exod 20:2; Deut 5:6, see also Lev 26:13). This reference to the covenant name of God evokes an entire complex of texts, concepts, and images, such as the patriarchal promises, the exodus, the Decalogue, the covenant at Sinai, and even the Shema.[77] In this setting the psalmist uses the covenantal name and self-declaration formula in order to establish that he is speaking of Israel's covenant-making and covenant-keeping God.[78]

This writer posits that the psalmist's use of the self-declaration formula is more than a subtle intertextual echo to covenantal concepts and images, it is an allusion to Exod 6:2–8; 20:2 and Deut 5:6. The self-declaration formula appears prominently in Exod 20:2/Deut 5:6 as the opening identification of the covenant sovereign in relation to the Decalogue. The use of the divine name in this setting identifies Yahweh with the nation of Israel and the constitutive Mosaic covenant. Though not as obvious, Exod 6:2–8

---

75. There are poetic parallels involving the use of the Davidic terms "chosen" and "servant" in Pss 89 and 105. Gosse, "Le quatrième livre," 246–47.

76. Kraus, *Psalms 60–150*, 310.

77. Harman sees the use of "Yahweh, our God" as a way of linking God to the exodus and to the covenant relationship established with Abraham and the patriarchs. Harman, *Commentary*, 753. Kidner sees this name as an echo back to the exodus and the Mosaic covenant. Kidner, *Psalms 73–150*, 407. McKelvey sees this as an echo of the *Shema* in Deut 6:4. McKelvey, *Moses, David*, 232.

78. Stuart notes that the self-declaration "I am Yahweh" functions effectively as a synecdoche for the Sinaitic covenant. Stuart, *Exodus*, 172–73. Garrett adds that the covenant name emphasizes the continuity between the promises to the patriarchs (who knew God by the name Yahweh) and the fulfillment of those promises in relation to the covenantal relationship established at Sinai. Garrett, *Commentary*, 252.

has covenantal significance as a prelude to the Sinai covenant, and also as a bridge between the Abrahamic and Mosaic covenants (e.g., Gen 17).

The remainder of v. 7 affirms that this same God, who is Israel's covenant sovereign, has universal authority since his judgments are effective throughout the earth. This is likely a reference to Abraham's divine appellation, "the judge of all the world" (השפט כל־הארץ) in Gen 18:25.[79] This is the psalmist's first indication regarding a major theme of Ps 105, which is God's absolute sovereignty over all realms of creation.[80] In Ps 105, Passaro observes that one of the main goals of the psalmist's editorial activity and curation of the historical material is to identify God as the ultimate agent of history by attributing major moves in history to God's influence or control.[81]

This next passage (vv. 8–11) is worth examining closely since this is where the first explicit mention of the Abrahamic covenant occurs. The two references to the Abrahamic covenant are found in verses 8–11 and 42, which form an *inclusio* around the narrative body of the psalm. The opening reference places the covenant with Abraham in the context of the patriarchs and focuses on the land promise component of the Abrahamic covenant (Gen 15:18–21; 17:8).

Verse 8 opens with the statement that Yahweh "remembers forever" (זכר לעולם) his covenant. This expression means more than recollection, for Yahweh does not simply forget. This idea of "remembers forever" includes the ideas of commitment, loyalty, and appropriate action (e.g., Pss 74:2; 79:8).[82] Hartley notes that "to remember covenant" (זכר ברית) stands in opposition to הפר ("breaking" covenant), not שכח ("forgetting" covenant), and refers exclusively to God acting in the present in a manner consistent with past promises.[83] In fact, the perfect verb form (זָכַר), used in the gnomic sense, means Yahweh's "mindfulness" of the covenant has already begun and has been effective for numerous generations with the implication that his "mindfulness" will persist.[84] As an establishing statement, v. 8 is reminiscent of Exod 2:24 where it is Yahweh's remembrance of his covenant with

---

79. Emanuel, *From Bards*, 34–35.

80. Clifford notes that other gods only had power in their own territories, but Yahweh's power transcends boundaries. For example, he can summon drought in Canaan (v. 16) and summon plagues in Egypt (vv. 23–38). Clifford, "Style and Purpose," 424.

81. Passaro, "Theological Hermeneutics," 43–44, 47, 50–51. See also Emanuel, *From Bards*, 70–71.

82. Anderson, *Psalms: Vol. II*, 579, 728. See also Ross, *Commentary*, 265.

83. Hartley, *Leviticus*, 469.

84. Ross, *Commentary*, 207. The usage of the verb here suggests that זכר has a gnomic or characteristic sense.

the patriarchs that initiates the events that culminate in the exodus.[85] The specific language of "remembrance" in v. 8 calls to mind Exod 2:24 and Lev 26:42, 45, which affirm that Yahweh has "remembered" his covenant in the past, reinforcing the point that Yahweh will maintain his covenant in the future.[86]

According to the parallelism of v. 8, the phrase "the word he commanded to a thousand generations" (דבר צוה לאלף דור) also describes Yahweh's covenant with Abraham. In effect, v. 8b can be read as parenthetical to v. 8a. The phrase דבר צוה has the sense of divine declaration. Though the verb צוה is often rendered "to command," its use in this context is related to the idea of a divine pronouncement, declaration, or decree, especially when paired with the term דבר.[87] Another relevant nuance of this expression is an emphasis on divine initiative in making the covenant, which is consistent with the manner in which Yahweh established his covenant with Abraham.[88]

The expression "to a thousand generations" (לאלף דור) is a figurative way of expressing the perpetual or eternal nature of the covenant. This expression is also a textual marker that signals an allusion to Deut 7:9 and Exod 20:6 where this exact expression is used to describe the enduring nature of Yahweh's covenantal faithfulness (חסד) to the Mosaic covenant, namely to those who show covenantal love to Yahweh and obey the Mosaic law.[89] The crucial implication is that Yahweh's *ḥesed* is not shown to those who violate the covenant, meaning the blessings of the Mosaic covenant cannot be experienced unless the covenant relationship is renewed. Thus, v. 8 reinforces the fact that the Abrahamic covenant's sworn promise of land is a divine decree that is effective into perpetuity, but the allusion to Deut 7:9–10/Exod 20:6 tempers this by reminding the reader that the Mosaic covenant's blessings will only be experienced by those who love Yahweh and keep his commandments.

The first part of v. 9 explicitly identifies the covenant in v. 8 as the patriarchal covenant. In v. 9b, Isaac is identified as an additional recipient

85. McCann, "Book of Psalms," 1105.

86. For a discussion of זכר in the context of God "remembering" covenant, see Eising, "זכר," 4:70–71.

87. In Pss 42:9 and 111:9 the verb צוה is used to describe the LORD's "declaration" of his loyal love and his covenant, respectively. Kraus sees the collocation of דבר and צוה as having the sense of a prophetic announcement or decree. Kraus, *Psalms 60–150*, 310. The use of דבר צוה can also emphasize the commitment Yahweh has made in establishing the Abrahamic covenant. Goldingay, *Psalms 90–150*, 207.

88. Kidner, *Psalms 73–150*, 408.

89. The expression לאלף דור occurs verbatim in Deut 7:9. A similar expression, לאלפים, is used in Exod 20:6. Per Sarna, the correspondence with Deut 7:9 means "to a thousand generations" is the preferred reading in Exod 20:6. Sarna, *Exodus*, 111.

of the covenantal promise first made to Abraham.[90] Note that the colon in v. 10 is comprised of a colon with a verb, "he established it for Jacob . . . " (ויעמידה ליעקב), that is followed by a colon without a verb, "to Israel as an eternal covenant" (לישראל ברית עולם). This parallels the poetic structure of v. 9, which is comprised of an initial colon with a verb, "which he ratified" (אשר כרת), followed by a colon without a verb, "his sworn promise to Isaac" (ושבועתו לישחק). The syntactical structure of vv. 9 and 10 highlights the fact that the same core covenant that was established with Abraham was confirmed with Isaac and Jacob.[91] In a manner similar to the use of דבר צוה ("the word he commanded") in v. 8, the legal term חק ("statute" or "decree") is used here to reinforce the commitment Yahweh has made to Abraham and his descendants.[92]

Verses 8–10 not only include the patriarchs in the covenantal promise made to Abraham, there is also a subtle *inclusio* involving the terms ברית and עולם (see vv. 8a and 10b) that relates the Abrahamic covenant to the patriarchal promise of land (e.g., Gen 50:24; Exod 2:24; 6; Num 32:11; Deut 1:8). There is a minor question as to the meaning of "Israel" (ישראל) in v. 10. Though it is possible that the nation is the referent, a later shift to "his people" (עמו) from v. 24 to the end of the psalm seems to indicate that "Israel" refers to Jacob in this context.[93] In sum, vv. 9–10 link the original covenant with Abraham to the promise made to Isaac and the decree established with Jacob. In addition, the perpetual, multi-generational nature of the Abrahamic covenant is seen in the way it is effective for Abraham's descendants, Isaac and Jacob. The involvement of several generations of patriarchs reinforces these promises as a covenant made for a "thousand generations." The ensuing historical narration only further reinforces this notion as the promise to the patriarchs comes to fruition via wondrous acts of God that are experienced by later generations of Abraham's descendants.

The actual content of the covenantal promise to the patriarchs is made explicit in v. 11. Allen observes that only the promise of the land is featured

---

90. In v. 9b, the verb form שְׁבוּעָתוֹ can be read in two different ways. Most render שְׁבוּעָתוֹ as the construct form of the noun שבע with a 3p, m. sg. pronominal suffix ("his sworn promise"). Dahood reads שְׁבוּעָתוֹ as a *Qal* f. passive participle of the verb שבע with a dative suffix expressing agency ("sworn by him"). Dahood, *Psalms III*, 54. Dahood's reading is a rare and unlikely construction. In addition, the synonymous parallelism involving vv. 9 and 10 favors the customary reading, "his sworn promise."

91. Per Harman, the terminology used in v. 10 is highly unusual. The verb form וַיַּעֲמִידֶהָ (*Hif.*) is a *hapax legomenon* and it is uncommon to see חק used by itself. The verse still reinforces the fact that the covenant with Jacob is the same as the covenant with Abraham. Harman, *Commentary*, 754, 754n6.

92. Goldingay, *Psalms 90–150*, 207.

93. Allen, *Psalms 101–150*, 37n10a.

here even though the Abrahamic covenant entails other promises, such as that of numerous descendants, great nations, and even kings from the Abrahamic line.[94] The opening verb in v. 11 "saying" (לאמר) may be a subtle way of pointing specifically to the promise of land. Emanuel notes that direct quotations are usually unmarked in the Psalter (e.g., Ps 105:15), thus the use of the explicit marking of Yahweh's speech seems to point the reader to Gen 15:18.[95] Kraus also points out that in the pentateuchal historical narratives, the promise of land appears to be the core of the covenant with the patriarchs (e.g., Gen 50:24; Exod 2:24; 6:3–8; Num 32:11).[96]

The expression "share of your inheritance" (חבל נחלתכם) brings to mind Yahweh's sovereign authority to parcel out land among the nations (e.g., Deut 32:9). The word חבל ("share" or "portion") literally refers to a cord or length of rope that was used to measure a section of land for distribution (e.g., Amos 7:17).[97] Thus, the Lord has "measured out" a parcel of land to give to Israel as a permanent inheritance. While some see the second person singular (לך) in the first colon and the second person plural (נחלתכם) in the latter colon to be a text critical issue, it is more likely that the oscillation in number reflects the collective extension of the Abrahamic covenant to the entire nation.[98] This section (vv. 7–11) firmly establishes Abraham as the "carrier of the promise" and the descendants as the "continuing carriers of the divine promise."[99]

Psalm 105:12–15: Yahweh Guides the Patriarchs to Egypt

Verses 12 and 13 open with a description of the patriarchal generation and how they were few in number when they wandered and sojourned among the nations. These verses reflect Deut 7:7–8 where Yahweh stresses that his covenantal selection of Israel was in spite of how few in number and powerless they were. This allows the psalmist to highlight Yahweh's power and sovereignty against the backdrop of the people's helplessness and homelessness. The infinitive construct that opens this section (בהיותם) has a temporal

94. Allen, *Psalms 101–150*, 37n11c.

95. Emanuel, *From Bards*, 38. In Gen 15:18, לאמר marks the promise of land as Yahweh's quoted direct speech.

96. Kraus, *Psalms 60–150*, 310. Clifford argues that it is because the core of the promise is the land that the psalmist features the patriarchs so prominently. Clifford, "Style and Purpose," 422–23.

97. Goldingay, *Psalms 90–150*, 208.

98. Allen, *Psalms 101–150*, 37n11b. See also Goldingay, *Psalms 90–150*, 208; Hossfeld and Zenger, *Psalms 3*, 67.

99. Brueggemann and Bellinger, *Psalms*, 452–53.

function and signals that the narrative core of the psalm begins in earnest here.[100] The wandering of the sojourning patriarchs is a theme that is well-known in Israel's historical traditions and likely reflects the influence of a known credo-like formula (see Deut 26:5; cf. Deut 7:7–8; Josh 24:2).[101] In fact, this description of the sojourning patriarchs is one of several places in Ps 105 where the psalmist's historical narration reflects the discernible influence of language and imagery from Deuteronomy (see Ps 105:7, 12, 42–45).[102]

It is also noteworthy that Deut 7:7–8 precedes an axiomatic Mosaic covenant text where Yahweh characterizes his covenantal faithfulness as favor that is exclusively shown to those who love him and keep his commandments (Deut 7:9–10; Exod 20:6). The allusion in Ps 105:8b evokes this reciprocal aspect of the Mosaic covenant relationship, and the description of the people in Ps 105:12–13 can be considered a recollection or echo of Deut 7:7–8, which has a synergistic rhetorical effect. In essence, the people have been chosen by grace and shown favor, but the Mosaic covenant relationship means this covenantal faithfulness is for those who keep the covenant.

In verses 14 and 15, Yahweh's protection of his sojourning people stands out against the backdrop of helplessness and homelessness. His people were itinerant and few in number as they wandered among stronger nations, but Yahweh responded by "rebuking" any ruler that would oppress them and forbidding any power to harm his "anointed ones." In vv. 14–15, as in v. 6, the psalmist again introduces two meaning-laden terms and applies them in a novel way to the patriarchs. In the OT, "anointed" (משיח) is used of kings, prophets, and priests and it is possible that the psalmist had in mind the promise of royal descendants (Gen 17:6), the identification of Abraham as a priest (Gen 12:7–8), or even as a prophet (Gen 20:7).[103] In any case, the psalmist's usage of "anointed" in reference to the sojourning patriarchs is highly unusual.[104] Kraus additionally posits that משיח might be an allusion to the general anointing of prophets (e.g., 1 Kgs 19:16) or the

---

100. Hossfeld and Zenger, *Psalms 3*, 67.

101. Olbricht notes that vv. 12–13 are reminiscent of the so-called "little credo" in Deut 26:5–9. Olbricht recognizes the credo genre, which is as a formulaic listing of God's acts in a traditional order. This genre elicits "at various junctures theological reflection and commitment." Olbricht, "Rhetoric," 160, 164.

102. Tucker and McKelvey see evidence of Deuteronomic features in the psalm's historical narration, indicating the use of pentateuchal historical materials. Tucker, "Revisiting the Plagues," 409–11; McKelvey, *Moses, David*, 232–34.

103. Jacobson, "Psalm 105," 790. Römer notes that the "astonishing title משיחים is without parallel in the Ancestral Narratives." Römer, "Abraham Traditions," 175n86.

104. Römer, "Abraham Traditions," 175n86.

"democratizing" of the title of king to Abraham (see Exod 19:6; Isa 61:1).[105] It is difficult to say with certainty which of these references the psalmist had in mind, but the point is to remind the audience of the "inviolability and unassailability" of Yahweh's anointed ones (see 2 Sam 1:1–16).[106] Gerstenberger sees the emphasis on sojourning under divine guidance and protection as a prelude to the eventual possession of the land that was promised to the patriarchs, which is a typical theme of exilic/postexilic writings.[107]

In the process of introducing his historical narrative it is significant that a confluence of the expressions, "chosen ones" and "servants" (v. 6) along with "anointed ones" and "prophets" (vv. 14–15) has been applied in a novel way to the patriarchs, and by extension, to the people of Israel. By intertwining these meaning-laden terms, the psalmist highlights the continuity of Yahweh's covenantal faithfulness, which begins with Abraham and the patriarchs, then applies to Moses, and ultimately to David.

The next section transitions from the patriarchal sojourn into the Joseph narrative. The epic, broad retelling of history is signaled by a long sequence of preterite verbs, or narrational *waw*-imperfects, that direct the narrative flow (vv. 16, 20, 23, 24, 29, 33, 35–37).[108] The verbs occurring at the beginning of each new line syntactically emphasize the sovereign activity of Yahweh in history, which is in keeping with one of the main themes of Ps 105.[109] In the Joseph narrative it is apparent that the psalmist actively shapes the historical material in order to draw attention to divine sovereignty.

The psalmist's inclusion of the Joseph story is somewhat surprising since it is not featured prominently in the OT outside of Genesis.[110] The psalmist's retelling of Joseph's captivity and rise to power in Egypt follows the broad contours of the Genesis account (Gen 37; 39–50), but there are some notable points of divergence. The psalmist makes use of poetic techniques in order to tell the story in a way that draws the reader's attention to God's role and sovereignty. While the Genesis narrative highlights God's sovereignty in his "behind-the-scenes" orchestration of events (Gen

---

105. Kraus, *Psalms 60–150*, 311.

106. Kraus, *Psalms 60–150*, 311. Jacobson also notes that "anointed" evokes the idea that Yahweh's anointed are to be protected (e.g., 2 Sam 1:1–16) since kings were known to persecute prophets. Jacobson, "Psalm 105," 790.

107. Gerstenberger, *Psalms*, 232.

108. Gerstenberger, *Psalms*, 232.

109. Kraus, *Psalms 60–150*, 311. Beginning in v. 7 the psalmist introduces the theme of divine sovereignty, which is emphasized both syntactically and by the editorial reworking of narrative details.

110. Brueggemann and Bellinger, *Psalms*, 453. Psalm 105 is the only psalm that features the Joseph narrative. Ruppert, "Neuinterpretation der Josefstradition," 116.

45:5-6; 50:20), the psalmist attributes even the famine in the land to God and implies that this is what actually prompted the need for Joseph's captivity and rise in Egypt (Ps 105:16).[111] The language of Ps 105:16 shows God actively and intentionally "summoning" a famine (ויקרא רעב על־הארץ) and cutting off all supplies of food (כל־מטה־לחם שבר, lit. "he broke every staff of bread") which differs from the Genesis narrative.[112]

In a related piece of analysis, Passaro has noted an inverted chronology involving the patriarch's sojourn in Egypt and Joseph's captivity.[113] In the patriarchal narratives, Joseph is first sold into slavery and then rises to prominence before the famine strikes the land, but the psalmist's narrative inversion places the famine first and implies that Jacob/Israel entered Egypt (Ps 105:23) because of the way the Joseph story developed.[114] In effect, the psalmist depicts God as causing Israel to be fruitful and grow strong in Egypt (Ps 105:24; cf. Exod 1:7), which shows how the promise of descendants begins to be fulfilled.[115] Per Passaro, the psalmist uses narrative inversion to position the Abrahamic covenant as the basis for the fruitfulness that was experienced in Egypt.[116] This narrative effect strengthens the notion that the Abrahamic covenant is a firm foundation for the land promise.

Another noticeable divergence from the Genesis account is the psalmist's description of Joseph's captivity in v. 18 where the psalmist depicts Joseph with painful fetters on his feet and neck in irons.[117] The psalmist is adding details absent in the pentateuchal narrative (cf. Gen 39:20) for there is no mention of Joseph being kept bound in this severe a manner. While it may be possible that the psalmist's language is influenced by other psalms (cf. Pss 107:10; 149:8), it is more likely that the psalmist is exercising poetic license to enhance a well-known story for present relevance and rhetorical

---

111. The Psalmist omits the brothers selling Joseph into slavery, but depicts the famine as God's intentional act. Ruppert, "Zur Neuinterpretation," 121.

112. Goldingay posits v. 16 may imply chastisement (e.g., Jer 29:17). In v. 16b the expression, "staff of bread" (מַטֵּה־לָחֶם) may indicate supplies/support (e.g., Isa 3:1), which is consistent with the idea of divine chastisement. Goldingay, *Psalms 90–150*, 210. See also Grogan, *Psalms*, 177. Others see "staff of bread" as a literal staff with hanging bread rings to keep bread away from pests (see Lev 26:26; Ezek 4:16; 5:16; 14:13). Koehler et al., *HALOT*, 1:573. See also Jacobson, "Psalm 105," 790.

113. Passaro, "Theological Hermeneutics," 47.

114. Passaro, "Theological Hermeneutics," 47.

115. Passaro, "Theological Hermeneutics," 47.

116. Passaro, "Theological Hermeneutics," 47.

117. In v. 18b there is some question as to the meaning of נַפְשׁוֹ ("his soul"). While it could be read figuratively as Joseph's very soul or life bound in slavery, it likely means "neck" when taken in parallel with "feet" in the previous colon. *Psalms 101–150*, 38.

impact.¹¹⁸ The first clue is the use of the term ענה ("affliction"), which is the same root found in Gen 15:13 where Yahweh predicts enslavement and oppression for Abraham's descendants (see Exod 1:11).¹¹⁹ The psalmist uses the Joseph story and embellished enslavement imagery to draw attention to the broader theme of Israel's subjugation under foreign rulers culminating in the Babylonian exile.¹²⁰

There is some discussion regarding the reading of v. 19. The reading that aligns best with the narrative in Genesis would be that Joseph was bound and shackled until Yahweh validated his dream reading. However, some read v. 19 to mean Joseph was actually the one being tested and refined by trials resulting in his validation.¹²¹ The alternative readings do not drastically change the overall narrative, but it seems that the psalmist is not as concerned with Joseph's development as he is with Joseph's ascendance to power. In either case, the psalmist continues the motif of divine sovereignty by emphasizing that it is Yahweh who refines Joseph, whether as a test or as validation.

In v. 20, the psalmist uses the term "king" and the expression "the one who rules nations" (משל עמים) in reference to the Egyptian ruler who freed Joseph. Since the term "pharaoh" was not specifically used of the Egyptian ruler at the time when Joseph entered Egypt, the absence of the term pharaoh is historically accurate. However, it is noteworthy that the title pharaoh would have been a well-known, though anachronistic, title for the Egyptian ruler from the perspective of the psalmist's audience. In this context, it is possible that the customary title of pharaoh is bypassed because the psalmist is shifting into a more general perspective where the focus is on a gentile ruler that has freed Joseph. Goldingay suggests that the narrative of a "heathen king" freeing Joseph, who represents Israel in captivity, would resonate with those who experienced the emancipation of the Persian kings.¹²² In fact, Gerstenberger notes that "ruler of nations" (משל עמים) is a title that

---

118. Gerstenberger posits that the psalmist may be following some psalmic traditions in using such expressions. Gerstenberger, *Psalms*, 232.

119. Goldingay, *Psalms 90–150*, 210.

120. Holm-Nielsen, "Exodus Traditions," 24–25.

121. Jacobson views Joseph as the one being tested by God's word, which refined him as in a blacksmith's forge. He bases his reading upon צרף, which means "refined, tested" (cf. Ps 12:6; 26:2 *Qere*). Jacobson, "Psalm 105," 791. Goldingay also favors this approach as he notes how much Joseph seems to have grown (been refined) between the time he was enslaved and later showed grace to his brothers. Goldingay, *Psalms 90–150*, 210. Ross also posits that Joseph's refinement refers to the process by which Yahweh prepared Joseph for greater purposes as a ruler in Egypt. Ross, *Commentary*, 267.

122. Goldingay, *Psalms 90–150*, 211.

would be appropriate for a Persian great king (e.g., 2 Chr 9:26; 20:6) in a postexilic setting.[123] This would cohere with the sense that the psalmist is modifying the traditional narrative in order to speak in a multi-valent manner of past history, while also speaking of its relevance to a present postexilic community.

In vv. 21–22, the Joseph narrative concludes without major divergence from the Genesis account. Joseph is given administrative authority, which includes authority over the palace and property as well as over officials and advisors. The psalmist employs a clever wordplay in v. 22 to highlight the stunning turn of events. In v. 18, it was Joseph's נפש that was bound in iron, but in v. 22 Joseph has the authority to bind the נפש of the officials of Egypt.[124]

In vv. 23–25 the narrative shifts from Joseph to the arrival of Jacob and his clan in the land of Egypt. In v. 23 the use of "Israel" presents an ambiguity in that it could be Jacob the patriarch or the nation of Israel. Hossfeld proposes a helpful reading of "Israel" in these verses by viewing v. 23 as the conclusion to the Joseph story, which means "Israel" is Jacob, while v. 24 is the start of the nation's story as it sojourns in Egypt (cf. Exod 1:7).[125] The psalmist seems intentionally to play off the ambiguity of the term "Israel" to create a poetic transition from the story of Joseph and his father, Israel, to the story of Israel, the nation.[126]

The psalmist transitions into the Moses portion of the narrative by establishing that it was actually God who caused the Egyptians to "hate" his people (v. 25).[127] Once again, the theme of divine sovereignty comes to the fore as God is portrayed as the one who sent the famine that led to Israel's sojourn in Egypt and then bookends this with God causing the Egyptians to oppress the Israelites, which initiates the events that will culminate in the exodus.[128] God's direct intervention is most dramatically seen in the psalmist's use of the transitive verb "turn" (*Qal* perfect of הפך) to depict how God actively "turned" the hearts of the Egyptians against Israel instead of the

---

123. Gerstenberger, *Commentary*, 233.

124. Harman, *Commentary*, 756.

125. Hossfeld and Zenger, *Psalms 3*, 67.

126. Hossfeld adds that this approach to "Israel" in v. 23 actually clarifies that it is the LORD who is the subject of v. 24. Hossfeld and Zenger, *Psalms 3*, 67.

127. Chisholm notes that it is possible to translate הפך as an intransitive verb, which would read, "their heart turned to hate." Chisholm notes that the marginal reading in the New JPS Tanakh Translation, "Their heart changed," reflects this reading. Though the *Qal* form is normally transitive, 2 Kgs 5:26 seems to be a grammatical parallel where הפך is an intransitive verb (כאשר הפך־איש, "when a man turned ... "). Dr. Robert Chisholm's personal input on this translation issue is greatly appreciated.

128. Grogan, *Psalms*, 177.

passive form of the same verb (*Nifal waw*-consecutive, ויהפך) found in Exod 14:5, which softens the manner in which pharaoh's heart "was turned."[129]

Psalm 105:26–36: Moses and the Exodus

As the narrative core of the psalm reaches its central section, some detect a chiasm involving vv. 25–29, which emphasizes Yahweh's total control over both Egypt's attack and his own counter-attack.[130]

    A. He *turned* their hearts (v. 25)
        B. He *sent* Moses and Aaron (v. 26)
            C. They *performed* his signs and miracles (v. 27)
        B'. He *sent* darkness (v. 28)
    A'. He *turned* their waters into blood (v. 29)

The psalmist's version of the account of the plagues is one of the most dramatic examples of modifying the historical tradition for rhetorical effect. The plagues are ordered differently from the Exodus account with the psalmist emphasizing darkness (the ninth plague) and death (the tenth plague) by using them as an *inclusio* around the other plagues.[131] The order of the plagues in Ps 105 is darkness (ninth), waters turned to blood (first), frogs (second), flies (fourth), gnats (third), hail (seventh), locusts (eighth), and then death (tenth) as the ultimate plague. The reconfiguration of the plagues in Ps 105 has engendered much scholarly discussion. Mascarenhas posits that the placement of the darkness plague at the very beginning represents the defeat of the Egyptian sun god.[132] Goldingay adds that darkness may be a more general portent of disaster/judgment linked to "the day of the LORD" (e.g., Isa 13:10; 45:7; 47:5).[133]

Clifford's novel proposal is that the positioning of darkness as the first plague is done in light of the contrast between Egypt and the wilderness since the first plague of darkness (v. 28) corresponds to the first act in the wilderness of "lighting the night" (v. 36).[134] In fact, Clifford discerns a

---

129. Goldingay, *Psalms 90–150*, 212.

130. Clifford, "Style and Purpose," 425. Harman also discerns this chiastic structure. Harman, *Commentary*, 757. Goldingay notes the way הפך is used in both vv. 25 and 29. Goldingay, *Psalms 90–150*, 214.

131. Harman, *Commentary*, 757.

132. Mascarenhas, "Psalm 105," 87–88. Grogan similarly posits that darkness in the first position represents a judgment on the sun god. Grogan, *Psalms*, 177.

133. Goldingay, *Psalms 90–150*, 213.

134. Clifford, "Style and Purpose," 426.

repeated formula involving the theme of land that is used stylistically to contrast Yahweh's attack on the rich, abundant land of the Egyptians against the abundance Yahweh provides for Israel in the sparse desert of the wilderness (vv. 31, 34, and 40).[135] These three verses open with a verb sequence that highlights the power of God's word via speech that results in some sort of divine activity. In vv. 31 and 34, אמר ויבא describes how Yahweh speaks and summons flies and then locusts, and this attack on Egypt's good land is contrasted with v. 40 where the Israelites ask and Yahweh summons quail in the desert (שאל ויבא).[136]

One of the more compelling studies of the plagues in Ps 105 is that of Lee who notes that the reconfigured plagues parallel the creation account of Gen 1 by moving from heaven, to waters, then to earth.[137] Lee demonstrates how the sequence of the plagues corresponds to the structure of creation order in Gen 1; for example, the swarming of frogs then flies disrupts the created order and then the consumption of all vegetation reverses the creation acts in Gen 1.[138] Furthermore, Lee notes that all the plants and fruit trees were "given" (נתן) to mankind in Gen 1:29, but in Ps 105:32, God "gives over" (נתן) food bearing vegetation to destruction by hail and fire.[139] Finally, both Gen 1 and Ps 105 culminate their respective narratives with man in that the creation of the first man is the final act in Gen 1, while in Ps 105 the killing of the firstborn is the final plague.[140]

According to Averbeck, there may be a more proximal psalmic influence that explains the psalmist's particular plague sequence.[141] Like Lee, Averbeck sees creation as a possible template for the psalmist's version of the plague account; however, Averbeck suggests that the creation material in Ps 104, rather than Genesis, might be the literary background for the plagues in Ps 105. Though Ps 104's creation account is poetically stylized, it

---

135. Clifford, "Style and Purpose," 425–26.

136. In v. 40, Clifford correctly reads שאלו for שאל since haplography likely led to the loss of the ו. This reading is more consistent with the context since it is likely that it is Israel ("they") that is "asking" and Yahweh who causes the quail to arrive in response. Clifford, "Style and Purpose," 425–26.

137. Lee, "Genesis I," 257–63. Hossfeld also takes Lee's view in his analysis of the poetry in the historical narrative of Ps 105. Hossfeld, "Eine poetische Universalgeschichte," 300–303.

138. Lee, "Genesis I," 260.

139. Lee, "Genesis I," 260.

140. Lee, "Genesis I," 260.

141. This writer appreciates Dr. Richard Averbeck's personal insights regarding the possible influence Ps 104's creation account might have had on the plague narrative in Ps 105.

still follows the basic contours of the Gen 1 account.[142] There is a discernible movement from the heavens (Ps 104:2–4), to waters (vv. 6–10), and then to earth, including vegetation (vv. 14–18), animals (vv. 10–13, 19–21, 24–30), and ultimately man (vv. 27–30). The plagues in Ps 105 similarly move from the heavens (darkness, Ps 105:28), to the waters (blood in the Nile, v. 29), and then to the earth, including swarms of frogs, flies and gnats (vv. 30–31), vegetation destroyed by hail and lightning (vv. 32–33), locusts (vv. 34–35), and ultimately the death of the firstborn (v. 36). In terms of sequence and the individual elements, it is tenable that Ps 105's plague order reflects the influence of the creation account in Ps 104. Though they are juxtaposed in Book IV of the Psalter, this is the work of a later editor/compiler; therefore, the main question is whether Ps 104 has literary priority over Ps 105.

Since Ps 105 is relatively late (late exilic to postexilic), it is not unreasonable that Ps 104 has literary priority. Unfortunately, there is no consensus as to Ps 104's date of composition. Various studies suggest dates from as early as the period of the monarchy to as late as the postexilic period.[143] One particular feature of Ps 104 that may provide a clue regarding the date of composition is the notable similarity between Ps 104 (especially vv. 20–30) and the Egyptian Great Hymn to the Aten (sun god) from the period of Amenhotep IV (Akhenaten, fourteenth century BCE).[144]

There are some genuine parallels between the Aten hymn and Ps 104:20–30, but there are also significant contrasts, therefore, some tend to attribute the similarities to the common ANE cultural milieu with regard to cosmology and cosmogony.[145] In an interesting study by Dion, he analyzes not only the similarities between Ps 104 and the Aten hymn but also identifies imagery in Ps 104 that has affinities to Late Bronze Age (LBA) Syrian storm-god materials.[146]

The highlight of Dion's study is the analysis of treaties from the treaty period between Egypt under Ramesses II and Hatti (ca. thirteenth century BCE). Dion identifies several treaty documents that seem to depict the joint

142. Averbeck, "Psalms 103 and 104," 141.

143. For example, Hossfeld's analysis of Ps 104's composition history results in a core that dates from as early as the royal period to portions that can be postexilic. Hossfeld and Zenger, *Psalms 3*, 46–48. In a separate study, Hossfeld posits that Ps 104 may have been redacted at a later date to cohere with Gen 1 and the plague account of Ps 105. Hossfeld, "Eine poetische Universalgeschichte," 305. Kraus sees no clear date of composition, cautiously noting that a preexilic date is possible. Kraus, *Psalms 60–150*, 299.

144. Averbeck, "Psalms 103 and 104," 144.

145. Averbeck, "Psalms 103 and 104," 144–45. See also Allen, *Psalms 101–150*, 30; Ross, *Commentary*, 245–46.

146. Dion, "YHWH as Storm-god," 44–45, 59, 61–62.

supremacy of the Egyptian sun god and the Mesopotamian storm god, and it is this confluence of religious imagery that can be seen in Ps 104.[147] Though Dion stops short of seeing this intriguing confluence as evidence that Ps 104 may have an early date of composition, this unique religious imagery seems a viable influence for Ps 104.

The influence of Egyptian and Hittite cultures would have been felt throughout the ancient Near East long after the thirteenth century BCE, but at the very least, Dion's work identifies a scenario in which Egyptian and Mesopotamian imagery was collocated in the same context. Despite the lack of consensus regarding the date of Ps 104, the affinities between Ps 104 and ANE cosmology/cosmogony from as early as the thirteenth century BCE suggest that a preexilic date of composition is possible.

In addition to a rhetorical or hermeneutical purpose for the psalmist's modification of the plague account, Holm-Nielsen points out the possibility that some of the changes may be poetic in nature. In vv. 29–30, Holm-Nielsen sees the description of the Nile turning to blood followed by the swarm of frogs as a formal parallelism in which the plague of water turning to blood (v. 29) results in the frogs overrunning the land (v. 30).[148] Mascarenhas sees the modified plague accounts as demonstrating the sovereignty of God, which he sees in several realms, such as supremacy over Egyptian gods, darkness, and creation.[149] Brueggemann and Bellinger note that the shift in emphasis in the plague narrative seems to reflect Exod 10:2, which exhorts the Israelites to tell these stories to their descendants that they may remember how Yahweh humbled Egypt by his signs and wonders so that they will know that Yahweh is Lord.[150]

Psalm 105:37–41: The Wilderness Journey to Canaan

Beginning in v. 37 the narrative shifts to the wilderness journey following the exodus. In vv. 37–38, the psalmist highlights the plunder that the Israelites took out of Egypt and the celebration of the Egyptians who dreaded the Israelites and celebrated their departure. In this selective account of the exodus and wilderness journey, the psalmist mentions events from Exod

---

147. Dion notes that this depiction of each superpower's gods seemed to be an important concept in the religious setting of both Egypt and Hatti. Dion, "YHWH as Storm-god," 65–66.

148. Holm-Nielsen, "Exodus Traditions," 26. This could also be synthetic parallelism since the Nile turning to blood could cause the swarm of frogs.

149. Mascarenhas, "Psalm 105," 87–88.

150. Brueggemann and Bellinger, *Psalms*, 453.

3:21–22 (Ps 105:37); 15:16 (v. 38); 13:21 (v. 39); 16:4, 13 (v. 40); and Num 20:11 (v. 41). Harman notes that the selection and narration of these historical elements highlight God's provision for his people's needs.[151]

The conspicuous omissions here are related to the Sinai narrative, including the giving of the law at Sinai, the Sinai covenant, and the rebellion of the people.[152] Jacobson posits that the omission of the Sinai covenant and an emphasis on God's election and faithfulness to the Abrahamic covenant subordinate the Sinai covenant to the Abrahamic covenant.[153] Omission of the Sinai elements may also reflect the psalmist's intentional emphasis upon the promissory aspects of the Abrahamic covenant. Rather than dwell on the giving of the law and the covenant stipulations that would draw attention to the nation's failures in history, the psalmist keeps the reader's focus squarely upon Yahweh's promises and faithfulness. It is helpful to note that the omission of the covenant-making events at Sinai only refers to explicit narration since allusions to the Mosaic covenant frame the narrative portion of Ps 105. In fact, this writer sees the explicit references to the Abrahamic covenant combined with allusions to the Mosaic covenant as a poetic feature that serves the psalmist's rhetorical purposes.

Interestingly, v. 39 does not indicate a pillar of cloud, but cloud cover. Goldingay notes this imagery seems more indicative of the cloud cover at Sinai or perhaps depicts Yahweh as covering his people like a tabernacle (e.g., Exod 37:9; 40:19, 21, 34–38).[154] Kraus also notes that the reworking of the cloud presence emphasizes a "covering, protective power" (e.g., Exod 14:19 and on למסך see Isa 22:8).[155] Ross suggests that the cloud may have been a traveling pillar that also provided some protection from the intense sun out in the wilderness.[156] This subtle shift in the effect of the cloud adds an active dimension of divine care and protection that is consistent with the psalmist's focus on Yahweh's provision and faithfulness.

In vv. 40–41, the omission of details about Israel's sins in the wilderness is conspicuous. The psalmist avoids a pejorative depiction of Israel while focusing positively on Yahweh's provision.[157] Goldingay notes that the word "asked" in v. 40 (שאל) is "understated" and the term for water "flowing" (זוב)

---

151. Harman, Commentary, 177.
152. Jacobson, "Psalm 105," 793. See also Goldingay, Psalms 90–150, 215.
153. Jacobson, "Psalm 105," 793. 793.
154. Goldingay, Psalms 90–150, 215.
155. Kraus, Psalms 60–150, 312.
156. Ross, Commentary, 271. See also Kirkpatrick, Book of Psalms, 623.
157. Ross, Commentary, 271.

in v. 41 is the same verb used to describe the "flowing" of milk and honey in the promised land (Exod 13:5).[158]

This section provides a good look at the various ways in which the psalmist exercised poetic license in portraying a positive account of the wilderness journey. The language and rhetorical flow as well as the selective retelling of the history emphasize Yahweh's gracious provision and care while avoiding Israel's sins and failures. The psalmist invites the reader to maintain hope by fixating on Yahweh's covenantal faithfulness and power while minimizing Israel's unworthiness.

Psalm 105:42–45: The Promise of Land Fulfilled

The close of Ps 105 merits a detailed look since this is where the Abrahamic covenant is referenced (v. 42) in relation to an allusion to the Mosaic covenant (v. 45). In addition to closing the *inclusio* opened in v. 8, the reference to the Abrahamic covenant in v. 42 summarizes the first reference in v. 8. This final strophe is significant in that the closing colon (v. 45) addresses the Mosaic law and connects the Abrahamic and Mosaic covenants. In v. 42, the opening כי construction signals the end of the narrative portion and the start of the closing section of the psalm.[159]

As noted earlier, the phrase כי זכר את־דבר קדשו ("for he remembered his holy word") forms an *inclusio* when paired with זכר לעולם בריתו ("he always remembers his covenant") in v. 8, especially since דבר צוה ("the word he decreed") is the parallel colon in v. 8. The poetic and syntactical placement of v. 42 is significant for the psalmist signals the importance of this verse by setting it apart without any parallelism, either within the verse or with surrounding verses.[160] This statement in v. 42 is significant, for it serves as an authorial interjection that provides the reader with an important interpretational key: all that Yahweh did for Israel was in remembrance of his promise to Abraham and a demonstration of his covenantal faithfulness.[161]

There is some question as to the construction את אברהם in v. 42b. Some, such as Goldingay, render this as "Abraham," with the direct object marker (את, *nota accusativi*), which would then read, "For he remembered his holy word and his servant Abraham."[162] However, it is preferable to read את as a preposition, which would be consistent with its usage in v. 9

---

158. Goldingay, *Psalms 90–150*, 215–16. See also Ross, *Commentary*, 271.
159. Hossfeld and Zenger, *Psalms 3*, 67.
160. Emanuel, *From Bards*, 67.
161. Emanuel, *From Bards*, 67.
162. Goldingay, *Psalms 90–150*, 216. Note also ASV, NRSV.

(אשר כרת את־אברהם), "which he made with Abraham").[163] In light of the context, reading את as a preposition is a preferable rendering of v. 42, "For he remembered his holy word to Abraham his servant." In effect, the main body of historical narration celebrating God's great saving works is framed in terms of God's faithfulness to the covenant with Abraham and specifically his promise of land. The title "servant" (עבד) which was used of Abraham earlier in v. 6 is used once again in v. 42, reinforcing the *inclusio* effect of the Abrahamic covenant references in vv. 8 and 42. As it is used in v. 6, עבד functions as an honorific title that imbues Abraham with a significance akin to that of Moses and David.[164]

The imagery of God's people being delivered from Egypt with "joy" (בששׂון) and "shouts" or "songs" of "gladness" (ברנה) is reminiscent of Exod 15.[165] The exodus-like imagery seems to be a rhetorical touch by the psalmist. McCann sees the return to the land as a "new exodus" (see also Isa 55:12), which reinforces the sense that Ps 105 is intended to address the crisis of exile through the lens of past history.[166] The significant term בחיריו ("his chosen ones") reinforces the concept of divine election in God's covenant with Abraham. In v. 43, the concept of election is transferred from the election of an individual in Abraham and the patriarchs (cf. v. 6) to the election of Abraham's descendants.[167] This concept of Abraham's descendants, the nation of Israel, being "chosen ones" through Abraham's election is especially relevant to the discussion of the continuity between the Abrahamic and Mosaic covenants.

In v. 44, the psalmist transitions from the exodus into the conquest of Canaan. The use of the plural "lands" (ארצות) rather than the singular for the territory of Canaan is likely an echo of Exod 15:11–18 (cf. Ps 105:13) where Canaan is described as being comprised of various nations and their respective territories. However, others posit that this may reflect the geopolitical reality of the Second Temple period when various "peoples of the

---

163. Dahood notes that Ps 105:9 in 11QPsa frag. E reads עם ("with") in place of the MT's את. Dahood, *Psalms III*, 62. Per Allen, the collocation of את and דבר supports a prepositional understanding of את (see Gen 17:3, 22, 23; 21:2). Allen, *Psalms 101–150*, 39n42a.

164. Römer, "Abraham Traditions," 176.

165. These specific terms are not collocated elsewhere in the Psalms, but they are found in Isa 35:10; 51:11; 55:12, which could indicate an exilic or postexilic date for Ps 105. Anderson, *Psalms 73–150*, 734–35. See also Allen, *Psalms 101–150*, 216.

166. McCann, "Book of Psalms," 1105. Emanuel notes that the wording of v. 43 is reminiscent of Isa 51:11, which also refers to the postexilic return as an exodus. Emanuel, *From Bards*, 68.

167. Kraus, *Psalms 60–150*, 312.

land" inhabited the area around Yehud (e.g., Ezra 9:1, 2, 11).[168] Ceresko notes that there is an ironic effect involving the tenfold mention of "land" (ארץ) in Ps 105 and the key to this ironic effect is the relationship between vv. 7b and 44.[169]

Throughout the psalm, possession of the land is in jeopardy and it is seen as belonging to others (primarily the Canaanites and the Egyptians), but in v. 7b the psalmist had stated that Yahweh's judgments are effective in all the earth. In v. 44 the psalmist then demonstrates the truth of this proposition since Yahweh has apportioned to Israel the land that belonged to greater nations. The theme of divine sovereignty that the psalmist had been developing throughout the psalm culminates in the fulfillment of the land promise. Yahweh's granting of the land to Israel in v. 44 is the ultimate proof of Yahweh's sovereignty (v. 7b). The expression עמל לאמים literally means the "toil" or "trouble" of the peoples, but עמל is a metonymic term for the product of labor and toil. The use of the verb ירש ("take possession" or "dispossess") recalls the Deuteronomic depiction of conquest (e.g., Deut 3:18; 19:1-2). Furthermore, the idea of the Israelites possessing the fruit of other peoples' labor (ועמל לאמים יירשו) echoes Deuteronomic descriptions of the conquest in which the Israelites would inhabit houses others built (e.g., Deut 6:10; 19:1-2; Josh 24:13).[170]

In this strophe, the Abrahamic covenant is specifically connected to the exodus and the conquest of Canaan. Interestingly, the psalmist's curated account of Israel's national history, including Jacob's sojourn in Egypt, Israel's slavery, the exodus, and the occupation of Canaan, parallels the covenantal prophecy of Gen 15:13-21. The psalmist makes the compelling case that God's covenantal faithfulness to Abraham and the patriarchs is validated by Israel's history.

Verse 45 not only closes the psalm, it is a key to understanding the relationship between the Abrahamic and Mosaic covenants. The historical survey ends in v. 44 with a reference to the conquest of Canaan, thus v. 45 stands out as a didactic concluding statement. Up to this point, the absence of an explicit reference to the giving of the law and the covenant at Sinai seemed a glaring omission. This makes the sudden appearance of the Mosaic law a curious and significant feature. The first colon begins with a statement of purpose בעבור ("for the sake of")[171] that highlights the explan-

---

168. Goldingay, *Psalms 90-150*, 216.

169. Ceresko, "Poetic Analysis," 44-45.

170. Goldingay, *Psalms 90-150*, 216.

171. The form בַּעֲבוּר is comprised of עבור + the preposition ב. When combined, this expression means "because of" or "for the sake of." Koehler et al., *HALOT*, 1:778. Hence, "So that . . ."

atory/expository nature of v. 45. This is followed by two parallel statements regarding obedience to the Mosaic law. The first statement ישמרו חקיו ("they might keep his decrees/statutes") uses two terms that are typical of pentateuchal language on adherence to the Mosaic law (e.g. Exod 15:26; Deut 4:40; 7:11; 11:32). The syntax of v. 45 signals a didactic statement of purpose and explanation. In effect, the psalmist explains why Yahweh has established his covenant with the patriarchs and to what end he has guided Abraham's descendants through an eventful history into the land of promise.

The term חק also calls back to v. 10 creating a semantic link that reinforces the connection between the Abrahamic and Mosaic covenants. The second parallel statement, ותורתיו ינצרו ("and obey his laws") is synonymous with the first, but explicitly uses the key Mosaic term תורה ("law"). The two verbs שמר and נצר mean "to keep" with regard to the Mosaic law (e.g., Deut 33:9; Prov 5:2).[172] The term חק ("statute, decree, ordinance") is one of three law terms (חקים, מצוה, משפטים) that are used throughout Deuteronomy to refer to the statutes, commandments, decrees, and ordinances of the Mosaic law. These three terms are used most prominently in the context of Moses's description of the things that Yahweh had instructed (i.e., covenant stipulations) and commanded him to teach Israel on the verge of entering Canaan.[173] In fact, the pairing of חק and תורה often refers to the Mosaic law (e.g., Deut 4:8; 17:19; 30:10) in the context of covenant ratification, violation, or renewal.[174] Thus, the use of חק and תורה metonymically highlights the giving of the law at Sinai and ratification of the Mosaic covenant.

Though Ps 105 began with a hymnic introduction it now closes with a didactic conclusion.[175] The psalmist concludes that obedience to the Mosaic law is the purpose for Yahweh's fulfillment of the Abrahamic promise of land. Thus, the Mosaic covenant cannot be separated from the Abrahamic covenant since the law given at Sinai is inextricably tied to the covenant made at Sinai. Gerstenberger observes that life in the promised land under the rule of the Mosaic law would be the highest blessing for the psalmist in

---

172. Emanuel, *From Bards*, 69.

173. Per Merrill, when these three terms occur together (e.g., Deut 5:31; 6:1; and 7:11) there is a connection to the Mosaic law and the Mosaic covenant. Merrill refers to these as "command-response" formulas since Moses responds to the LORD's command to teach the terms and stipulations of the covenant to the people prior to the conquest. Merrill, *Deuteronomy*, 161. See also Craigie, *Book of Deuteronomy*, 167–68.

174. Emanuel, *From Bards*, 69n98. For examples where חק and תורה are used of the law in the context of making, keeping, or violating the Mosaic covenant, see Deut 17:19; 2 Kgs 17:37; Amos 2:4; Mal 3:22 [MT]; Neh 9:13; 10:30 [MT]; 2 Chr 33:8.

175. Mascarenhas, "Psalm 105," 85. See also McCann, "Book of Psalms," 1103.

a postexilic context.¹⁷⁶ In fact, closely tying prosperity in the land to keeping the laws of the Mosaic covenant is an important thesis in the book of Deuteronomy. McKelvey observes:

> [Verse 45] reflects a classically Deuteronomic understanding of the Mosaic/Sinaitic covenant and the responsibility of Israel to obey God's commandments. The element of necessary obedience in relation to the promise of the land is an important theme in Deuteronomy, linking this psalm and collections of psalms, once again, with Moses.¹⁷⁷

Clearly, a key rhetorical emphasis is that blessing in the land is tied to covenant obedience. Though Sinai is not explicitly mentioned, the Mosaic law and covenant are not forgotten for the specific link between continued life in the promised land and obedience to the law is part of the central theme of Deuteronomy.¹⁷⁸ As the postexilic community settles anew in the land of promise, the psalmist evokes this Deuteronomic principle to make this crucial point to his audience.¹⁷⁹ Just as the generation of the conquest was required to obey the Mosaic law and show covenant loyalty in order to prosper in the land, the postexilic community must also be committed to honoring the law as a sign of loyalty to the Mosaic covenant relationship that is still effective in this postexilic generation.

In effect, this pivotal verse depicts Israel's obedience to the law in accordance with the Mosaic covenant as the purpose of the special relationship God has established with "chosen" Israel via his covenant with Abraham. This dynamic involving the gift of land and ongoing blessing in the land takes on increased relevance for the postexilic community as they wrestle with the tension between being back in the land in accordance with the patriarchal promise and the absence of anticipated Mosaic covenant blessings.

---

176. Gerstenberger, *Psalms*, 233–34.
177. McKelvey, *Moses, David*, 233–34.
178. McKelvey, *Moses, David*, 303.
179. Hossfeld, "Eine poetische Universalgeschichte," 303.

5

A Rhetorical Reading of Psalm 105
Text and Subtext

ACCORDING TO CHOI, "WORKS of history are necessarily ideological and subjective, and in terms of literary form, works of history are nearly identical to works of fiction."[1] In theoretical studies of history writing, it is understood that the significance of an event is only established when that event is placed into a particular context and the selection and connection of these events results in a narrative that is subjective and interpretive.[2] In this sense, Choi contends that even the Pentateuch is the "product of an ideologically driven process of selection and narrativization," which means that other historical texts in the OT must also be, in some sense, a selective, subjective interpretation of historical events.[3] Aaron notes that historical retrospectives in the OT serve a specific purpose and are characterized by polemical or ideological priorities that reflect the expectations of the audience as well as the author's socio-cultural and historical context.[4] It is this characteristic of historical writing that is actually a feature, not a bug, so to speak. In Ps 105, the psalmist is subjectively and ideologically placing the events of Israel's history into a particular narratival context and the rhetori-

---

1. Choi, *Traditions*, 107.

2. Choi, *Traditions*, 109–10. Choi's understanding of the philosophy of history-writing draws on Danto's work. Danto stresses that historians produce more than records of past events, they interpret the events of the past in a way that establishes patterns and significance. Danto, *Analytical Philosophy*, 115, 117–18, 139–42.

3. Choi, *Traditions*, 117.

4. Aaron, *Etched in Stone*, 67.

cal features of the narrative reveal insights into the psalmist's interpretation of Israel's history and his understanding of the covenants.

Brueggemann, delving into the historical psalms, posits that the recitation of history in the Psalter is a "stylized retelling of the past, and therefore an intentional shaping of the present and a passionate yearning for a specific future."[5] Brueggemann affirms that part of the reason for historical psalms is to remember the original events by reenacting the "abiding astonishment" of the original experience, but the ongoing recitation of history is meant to provide patterns for understanding the present that are ultimately "affirmative and polemical."[6] It is in this sense that Ps 105 is a welcome opportunity to gain insight into the covenant theology of a later Israelite community via the historical interpretation and rhetorical imagination of the psalmist.

In analyzing the rhetorical features of Ps 105, it is this writer's aim to discern what the psalmist wanted to convey to his audience about the covenants and how that was to affect their thinking. Choi's comparison of the historical narrative in Ps 105 with the corresponding narratives in the Pentateuch leads him to conclude that the psalmist "had access to a wide range of historical traditions, some of which he included in his text and others which he excluded in accordance with his compositional intent."[7] While this study ultimately diverges from Choi's approach to tradition history, a close reading of Ps 105 supports his general characterization of the psalm as a selective narration of Israel's history where deviations from pentateuchal accounts indicate interpretive and rhetorical intent.

CLASSICAL RHETORIC AND POETICS

An interesting starting point for an analysis of the psalmist's rhetoric is found in Olbricht's study of Ps 105. Olbricht begins his study of Pss 105 and 106 with a helpful overview of classical rhetoricians and the various principles and concepts they address in relation to the genre of narrative.[8] Classical rhetoricians generally focus on speech in the courtroom, political assembly, or the marketplace (including the palace or temple), thus the

---

5. Brueggemann, *Abiding Astonishment*, 29.
6. Brueggemann, *Abiding Astonishment*, 34.
7. Choi, *Traditions*, 124.
8. Olbricht surveys works by Aristotle, Cicero, and Quintilian regarding the use of narrative in different types of rhetoric. The principles of classical rhetoricians provide a helpful means of understanding the rhetorical activity taking place in Pss 105 and 106. Olbricht, "Rhetoric," 156–59. It is worth noting that Olbricht's application of classical rhetorical concepts assumes a degree of universality in these concepts when applied to other cultures in other times.

types of speech they engage in are forensic, deliberative, and epideictic, respectively.[9] Olbricht notes that the psalms do not fit into the traditional categories favored by rhetoricians, but he does find some useful insights from the way classical rhetoricians evaluate the use of narrative.

In general, rhetoricians use narrative to do more than convey facts. In eulogistic and forensic discourse, narrative can be used to "enhance the character of the speaker and to vilify his detractors," which prompts Olbricht to anticipate such rhetorical activity in the praise narrative of Pss 105 and 106 as God is praised and Israel denounced for her failure to respond appropriately.[10] Classical rhetoricians espoused the use of narrative reworked in a "lively style" to enhance an argument in forensic speech.[11] In other words, the use of narrative is not bound by a slavish adherence to facts but can present an account that is designed to evoke certain emotions and emphasize certain points so as to persuade the listener.[12] In this way, Olbricht examines the manner in which the psalmists composed Pss 105 and 106, especially in light of how these psalms rework and modify the historical traditions found in the Pentateuch. Olbricht's form-critical and rhetorical analysis of the two psalms focuses on four basic aspects of the text: structure, setting, genre, and intent.[13]

In terms of structure, Ps 105 features a series of chronological narratives that follow the formulaic pattern of the credo genre.[14] In terms of social setting, Ps 105 was likely composed to be used in some sort of communal worship setting, but a specific reconstruction of the original *Sitz im Leben* is elusive due to a dearth of concrete indicators.[15] Part of the rhetorical shaping of the psalm includes selecting what historical narratives would be

---

9. Olbricht, "Rhetoric," 158.

10. Olbricht discusses Aristotle's principles on the use of narrative in epideictic speech and applies these concepts to the rhetorical activity in Pss 105 and 106. Olbricht, "Rhetoric," 157.

11. Olbricht outlines principles found in *Rhetorica ad herennium*, which was originally attributed to Cicero but is now understood to be the work of an anonymous author. Olbricht also cites principles from Quintilian's *Institutio Oratoria*, which provides guidelines on the use of narrative in forensic speech. Olbricht, "Rhetoric," 157–58.

12. Olbricht, "Rhetoric," 157–58.

13. Olbricht notes that the emergence of rhetorical criticism in biblical studies is related to scholarly questions regarding the merits of form criticism. He notes Muilenburg's well-known call to move toward rhetorical criticism while still seeing the value of form criticism. Olbricht, "Rhetoric," 159.

14. Olbricht, "Rhetoric," 161.

15. Olbricht, "Rhetoric," 161–62. Martilla cautions against detailed conclusions regarding cultic setting and usage due to the lack of concrete data and evidence. Marttila, *Collective Reinterpretation*, 236.

featured. Olbricht helpfully observes: "the mighty actions of God in terms of specifics had previously been identified in template fashion. Each author who iterated these actions, however, was free to select among the proscribed entities in this catalog."[16] In looking at the particular historical survey in Ps 105, Olbricht notes that the rhetorical structure points to the gifting of land to Abraham, which was then re-promised to Isaac and Jacob, as the key action in Ps 105.[17] Thus, Olbricht posits that Ps 105 fits the classical genre of forensic rhetoric where the main proposition of the psalm is Yahweh's faithfulness to the covenant made with Abraham (vv. 7–11).[18] Therefore, the rhetorical makeup of the main body argues for Yahweh's covenantal faithfulness and this is positively affirmed a final time in the concluding section (v. 42).[19] The concept of Yahweh's covenantal faithfulness will become germane to understanding the interplay between the Abrahamic and Mosaic covenants in this psalm. While the Abrahamic covenant is used to stress Yahweh's unimpeachable covenantal faithfulness, the allusions to the Mosaic covenant make the crucial point that this faithfulness will only be experienced by those who show covenantal love and obedience to Yahweh.

In terms of rhetorical style, Olbricht also observes that the psalmist takes poetic liberties with the historical narrative traditions found in the Pentateuch. This enhancement of the traditional material fits the pattern of enhancing the narrative for rhetorical effect.[20] For example, the detail that Joseph was in fetters and chains is not found in the original Genesis account, but serves to make the narrative "lively and magnificent," which Olbricht sees as akin to a classical rhetorical device.[21] On the whole, the psalmist's rhetorical approach is effective from a classical rhetorician's point of view. Psalm 105 validates and praises Yahweh's covenant faithfulness causing the reader to reflect on past history and conclude that Yahweh can be trusted in the present.[22]

In Hildebrandt's reflection on the relationship between historical narrative and poetry, he views the psalmist as a poet who reshaped historical events to create Ps 105.[23] Hildebrandt identifies a representative sampling

16. Olbricht, "Rhetoric," 162. Olbricht's observation is consistent with the general understanding of historiography as a selective, curated narrative with a particular viewpoint and even ideological aims. Choi, *Traditions*, 117.

17. Olbricht, "Rhetoric," 162.

18. Olbricht, "Rhetoric," 163.

19. Olbricht, "Rhetoric," 163.

20. Olbricht, "Rhetoric," 164.

21. Olbricht, "Rhetoric," 164.

22. Olbricht, "Rhetoric," 165–66.

23. Hildebrandt, "Song of Our Father," 51–52.

of eight poetic devices that illustrate how the psalmist works as a bricoleur "shaping and fitting fragments of colored glass into a beautiful stained glass window."[24] The eight poetic devices Hildebrandt identifies are:

1. *Selection*. This is the deliberate inclusion or exclusion of certain historical events and narratives in his narrative.

2. *Compression*. The joining/fusing of different narratives into a single narrative.

3. *Reordering*. The changing of sequences of events for poetic or rhetorical purposes.

4. *Attribution*. The attribution of agency and/or motive where there was none in the earlier tradition.

5. *Image enhancement*. The poetic enhancement of details or elements in a known narrative.

6. *Interpretive addition*. The interjection of the poet's interpretation of the past into the present work.

7. *Concatenation of disparate events*. The juxtaposition/relating of events and elements in a way that implies new meaning.

8. *Perspective shift*. This device changes the perspective of a certain narrative to provide a different understanding of the event.[25]

In analyzing the psalmist's use of these poetic devices, Hildebrandt concludes that these "poetic methods create a focus in this psalm on the absolutely sovereign movements of God and give historical support to the major theme of Book IV: the LORD reigns."[26]

Ceresko's study of Ps 105 is helpful in its analysis of poetic structure, chiasm, lexical repetition, distant parallelism, and even irony in the Joseph narrative.[27] The presence of a chiasm in Ps 105:25–29 has been suggested by other commentators and the general consensus is that the chiasm highlights Yahweh's direct control over the plagues loosed upon Egypt.[28] One of Ceresko's novel findings is discerning two different structures that function simultaneously within the psalm. He discerns both a chronological

---

24. Hildebrandt, "Song of Our Father," 52–53.
25. Hildebrandt, "Song of Our Father," 52–53.
26. Hildebrandt, "Song of Our Father," 53.
27. Ceresko, "Poetic Analysis," 20–46.
28. Clifford, "Style and Purpose," 425.

structure, which is based on the sequential narration of events, and a poetic structure based on the use of initial verbs.[29]

Ceresko also sees a bifurcation in the psalm based on movement from Canaan into Egypt in the first half and from Egypt into Canaan in the second half with the pivot being v. 23.[30] Ceresko sees this macrostructure as a sign of poetic design and literary unity.[31] In terms of rhetorical significance, Ceresko sees the complementary structures and the poetic use of repetition and parallelism as creating a net rhetorical effect that affirms "both the example (Abraham, vv. 6, 42; Joseph, v. 17; Moses, v. 26) and the necessity (v. 45) of grateful obedience; such obedience is possible in any land in which God's servants may find themselves."[32]

With regard to the central concept of land, Clifford sees a poetic contrast between the land of Egypt and the wilderness in Ps 105:31–40. Clifford identifies a threefold repetition of an expression that describes the power of God's word, both in summoning plagues in Egypt (vv. 31, 34) and in summoning life-giving food in the wilderness (v. 40).[33] Ceresko also sees poetic irony at work in relation to the prominence of land in the psalm. The land is mentioned in multiple places and in different ways (e.g., references to the land of Canaan, land of Ham, "their land," "land of the nations," and land belonging to Egypt). Ceresko notes that in v. 7 there is a crucial statement affirming that the "whole earth," which includes all lands, belongs to Yahweh giving him the authority to apportion land to Israel as he sees fit.[34] Ceresko's poetic analysis surfaces a poetic-rhetorical emphasis on the promise of land and its fulfillment as well as the importance of obedience to the Mosaic law as a crucial aspect of possessing the land.

In summing up these various studies of Ps 105 in terms of both classical rhetoric and poetics, certain clear emphases emerge. Olbricht's analysis through the lens of classical rhetoric suggests that the main proposition of Ps 105 is the affirmation of Yahweh's faithfulness to the Abrahamic promises.[35] In studying the poetic shaping of the historical narrative, Hildebrandt concludes that the emphasis of the psalm is on Yahweh's absolute sovereignty.[36]

---

29. Ceresko, "Poetic Analysis," 43–44.

30. Ceresko, "Poetic Analysis," 26.

31. Ceresko notes, not only are there an equal 22 verses before and after v. 23, there are even 347 syllables before and 343 syllables after in the MT vocalization. Ceresko, "Poetic Analysis," 26.

32. Ceresko, "Poetic Analysis," 44.

33. Clifford, "Style and Purpose," 425–26.

34. Ceresko, "Poetic Analysis," 44–45.

35. Olbricht, "Rhetoric," 163.

36. Hildebrandt, "Song of Our Father," 174.

Clifford's analysis of the poetic style in Ps 105 leads to the conclusion that it is a hymn to Yahweh based on the certainty of his promises, which are effective in all places and all times.[37] Ceresko similarly concludes that a major emphasis is Yahweh's sovereignty over all the earth, which gives him the right to grant Israel land as he promised.[38] Ceresko also notes that the various levels of poetic structure function to emphasize the essential nature of obedience to the law, as exemplified by Abraham, Joseph, and Moses, in whatever land Yahweh grants his servants.[39] The psalmist's poetic and rhetorical design consistently points to three major emphases: (1) divine sovereignty; (2) Yahweh's faithfulness to the land promise of the Abrahamic covenant; and (3) the necessity of obedience to the Mosaic law when inhabiting the land.

THE PSALMIST'S VOICE: THE RHETORICAL STRUCTURE AND ARGUMENT

A rhetorically-informed reading discerns the development of themes and arguments via literary devices and rhetorical design. Unlike didactic or epistolary literature, which tends to exhibit a linear, explicit rhetorical structure, poetry conveys the writer's message and argument through the artful use of literary and poetic devices. Though the rhetorical features of Ps 105 are based in poetry and narrative, there is a rhetorical framework that reflects the psalmist's purpose, arguments, and conclusion.

Psalm 105 is not structured as a linear discourse but features a clever rhetorical design. The following is a skeletal overview of the psalm's rhetorical design. The psalm opens with a standard hymnic call to worship (vv. 1–6) and then the rhetorical structure becomes sophisticated. There is an introductory section (vv. 7–11) where the psalmist states the *argument* or thesis, identifies a *problem*, and introduces a key *subtext* that will resolve the issue. The body of the psalm (vv. 12–41) features the psalmist's curated historical narrative, which validates the argument. Then the psalm reaches a conclusion where the subtext clarifies the problem and concludes with a didactic solution (vv. 42–45).

Within this rhetorical framework, the *argument* consists of the central propositions that are developed and validated in the psalm. In Ps 105 the argument consists of two propositions: (1) Yahweh's covenantal faithfulness is unfailing and (2) Yahweh's absolute sovereignty guarantees the fulfillment

37. Clifford, "Style and Purpose," 427.
38. Ceresko, "Poetic Analysis," 44–45.
39. Ceresko, "Poetic Analysis," 44.

of his covenant promises. In the body of the psalm the historical narrative is shaped to validate this argument. From a historical perspective, the dramatic fulfillment of the patriarchal land promise validates the propositions that comprise the psalm's argument.

The *problem* is the issue that stands in tension with the main argument. In this case, the postexilic remnant has returned to the land but has not experienced the anticipated blessing promised in the Mosaic covenant. Thus, the covenantal faithfulness of Yahweh comes into question. In literary terms, the *subtext* is a theme or argument that is not explicitly stated, but implicitly understood.[40] In this context, the psalmist uses three allusions involving the Mosaic covenant in order to address the problem. These three allusions create a subtext that explains how the violation of the Mosaic covenant has led to the forfeiture of Yahweh's covenant faithfulness (*ḥesed*) and blessings in the Mosaic covenant relationship.

The *conclusion* assumes the validation of the argument and entails the resolution of the problem, culminating in a didactic prescription. In Ps 105 the conclusion affirms that Yahweh is faithful in keeping covenant and capable of fulfilling his promises. Thus, the problem is the nation's failure to keep the Mosaic covenant, and the solution is covenant renewal resulting in covenant faithfulness and obedience to the law.

The Call to Worship (Ps 105:1–6)

Rhetorically speaking, this opening section emphasizes God's praiseworthy deeds and prepares the audience to delve into the meaning of his great divine acts. Next, the psalmist identifies the intended audience, the postexilic community in the land, as Abraham's and Jacob's descendants. This is where the psalmist introduces two theologically significant expressions in order to prepare his argument. In v. 6a the psalmist refers to Abraham as God's

---

40. According to Elam, the structuralist understanding of a subtext is a "destabilizing element" that "works against and undermines a text's potential reading." Per Elam, a subtext is "not what is 'meant' or 'expressed,' but rather that which tends to 'dissimulate or forbid' and which it nonetheless makes evident at certain points of stress or conflict. The subtext functions as a text's unconscious—what it does not know it knows—and indicates a reading against the grain." Elam, "Textuality," 1277. For an example from a biblical study, see Ferda, "Reason to Weep," 30–60. For the purposes of this study, the *subtext* is an implicit line of thought that becomes evident as a text unfolds. The subtext can but does not necessarily undermine the main text. The subtext fills gaps and functions dialectically in relation to a main text. Thus, the subtext is an implicit feature of a text featuring narrative elements, intertexts, and other literary devices that conveys an underlying argument or line of thought. See Cohen, "Exploring Subtext Processing," 274–76.

"servant," which is a term that is traditionally associated with Moses and David. In v. 6b, the descendants of Jacob are called "God's chosen ones," which is also an expression pregnant with meaning.

Clifford posits that in this hymnic introduction the identity of the readership is actually held off until the end of the section for dramatic emphasis.[41] This is a rhetorical clue regarding the significance of the two terms "servant" and "chosen." Clifford notes that these two terms are repeated in each major section so that whenever there is danger in the narrative, "there are servants, offspring of Abraham and Jacob, in whom the promise appears."[42] The final occurrence of these two terms is in the concluding section (vv. 42–43) where the reference to Abraham as Yahweh's "servant" and to the people as his "chosen ones" mirrors the usage of these terms in v. 6.[43] Clifford posits that the occurrence of these two terms in the conclusion (vv. 42–43) reinforces what was stated in v. 6, that "the promise of the land applies to all Israel."[44] The psalmist's use of these terms draws the reader's attention to the thesis that Yahweh will faithfully fulfill his promise of land to future generations, including the postexilic generation.

Rhetorical Introduction (Ps 105:7–11)

The psalmist opens in v. 7a with the covenant expression, "He is Yahweh our God." This self-declaration formula has its roots in the seminal exchange between Yahweh and Moses in Exod 6:2–8 and is used prominently in the title-line of the Decalogue (Exod 20:2/Deut 5:6). This self-declaration formula is an allusive textual marker that signals the first of three Mosaic covenant allusions that make up the psalm's subtext. This allusion evokes the Mosaic covenant relationship established at Sinai.[45] Within the psalm, this self-declaration formula links the God who does wonders (vv. 1–6) with the God who keeps covenant (vv. 7–11). There is also an inter-covenantal continuity involving the name Yahweh since this name is also known in the

---

41. Clifford, "Style and Purpose," 422.

42. Note that Joseph is sold as a "servant" in v. 17, the people oppressed in Egypt are called "servants" in v. 25, Moses and Aaron are called Yahweh's "chosen" in v. 26, and in vv. 42–43, Abraham is Yahweh's "servant," and the people are his "chosen ones." Clifford, "Style and Purpose," 423.

43. Clifford, "Style and Purpose," 423.

44. Clifford, "Style and Purpose," 423.

45. Kidner sees an echo of Exod 20:2 where Yahweh opens the Decalogue by identifying himself as "the LORD your God." Kidner, *Psalms 73–150*, 407. McKelvey sees an echo of the Shema from Deut 6:4. McKelvey, *Moses, David*, 232.

context of the patriarchal narratives and the Abrahamic covenant (see Gen 15:7; 22:14).[46]

The self-declaration formula is based on the self-revelation of the divine name in conjunction with a relational understanding of God—"He is Yahweh our God" (הוא יהוה אלהינו). In essence, Yahweh, the God of the patriarchs, of Moses, and of his covenant nation, Israel, is also the God of the postexilic community (Exod 6:3–7). It is noteworthy that the complex of the terms "Canaan" in v. 11 and the three patriarchs in vv. 9–10 corresponds with Exod 6:3–4 where Yahweh introduces himself as the God of the patriarchs who promised the land of Canaan to them.[47] Rhetorically, the psalmist uses the self-declaration formula to construct an inter-covenantal bridge between Yahweh the covenant God of the patriarchs (Abrahamic covenant) and Yahweh the covenant lord of Israel (Mosaic covenant). The self-declaration formula identifies God by his covenant name and reflects the fact that Yahweh's covenantal faithfulness (חסד) is a defining trait.

The fact that Yahweh's covenantal faithfulness is steadfast is the first proposition of the psalm's argument. In addition, the allusion to the self-declaration formula introduces the subtext into the rhetorical framework of the psalm. The statement "He is Yahweh our God" identifies Yahweh with the Mosaic covenant. This Mosaic covenant allusion signals a subtext since it is never mentioned explicitly in the plain text of Ps 105:7–11. The psalmist introduces the Mosaic covenant into the discussion since the absence of covenant blessing in the postexilic setting is best explained in terms of the Mosaic covenant.

The second important rhetorical feature of v. 7 is the second colon where it is stated that Yahweh's "judgments are in all the earth." This statement reveals the second proposition of the psalm's argument, which is that Yahweh is an all-powerful God.[48] This theme of divine sovereignty is

---

46. Garr's in-depth study of Exod 6:3 demonstrates that the self-declaration of the divine name does not mean that this name was unknown prior to Yahweh's dialogue with Moses. The core issue is not knowledge of a name but experiencing God relationally in a covenantal context that the patriarchs did not know. Garr, "Grammar and Interpretation," 402–8. Janzen's insights regarding Exod 6:3–7 shed some light on the possible significance of the self-declaration formula in Ps 105:7. Janzen sees Exod 6:3 as an "epoch-making shift from one paradigm of divine-human relations to another." Per Janzen, the two paradigms are: The Abrahamic paradigm, which is centered around familial relationships characterized by *ḥesed*, and the Mosaic paradigm, which is based on covenant and law under the administration of Yahweh, the divine King of Israel. Janzen, *At the Scent of Water*, 24–33.

47. Gosse, "Abraham dans les Ps 105," 86.

48. This may also be a reference to Gen 18:25 where Yahweh is called the "judge of all the earth" (השפט כל־הארץ). Emanuel, *From Bards*, 34–35.

developed within the psalm as Yahweh is shown controlling key historical events. His sovereignty and power are demonstrated in multiple realms, such as creation, among the nations, and in historical events. The use of the term, "judgments" (משפטים), speaks to the universal scope of Yahweh's authority as he enacts his will throughout the earth. This term also has rhetorical value as a bridge to the Mosaic law reference in v. 45. In addition, the use of משפטים coheres with the covenantal emphasis of vv. 7–11 where Yahweh remembers his eternal covenant (זכר לעולם בריתו), which is a "word commanded to a thousand generations" (דבר צוה לאלף דור) and a promise "sworn" to Isaac and "established as a decree" to Jacob.[49] In this constellation of covenantal and promissory terms, the term "judgments" in v. 7 establishes the authoritative and trustworthy nature of Yahweh's covenantal word. Since Yahweh is sovereign over all things he is certainly able to fulfill his covenant promises.

In v. 8b the expression "to a thousand generations" (לאלף דור) describes the enduring nature of the sworn covenant promise. This same expression allusively evokes Deut 7:9/Exod 20:6, which feature an axiomatic description of Yahweh's covenant loyalty (חסד) to the Mosaic covenant. Whereas the self-declaration formula in v. 7 allusively identifies Yahweh as Israel's covenant partner in the Mosaic covenant, this allusion to Deut 7:9/Exod 20:6 points out a crucial aspect of the Mosaic covenant relationship. Though Yahweh's covenant loyalty is shown to a "thousand generations," it is only for those who love him and keep the law. This allusion explains why the postexilic remnant is unable to experience the expected blessing after returning from exile (cf. Deut 30:1–10; Lev 26:40–45).

In terms of the rhetorical framework, v. 7 introduces the argument, which is that Yahweh is a faithful, covenant-keeping God (v. 7a) and that his sovereignty ensures the fulfillment of his covenant promises (v. 7b). The subtext is also introduced by the self-declaration formula allusion in v. 7a, which identifies Yahweh as Israel's covenant God in accordance with the Mosaic covenant. The allusion in v. 8b explains why Israel no longer experiences Yahweh's Mosaic covenant loyalty and blessing. Per Deut 7:9–10 and Exod 20:6, only those who love Yahweh and keep his commandments will experience covenantal blessing. This allusion reveals the problem that the psalmist seeks to resolve, which is that Israel's failure to keep the Mosaic covenant has resulted in the forfeiture of covenant blessing. The psalmist has now stated the argument (v. 7), introduced the Mosaic covenant subtext (vv. 7a, 8b), and revealed the problem (v. 8b).

---

49. The use of משפט/משפטים, חק/חקים/חקות, and verbs, such as נצר, שמר, צוה, and כרת, are terms related to the Mosaic covenant and the law.

The Historical Narrative (vv. 12–44)

Brueggemann and Bellinger note that the promise of land in v. 11 and the fulfillment in v. 44 serve as the "envelope for the entire memory of Israel" and that the divine grant of land is the "antidote to the crisis of exile."[50] Though they have returned from exile there are still external threats and internal unrest as they attempt to rebuild Jerusalem's walls and the temple (see Ezra–Nehemiah). In vv. 7–11, the psalmist has established that the covenant Yahweh made with Abraham is "eternal" and effective for a "thousand generations." The historical narrative section is not a simple rehearsal of Israel's history, but a selective narration that validates Yahweh's covenantal faithfulness and ability to fulfill his promises. The psalmist also uses the historical narrative to convince the postexilic reader that they are part of the Israel of history and can, therefore, trust in the God of Israel's history.

The poetic structure of the historical survey serves the psalmist's rhetorical purposes.[51] The historical narration in the first half of the psalm describes Yahweh's agency in bringing the wandering patriarchal sojourners out of Canaan and into Egypt via famine and Joseph's enslavement. In poetic parallel, the second half of the historical section demonstrates Yahweh's power and protection in bringing his people out of Egypt, through the wilderness, and into the land. Wherever the psalmist diverges from the pentateuchal tradition, whether by poetic enhancement, omission, or inclusion of non-pentateuchal details, these rhetorical features draw attention to Yahweh's sovereignty and covenantal faithfulness.

Overall, the psalmist uses poetic and rhetorical devices to craft a historical narrative that validates his two-pronged argument regarding Yahweh's faithfulness to the Abrahamic covenant and his sovereignty in fulfilling the promise of land. The shift in perspective keeps the reader's attention trained on Yahweh's sovereign activity and covenant faithfulness while minimizing the role of human intermediaries and the devastating effects of Israel's sinful disobedience. From the patriarchs to Moses, it is consistently Yahweh who providentially and sovereignly directs the movement of his people from Canaan into Egypt and back to the land. The conclusion of the historical movement at the conquest of the land demonstrates that Yahweh has been faithful to his promise by giving Israel the land and all of its abundance.

---

50. Brueggemann and Bellinger, *Psalms*, 454.

51. Ceresko discerns a macrostructure as well as a microstructure, which function in a complementary manner. Ceresko, "Poetic Analysis," 21–44.

The Conclusion (v. 45)

The rhetorical conclusion to the psalm is v. 45, but there is some overlap in terms of the structure and function of the final four verses. The *inclusio* formed by vv. 8 and 42 as well as the כי construction in v. 42 signal that the psalmist is transitioning to the conclusion. However, there is still some narrative material regarding the conquest and possession of the land in vv. 42–44. The closing of the *inclusio* affirms that Yahweh has proven faithful to the covenant promise of land that he made with Abraham and confirmed with the patriarchs (cf. v. 8). This is reinforced by the secondary *inclusio* formed by v. 6 and vv. 42–43 where the psalmist has introduced and echoed the terms "servant" and "chosen" as a way of demonstrating that the land promise has been fulfilled for all Israel.[52] This poetic use of recurring terms and *inclusios* draws the reader's attention to Yahweh's proven covenant faithfulness.

Having demonstrated Yahweh's covenant faithfulness and the sovereign authority necessary to fulfill his promises, the psalmist closes with a didactic purpose statement in v. 45. The fulfillment of the land promise has resulted in possession of the land and the psalmist concludes that the ultimate purpose is for Israel to keep the covenant's statutes and laws (ישמרו חקיו ותורתיו ינצרו). The terms, חקות/חקים ("statutes") and תורות ("laws"), refer to the Mosaic law.[53] The inter-covenantal dynamic in Ps 105 is informative for it is Yahweh's faithfulness to the patriarchal promises that leads Abraham's descendants into their own land (vv. 8–44). With all the elements of nationhood in place, the Mosaic covenant constitutes the people into a nation and provides the nation with a law code that defines its national character (v. 45) and status in the land.

In v. 45 the collocation of Mosaic law terms and the language of covenant obedience signals the final allusion to the Mosaic covenant. This allusion concludes the subtext that was introduced in vv. 7a and 8b. The subtext affirms that Israel's relationship to Yahweh is defined by the Mosaic covenant, but Yahweh's covenantal loyalty is only for those who love him and keep his commandments. The fact that Israel's failure to keep the Mosaic covenant can result in forfeiture of covenantal blessing clarifies the problem facing the postexilic community. Verse 45 closes the subtext by providing a prescriptive solution to the problem. Just as the forefathers experienced

---

52. Clifford, "Style and Purpose," 423.

53. See Exod 15:26; Duet 4:40; 7:11; 11:32. The specific combination of חק and תורה refers to the Mosaic law (Deut 4:8; 17:19; 30:10). Emanuel, *From Bards*, 69n98. Per Tigay, various combinations of legal terms (e.g., משפט, מצות, חק, תורה, and עדות) can be used without etymological distinction as a reference to the law. Tigay, *Deuteronomy*, 43.

blessing in the land by keeping the Mosaic covenant, the postexilic community can experience blessing by renewing the covenant, showing covenantal love to Yahweh (חסד), and observing the Mosaic law (Deut 7:9–10; Exod 20:6).

In terms of the rhetorical framework, the main argument (v. 7) and historical narration (vv. 12–44) validate Yahweh's covenant faithfulness and sovereignty. In the case of the Abrahamic covenant, history has proven that Yahweh is faithful and able to fulfill the patriarchal promise of land (vv. 8–11, 42–44). Though the postexilic return to the land ostensibly demonstrates Yahweh's faithfulness to the Abrahamic covenant, the lack of blessing and the struggles of reconstruction stand in tension with the thesis of the psalm. This is why the subtext consisting of the three Mosaic covenant allusions (vv. 7a, 8b, and 45) is crucial to the rhetorical dynamic of this psalm. The subtext brings the Mosaic covenant relationship into the discussion and explains why Israel's covenant failure has resulted in the loss of covenant blessing and the forfeiture of Yahweh's *ḥesed*.

Israel's violation of the Mosaic covenant explains the stark realities facing the postexilic community. Taken together with the main argument, the psalmist has demonstrated that Yahweh can rightfully withhold his *ḥesed*, but it is impossible for Yahweh to violate a covenant. Therefore, the absence of blessing and prosperity in the postexilic setting has to be the result of Israel's failure to keep the Mosaic covenant. The concluding verse demonstrates the psalmist's recognition of this fact. Just as the Moab generation would only experience blessing in the land if they loved Yahweh and kept his commandments, the postexilic generation must also renew the covenant and do likewise.

6

The Abrahamic Covenant
Patriarchal Promises

HAVING EXAMINED Ps 105 and discerned the psalmist's rhetorical strategy and argument, the next phase of this intertextual study entails an overview of the Abrahamic and Mosaic covenants as the referents in the psalm's intertextualities. The references to the Abrahamic covenant are literary references, thus, they are rhetorically straightforward. As such, the Abrahamic covenant references have no imported meaning that rhetorically affects Ps 105. Though the Abrahamic covenant is not an allusive referent, it is still worth addressing this covenant in order to facilitate the discussion of inter-covenantal dynamics in Ps 105.

ONE COVENANT OR MULTIPLE COVENANTS?

The marked disparity in the nature of the covenant terms and narratives in Gen 15, 17, and 22 presents a difficulty that is worth visiting before addressing the Abrahamic covenant and its progressive development. Historically, mainstream scholars have approached this problem from a source-critical, form-critical, and tradition-historical perspective. Westermann views the covenant in Gen 15 as a divine oath, a solemn assurance, and even as an obligation.[1] Whereas earlier scholars attributed Gen 15 to the Yahwist (J)

---

1. Westermann's view is influenced by Jepsen, Lohfink, Kutsch, and Perlitt, who define a *berit* as a bilateral relationship involving mutual obligations. Westermann, *Genesis 12–36*, 112–13.

and the Elohist (E), recent scholarship favors a late date.[2] Westermann assigns Gen 15 to "a late stage in the history of the patriarchal promises ... when possession of the land (vv. 7–21) and the survival of the people (vv. 1–6) was in danger, and the old patriarchal promises were revived so as to give surety to God's promise in a time of national danger."[3] In fact, Westermann goes as far as to state that Gen 15 "ceases to have any relevance for the whole question of a patriarchal covenant or a covenant between God and Abraham."[4]

In this sense, Westermann views Gen 17 as a true *berit* since it establishes a relationship characterized by mutual obligations.[5] Mainstream scholars view the differences between Gen 15 and 17 as evidence of different sources operating in different historical and theological contexts. For example, Gen 17 is seen as a late Priestly text that addresses Yahweh's relationship with the nation in a manner that aligns with the Sinai covenant tradition.[6]

The recent trend of assigning a late date to Gen 15 has led to a lack of consensus regarding its underlying source(s). The dating of Gen 15 to an exilic or postexilic period also seems to be influenced by the view that Israel's covenant theology is a late development shaped by the crisis of exile. For example, Ha posits that Gen 15 is a late work intended to revise the covenant theology of the postexilic community so that the hope of a divine oath can supplant the nation's failure to keep the Mosaic covenant.[7]

Williamson's well-known monograph posits that there are actually two independent but related covenants that involve Abraham.[8] Those who

---

2. For example, Ha sees Gen 15 as a late "compendium of the Pentateuchal history" that reinterprets the covenant-theology to be more consistent with the concept of a unilateral divine oath. Per Ha, the author understood the tension related to the Deuteronomic emphasis on obedience to the law, which motivated him to address the exile by emphasizing divine promise over Israel's covenantal failure. Ha, *Genesis 15*, 194–95, 215–16.

3. Westermann, *Genesis 12–36*, 217.

4. Westermann, *Genesis 12–36*, 113.

5. Westermann, *Genesis 12–36*, 113.

6. Westermann attributes the Noachian and Abrahamic covenants to P, but not the Sinaitic covenant. In a source-critical framework, this is why the covenant in Gen 17 features the mutuality and conditionality that is a hallmark of the Sinaitic covenant. Westermann, *Genesis 12–36*, 113.

7. Ha, *Genesis 15*, 216.

8. Williamson, *Abraham, Israel, and the Nations*. Hahn sees two Abrahamic covenants, but does so based on a source-critical framework. Hahn, *Kinship by Covenant*. Alexander sees two complementary covenants in Gen 15 and 17 where Gen 15 focuses on descendants and land, while Gen 17 focuses on Abraham as a mediator of blessing. Alexander sees the divine oath in Gen 22 as the point when the Abrahamic covenant is established. Alexander, *From Paradise*, 52–54.

see only one covenant view the differences between Gen 15 and 17 as indicative of multiple stages in the development of the Abrahamic covenant.[9] Williamson, however, sees the differences as evidence of two independent covenants involving Abraham.[10] Genesis 15 depicts a unilateral, unconditional covenant while Gen 17 describes a bilateral, conditional covenant. Williamson also argues that the notable time gap between the events of Gen 15 and 17 is further evidence for two distinct covenants.[11] In this construct, Williamson sees the events of Gen 22:16–18 as the climactic ratification of the bilateral, conditional covenant initiated in Gen 17.[12] In essence, Abraham's willingness to sacrifice Isaac fulfills the prerequisite for blameless conduct found in Gen 17:1 and finally establishes Abraham as a model of the righteous behavior that will eventually be expected of Abraham's descendants and heirs (Gen 18:18–19; 26:5; cf. Neh 9:13).[13]

Williamson's two-covenant construct is tenable, but the issues he raises do not necessitate such a framework.[14] Chisholm's approach addresses the same disparities, but he sees these tensions through the lens of a cohesive narrative that describes a developing covenantal relationship.[15] Chisholm acknowledges that the covenant in Gen 15 is technically distinct from the one in Gen 17 but posits that Gen 17 serves as an expansion of Gen 15 once Yahweh's solemn oath (Gen 22) definitively ratifies all the promises as a single covenant.[16] Chisholm's approach is appealing in that he discerns a process of progressive covenant ratification that organically follows the contours of the narrative.[17] Niehaus also discerns a larger pattern in which God

---

9. See Chisholm for an exegetical and narrative analysis that is representative of this view. Chisholm, "Evidence from Genesis," 35–54.

10. Williamson, *Abraham, Israel, and the Nations*, 212–14.

11. Williamson points to an approximate 13-year gap between Gen 15 and 17. He also notes that Gen 17 repeatedly projects the ratification of the covenant into the future, which is consistent with reading Gen 22 as the formal ratification of the covenant in Gen 17. Williamson, "Covenant," 147–48.

12. Williamson, "Covenant," 147–48.

13. Williamson, "Covenant," 147–48.

14. Niehaus, "God's Covenant with Abraham," 249–71, 249n4.

15. Like Williamson, Chisholm sees Gen 22 as a climactic moment in the relationship between God and Abraham; however, he sees this as the final test that prompts Yahweh to ratify the covenant promises as an irrevocable divine oath. Chisholm, "Evidence from Genesis," 46–50.

16. Chisholm, "Evidence from Genesis," 44n30.

17. Beginning with Abraham's obedient move to Canaan in Gen 12 and culminating with Abraham's offering of Isaac in Gen 22, Abraham's obedience over the course of several years results in the ratification of the covenantal promises (see Gen 26:3–5). Chisholm notes that Abraham's initial obedience causes God to begin fulfilling his

initiates a covenant relationship and then reveals "supplemental" information, thus Gen 15 can be seen as the initiation with Gen 17 and 22 representing the "supplemental" elements.[18] Even Hahn, who favors Williamson's multiple covenant framework, affirms that there is a developmental process in Abraham's covenantal relationship that culminates with the divine oath sworn in Gen 22.[19]

Niehaus argues that the broader biblical context indicates that there is one covenant that defines Yahweh's promises to Abraham and the patriarchs, which is indicated by the way later references to the Abrahamic covenant point back to a single covenant (e.g., Exod 2:24; Lev 26:42; 2 Kgs 13:23; 1 Chr 16:16; Ps 105:9 and Acts 3:25).[20] Niehaus also notes that in the progress of the OT narrative, the Abrahamic covenant becomes the covenant with Isaac and Jacob, which eventually becomes known as the covenant with the "fathers."[21] The manner in which the psalmist refers to the Abrahamic covenant in Ps 105 coheres with Niehaus's observation (see Ps 105:7–11).

Interestingly, in comparing the two-covenant frameworks of Williamson and Hahn with the single covenant view represented by Chisholm's reading, one finds that there are notable similarities in the details. There is a general consensus that the covenantal content in Gen 15 differs from that in Gen 17. There is also a common understanding of the divine oath in Gen 22 as the climactic, defining moment in the Abrahamic covenant narrative. Yet two features commend Chisholm's approach. First, his interpretation of the progressive ratification process accounts for the cohesive narrative dynamic of the literary unit marked by the *inclusios* in Gen 12 and 22. Second, Chisholm's approach acknowledges the tensions between the covenant pericopes (Gen 15, 17, and 22) but accounts for them via the developing interplay between Abraham's obedience and Yahweh's progressive covenant ratification. As Abraham demonstrates his faith and obedience Yahweh strengthens the promissory aspects of the covenant. This is consistent with Averbeck's characterization of each major biblical covenant as having both promissory and obligatory aspects.

---

promises even before they have been finally ratified. Chisholm Jr., "Evidence from Genesis," 36–38, 38n9.

18. Niehaus notes that the Mosaic covenant is made in Exod 20–24, followed by additional content in the remainder of Exodus, Leviticus, Numbers, and Deuteronomy. He also sees this pattern in the NT where the new covenant is inaugurated in Matt 27–28, followed by supplemental information in the remainder of the NT books. Niehaus, "God's Covenant with Abraham," 253–54.

19. Hahn, *Kinship by Covenant*, 134.

20. Niehaus, "God's Covenant with Abraham," 249n4.

21. Niehaus, "God's Covenant with Abraham," 249–71.

THE DEVELOPMENT OF THE ABRAHAMIC COVENANT

The Abrahamic covenant texts are found in Gen 12:1-9; 15; 17; and 22, but there are also supplemental texts in Gen 18:18-19 and 26:3-5 that provide insight into the nature of the covenant's stipulations and fulfillment. The core of the Abrahamic covenant narrative is framed by an *inclusio* featuring the divine command "*you* go . . . " (לֶךְ־לְךָ) in Gen 12:1-9 and 22:1-19.[22] The divine call and pronouncement in Gen 12:1-9 is not part of the covenant proper, but it is a prelude that reveals the first indication of the promissory program that will be developed into the Abrahamic covenant over the course of three pivotal divine encounters (Gen 15, 17, and 22). Though the specific nuances of the divine promises are open to discussion, the basic promises can be characterized as great nationhood, a great name, and blessing for all nations with a hint regarding the promised grant of land (Gen 12:1, 7).[23]

Prelude and Preview: Genesis 12:1-9

A good deal has been written regarding the syntax and grammatical structure of Gen 12:1-3 yielding varying views on the nature of the divine command and promises.[24] For the purposes of this study, the pertinent issue is the degree of obligation and promise that is related to Abraham's obedience to the initial imperative (לֶךְ־לְךָ) in v. 1a and Yahweh's programmatic promises in vv. 2-3. Interpretations range from a virtual "partnership" between Yahweh and Abram to a purely obligatory relationship between Abram's response and Yahweh's fulfillment of his promises.[25] Chisholm's analysis

---

22. Williamson, *Abraham, Israel, and the Nations*, 18, 136, 217-20. See also Mathews, *Genesis 11:27—50:26*, 105; Hamilton, *Genesis 1-17*, 370-71.

23. There are complexities regarding the syntax of Gen 12:1-3, but identifying the basic promises suffices in surveying the subsequent development process. For a detailed delineation of seven elements in the promises of Gen 12:1-3, see Sarna, *Genesis*, 88-90. Hahn's distillation of the promises to three fundamental elements reflects the approach of this study. Hahn, *Kinship by Covenant*, 103. It is also significant that the promise of a great name is unique to Abraham and not extended to the other patriarchs. Clines, *Theme of the Pentateuch*, 32-50.

24. The following are helpful discussions on the syntax and grammar of Gen 12:1-3: Baden, "Morpho-Syntax," 223-37; Chisholm, "Evidence from Genesis," 37-39; Jeppesen, "Promise and Blessing," 32-42; Hamilton, *Genesis 1-17*, 370-76; Miller, "Syntax and Theology," 472-75.

25. Baden's novel interpretation suggests an agreement or " . . . a partnership between Yhwh and Abraham, one in which both sides are "equally responsible for their set of actions." Baden, "Morpho-Syntax," 237. Chisholm concludes that there are two viable readings based on the syntax/grammar: (1) the cohortatives of vv. 2-3 are sequential,

of the syntax and grammar suggests that the relationship between the imperative and the cohortatives can be read as sequential or consequential, therefore, both a promissory or obligatory nuance are possible in Yahweh's speech.[26] In terms of the larger context, there is a discernible thread in the Abrahamic narrative that links Abraham's obedience and faith to the progression of the covenant program. In light of this larger literary context, it is reasonable to see a conditional nuance in the relationship between Yahweh's command in Gen 12:1 and the cohortatives in vv. 2–3.

Hahn's analysis of the relationship between Gen 12:1–3 and the covenant texts in Gen 15, 17, and 22 provides a helpful framework for understanding the development of the promulgated promises of Gen 12. Hahn observes a framework in which each of the three main promises of Gen 12:1–3, great nationhood, a great name, and blessing for all nations, is addressed in Gen 15, 17, and 22, respectively.[27] In Gen 15 the focus is upon numerous descendants and land, which are the fundamental elements of nationhood (Gen 12:2a).[28] In Gen 17, the promise of nationhood is confirmed (e.g., land and descendants addressed in Gen 17:6–8), but the promise of a "great name" (Gen 12:2c) comes to the fore as Yahweh builds upon the covenant content revealed in Gen 15.[29] Hahn makes the connection between the promise that Abraham would be the "father" of many nations and the concept of suzerainty through the ANE use of kinship terms ("father" for suzerain and "son" for vassal) in international treaties.[30] Genesis 17 also expands on the covenantal promise of a "great name" and kingship

---

implying that the promises are unconditional and not dependent on Abram's response; (2) the cohortatives are consequential, meaning there is a degree of conditionality based on Abram's response. Chisholm, "Unpacking Yahweh's Promise," 20–21.

26. Chisholm, "Unpacking Yahweh's Promise," 20–22.

27. Hahn, *Kinship by Covenant*, 103–11.

28. Per Hahn, the first occurrence of the term גוי ("nation") after Gen 12:2a is in Gen 15:14. Hahn, *Kinship by Covenant*, 104. Williamson notes that the two main conditions for nationhood (people and land) are emphasized in Gen 15. Williamson, *Abraham, Israel, and the Nations*, 99, 140.

29. Hahn notes that the expansion of Abraham's and Sarah's names highlights the theme of a "great name." The promise of kings from Abraham's line (Gen 17:6, 16) adds royal lineage to the covenant promises, which is also related to a "great name." Hahn, *Kinship by Covenant*, 105–6.

30. Hahn posits that "father" is used metaphorically of Abraham as a suzerain since his royal descendants David and Solomon later rule as "suzerains" over all nations from Egypt to the Euphrates (see 2 Sam 8 and 1 Kgs 4:21; cf. Ps 2:7–12; 72:8–11; 89:25–27). Hahn, *Kinship by Covenant*, 106–7.

by promising Canaan as the future homeland of the kingdom issuing from Abraham.[31]

The cumulative nature of the inchoate covenants in Gen 15 and 17 culminates in Gen 22. Genesis 22:15–18 is the climax of the Abrahamic covenant narrative, but Hahn goes as far as to suggest that the divine oath also functions as a major focal point of the Pentateuch.[32] Hahn notes that Gen 22:15–18 is the first and only account of God swearing an oath to any patriarch and that it is specifically this oath that becomes the "clearest textual referent for the recurring allusions to the oath to the patriarchs or the covenant sworn to the patriarchs, in the rest of the Old Testament."[33] The fact that God has bound himself by oath represents the culmination of a cumulative process resulting in an irrevocable covenant with God assuming full responsibility for the promises.[34]

Though there are difficulties with Hahn's view that Gen 15, 17, and 22 are separate covenants, his recognition of a cumulative nature to these covenants is a helpful way to understand the progressive covenant narrative. The following summary statement effectively describes the dynamic between the covenant pericopes in Gen 15, 17, and 22:

> Genesis 15, 17, and 22 represent a succession of covenant episodes involving increasingly greater sacrifices from Abraham (i.e., animals, circumcision, Isaac), and at the same time increasingly greater blessings are divinely pledged by covenant (i.e., land, dynasty, worldwide blessing). The oath that God swears to Abraham in Genesis 22 represents the sum and substance of the covenant grant, particularly as it relates to the worldwide blessing and future triumph of Abraham's 'seed.'[35]

Interestingly, the above summary does not require understanding Gen 15, 17, and 22 as independent covenants. Though this writer takes the view that Gen 12–22 reflects the progressive development of a single covenant, Hahn's summary of Abraham's increasing acts of obedience and Yahweh's

---

31. The promised land in Gen 17 is smaller than the land in Gen 15, which may reflect that Canaan is for Isaac and refers specifically to Israel's homeland. Hahn, *Kinship by Covenant*, 107.

32. Hahn, *Kinship by Covenant*, 108.

33. Hahn, *Kinship by Covenant*, 108. See esp. Gen 26:3 and Exod 32:13, also Gen 24:7; 50:24; Exod 13:11; 33:1; Num 14:23; 32:11; and Deut 1:8, 34; 6:10, 18, 23; 31:20–21; 34:4.

34. Hahn, *Kinship by Covenant*, 127–28.

35. Hahn, *Kinship by Covenant*, 134.

commensurate responses is an apt description of the Abrahamic covenant's development into an irrevocable promissory covenant.

A Unilateral Promise: Genesis 15

Keeping in mind Hahn's summarization of the cumulative covenant-making process, it is now important to examine the covenant narrative and see how an obligatory dynamic based on Abraham's obedience develops into an irrevocable divine oath.[36] The bilateral dynamic between Abraham's obedience and Yahweh's covenantal response manifests early in the Abraham narrative. For example, in a rhetorical and literary analysis of Gen 13, Rickett concludes that the actual focus of the narrative is twofold: (1) the separation of Abraham from Lot as a step in obeying God's earlier mandate to leave his father's household and (2) occupying the land of promise (see Gen 12:7), which can only happen once Abraham has broken ties with his father's household as commanded in 12:1.[37] Rickett's findings suggest that the narrative focuses on Abraham's obedience as a major factor in inhabiting the land of promise. Though the promise of land was not as prominently featured in Gen 12:1–9, it takes on greater significance as the narrative progresses. Furthermore, the promise of great nationhood inherently includes the idea of a land grant since this is a defining characteristic of national sovereignty.

The first covenantal encounter in Gen 15 features a sacrificial ritual involving the slaughter and halving of various animals (Gen 15:9–10). The exact meaning of this sacrificial ritual has been the subject of much discussion. While the exact significance may not be certain, this ritual is understood as a self-imprecation act in which the slaughter of the animals vividly demonstrates the fate of the one who violates the terms of the given covenant (e.g., Jer 34:18).[38] However, Hamilton suggests that this is a covenant ritual ceremony expressed in theophanic terms without self-imprecatory

---

36. There is a veritable plethora of research concerning the relationship between a covenant and an oath in ANE contexts. For the purposes of this study, there is a distinction, but the solemn divine oath in Gen 22 is inextricably linked to the Abrahamic covenant (Gen 15 and 17) and defines the final form of the covenant. This final form is restated to Isaac and Jacob. For more on "covenant" vs. "oath," see Hugenberger, *Marriage as a Covenant*, 168–215.

37. Rickett, "Rethinking the Place," 41–42; 50–53.

38. McCarthy, *Treaty and Covenant*, 93–94. Weinfeld sees significance in the inferior party providing the sacrificial animals for the superior party. Weinfeld, "Covenant of Grant," 197. For a comparative study of the slaughter of animals in Gen 15 in the context of ANE evidence, see Hess, "Slaughter of Animals," 55–65.

implications.³⁹ As a theophanic covenant ratification ritual, the manner in which the theophanic elements of fire and smoke pass between the sacrificial animal parts signifies that God is unilaterally ratifying this covenant (Gen 15:17).⁴⁰ Williamson further notes that the absence of any particular covenantal sign may be due to the absence of human obligations in this covenantal context.⁴¹

As for the actual substance of the covenantal terms in Gen 15, the primary focus is the establishment of a "great nation" within specific geographic boundaries (Gen 15:18–21; cf. Gen 12:2).⁴² The various covenant promises can reasonably be packaged within the general rubric of a "great nation" since a large population, land, and blessings are all characteristics of a great nation in ANE contexts. Therefore, the unilateral, promissory nature of the first covenant encounter in Gen 15 creates the context in which subsequent covenant-making episodes are read.

Abraham's Obligations: Genesis 17

Unlike Gen 15, the covenant encounter in Gen 17 suggests a bilateral covenant relationship. Chapter 17 begins with a command for Abraham to conduct himself blamelessly before the Lord (התהלך לפני והיה תמים, "walk before me and be blameless"), which is then followed by an apparently conditional offer of a ratified covenant (ואתנה בריתי ביני ובינך, "Then I will confirm my covenant between me and you").⁴³ The command to Abraham consists of two imperative verb forms, "walk" (התהלך) and "be" (והיה), followed by a

---

39. Hamilton sees Gen 15:17 in light of Exod 33–34 and Josh 3–4, and the common elements are the the divine name, the cutting of animals, Yahweh's "passing through" described by the verb, עבר, a list of nations to be expelled, and the context of a covenant ceremony. Hamilton, *Genesis 1–17*, 437. For a helpful study on the significance of עבר in theophanic covenant ratification/renewal, see Hauan, "Background and Meaning," 337–48.

40. Hamilton, *Genesis 1–17*, 437. Sarna also sees the covenant as an unconditional grant with grant treaty elements. Sarna, *Genesis*, 117.

41. Williamson, "Covenant," 146.

42. Chisholm views the ritual in Gen 15:9–17 as indicative of an unconditional gift of land. However, he also notes that the promises of Gen 12:2 (great nation, personal blessing, great name) as well as eternal possession of the land (Gen 13:15) and numerous offspring (Gen 13:16; 15:5) are still unratified and conditional at this point. Chisholm, "Evidence from Genesis," 40, 42.

43. Per Chisholm, "walk before me" is an idiomatic expression for an "intimate relationship with God that is characterized by faithful, obedient behavior." This is understood to be a condition that must be fulfilled for God to "ratify" and make certain the promises outlined in vv. 4–8. Chisholm, "Evidence from Genesis," 43.

cohortative verb form "Then I will establish" (ואתנה) that indicates consequence in light of the preceding imperatives.[44] In addition, the dichotomy between Yahweh's terms and Abraham's terms ("As for me . . . As for you . . . in Gen 17:4, 9) suggests a bilateral dynamic in this covenantal framework.

In this passage, Abraham's covenantal obligations are faithful and blameless conduct (17:1) accompanied by the covenant sign of male circumcision for him and his descendants (17:10–14).[45] Contingent on Abraham honoring his terms, Yahweh promises to make Abraham the father of many nations (17:5–6, 16) and the progenitor of a great multitude of descendants (17:2).[46] In addition, the Lord promises that kings will be amongst his descendants (17:6, 16), thus adding a dimension of "international significance" to Abraham's covenantal legacy.[47] Hahn rightfully sees the promise of kingship as an additional aspect of the "great name" promise.[48]

Rendtorff analyzes the covenant speech of Yahweh and notes that the first part of the covenant formula ("I will be your God.") is reflected in 17:7 and 17:8b, which frames the promise of land and serves to highlight it.[49] Rendtorff's observation is also significant for he sees Yahweh's formulaic

---

44. There is some question as to the relationship between the two imperative verbs התהלך ("walk") and והיה ("be"). Sarna sees a parallel relationship between "walk before me," which he reads as "walk in my ways," and "be blameless." He sees these parallel commands in relation to the covenantal expectation of allegiance ("walk in my ways") and the covenant sign of circumcision, which he sees as symbolizing the removal of blemishes ("be blameless"). Sarna, *Genesis*, 123.

45. Rendtorff states that Abraham's obligations, along with Yahweh's promises, make up the foundation of the covenant (v. 9). Rendtorff sees a key point of continuity here between the Abrahamic and Mosaic covenants, since Gen 17 and Exod 19 share the same formula regarding the obligation to "keep covenant" (see Gen 17:9; Exod 19:5). Rendtorff, *Covenant Formula*, 84, 88.

46. Williamson notes that only the Israelites and Edomites can literally trace their ancestry to Abraham. Thus, God's promise of many nations entails more than biological ancestry. When the preposition ל is joined to אב ("father") in a resultative sense (GKC §119t), this can indicate a metaphorical sense of fatherhood (Gen 17:4). Williamson, "Covenant," 147. Hahn also views the status of "father of many nations" metaphorically based on the concept of kinship that was used in ANE international treaties. Hahn, *Kinship by Covenant*, 106–7.

47. The added element of kings coming from Abraham and Isaac's line (Gen 17:6–8, 16; see also 17:19–21; 35:11) becomes an important backdrop for later revelation regarding David's royal line, the Davidic covenant, and the Messiah. Hahn, *Kinship by Covenant*, 106–7.

48. Hahn, *Kinship by Covenant*, 106–7.

49. Rendtorff sees significance in the double use of Formula A (the first half of the covenant formula) in Gen 17 for it ties the covenant formula to the concept of covenant. Rendtorff, *Covenant Formula*, 14–15. See Appendix B for the covenant formula and its variants.

statement that " ... I will be your God and the God of your descendants after you" (v. 7) as a defining statement about the content of the Abrahamic covenant.[50] According to Rendtorff, Gen 17:7-8 represents the first occurrence of the covenant formula and helps define the significance of *berit* for Abraham and his future descendants.[51] The link between the covenant formula and the developing concept of covenant will prove useful later in the analysis of the Mosaic covenant allusions in Ps 105.

The bilateral aspect of the covenantal exchange in Gen 17 is further reinforced in subsequent episodes of the progressing narrative. In Gen 18:18-19, Yahweh makes a statement that affirms his intentions to make Abraham the patriarch of a great nation and the agent of international blessings based on Abraham's name. In Gen 18:19, Yahweh explains that Abraham has been chosen in order to instruct his family and his descendants to live in a righteous manner so that the promises may be fulfilled. The language of Yahweh's statement indicates that the obedience of Abraham's descendants is an obligation that affects the fulfillment of the covenant promises.[52] The tension between promise and obligations is difficult, but Chisholm resolves this tension by giving priority to Yahweh's oath in Gen 22, meaning ratification by divine oath divinely ensures the ultimate fulfillment of the promises while also allowing for human response to play a part in the manner of realization.[53]

The obligatory aspect of the covenant-making process is most clearly addressed in Gen 26:3-5 when Yahweh declares that Isaac is an heir to the promises of the Abrahamic covenant. This exchange takes place after the defining oath-making moment in Gen 22 and offers insight into the covenant-making process. In vv. 3-4 Yahweh commands Isaac to stay in the promised land (Canaan) during a time of famine and then declares that Isaac will be the recipient of the same promises that were made to Abraham. Chisholm notes that the grammatical structure of Gen 26:3 suggests that Isaac receiving the promises is conditioned upon his obedience to the command to stay in the land (גור).[54] There are verbal parallels between Gen 22:17-18

---

50. Rendtorff, *Covenant Formula*, 15.

51. Rendtorff, *Covenant Formula*, 15.

52. Sarna, *Genesis*, 131. See also Haran, "The *Berît* 'Covenant,'" 206-7.

53. Chisholm views the statement in Gen 18:19 as focused on realization/fulfillment of the promises, not on the ratification of the promises, which takes place in Gen 22. Once the promises are ratified by divine oath, whatever conditions are required for the promises to be realized will be divinely fulfilled. Chisholm, "Evidence from Genesis," 46 and 46n36.

54. The imperative followed by two imperfect forms + simple *waw* verbs (possibly cohortatives) indicates a conditional relationship between Isaac's obedience and

and Gen 26:3-4 that make it clear that Isaac is now being included in the Abrahamic promises.

The obligatory aspect of the covenant-making process runs like a thread through the narrative and even beyond the Abraham narrative. The key revelation is found in v. 5 where it is explicitly stated that the basis for the fulfillment of the covenantal promises is Abraham's obedience to Yahweh's commandments (מצות), statutes (חקות), and laws (תורות).[55] This is one of the few places where three of the legal terms used of the Mosaic law are collocated in one statement (e.g., Deut 4:1-2; 6:1), which indicates that the emphasis is upon the whole law of Moses.[56] While this reference to the Mosaic law is narratively anachronistic, it is striking that Abraham's adherence to the covenantal obligations Yahweh presented is described in such terms. Genesis 18:19 and 26:5 attribute Yahweh's solemn oath and confirmed promises to Abraham's faithful obedience. This obligatory aspect of the Abrahamic covenant is a key point of continuity in the relationship between the Abrahamic and Mosaic covenants.

Yahweh's Solemn Oath: Genesis 22

In Gen 22, the climactic offering of Isaac (the *Akedah* narrative) results in God's restatement of the promises, but this time the three primary elements (offspring, blessing, and land) are combined and promised by a solemn divine oath (Gen 22:15-18). Sarna sees the divine oath in vv. 15-18 as a reaffirmation of the previous promises, but he acknowledges that the oath is uniquely presented as a reward for Abraham's obedience.[57] Chisholm views this as the final ratification of the promises in light of Abraham's faithful response, which means the promises are now irrevocably sealed by divine oath.[58] Alexander takes the view that Gen 17 represents a distinct "covenant of circumcision" that is finally ratified in Gen 22 in response to Abraham's

---

Yahweh's promises. Chisholm, "Evidence from Genesis," 51n44.

55. These Mosaic legal terms (חקות, מצות, and תורות) are used anachronistically to characterize Abraham's obedience in Mosaic law terms. Waltke notes that these terms can be read within the larger context of the Pentateuch and understood as an idiomatic way of relating Abraham's obedience to the standards revealed in the law. Waltke and Fredricks, *Genesis*, 368. For more on the legal terms, see McConville, *Deuteronomy*, 102-3.

56. Per Tigay, all of the well-known legal terms used in relation to the *torah* have distinct etymological backgrounds but are often used without functional distinctions (e.g., the English idiom "rules and regulations"). Tigay, *Deuteronomy*, 43.

57. Sarna, *Genesis*, 154. See also Hamilton, *Genesis 18-50*, 115-16.

58. Chisholm, "Evidence from Genesis," 46-50.

proven record of obedience.[59] Though this writer does not see Alexander's "covenant of circumcision," his conclusion regarding Gen 22 and Abraham's obedience gives credence to the view presented here.[60] Genesis 22:15–18 and the language of obedience in Gen 17:1 (cf. Gen 18:19; 26:5) indicate that the development of this covenant and the final divine oath are directly related to Abraham's obedience.[61]

Boda also sees obedience as a key to understanding Yahweh's recognition of Abraham but argues from a novel perspective. In his study of Neh 9, Boda notes that most studies view Gen 15:6 as the background for Neh 9:8 where Yahweh "perceives Abraham's heart is faithful," but he argues that this may actually be influenced by Deuteronomic thought where the "realm of the heart cannot be disconnected from the realm of actions."[62] Therefore, Boda posits that the expression "a faithful heart" (Neh 9:8) has covenantal significance as a description of the ideal covenant partner.[63] The idea of Abraham as an ideal covenant partner is consistent with the Gen 22 portrayal of a covenant relationship with bilateral characteristics.

SUMMARY OF THE ABRAHAMIC COVENANT

In sum, the Abrahamic covenant is revealed, developed, and ratified within the context of the Abraham narrative (Gen 12–22). It is significant that even when scholars have differing views about the exact number of distinct covenants present in Gen 15, 17, and 22, there is consensus regarding three important aspects of the Abrahamic covenant narrative. First, there is agreement that there is progressive development of covenant promises as the program pronounced in Gen 12:1–3 becomes fleshed out in Gen 12–22. Second, there is consensus regarding the climactic nature of the divine oath Yahweh swears in Gen 22:15–18. Whether there are multiple Abrahamic covenants or one, the unilateral and irrevocable nature of the divine oath in Gen 22:15–18 is broadly accepted. Finally, there is consensus regarding the obligatory dynamic at work in Yahweh's response to Abraham's repeated acts of obedience and sacrifice. As Abraham proves himself to be faithful in "walking" according to Yahweh's ways (i.e., in torah obedience), Yahweh responds accordingly in increasing the promissory stakes and ultimately swearing an oath that irrevocably seals the Abrahamic covenant promises.

59. Alexander, *From Paradise*, 52, 61n6.
60. Alexander, *From Paradise*, 52–54.
61. Hamilton, *Genesis 18–50*, 116.
62. Boda, *Praying the Tradition*, 104–5.
63. Boda, *Praying the Tradition*, 104–5.

Thus, the Abrahamic covenant is not as simplistically unconditional as it is often characterized. The conditional give and take early on in the process is genuine, and it only becomes irrevocable once Yahweh ratifies it by divine oath. The underlying relational dynamics involving Abraham indicate that Yahweh's sovereignty and covenantal faithfulness render his covenantal promises irrevocable, even when human response is part of the covenant's establishment and fulfillment.

7

The Mosaic Covenant
From Covenant People to Chosen Nation

WHEREAS THE ABRAHAMIC COVENANT is evoked through literary references, the Mosaic covenant is evoked through three allusions (Ps 105:7, 8 and 45), therefore, these intertexts will be examined according to the method for validating an allusion detailed in chapter 3 of this work. In terms of a valid allusion, a study of the Mosaic covenant addresses the stable meaning of the *alluded* text. This overview sets the stage for an analysis of the rhetorical interplay between the psalm's developing message and the intertextual use of both covenants.

Though there are numerous Mosaic covenant-related texts throughout the Pentateuch, the present investigation focuses on the seminal covenant-making events at Sinai. For the purposes of this study, the covenant renewal on the plains of Moab (the so-called Deuteronomic covenant) is treated as a reiteration of the Mosaic covenant for a new generation and not a separate covenant.[1] The Mosaic covenant narrative begins in Exod 3:1–10 and 6:2–8 with Yahweh's self-revelation and commissioning of Moses, which serves as a prelude to the Mosaic covenant narrative. Interestingly, the call of Moses and Yahweh's announcement of his relational intentions in the discourses of Exod 3 and 6 function similarly to Gen 12:1–9 in that both narrate the call of the central covenant mediator and both include Yahweh's self-revelation regarding his covenantal intentions.

---

1. Hahn represents an additional view that considers the Levitical covenant to be a separate covenant in addition to the Sinai and Moab covenants. Hahn, *Kinship by Covenant*, 136–75.

The core Mosaic covenant text is Exod 19–24, which includes the seminal covenant-making events at Sinai as well as the Covenant Code, or Book of the Covenant (Exod 20:19—23:33). The Covenant Code consists of the Decalogue and the main corpus of Mosaic law.[2] Exodus 32–34 are also of interest since the golden calf apostasy and first instance of covenant renewal are addressed in these chapters. The Holiness Code (Lev 17–26) and additional cultic instructions in Numbers (Num 5—10:10; 28–30) provide detailed instructions on the proper cultic and ceremonial practices that govern formal interactions between Yahweh and his covenant people. Finally, Deut 12–26 contains the majority of the casuistic laws that make up a significant portion of the Mosaic law code. At its heart, the Mosaic covenant constitutes a nation and provides the moral/ethical/legal framework for maintaining this unique covenant relationship between a holy God and his sinful people.[3]

COVENANT RENEWAL OR SEPARATE COVENANTS?

Before examining the Mosaic covenant, it is helpful to clarify one particular question that affects the manner in which the covenant-making events in Exod 19–24; 34; and Deuteronomy are understood. Some consider the Mosaic covenant to be instituted at Sinai, renewed following the golden calf apostasy, and then renewed on the plains of Moab prior to the conquest. Others see the covenant-making episodes in Exod 34 and Deuteronomy as the formation of distinct covenants. This issue will be addressed so that there is clarity as to the use of certain terms as well as how these covenant events will be characterized.

After the Golden Calf Apostasy: Exodus 34

The earliest and most serious existential threat to the nascent covenant relationship involves the golden calf apostasy (Exod 32–34), which jeopardized Israel's position as Yahweh's covenant partner (Exod 32:9–10). Historically, source-critical readings of Exod 34 have identified this covenant ceremony as a parallel account to the events in Exod 19–24, but this reading does not adequately account for the literary and narratival context.[4]

---

2. ANE law codes did more than legislate the conduct of the citizenry. They could also make "a statement about the king who promulgated them." Williamson, "Covenant," 151.

3. Williamson, "Covenant," 151.

4. Scholarly discussion regarding the covenant ceremony in Exod 34 has

When reading Exod 34 in its canonical and narratival context, the differences between Exod 34 and Exod 19–24 can be explained in light of Israel's first major breach of covenant.⁵ Garrett sees the similarity in ceremonial rules as an indication that the covenant ceremony marks a remaking of the original covenant rather than the making of a new covenant.⁶ Davis believes that the differences in legal content and narrative details make sense, considering that the renewal must address the golden calf apostasy and the ensuing existential threat to the inchoate covenant relationship.⁷ In fact, Sarna notes that the new laws are actually stricter, which would be expected in light of the apostasy.⁸ Hamilton highlights creation language in the covenant renewal narrative, which he reads as an affirmation that Yahweh's "re-creation" of the covenant is miraculous like the original act of creation.⁹ Stuart makes the interesting suggestion that Moses's hand-engraving of the second set of tablets, as opposed to the first set which were engraved by God, signifies that Israel will now have to initiate and work for covenant renewal and restoration whenever the need arises.¹⁰

On the Plains of Moab: Deuteronomy

A similar question surrounds the covenant event at Moab (the so-called Deuteronomic or Moab covenant), which some consider to be a separate covenant.¹¹ Hahn sees two separate covenants at Sinai and Moab and his view is based on the premise that Sinai and Moab are two different types of covenants. Hahn classifies the covenant at Sinai as a divine kinship

---

traditionally focused on a source-critical framework in which this covenant event is J's parallel account to E's Sinai covenant account. For a helpful survey see Childs, *Book of Exodus* 604–7. See also Stuart, *Exodus*, 713n151.

5. Davis, "Rebellion, Presence, and Covenant," 81–84. See also Hamilton, *Exodus*, 577–78; Sarna, *Exodus*, 217. Stuart, *Exodus*, 712n150.

6. The two tablets Moses brings up (Exod 34:1–6), the prohibition of anyone ascending (Exod 19:12–13), and the theophany in a cloud (Exod 19:18) indicate that the ceremonial rules are the same, which indicates covenant renewal. Garrett, *Commentary*, 652.

7. Davis, "Rebellion, Presence, and Covenant," 81–84.

8. Sarna, *Exodus*, 217.

9. Hamilton sees intentional wordplay involving the verbs, עשׂה and ברא (Exod 34:10), which he connects with Gen 1. Hamilton, *Exodus*, 577–78.

10. Stuart, *Exodus*, 712n150.

11. Barrick acknowledges the similarities between the two covenants but views Sinai and Moab as two distinct covenants. Barrick, "Mosaic Covenant," 214n8.

covenant, whereas the covenant at Moab is a treaty-type covenant.[12] Hahn broadly characterizes the ANE kinship covenant as one in which "kinship bonds are extended to bind two parties in a *mutual* relationship based upon a *joint* commitment under divine sanctions."[13] A key to understanding the kinship covenant as the possible pattern for a divine-human covenant is the patriarchal concept of the father as a figure of "power and authority" more than one of "affection and benignity."[14] Thus, the kinship covenant was a patriarchal "social matrix" in which the concepts of "sonship" and "servanthood" were closely correlated.[15] Per Hahn, the covenant-making ceremony in Exod 24, including cultic sacrifice, meal-sharing, and oath-swearing, extends "kinship-by-covenant," and the ceremonial symbols indicate mutual obligations since the sprinkling of blood signifies that both parties have accepted the oath-sign.[16] The defining analogy in this covenant is the father-son relationship (Exod 4:22) between Yahweh and Israel with the clear implication that Israel is now part of Yahweh's family.[17]

As for the Moab covenant, Hahn considers Deuteronomy to be a typical example of an ANE treaty-covenant.[18] Hahn lists an impressive array of ways in which Deuteronomy is distinct from the Sinai covenant in terms of form, legal content, cultic regulations, and narrative since Deuteronomy is Moses's farewell discourse.[19] Yet, Hahn concludes that the essential difference is relational since the distinctive nature of the Moab covenant is a result of Israel's sin and rebellion, which has necessitated a "probationary vassalage" characterized by less intimacy and a diminished emphasis on sonship.[20]

Though Hahn's thesis is tenable, the prevalent view identifies the Moab covenant event as a renewal or reiteration of the Sinai covenant.[21]

---

12. Hahn, *Kinship by Covenant*, 44–48, 62–80.

13. Hahn, *Kinship by Covenant*, 37. For helpful explanations of this covenant type, see McCarthy, *Treaty and Covenant*, 254–73 and Kalluveettil, *Declaration and Covenant*, 130–35, 203–10.

14. Kalluveettil, *Declaration and Covenant*, 131–32.

15. Hahn, *Kinship by Covenant*, 40. Hahn bases his understanding of the "father" concept on the work of Kalluveettil and McCarthy. See Kalluveettil, *Declaration and Covenant*, 132–33 citing McCarthy, "Love of God," 145.

16. Hahn, *Kinship by Covenant*, 48.

17. Hahn, *Kinship by Covenant*, 48.

18. Hahn, *Kinship by Covenant*, 62. See also Moran, "Ancient Near Eastern Background," 82.

19. Hahn, *Kinship by Covenant*, 67–74.

20. Hahn, *Kinship by Covenant*, 74.

21. Tigay provides a helpful discussion of the continuity between Sinai and Moab,

Considering the apparent historical provenance, Merrill observes that the Moab covenant "reiterates the [Sinai] covenant, but it does so in a greatly expanded form and in terms appropriate to a new generation, one about to enter a new life experience and engage in a new realm of responsibility."[22] McConville sees the Sinai covenant as constitutive and the Moab covenant as a "re-realization" of that covenant, which he sees as happening repeatedly with God's people in history.[23] Craigie suggests that covenant renewal was intended to be a regular occurrence in which the Sinai covenant is recalled so that each new generation could "recommit itself regularly in love and obedience to the Lord of the covenant."[24]

The notable differences between the covenant at Sinai and the covenant at Moab can be attributed to the progression of Israel's story.[25] The Sinai covenant functions as a constitutive, seminal covenant, while the Moab covenant serves as a "national constitution" that features, not only extensive laws, but sermonic, didactic discourse "intended for religious instruction and education in ancient Israel."[26] This study proceeds with the view that Exod 32–34 and the covenant at Moab are covenant renewal events that are rooted in the Sinai covenant. The additions to the legal code that are part of the covenant renewal in Exod 34 and at Moab are best understood as supplementation and practical applications of the axiomatic principles established in the Decalogue and the Covenant Code of Exodus. Christensen aptly observes that Deuteronomy "expounds the implications of the historic agreement at Mount Sinai between God and Israel by which the latter became the chosen people."[27]

In light of the narrative context and the functional complementarity of the Sinai and Moab covenant materials, the expression "Mosaic covenant" will be understood as a broad term encompassing the foundational covenant-making event at Sinai, the legal material in the Covenant Code, the

---

concluding that the giving of the law at Moab is a continuation of the revelation at Sinai, not a separate revelation. Tigay, *Deuteronomy*, 60, 74. Based on a source-critical approach, Weinfeld sees Sinai as an early covenant of laws and Moab as a later vassalship treaty-type covenant that was eventually blended to enrich the Sinai covenant with vassal-treaty elements. Weinfeld, *Deuteronomy and the Deuteronomic School*, 156–57.

22. Merrill, *Deuteronomy*, 26.
23. McConville, *Deuteronomy*, 29–30.
24. Craigie, *Book of Deuteronomy*, 36–38, specifically 37.
25. Williamson discusses Sinai and Moab in similar terms. He views Moab as a covenant renewal but with significant modifications. Williamson, *Sealed with an Oath*, 111–15.
26. Christensen, *Deuteronomy 1:1–21:9*, lvii.
27. Christensen, *Deuteronomy 1:1–21:9*, lvii.

covenant renewal of Exod 34, the Holiness Code of Leviticus (Lev 17–26), and the Moab covenant renewal depicted in Deuteronomy. The terms Sinai/Sinaitic covenant and Moab/Deuteronomic covenant will be used for the disambiguation of narrative details and covenant content that are specific to either the Sinai or Moab narrative.

THE FORM AND BACKGROUND OF THE MOSAIC COVENANT

The actual Covenant Code (Book of the Covenant) is found in Exod 20:19—23:33, but the covenant-making narrative begins in Exod 19 and the description of the covenant ratification ceremony is detailed in Exod 24. After the seminal comparative study of Mendenhall, it has become widely held that the Mosaic covenant reflects the basic structure and relational dynamics of an ANE suzerain-vassal treaty.[28] Amongst conservative scholars, the Mosaic covenant is viewed as an analogue of the late second millennium Hittite suzerainty-type treaties (ca. 1340–1180 BCE), which generally consist of the following six components: (1) a preamble identifying the covenant parties, namely the great king (suzerain) and the vassal party, (2) a historical prologue that reviews the relationship between the suzerain and the vassal, (3) a stipulations section that delineates the terms and requirements of the given covenant, (4) a document deposit/public reading section in which the storage and occasional public reading of the covenant is detailed, (5) a witness list that would normally consist of various deities that served as divine witnesses and arbiters holding the covenant parties to account, and (6) a curses and blessings section that lists various curses and blessings that the vassal could expect to experience in relation to covenant violations or faithfulness to the covenant.[29]

---

28. As noted, Mendenhall's seminal study inspired much subsequent discussion and analysis comparing ANE suzerainty-type treaties with the Mosaic covenant. Mendenhall specifically relates the Sinai covenant (Exod 20–24) to Hittite suzerain-vassal treaties from the ancient Hittite capital of Ḫattuša (1700 BCE to 1200 BCE). Mendenhall, "Covenant Forms," 50–76.

29. The most comprehensive comparative data is currently found in Kitchen and Lawrence's work. Kitchen and Lawrence argue that the late second millennium Hittite treaty-law form is the closest analogue to the Mosaic covenant form found in Exodus-Leviticus, Deuteronomy, and Josh 24. Kitchen and Lawrence, *Treaty, Law, and Covenant*, 3:103–213, 250–66. For a helpful review of influential comparative studies of ANE treaty forms and the Sinai/Moab covenant forms, see Kline, *Treaty of the Great King*, 47–149; McCarthy, *Treaty and Covenant*, 157–99, 243–98; Weinfeld, *Deuteronomy and the Deuteronomic School*, 59–157; Kitchen, *Reliability of the Old Testament*, 283–94.

Though Mendenhall initially compared the Covenant Code to the Hittite treaty form, Kline's work on the treaty-covenant structure of Deuteronomy would lead to a broad consensus regarding the pronounced treaty structure of the book.[30] Though the comparisons do seem favorable, the analogy is not without issues. Following McCarthy's influential work on ANE treaty and covenant forms, mainstream scholars now favor the first-millennium Neo-Assyrian treaty form (e.g., Esarhaddon's vassal treaty) as the basis for the Mosaic covenant.[31] Recent studies addressing the most current documentary data have given scholars cause to revisit the late-second-millennium Hittite treaty form as a viable analogue for the covenant form reflected in Exodus-Leviticus and Deuteronomy.[32]

In their comprehensive study of ANE treaty, law, and covenant documents, Kitchen and Lawrence marshal the most current documentary evidence in order to present a compelling case for identifying the Mosaic covenant's form with late-second-millennium Hittite treaty and law documents.[33] Kitchen and Lawrence cover a corpus of ANE treaty and law texts that has already been detailed in major works by scholars, such as McCarthy and Weinfeld, thus their findings are generally in line with earlier research when it comes to the formal characteristics of ANE treaty and law documents from the third to the first millennium. Through meticulous cataloging of documentary data Kitchen and Lawrence have built a comprehensive database that will prove invaluable for any future comparative studies. In addition, Kitchen and Lawrence's novel methodology has resulted in fresh insights regarding the relationship between relevant ANE documents and the Mosaic covenant form.

One key methodological innovation involves the manner in which Kitchen and Lawrence identify a distinct public covenant form associated

---

30. Following Mendenhall's approach, Kline outlined the similarities between the Hittite suzerain-vassal treaty form (second millennium) and the structure of Deuteronomy. Kline, *Treaty of the Great King*, 47–48. For a recent comparative study of second millennium Hittite treaty forms, see Kitchen and Lawrence, *Treaty, Law, and Covenant*, 3:103–213, 250–66.

31. McCarthy's work has led to the widely-held position that the Neo-Assyrian vassal treaty form (e.g., Esarhaddon's treaties from the first millennium) is the likely template for the treaty structure of Deuteronomy. McCarthy, *Treaty and Covenant*, 157–99, 243–98.

32. See Kitchen and Lawrence's comparison of the biblical public covenant form (Mosaic covenant) with Egyptian, Hittite, and Neo-Assyrian forms. Kitchen and Lawrence, *Treaty, Law, and Covenant*, 3:117–214, 250–61. See also Kitchen, *Reliability of the Old Testament*, 283–94.

33. For a helpful summary of Kitchen and Lawrence's detailed comparison of the biblical covenant form in Exodus-Leviticus, Deuteronomy, and Josh 24 with ANE treaty and law texts, see Kitchen and Lawrence, *Treaty, Law, and Covenant*, 250–66.

with the Sinai covenant and its successive renewals and reiterations. Kitchen and Lawrence refer to this process as "detaching" or "liberating" the covenant proper from its surrounding literary "matrix."[34] Whereas previous studies had recognized Deuteronomy as an example of a Hittite suzerainty treaty, there was a tendency to equate the structure of Deuteronomy with second-millennium Hittite suzerainty treaties in broad, generic terms.[35] The value of Kitchen and Lawrence's approach is in recognizing that no biblical covenant has been preserved and transmitted to the modern reader in its original documentary form as have some ANE exemplars.

The biblical covenants are "major *transmitted* documents (not original copies), embedded in larger contexts of later construction."[36] Kitchen and Lawrence refer to the larger literary context as the "matrix" and proceed to "detach" the covenant document from this literary "matrix" which primarily consists of a narrative "report."[37] The result of this process is three discernible covenant documents found in Exodus-Leviticus, Deuteronomy, and Josh 24.[38] The isolation of these three covenant documents suggests a public covenant form in the Hebrew Bible that is a noteworthy confluence of elements that were characteristic of both law-collections and treaties from the Kassite phase of the fifteenth and fourteenth centuries BCE.[39] In fact, the most dramatic correspondence between the biblical public covenant form

---

34. Kitchen and Lawrence specifically identify three distinct covenant documents associated with the Mosaic covenant. The first is the Sinai covenant embedded in Exodus-Leviticus, the second is the Mosaic covenant embedded in Deuteronomy, and the final document is a later renewal of this covenant in Josh 24. Kitchen and Lawrence, *Treaty, Law, and Covenant*, 3:117–32.

35. For example, see Kline's work on Deuteronomy as a suzerain-vassal treaty. Kline, *Treaty of the Great King*. Kitchen and Lawrence identify a covenant document "contained within the present book of Deuteronomy but not co-extensive with it. This existing book contains additional elements that are NOT in themselves part of the covenant as narratively renewed (reaffirmed) in this book, and which, therefore we need to detach for our purposes." Kitchen and Lawrence, *Treaty, Law, and Covenant*, 3:121.

36. Kitchen and Lawrence, *Treaty, Law, and Covenant*, 3:117–18.

37. Kitchen and Lawrence note that the way the biblical covenant is embedded in a "narrative report" coheres with similar reports found at Mari. The biblical reports are consistent in form, thus providing a "solid basis for comparison" with similar ANE documents. Kitchen and Lawrence, *Treaty, Law, and Covenant*, 3:118.

38. Kitchen and Lawrence, *Treaty, Law, and Covenant*, 3:118.

39. Kitchen and Lawrence, *Treaty, Law, and Covenant*, 3:128, 132–35. For helpful tables that summarize the structure and form of law-collections, late second millennium treaties, and biblical public covenants, see Kitchen and Lawrence, *Treaty, Law, and Covenant*, 3:134–35.

and ANE documents is found among Hittite treaties and law-collections of the later second millennium (especially from ca. 1380 to 1180 BCE).[40]

Kitchen and Lawrence's analysis has unearthed a particularly fascinating example of correspondence. This feature is related to the title section in which the major treaty figures are identified along with any pertinent titles and descriptors. Kitchen and Lawrence identify different expressions and forms these formal title-lines can take in terms of syntax and style.[41] In the biblical covenants, Exod 20:1, Deut 1:5, and Josh 24:2b represent an elliptical verbal speech form in the title line ("Thus (speaks) X . . . "), but in Deut 1:1, there is a substantival variant ("these are the words . . . "), which is unusual since the elliptical form ("Thus (speaks) X . . . ") is characteristic of later second millennium Hittite treaty and law texts.[42] However, Kitchen and Lawrence found one intriguing exception in the Hittite corpus where both forms are used in tandem as in Deut 1:1–5.[43] This particular text turns out to be an intriguing example for it is the great Hittite-Egyptian treaty of 1259 BCE and the Akkadian version of this document uses both the substantival (descriptive) and elliptical (verbal) title-lines in a manner that is remarkably similar to the dual modes found in Deut 1:1–5.[44] Along with other similarities, the unique and unusual correspondence between Deut 1 and the title-lines in the great Hittite-Egyptian treaty of 1259 BCE stands out as a noteworthy finding.

In addition to Kitchen and Lawrence's important work, other recent works, such as the aforementioned studies by Weeks and Taggar-Cohen, add fresh support for the Hittite treaty form as a viable analogue for the Mosaic covenant form.[45] In the very least, recent scholarship shows that the

40. Kitchen and Lawrence, *Treaty, Law, and Covenant*, 3:134–36. For a summary of the comparative analysis and arguments for correlating the biblical covenant form with late-second-millennium Hittite treaty and law texts, see Kitchen and Lawrence, *Treaty, Law, and Covenant*, 3:250–66.

41. For a detailed explanation of the history and distribution of the various types of title lines and their respective syntactical and stylistic traits, see Kitchen and Lawrence, *Treaty, Law, and Covenant*, 3:118–19, 122–23.

42. Kitchen and Lawrence, *Treaty, Law, and Covenant*, 3:122.

43. Kitchen and Lawrence, *Treaty, Law, and Covenant*, 3:122, 255.

44. This unique convergence of a Hittite treaty form in an Egyptian context means that there would have been a significant international treaty form publicly accessible in Egypt at a time when Moses and Israel were purported to be present. While this scenario can be dismissed as "whimsical" or "imaginary," he notes that a rare "dual-genre" form present only in a major Hittite-Egyptian treaty and Deuteronomy is not imaginary. Kitchen and Lawrence, *Treaty, Law, and Covenant*, 3:122.

45. Weeks's 2004 work arrives at a similar conclusion regarding the second-millennium Hittite treaty form via a fresh analysis of documents from Egypt, Hatti, Syria, Mesopotamia, and Israel. Weeks, *Admonition and Curse*. Taggar-Cohen's study of the

place of the Mosaic covenant form within the corpus of ANE treaty and law texts is not as settled as previously thought.

Though scholarly attention has historically focused on the form-critical study of ANE covenant and treaty forms, another aspect of ANE backgrounds that informs the biblical concept of covenant is kinship relationships. There is good evidence that the Mosaic covenant may actually represent relational dynamics reflected in both kinship and marriage relationships in the ANE. As noted above, Hahn sees the Sinai covenant in Exodus as indicative of a kinship covenant where Yahweh assumes the role of the patriarch to Israel's son. In Sohn's study of the covenant formula ("I will be your God and you will be my people."), he makes the point that the language of the formula, which is especially relevant to the Mosaic covenant, is rooted in marriage language with Yahweh assuming the role of the husband to Israel's bride.[46]

In Hugenberger's study of marriage and covenant in the Bible, his lexical study yields this helpful definition of a biblical covenant: "an elected, as opposed to natural, relationship of obligation established under divine sanction."[47] An important observation is that a biblical covenant involves the forging of a relationship with a non-relative, which results in a formal relationship that is characterized by kinship terms that can be fraternal or marital.[48] This aspect of the covenant relationship is informative, for it implies that kinship is extended to a non-relative through the making of a covenant. The manner in which Yahweh relates to Israel reflects a distinct sense of a marriage relationship in which loyalty (faithfulness) is the hallmark of the relationship.

Alexander adds that Deuteronomy emphasizes marital love and loyalty as the essence of the relationship between Yahweh and Israel.[49] McCarthy addresses a related question when he examines the relationship between covenant and law in the exilic to postexilic period and concludes that law is an essential part of the covenant concept, for it governs the expression of loyalty to Israel's covenant lord, Yahweh.[50] The covenant made at Sinai is affirmed and reestablished in Deuteronomy, but there is a clear sense that love and loyalty are foundational for a relationship in which the law is the

---

Hittite *išḫiul* (a type of treaty text) also supports the Hittite tradition as a tenable influence on the Mosaic covenant form. See Taggar-Cohen, "Biblical Covenant."

46. Sohn, "I Will Be Your God," 367.
47. Hugenberger, *Marriage as a Covenant*, 215.
48. Hugenberger, *Marriage as a Covenant*, 176–81.
49. Alexander, *From Paradise*, 166–72.
50. McCarthy, "Covenant and Law," 25–44.

means of expressing this love and loyalty.⁵¹ Thus, love and loyalty are the essence of the bilateral, mutual relationship that characterizes the Mosaic covenant, but the law must be properly understood as a practical expression of covenant love and loyalty.⁵²

THE MAKING OF THE MOSAIC COVENANT

Prelude: Exodus 3:1-10; 6:2-8

In surveying the Abrahamic covenant, the divine speech of Gen 12:1-3 proved crucial as a covenantal syllabus that lays out the divine promises and also establishes the nature of the covenantal relationship between Yahweh and Abraham. In the framework of the Mosaic covenant narrative, the divine speeches in Exod 3:1-10 and 6:2-8 serve a similar narrative purpose. Exodus 3:1-10 narrates the call of Moses, Yahweh's self-revelation to Moses, and Yahweh's announcement of his intentions to deliver his people. Exodus 6:2-8 advances Yahweh's dialogue with Moses by announcing his covenantal intention in the language of the covenant formula (Exod 6:7; cf. Gen 17:7-8). Meyers points out that Exod 6:6-8 rhetorically emphasizes the impending deliverance and fulfillment of the land promise through a "staccato" series of nine action verbs that culminate with the emphatic declaration of authority, "I am Yahweh!"⁵³

A notable feature of the prelude discourses in Exod 3 and 6 is the significance of Yahweh's relational and covenantal connection to the patriarchs. In Exod 3:6 and 6:3-4, Yahweh identifies himself as the covenant-making God of Abraham, Isaac, and Jacob.⁵⁴ The key covenantal promise in these introductory speeches is the promise of land (Exod 3:8; 6:4) and it is

---

51. Christensen, *Deuteronomy 1:1-21:9*, lvii.
52. Alexander, *From Paradise*, 167-68.
53. Meyers cites seven main verbs with Yahweh as the subject: free, deliver, redeem, take, will be, will bring, will give. In addition, she cites two more verbs in dependent clauses: swore, freed. Meyers, *Exodus*, 68.
54. The solemn mode of self-identification, "I am God," echoes the way Yahweh addressed the patriarchs and would resonate in this context (Gen 15:7; 17:1; 26:24; 28:13; 35:11; 46:3). The expression "God of your father" becomes "the God of the fathers" in the exodus period as the reference to the three patriarchs becomes formulaic. Yahweh's self-identification connects Moses and the Israelites to the patriarchs and the patriarchal promises. God identifies himself as the one who made the covenant promises with Abraham and the patriarchs (see Exod 2:24). Sarna, *Exodus*, 15.

noteworthy that the list of the land's inhabitants in Exod 3:8 is similar to the list of inhabitants in Gen 15:18–21.[55]

Rendtorff examines Exod 6 against Gen 17 and unearths several lexical and syntactical features that connect the divine covenant speech of Gen 17:7–8 with Yahweh's speech in Exod 6:5–7.[56] Rendtorff sees the divine speech of Exod 6:2–8 as a dense text since all the major covenant themes are mentioned in concentrated form, including the self-declaration formula (Exod 6:2), the full covenant formula (Exod 6:7), the exodus deliverance (Exod 6:6), the formulaic remembrance of the covenant (Exod 6:5), and the promise of land (Exod 6:4).[57]

There is some discussion over what is meant when Yahweh tells Moses that he did not make himself known to the patriarchs by the divine name (Exod 6:2–3). Historically, this question has been dealt with in terms of higher critical solutions involving different sources and the various divine appellations that reflect historical, cultural, and theological backgrounds.[58] Most contemporary scholars do not understand Yahweh's statement to mean that this is literally the first unveiling of the divine name; however, there is some discussion as to the significance of this statement.[59]

---

55. In Gen 15:18–21, the inhabitants list consists of the Kenites, Kenizzites, Kadmonites, Hittites, Perizzites, Rephaites, Amorites, Canaanites, Girgashites, and Jebusites. In Exod 3:8 the listing consists of the Canaanites, Hittites, Amorites, Perizzites, Hivites, and Jebusites. Genesis 15 has the most comprehensive list with ten people groups whereas some list as few as three. Exodus 3:8 is fairly extensive with six groups. Sarna, *Exodus*, 16.

56. Rendtorff notes the common use of the expression "establish covenant" (הקים+ברית) in Gen 17:7 and Exod 6:4, as well as the emphasis on the promise of land in both speeches. Rendtorff also discerns a chiasm-like feature involving the order of covenant and God's covenantal act where Gen 17:7 mentions the covenant formula first then the possession of land, whereas Exod 6:6 places deliverance before the covenant formula in v. 7. Rendtorff, *Covenant Formula*, 15–17.

57. Rendtorff, *Covenant Formula*, 51. See Appendix B for the major covenant-related formulas.

58. Garrett points out that Exod 6:2–3 is a pivotal text for adherents of the documentary hypothesis since it is considered a definitive P text where the divine name defines a P text as opposed to an E text in Genesis and Exod 1–5. Garrett, *Commentary*, 250. See also Childs, *Book of Exodus*, 112–14. Hamilton provides an overview of scholarship regarding the meaning of El Shadday and Yahweh's statement about the self-declaration of his divine name. Hamilton, *Exodus*, 98–101. See also Garrett, *Commentary*, 250–52. For a grammatical analysis of Exod 6:3 from a source-critical perspective, see Garr, "Grammar and Interpretation," 385–408.

59. The following are a sampling of commentators who eschew the view that this is the first revelation of the divine name. Sarna, *Exodus*, 31; Garrett, *Commentary*, 252–53; Hamilton, *Exodus*, 101–2.

Sarna provides an interpretation that guides the readings of others who take the view that Yahweh is not speaking of intergenerational ignorance regarding his divine name.[60] Per Sarna, the self-declaration of the divine name would undermine, not enhance, a divine pronouncement if it were an unknown name, and he adds that ANE self-declaration formulas are effective precisely because the one making such a declaration is well-known.[61] Thus, Sarna concludes that Yahweh is referring to the identification of his sacred name with his attributes, power, and character, which means that the patriarchs had not experienced the full power and significance of Yahweh's covenant promises.[62]

Garrett follows Sarna's reading and adds that the revelation of the divine name is not something novel but the "completion of something very old," in that Yahweh is emphasizing continuity from the patriarchs to Moses.[63] Janzen goes as far as seeing the shift from El Shaddai/Shadday to Yahweh as signifying an "epoch-making shift from one paradigm of divine-human relations to another," namely from "Patriarchal Religion" to "Mosaic Faith."[64] While this writer does not see such a drastic delineation between the religion of the patriarchs and that of Moses, Janzen's point highlights the significance of the divine name shift as a signal of defining events to come. This reading accounts for the context in which Yahweh is preparing Moses for divine acts with profound implications for both the Abrahamic covenant and the impending Mosaic covenant.

Preparations: Exodus 19

The narrative of the covenant-making events at Sinai (Horeb) begins in earnest in Exod 19. Sarna describes the situation aptly:

> The arrival at Sinai inaugurates the culminating stage in the process of forging Israel's national identity and spiritual destiny.

---

60. Sarna's consultation of the Tosafists (Rashi, Rashbam, Bekhor Shor) adds the weight of tradition to his interpretation. Sarna, *Exodus*, 31.

61. Sarna, *Exodus*, 31.

62. Sarna, *Exodus*, 31. See also Hamilton, *Exodus*, 101–2. Seitz's study of Exod 6:2-3 uses a source-critical approach yet reaches a conclusion similar to Sarna's. He notes: Yahweh, in the impending deliverance of Israel, is making himself known " . . . fully rather than for the first time—as YHWH." Seitz, "Call of Moses," 145–61, specifically 158–59.

63. Garrett, *Commentary*, 252.

64. Janzen, *At the Scent of Water*, 24, 31. Janzen references the terms "Patriarchal Religion" and "Mosaic Yahwism" introduced in Moberly, *Old Testament of the Old Testament*.

The shared experiences of bondage and liberation are to be supplemented and given ultimate meaning by a great communal encounter with God. Henceforth, Israel is to be a people inextricably bound to God by a covenantal relationship.[65]

As the scene is set for the making of the covenant, Yahweh explains the relational essence of the anticipated covenant relationship. In Exod 19:5–6, Yahweh instructs Moses to declare the following programmatic statement to the people:

> 5 Now if you obey me fully and keep my covenant, then out of all nations you will be my treasured possession. Although the whole earth is mine, 6 you will be for me a kingdom of priests and a holy nation.' These are the words you are to speak to the Israelites." [NIV]

This is the first mention of *berit* in Exodus and it signals to the people that they are about to enter into a formal relationship with Yahweh since they would have been familiar with the ANE concept of covenant.[66] This is not a suggestion regarding a specific covenant form, but rather the general ANE concept of a *berit*, which would have been understood to encompass concepts, such as a formal relationship, obligations, loyalty, and divine oversight. Going back to Hugenberger's definition of *berit* in the OT, it is worth stressing that covenant entails "an elected, as opposed to natural, relationship of obligation established under divine sanction."[67] It seems reasonable to assume that the weight of the divine pronouncement in Exod 19:5–6 would not have been lost on the people at Sinai.

The expression "obey my voice" (תשמעו בקלי) is a distinctive idiom that hearkens back to Gen 22:18 and 26:5 where Abraham is described as one who has obeyed Yahweh faithfully. This affirms that Abraham's obedience was instrumental in Yahweh's final ratification of the covenantal promises by solemn oath (Gen 22:15–18). The obligatory aspect of the Mosaic covenant is clear based on the divine pronouncement in Exod 19:5. The

---

65. Sarna, *Exodus*, 102.

66. Hamilton notes that Israel had already been referred to as God's people in earlier texts (e.g., Exod 3:7, 10; 5:23) and even in kinship terms (Exod 4:22, 23), but the offer of covenant reflects a "... more intimate, dynamic level of an already-existing relationship between two parties." Hamilton, *Exodus*, 301. Hugenberger also observes: "... far from creating a relationship *de novo*, the making of a covenant seems to presuppose an existing relationship, to which explicit appeal is made during the negotiations to make a covenant." Hugenberger, *Marriage as a Covenant*, 169.

67. Hugenberger's lexical study resulted in four essential "ingredients" in an OT understanding of *berit*: (1) relationship, (2) with a non-relative, (3) involving obligations, and (4) established with an oath. Hugenberger, *Marriage as a Covenant*, 215.

second general stipulation is the obligation to "keep" Yahweh's covenant (וּשְׁמַרְתֶּם אֶת־בְּרִיתִי). The charge to keep covenant further emphasizes the formality of the relationship as well as the fact that the obligations of the impending covenant will be enforced by divine sanction. Garrett adds that "obeying Yahweh's voice" speaks to the internal obedience of the heart while "keeping Yahweh's covenant" speaks to the formal stipulations of torah that characterize covenant loyalty.[68] The poetic structure of the divine speech also reinforces the essential nature of obedience to the covenant. Garrett discerns the following chiastic pattern in Exod 19:3–6:

A: The command to speak to Israel (19:3cd)
   B: YHWH's past grace toward Israel (19:4abc)
      C: Condition of obedience to the covenant (19:5ab)
   B': YHWH's future grace toward Israel (19:5cd–6ab)
A': The command to speak to Israel (19:6cd)[69]

Equally important is the divine obligation in this bilateral covenant. The result of the covenant's fulfillment is characterized by two notable statements. First, the people will be considered Yahweh's "special possession" (סְגֻלָּה) from among all nations and peoples. Second, they will function as a "kingdom of priests" (מַמְלֶכֶת כֹּהֲנִים) and a "holy nation" (גּוֹי קָדוֹשׁ). The expression "special possession" has a literal meaning of valued property, but has the figurative meaning treasured or beloved.[70] As for "kingdom of priests" and "holy nation," nationhood is a key aspect of the Abrahamic covenant's fulfillment, but now nationhood is distinguished from a secular understanding by both Israel's function, which is to be a mediating people and a model for the nations, and also by Israel's holiness, i.e., separation from the profane. Hamilton notes that the expression "holy nation" (גּוֹי קָדוֹשׁ) echoes Yahweh's Abrahamic promises regarding a "great nation" (גּוֹי גָּדוֹל) in Gen 12:2 and 18:18, but Yahweh now develops the idea so that growth in numbers, which is already evident, is not the only measure of the nation's greatness.[71]

The covenant-making process begins in earnest as Moses is commanded to prepare the people for Yahweh's theophany on Sinai (Exod 19:9–25). The preparation emphasizes specific instructions for purification and ceremonial cleanness throughout the three-day duration of Yahweh's appearance. The preparatory activity is intended to protect the people since

---

68. Garrett, *Commentary*, 459–60.
69. Garrett, *Commentary*, 459.
70. Sarna, *Exodus*, 104.
71. Hamilton, *Exodus*, 304.

Yahweh's holiness means death to any who are unclean or too close to his presence (Exod 19:12, 21–23).

The account of the theophany is followed by the giving of the Decalogue (Exod 20) and the Covenant Code (Exod 21–23), which represents the first corpus of torah legislation.[72] It is noteworthy that Exod 20:2 (see also Deut 5:6 and Lev 26:13) demonstrates the covenantal significance of the self-declaration formula since the core of the Mosaic covenant (the Decalogue and the Covenant Code) is introduced by the self-declaration of Yahweh as Israel's covenant God. In essence, the divine name that was revealed to Moses in Exod 3 and 6 is now indelibly affixed to the Mosaic covenant and Israel's national identity. One additional intended effect of the theophany is to establish Moses's credibility and unique authoritative status as Yahweh's covenant mediator. In v. 9, Yahweh tells Moses that he will approach him in a visible and audible presence so that the people will always trust in Moses (וגם־בך יאמינו לעולם). The identification of this covenant with Moses as the mediator is established at Sinai and it is an unequivocally divine decision.

Ceremonial Ratification: Exodus 24

The covenant-making narrative resumes in Exod 24 as Moses is summoned into Yahweh's presence followed by Moses's public announcement of the Decalogue and the laws ("judgments," משפטים) of the Covenant Code (Exod 24:1–3). At this point, the people respond, *en masse*, to accept these covenant stipulations and declare that they will obey all that has been commanded (Exod 24:3). This is the first indication that the people are accepting the terms of the covenant as a willing covenant partner. Moses then proceeds to codify the covenant commands into what is called the "Book of the Covenant" (ספר הברית), which is consistent with the general ANE treaty-ratification practice of writing the terms to make them legally binding.[73]

The ratification of the covenant is finalized by ceremonial rites described in Exod 24:4b–18. The ceremonial acts and divine response in this section of the narrative represent the solemn oath and divine sanction element that is considered a necessary component of a proper *berit*.[74] The nar-

---

72. The Decalogue, called "the words," and the laws/rules, literally called "the judgments," represent the two types of laws in the initial legal corpus of the covenant. The Decalogue consists of apodictic commandments and the "judgments" (or "rules") of the Covenant Code are fitting of state regulations and law courts. Sarna, *Exodus*, 151.

73. Sarna, *Exodus*, 151.

74. For a helpful discussion of the oath, divine sanction, and other means of

rative describes several ceremonial elements of significance as part of the covenant-ratification process. First, is the solemn oath, or *verba solemnia*, that signifies the acceptance of the covenant or treaty terms. As noted above, the people initially responded to the pronouncement of the Decalogue and the Covenant Code by willingly committing to obey all that had been commanded (Exod 24:3). The following day, they reiterated their commitment to obey the terms and stipulations of the covenant following Moses's reading of the newly codified Book of the Covenant (Exod 24:7). Though McCarthy emphasizes the self-maledictory nature of any legitimate covenant-sealing oath, he concedes that the theophanic presence of Yahweh followed by the people's verbal commitment to obedience (Exod 24:3) meets the criteria for *verba solemnia*, which can function like a covenant-sealing oath.[75]

In the ensuing narrative, there is a dense ceremonial process that serves to ratify the Sinai covenant. The morning after the initial verbal pledge, Moses builds an altar and erects twelve symbolic stones. Sarna posits that the constructed altar and the twelve erected stones, symbolizing the twelve tribes of Israel, represent the divine presence and the people of Israel as the contracting parties of the *berit*.[76] The next major ceremonial element is the sacrifice of bulls that entails two types of offerings: a burnt offering (עלה) and a peace offering (שלמים), or as Sarna suggests, "a sacrifice of greeting."[77] The burnt offering is completely consumed in flames, but the peace offering involves burning certain parts and then serving the rest as a kind of shared sacred meal.[78]

Though the narrator does not explicitly describe the consumption of the peace offering, the traditional understanding of the ceremony implies that the people would have eaten the unburnt portions of the peace offering.[79] The meal that is shared later in Yahweh's presence by Moses, Aaron, and the elders is best understood as the shared meal that is an integral part

---

ratifying or sealing a covenant, see Hugenberger, *Marriage as a Covenant*, 185–214.

75. McCarthy, *Treaty and Covenant*, 253. Kalluveettil reaches a similar conclusion regarding the people's verbal assent (Exod 19:8) to the initial pronouncement of Yahweh's covenantal intentions in Exod 19. Kalluveettil, *Declaration and Covenant*, 157.

76. The use of pillars of stone as "mute witnesses" to treaty ratification is attested in Gen 31:45–54 and in Josh 24:27. Sarna, *Exodus*, 151.

77. Sarna, *Exodus*, 152.

78. Sarna, *Exodus*, 151–52.

79. Polak studied the covenant-making ceremony in Exod 24 in light of Mari texts on treaty-ratification ceremonies. Polak posits that there is a bi-local covenant meal in Exod 24 (see vv. 4–8 and 9–11), which follows the Mari practice of having a covenant meal in each party's home location. Polak, "Covenant at Mount Sinai," 125, 128–34.

of ANE covenant-ratification (Exod 24:11).[80] McCarthy adds that the meal may also have been a "reassuring gesture on the part of the superior toward the inferior, and not a pledge by the latter."[81] In light of the terror evoked by Yahweh's theophanic presence, McCarthy's comment has some merit, but the shared meal is most likely an oath-like covenant-ratification act reflective of analogous ANE practices.

The final ceremonial element of note is the sprinkling of blood (Exod 24:6) upon the altar and upon the people following their verbal pledge (v. 8). The specific meaning of the blood sprinkling is never made clear, but blood is generally understood to be a singular source of life, thus, sprinkling it on the altar and upon the people would indicate a sharing of life-essence between the covenant parties.[82] Meyers puts it more colloquially, referring to the blood rite as a symbolic way of showing that Yahweh and Israel are now bound as "blood brothers."[83] Though there is a temptation to see self-maledictory significance in the sprinkling of blood, there are difficulties regarding the idea of God making a self-maledictory pledge or oath.

Childs offers an innovative view in which the blood sprinkled on the altar represents an offering that speaks to God's gracious forgiveness, while the blood sprinkled on the people is seen as a self-maledictory act by which the people bind themselves to the covenant.[84] Despite the lack of concrete information regarding the specific symbolism of the blood, the overall meaning and functional significance seem clear. The sprinkling of blood upon both covenant parties signifies the solemn ratification and sealing of the covenant in bilateral terms.

In surveying the ratification ceremony of Exod 24 there is a telling contrast between the covenant rituals in Gen 15 and Exod 24. The similarity is in the divine theophanic presence, especially accounting for the visible features of smoke and fire. In both cases, there is the sacrifice of animals, but the key contrast is in Yahweh's solitary act of passing between the animal parts in Gen 15, which is different from the interactive ratification ceremony

---

80. Sarna, *Exodus*, 153. Hugenberger discusses the various symbolic common meals found in the OT and in the ANE and concludes that the common meal in Exod 24:11 is predicated on the offering in v. 5 and Israel's *verba solemnia* (v. 7), which indicates that this meal meets the criteria of a solemn covenant-ratifying meal. Hugenberger, *Marriage as a Covenant*, 210–11.

81. McCarthy's view of the meal in Exod 24 is colored by his thesis that a self-maledictory element is essential to any ratifying oath or analogous act. McCarthy, *Treaty and Covenant*, 254.

82. Sarna, *Exodus*, 152.

83. Meyers, *Exodus*, 206.

84. Childs, *Book of Exodus*, 506.

of Exod 24 where the people are present and involved via the mediation of Moses.[85] The contrast is telling for there is continuity in terms of Yahweh's presence and some ritual details, but the covenant at Sinai is best understood in bilateral terms with mutual covenant obligations.

THE CONTENT OF THE MOSAIC COVENANT

As for the actual substance of the Mosaic covenant, there is a clear moral/ethical standard required of God's covenant people, which is regulated through a combination of apodictic commandments (the Decalogue, see Exod 20; Deut 5), cultic regulations (e.g., the tabernacle instructions of Exod 25—31:18; the Holiness Code of Lev 17-26; Num 5—10:10; 28-30), and casuistic laws (e.g., the Book of the Covenant, Exod 20-23; Deut 12—26:15).[86] Williamson notes that this expected ethical distinctiveness was hinted at in the Abrahamic covenant (Gen 17:1; 18:19; 26:5) and ultimately sets Israel apart among the nations.[87]

The scholarly consensus appropriately affirms that the Mosaic covenant is obligatory with blessings and curses that are instituted as a means of ensuring Israel's faithfulness in keeping the stipulations and obligations of the covenant (e.g., Lev 26; Deut 27—29:1). In terms of the relationship between the various types of legal elements, the apodictic Decalogue (Exod 20:1-17) is the principle embodiment of Yahweh's moral/ethical standards (defining a "holy nation") and these principles are elaborated in specific and practical ways in the cultic regulations and casuistic laws found throughout Exodus to Deuteronomy.

---

85. Garrett, *Exodus*, 543. Hamilton also sees parallels between the theophanic covenant rituals in Gen 15 and Exod 34. Hamilton, *Genesis 1–17*, 436–37. See also Waltke and Fredricks, *Genesis*, 244.

86. Noth observes that "the law" is a complex collection of various types of legal material compiled into discrete literary units. He posits that the following literary units may have been independent texts: Law of Holiness (Lev 16–26), Covenant Code (Exod 20:23—23:19), sacrificial rituals (Lev 1–7), cultic laws on purity (Lev 11–15), the Passover and *Maṣṣoth* festivals (Exod 12:1-20, 43-49), the Day of Atonement (Lev 16), directions on sacrifice (Num 28–29), the Decalogue (Exod 22:2-17; cf. Deut 5:6-21), cultic instructions (Exod 34:11-26), and curses (Deut 27:15-26). Noth, *Laws in the Pentateuch*, 6.

87. Williamson, "Covenant," 150–51.

The Shema and Covenantal Love

Though there is a genuine tendency to reduce the Mosaic covenant to an obligatory, legalistic arrangement, this is a distortion of the covenant's essence. One of the distinctive aspects of the Mosaic covenant is the concept of covenant love that is presented as the essence of the covenant relationship. As noted, the Decalogue represents the "great principles of covenant relationship that outline the nature and character of God and spell out Israel's responsibilities to him."[88] It is first revealed in Exod 20 and then repeated nearly verbatim in Deut 5:6–21. After it is repeated for the Moab generation, the defining principles of the Decalogue are further distilled down to one statement: the Shema (from the first word of Deut 6:4, the imperative "hear," שְׁמַע). This is the definitive commentary on the Decalogue and the heart of the Ten Commandments: "Hear, O Israel: The LORD OUR GOD, THE LORD IS ONE. LOVE THE LORD YOUR GOD WITH ALL YOUR HEART AND WITH ALL YOUR SOUL AND WITH ALL YOUR STRENGTH" (Deut 6:4–5) [NIV]. This single command is considered the essence of the law and this is validated by Jesus' own citation of this command (along with Lev 19:18) as the greatest commandment (Matt 22:34–39; Mark 12:28–31; Luke 10:25–28).

The significance of the statement that "Yahweh is one" is the source of much discussion since there are several ways in which יהוה אלהינו יהוה אחד can be translated.[89] Tigay notes that a definitive interpretation of v. 4 is impossible since the language is open to several valid readings.[90] In surveying the various studies of this text, most commentators conclude that the text is either a defining statement on monotheism, a statement on the exclusivity of Israel's faith, or a statement on Yahweh's ontological or essential unity.[91] Based on a thorough study of the syntax and history of the Shema, Tigay observes that the best attested reading is to see v. 4 as a statement on the

---

88. Merrill, *Deuteronomy*, 162.

89. McConville engages with four possible translations and provides a helpful look at the syntax of the text. He ultimately reduces the issue to whether "one" (אחד) is adjectival ("one") or adverbial ("alone"). McConville, *Deuteronomy*, 140–41. Christensen cites three different translations and sees some validity in each. Christensen, *Deuteronomy 1:1—21:9*, 143.

90. Tigay, *Deuteronomy*, 76.

91. Nelson's survey of the three basic approaches summarizes the issue well. Nelson, *Deuteronomy*, 89–90. Craigie views this as a statement on monotheism. Craigie, *Book of Deuteronomy*, 169. Tigay emphasizes the exclusivity of Yahweh worship and Israel's relationship with him. Tigay, *Deuteronomy*, 76. McConville acknowledges the monotheistic angle but sees the primary emphasis on the exclusivity of Yahweh's relationship with Israel. McConville, *Deuteronomy*, 141. Christensen sees monotheism as implicit but sees Yahweh's "oneness" as the main emphasis. Christensen, *Deuteronomy 1:1—21:9*, 143.

exclusivity of Yahweh worship for his covenant people, but he also notes that the Shema also became a definitive statement on monotheism in the postexilic period.⁹² In addition, Tigay notes that the Shema functioned in Jewish liturgy with the force of a daily oath that pledged allegiance to Yahweh and to the covenant.⁹³

The language of covenant love, "loving" Yahweh (ואהבת את יהוה אלהיך) is significant and Deuteronomy is the first book of the Pentateuch that speaks of this. Tigay interprets "love" as more than an emotional attachment, though this idea is not excluded.⁹⁴ The love for God in this context is a loyal commitment that includes emotional affection, but necessarily "expresses itself in action."⁹⁵ The concept of covenant love is an important theme in Deuteronomy and the basis for Israel's love is consistently based in gratitude for Yahweh's love and deliverance (Deut 4:37–38; 6:10–11).⁹⁶

Moran addresses an interesting perspective on covenantal love in Deuteronomy in his important study of covenant love language in ANE treaties.⁹⁷ Moran views covenant love as a "profane love" that can be commanded in a covenant relationship and is "defined in terms of loyalty, service and obedience."⁹⁸ Whereas Moran's findings suggest a suzerain-vassal model for the "love" commanded in Deut 6:5, McCarthy weighs in with the relevant point that the father-son concept of kinship love is a likely model for the language of covenantal love in Deuteronomy.⁹⁹ Even McCarthy's understanding of the father-son bond in ANE treaties is mainly defined by reverence and loyalty, which coheres with the covenantal understanding of love that most see in Deut 6:5. An important lens for interpreting the love commanded in Deut 6:5 is Yahweh's love for Israel. More than simply using kinship concepts under the influence of ANE treaty language, Deuteronomy

92. See Excursus 10: The Shema (6:4) in Tigay, *Deuteronomy*, 438–41.
93. Tigay, *Deuteronomy*, 440.
94. Tigay, *Deuteronomy*, 76–77.
95. Tigay, *Deuteronomy*, 76–77.
96. McConville, *Deuteronomy*, 142.
97. Moran, "Ancient Near Eastern Background," 77–87.
98. Per Moran, Deuteronomy is both a book of love and an ANE treaty-type document. Thus, the love in Deuteronomy is the covenant love attested in ANE treaties. Moran, "Ancient Near Eastern Background," 81–82.
99. McCarthy argues that the Israelite concept of sonship under Yahweh, the father, is a more likely basis for the love concept in Deuteronomy. ANE father-son relationships were not simply tender bonds but included the central concept of reverential respect and obedience. McCarthy, "Love of God," 144–47. Cross's study affirms the notion that ANE kinship relationships and familial/tribal dynamics are the background for covenant concepts in the OT. Cross compares West Semitic tribal kinship relationships with biblical covenant concepts. Cross, "Kinship and Covenant," 3–21.

describes the love of God in relational terms that transcend simple treaty or kinship language.¹⁰⁰ Therefore, any command, including the Shema, is born out of a divinely initiated relationship characterized by grace in which obedience and loyalty are the proper response.¹⁰¹

The bilateral dynamic involving covenant love (אהב) is manifested in a seminal expression of Yahweh's covenant faithfulness, termed ḥesed (חסד), that is first stated in Exod 20:6 and then reiterated formulaically in Deut 7:9.¹⁰² In these passages, Yahweh is characterized as a loyal, loving God whose covenant faithfulness (ḥesed) is enduring (לאלף דור) but with the caveat that the recipients of his ḥesed are those who love him and keep his commandments (ועשה חסד לאלפים לאהבי ולשמרי מצותי, Exod 20:6).¹⁰³ Thus, the defining command to love Yahweh (ואהבת את יהוה אלהיך) given in the context of the Shema (Deut 6:5) is understood as a defining trait, along with obedience, of the covenant partner who bilaterally experiences Yahweh's covenant love (אהב) and covenant faithfulness (חסד).

Interestingly, the divine trait of ḥesed is used to characterize the faithfulness Yahweh has already exhibited by fulfilling the Abrahamic covenant's promises as seen in the events surrounding the exodus and the possession of the land (Deut 7:8, 12–13). Deuteronomy 7:7–13 indicates that Yahweh's template for being faithful to the Mosaic covenant is the faithfulness he had already demonstrated in fulfilling elements of the Abrahamic promises, such as numerous descendants, a newly constituted nation, and now the gift of the land. This indicates that there is considerable continuity between the Abrahamic and Mosaic covenants since the foundational characteristics of covenant love (אהב) and faithfulness (חסד) define Yahweh's relationship to both covenants. The dynamic of covenant love and faithfulness described in Exod 20:6; 34:6–7; and Deut 7:7–15 indicates that the covenant relationship

---

100. Wright observes that Yahweh's love for Israel is "axiomatic" in that it explains the covenant relationship from God's perspective, but there is no explanation behind Yahweh's decision to love Israel. Wright, *Deuteronomy*, 56.

101. Wright, *Deuteronomy*, 62–63.

102. Britt traces the formulaic use of ḥesed in the HB and concludes that Deut 7:9–20 is a "grace formula" that appears in both full and abbreviated forms numerous times in the canon. He paraphrases the so-called "covenant"/"grace formula" thusly: "Know therefore that the Lord your God is God, the faithful God who maintains the covenant and חסד with those who love him and keep his commandments, to a thousand generations, and who repays in their own person those who reject him." Britt, "Unexpected Attachments," 295.

103. Though the MT of Exod 20:6 literally reads "to thousands" (לאלפים), Sarna notes that this expression corresponds to Deut 7:9 where the equivalent expression explicitly reads "to a thousand generations" (לאלף דור). The JPS translation follows this rendering. Sarna, *Exodus*, 111.

with Israel, expressed in both covenants, is a relationship involving both promise and obligation.[104]

The threefold formula of "heart," "soul," and "strength," is understood to signify the comprehensive nature of the love Yahweh requires of his covenant people.[105] Though there is a real demarcation between the activities of the "heart," "soul," and "strength," the primary thrust of the command is that the people of Israel love Yahweh intensely in a single-minded, whole-hearted manner. In other words, this love must be loyal, undivided, and exclusive. In light of the love Yahweh has already demonstrated by remembering his promises and delivering his suffering people, nothing less could be expected in this covenant relationship. Therefore, the Shema is a crucial core element in the definition of the Mosaic covenant relationship that stresses the exclusivity of the relationship and demands a covenant love that is whole-hearted and completely reliable. The bilateral nature of the Mosaic covenant means loyal love is given and expected.

The Law: Terminology and Types

There is a history of helpful scholarship regarding the various legal terms used of different types of laws and regulations in the Mosaic covenant. A thorough treatment is not necessary in the context of this study, but a brief overview helps to elucidate the relationship between various types of Mosaic legal terms.[106] The term תורה is usually rendered as "law" and is used of a "divine standard of conduct," including both cultic/ceremonial matters and civil/social laws.[107] By the postexilic period, תורה became a standard term for the legal material in the Pentateuch.[108] The oft-paired terms משפטים and חקים/חקות are usually used of "judgments" and "statutes," respectively. "Judgments" (משפטים) is fittingly used of laws and ordinances

104. The dynamic involving both promissory and obligatory aspects in both the Abrahamic and Mosaic covenants coheres with Averbeck's thesis that both covenants entail varying degrees of "permanent promise and ongoing obligation." Averbeck, "Old Testament Treaties," 18.

105. Most scholars see some level of correspondence between "heart, mind, and strength," and the spheres of human activity characterized by intellect, emotion, and physical effort. However, some see a poetic or rhetorical significance more than a literal, ontological one. See Tigay, *Deuteronomy*, 76–77; Nelson, *Deuteronomy*, 91; McConville, *Deuteronomy*, 142.

106. For a helpful lexical study of each legal term, see van der Ploeg, "Studies in Hebrew Law (I)," 248–59; Falk, "Hebrew Legal Terms," 350–54; Falk, "Hebrew Legal Terms: II," 241–44; Falk, "Hebrew Legal Terms: III," 39–44.

107. Enns, "Law of God," 4:893.

108. Enns, "Law of God," 4:895.

(usually casuistic) that pertain to the realm of civil laws and court decisions.[109] "Statutes" (חקים/חקות) is generally used in the same semantic field as משפט, תורה, and מצוה but is often used specifically of cultic law.[110] The term מצוה is rendered commandment or command and is often paired with תורה.[111] The term עדות means statutes or stipulations and is generally used of nonspecified laws or commands or also as a reference to the law given to the exodus generation.[112] Finally, the term דבר can also be used of the Mosaic law, especially since it is used of the Decalogue in Exod 24 (see also Deut 4:2).[113]

Though each term has a specific meaning it is clear that actual usage has resulted in significant overlap in their semantic fields. Thus, various terms are used interchangeably as a synecdoche for the entire corpus of Mosaic covenant laws.[114] When used individually, these terms tend to keep their distinct meaning, but when paired or grouped (e.g., משפטים and חקים), they function idiomatically as a hendiadys-like expression for Mosaic laws.[115] In his thorough study of Hebrew law terms, van der Ploeg concludes that these terms are used as synonyms that refer to any divine commandment.[116] What is evident in the later writings, especially those from the postexilic period, is that the legal terms have become generic means of idiomatically referring to the Mosaic law. Various combinations of legal terms may reflect poetic or rhetorical function more than strict semantic meaning. This development parallels and reflects the manner in which the Mosaic covenant and its laws eventually come to be seen as a single, unified concept with an attendant constellation of legal and covenantal terms.

Future Failure and Hope for Restoration

One of the sources of tension between the Abrahamic and Mosaic covenants is the interplay between Yahweh's sworn oaths and the obligatory nature of the Mosaic covenant. As noted above, this dynamic is present in the very

---

109. Like תורה, the term משפטים can also be used as a reference to a corpus of laws, such as Deuteronomy. Enns, "משפט," 2:1142–43.

110. Enns, "חק," 2:250–51.

111. The term מצוה can also be used as a general reference to Mosaic laws. Enns, "מצוה," 2:1070.

112. Enns, "עדות," 3:328.

113. McConville, *Deuteronomy*, 103.

114. McConville, *Deuteronomy*, 102–3.

115. McConville, *Deuteronomy*, 102–3.

116. Van der Ploeg, "Studies in Hebrew Law: Conclusions," 296.

core understanding of Yahweh's covenant love and faithfulness (חסד). In Exod 20:6, 34:6–7, and Deut 7:7–13, Yahweh's enduring covenant faithfulness is exclusive to those who love him and keep his commandments. So, does the fact that the Mosaic covenant is contingent on the obedience and love of the people jeopardize the promises of land, nationhood, and blessing in any way? This important question is addressed at the end of Deuteronomy when Moses provides Israel with a word of warning and comfort regarding the future. In Deut 29, one of Moses's final speeches includes the dire prediction that Israel will forsake the covenant to the point of catastrophic failure, resulting in national destruction and exile among the nations (Deut 29:21–27). Later in history, the Babylonian exile will bear out the tragic reality predicted in Deut 29:21–27. At this point, it would seem that the jeopardy to the Abrahamic promises is very real.

It is in light of the dire prediction of Deut 29 that Moses's speech in Deut 30:1–10 elicits hope and allays fears regarding the ultimate fulfillment of Yahweh's promises to the patriarchs. In this follow-up speech, it is revealed that Yahweh will graciously leave the door open for Israel to return to Yahweh and be restored to a covenant relationship with him (Deut 30:1–3). McConville sees the significance of this speech in observing that this future reprieve is unprecedented in any ANE treaty form and that the "treaty pattern is, in a sense, overturned by this development."[117] There is an apparent condition that Israel must meet to be restored, and that is returning in repentance and committing anew to obey Yahweh (Deut 30:2–3). If the people genuinely repent and return then Yahweh will bring them back from exile, return them to the land, and bless them even more abundantly than he did their forefathers (Deut 30:4–5). On the surface, this enduring obligatory element means that nothing will mitigate against another generation failing to keep the covenant.

The key to the hope offered in this announcement is found in the novel concept of divine heart-circumcision (Deut 30:6). The closing to this speech hints at a divine work in the hearts of the people ("circumcision of the heart") that results in covenantal obedience, which then brings about Yahweh's ultimate favor and blessing (Deut 30:6–10).[118] Wright discerns a chiastic structure in Deut 30:2a–10a that highlights this divine work of heart-circumcision as the key to the eventual restoration of the people.[119] It

---

117. McConville, *Deuteronomy*, 425.

118. The new covenant (Jer 31:31–34; 32:39–40; Ezek 36:24–27) describes a new relational dynamic that is consistent with the divine work implied in Deut 30:6–10. This differs from the earlier exhortation for Israel to circumcise its own heart since it is not by human agency (cf. Deut 10:16).

119. In Wright's analysis of the chiasm and rhetorical structure, he surmises that the

is this "circumcision of the heart" that is the key to resolving the tension between the Mosaic and Abrahamic covenants for God's work will divinely enable the people to obey and fulfill their covenantal obligations.[120]

Moses's prediction of future exile and restoration is not wholly unfamiliar to the people, for a similar prediction was set in the context of the blessings and curses at the end of the Holiness Code (Lev 17–26). In Lev 26:27–39 the covenant curses reach their climax in war and exile. Wenham notes that the details of the curses in Lev 26:29–33 are more than the "ghastly" consequences of war: they represent the very dismantling of Israel as a great nation (cf. Gen 15, 17).[121] The curse of war gives way to a vivid description of exile (Lev 26:33–39) that is consistent with the threat of exile in Deut 29. Like Moses's speech in Deut 30, the end of Lev 26 anticipates the repentance of the people in exile (vv. 40–41), which will be met with Yahweh's gracious remembrance of the Abrahamic covenant (vv. 42–44). In v. 45, the eventual restoration of the people is compared to the first exodus, and this time it is the Sinai covenant that Yahweh remembers and restores.[122]

Leviticus 26:42–45 provides a remarkable clue regarding the postexilic understanding of the Abrahamic and Mosaic covenants. The postexilic restoration of the land is linked to Yahweh's remembrance of the Abrahamic covenant (v. 42), yet it is the Mosaic covenant that Yahweh remembers when he relents from judgment and brings the people out of exile. The organic blending of covenant obligations with the promised hope of future restoration, even in the face of Israel's failure to keep covenant, exemplifies Averbeck's thesis in which the major biblical covenants entail both permanent promise and ongoing obligation.[123]

"circumcision of the heart" ensures that the covenant's fundamental obligations will be met, albeit as the fruit of divine grace. Wright, *Deuteronomy*, 289.

120. Tigay understands "circumcision" here to mean God will remove "psychological impediments" to covenantal obedience and loyalty. Tigay, *Deuteronomy*, 285; see also Wright, *Deuteronomy*, 348–49. Others tend to view "circumcision" in the context of the new covenant, which suggests a divine empowerment and transformation. Though the nuances may differ, the net effect Tigay describes seems consistent with the type of spiritual work described in the new covenant. For example, see McConville, *Deuteronomy*, 427 and Merrill, *Deuteronomy*, 388–89.

121. Wenham, *Book of Leviticus*, 332.

122. Wenham considers the *berit* in v. 45 to be the Abrahamic covenant, but the appositive clause that modifies "ancestors" (ראשנים) indicates that these "ancestors" are of the exodus generation, which means the covenant is the Sinai covenant. Wenham, *Book of Leviticus*, 332. Hartley also reads the *berit* in v. 45 to be the Sinai covenant. Hartley, *Leviticus*, 471.

123. Averbeck, "Old Testament Treaties," 18.

The Mosaic speeches in Deut 30:1–10 as well as Lev 26:40–46 are the keys to understanding the disposition of the returnees following the exile. There is an expectation that nationwide repentance and a restoration of the Mosaic covenant relationship will cause Yahweh to return the people to the land and bless them in an unprecedented manner.[124] This expectation is also evident in later prophetic texts where the prophets anticipate a gathering of the diaspora and a glorious return to the land (e.g., Isa 40–66; Jer 29; Ezek 34). The anticipation of covenant restoration and divine blessing in the land provides an enlightening perspective on the actual expectations and actions of the postexilic community as depicted in Ezra-Nehemiah and other postexilic writings like Ps 105.

This Mosaic teaching on Israel's future failure and restoration provides the context for the covenant renewal described in Neh 8–10 as well as the manner in which exilic and postexilic writings relate to the Abrahamic promises and the Mosaic covenant. One major question facing the postexilic community is why they are back in the land, as predicted, but without unprecedented blessing in terms of population and prosperity. In postexilic Yehud, the community who returned from exile was dismayed at the oppressive foreign rule, the external threats from surrounding nations, and the poor condition of the land and its cities. From their perspective, some aspects of Moses's predictions seemed to be fulfilled, while others were clearly not. This background will prove invaluable to the rhetorical analysis of the intertextual phenomena in Ps 105.

SUMMARY OF THE MOSAIC COVENANT

The Mosaic covenant consists of several distinct elements, but the overall covenant can be outlined in a fairly straightforward manner. The constitutive covenant-making event takes place at Sinai following the exodus. This covenant-making event includes the defining theophany on Mount Sinai and the mediating activity of Moses. The revelation consists of the Decalogue and the Book of the Covenant. Covenant-ratification is enacted when the people accept the terms of the covenant in conjunction with a multifaceted series of solemn ratification acts. This is followed by the golden calf apostasy, which necessitates the restoration and renewal of the covenant

---

124. Note that Dozeman and Britt both posit that the formulaic use of *ḥesed* based on Exod 20:6; 34:6–7; and Deut 7:7–13 eventually becomes a part of later covenant renewal events. For a study of covenant renewal formulas based on Exod 32–34, see Dozeman, "Inner-biblical Interpretation," 218–23. On the liturgical use of *ḥesed* formulas in later biblical and post-biblical covenant tradition, see Britt, "Unexpected Attachments," 295–96.

with added stipulations that account for Israel's first major covenant violation. Deuteronomy represents a reiteration or renewal of the covenant for a new generation on the verge of entering the land. Deuteronomy includes instructions and casuistic laws that apply the axiomatic principles that were first taught at Sinai. By the time the Moab covenant events take place, the Decalogue and the essence of the covenantal relationship are distilled down to the command known as the Shema. This fundamental description of Yahweh is combined with the essential command for Israel to love Yahweh with heart, soul, and strength.

From the prelude to the covenant (Exod 3 and 6), it is apparent that Yahweh intends for the people to view their covenantal relationship, nationhood, and land possession in terms of the patriarchal promises that comprise the Abrahamic covenant. In fact, one can fairly characterize the Abrahamic covenant as a familial covenant for Abraham and the Mosaic covenant as a national covenant for the nation that issues from Abraham.[125] There is a significant sense of continuity involving Abraham's obedience and the obedience required of his descendants under the Mosaic covenant. There is also continuity in the fulfillment of the Abrahamic promises and the outworking of the Mosaic covenant.

Deuteronomy 7:7–15 describes Yahweh's covenantal faithfulness and love in terms that indicate a bilateral dynamic in which Yahweh's covenant faithfulness is enduring but only for those who love him and keep his commandments. Israel has been constituted into a great nation and is poised to enter the land where they can take their place among the nations. For a nascent nation, the law becomes a crucial set of instructions that shape Israel into the kind of society that blesses its people and the surrounding nations by its distinctive practice of righteousness and justice.[126] On the verge of entering the land, the people have become numerous and have begun to experience the blessings of being Yahweh's special possession. It is understandable that the focus of Deuteronomy would be upon *torah* instruction that leads to blessing in the land.[127] It is in this context that the relationship between the law and the land crystallizes into a major theme of Deuteronomy.[128]

---

125. Averbeck, "Israel, the Jewish People," 32.

126. Alexander, *From Paradise*, 178–79. Per Wright, possession of the land is a significant step in God's plan to bless the nations. Wright, *Deuteronomy*, 25.

127. Rendtorff, *Covenant Formula*, 62–64.

128. Alexander, *From Paradise*, 171–72.

INTER-COVENANTAL CONTINUITY

The Mosaic covenant is closely related to the Abrahamic covenant as evidenced by the various aspects of the patriarchal promises that are linked to the events of the exodus and the events at Sinai (Exod 2:23–25; Deut 7:8, 12–13). For example, Abraham's descendants becoming settlers in a foreign land (Gen 15:13a) becomes reality by the end of Genesis as Jacob and his family sojourn in Egypt and multiply (Gen 46:6–27; Exod 1:6–10). Not only have Abraham's descendants gone into a foreign land, the promise of numerous descendants is already coming to fruition by the beginning of Exodus (e.g., Exod 1:12).

The slavery of the Israelites in Egypt (Exod 1:11–14; 2:23–25; 3:7–10) further fulfills the earlier prediction regarding the oppression of Abraham's descendants (Gen 15:13b). Ultimately, these correspondences set the stage for the promised deliverance of Gen 15:14 and the Exodus narrative places the divine deliverance of Israel in the context of the Abrahamic promises (Exod 3:16–22; 6:2–8; 7:1–5; 11:1–3; Deut 7:8, 12–13). In light of the substantial promise-fulfillment continuity between the covenants, Anderson concludes that the Mosaic covenant is subordinate to the Abrahamic covenant when viewed through the lens of the final canonical form of the Pentateuch.[129] Rendtorff goes as far as to posit that the Abrahamic and Mosaic covenants are simply components of a single covenant between Yahweh and Israel.[130]

While intriguing, these views are not consistent with the approach taken in this study. Considerable inter-covenantal continuity does not completely erase the definitive distinctions between the Abrahamic and Mosaic covenants in terms of their form, purpose, historical setting, and biblical context. Fully subsuming the Mosaic covenant under the Abrahamic covenant or viewing them as a single covenant does not do justice to the biblical depiction of these covenants. Nonetheless, the significant degree of continuity between the two foundational covenants is clear. In the OT, there are very few passages where both covenants are explicitly addressed in relation to one other. Within the Pentateuch, there are two texts that provide valuable insight regarding the relationship between the Abrahamic and Mosaic covenants. A brief look at inter-covenantal continuity in the context of these two texts will be useful when delving into the inter-covenantal relationship addressed in Ps 105.

---

129. Anderson, *Contours*, 137.

130. Rendtorff traces the covenant formula synchronically through the OT and concludes that the continuity between the major biblical covenants means there is one covenant between Yahweh and Israel. Rendtorff, *Covenant Formula*, 78–87.

Exodus 6: A Prelude and a Bridge

In Rendtorff's study of the covenant formula, he traces this formula in its various forms and surveys the covenantal significance of the texts in which it appears.[131] One of the helpful aspects of Rendtorff's study is that his use of the covenant formula brings to light texts that have covenantal significance, even if the given text is not a traditional covenant text.[132] According to Rendtorff, Exod 6 is a text of theological density and significance in the elucidation of the inter-covenantal relationship between the Abrahamic and Mosaic covenants.[133] The importance of Exod 6:2–8 (and Exod 3:1–10) has already been addressed above, but there is a particular aspect in which Exod 6 serves as a prelude to the Mosaic covenant narrative as well as an important theological bridge between the Abrahamic and Mosaic covenants.[134]

Rendtorff notes that Exod 6 is an important bridge text because there is a rhetorical relationship with Gen 17 based on the patriarchal promise of the land, while also setting the stage for the coming Mosaic covenant and the relationship with Israel as his chosen people.[135] This observation coheres with the unique density of significant covenant-related formulas and motifs that are rhetorically significant in Exod 6.[136] First, there is the self-declaration formula, "I am Yahweh," which is featured three times (Exod 6:2, 6, and 8) with two instances framing the text as an *inclusio* that validates Yahweh's pronouncements (vv. 2 and 8).[137] The third instance involves the use of the divine name as a means of validation before the people (v. 6). Second is the theme of covenant with the patriarchs, which is evoked as the background to the impending covenant at Sinai (v. 4). Third, the "remembrance of the

---

131. Rendtorff's synchronic reading of the OT still relies on a source-critical framework. His insights based on this synchronic approach have proven valuable in elucidating the inter-covenantal dynamic between the Abrahamic and Mosaic covenants. Rendtorff, *Covenant Formula*, 14–37.

132. Rendtorff, *Covenant Formula*, 3–4, 25–26, 45, 57. See Appendix B for a list of covenant-related formulas.

133. Rendtorff, *Covenant Formula*, 51.

134. Rendtorff, *Covenant Formula*, 51, 69.

135. Rendtorff identifies a distant chiastic relationship between Gen 17 and Exod 6 in terms of the sequence in which the covenant formula and contents of the covenant are presented. This is one of several literary connections Rendtorff sees in Exod 6 and other key covenant texts, such as Gen 17 and Lev 26. Rendtorff, *Covenant Formula*, 16.

136. Rendtorff notes that the self-declaration formula, the covenant theme, the patriarchal promise of land, the recognition formula, the exodus, the conquest, and the covenant formula in its full form make Exod 6 a unique nexus of covenantal themes and formulas. Rendtorff, *Covenant Formula*, 51.

137. Rendtorff, *Covenant Formula*, 51.

covenant" motif in v. 5 is presented as the " . . . turning point in Israel's destiny."[138] Fourth, the exodus theme and the promised land theme are present as Yahweh discloses his intent to deliver Israel from slavery in Egypt and bring them into the land (vv. 6–8). Fifth, the recognition formula (" . . . they will know that I am Yahweh their God") appears in v. 7.[139] Finally, the covenant formula in its full two-part form can be considered the rhetorical center of this text (v. 7).

Rendorff's analysis of the covenant formula and related elements in Exod 6 demonstrates the unique accumulation of formulaic and thematic covenant-related elements in one literary unit. The significance of this text is that there are notable links looking back to the Abrahamic promise of land in Gen 17 as well as a look forward to the defining elements of Israel's national history, namely, the exodus, the Mosaic covenant, and the fulfillment of the land promise. Yahweh's relationship with the nation of Israel cannot be understood apart from his relationship with Abraham and the patriarchs.

Leviticus 26:40–46: Inter-Covenantal Continuity

One other pentateuchal text is worth addressing for its unique inter-covenantal perspective. As odd as it may seem, there are few places within the Pentateuch where the Abrahamic and Mosaic covenants are discussed within the same literary unit. Leviticus 26:40–46 is noteworthy in this respect. The chapter comes at the end of the Holiness Code (Lev 17–26) and contains the blessings and curses that stand as a motivation to keep the covenant made at Sinai, whether by the offer of blessing or due to fear of the curses.

As discussed earlier, the intensifying cycle of curses in Lev 26 culminates with war and exile (vv. 33–39). Like Deut 30:1–10, Lev 26:40–46 describes a movement of repentance that is met with divine grace and restoration. In v. 42, Yahweh remembers the Abrahamic covenant and begins restoring the land (v. 43). However, in v. 45 deliverance from exile is compared to the exodus, even to the point of evoking the Sinai covenant as the covenant Yahweh remembers and restores.[140] Averbeck notes the significance of the Sinai covenant in v. 45 where the reference to the "ancestors whom I brought out of Egypt" affirms that Yahweh's remembrance of the Sinai covenant takes place alongside his remembrance of the Abrahamic covenant

138. Rendorff, *Covenant Formula*, 51.

139. Rendorff, *Covenant Formula*, 16–17, 50–51.

140. As argued earlier, the syntax of v. 45 indicates that the "ancestors" are not the patriarchs, but the exodus generation who ratified the Sinai covenant with Yahweh.

(v. 42) as the basis for future postexilic covenant restoration and renewal.[141] The remembrance of the Sinai covenant is significant for the deliverance of the people and the renewal of the covenant in the postexilic period is now tied to the Sinai covenant. At the same time, v. 42 ties the restoration of the land to Yahweh's remembrance of the Abrahamic covenant. This exact dynamic will prove crucial in processing the postexilic understanding of the relationship between the two covenants.

There is one other feature of Lev 26:40–46 that is pertinent to this study. Like Exod 6:2–8, Lev 26:40–46 is rich in covenant-related formulas. In vv. 42 and 45 there are repeated occurrences of the remembrance formula, but it is striking that both the Abrahamic and Mosaic covenants are remembered in conjunction with the restoration of the people. The remembrance formula is not a statement regarding Yahweh's intellectual ability to recall a covenant, but rather a formulaic way of affirming the axiom that Yahweh never breaks his covenant.[142] In fact, Schottroff views Yahweh's act of "remembering" his covenant as a demonstration of his covenant pledge, "I am Yahweh your God" (the self-declaration formula).[143]

The self-declaration formula occurs twice in this passage (vv. 44–45) and in both cases, it is used to punctuate Yahweh's intention to remember and keep his covenant. Israel's violation of the covenant is expressed using Mosaic torah terms, such as "judgments" and "statutes" (v. 43), which brings together three covenant-related formulaic elements: the self-declaration formula, the remembrance formula, and torah terminology. This accumulation of formulas and themes, as in Exod 6:2–8, attests to the continuity between the Abrahamic and Mosaic covenants. In fact, Rendtorff sees a reciprocal relationship between Exod 6:7 and Lev 26:12 where the two-part (Variant C) covenant formula appears in an almost identical manner.[144] Rendtorff concludes that Gen 17-to-Exod 6:2-8-to-Lev 26 forms a discrete

---

141. Averbeck comments on the inter-covenantal continuity in Lev 26 by noting that the Mosaic covenant is a "natural extension of the Abrahamic covenant and, as a result, carries the promises of the latter forward into the future of Israel as a nation." Thus, "the Mosaic covenant promises of God are as permanent as the Abrahamic promises." Averbeck, "Old Testament Treaties," 25. See also Averbeck, "Israel, the Jewish People," 34–35.

142. In the remembrance formula, Schottroff observes that זכר ("remember") is the opposite of הפך ("break"), not שכח ("forget"). This idiom is about preserving covenant, not memory. The remembrance formula is most significant when Yahweh enters history to redeem his people, especially when the covenant is threatened by the people. Schottroff, *Gedenken*, 206. See also Hartley, *Leviticus*, 469.

143. Schottroff, *Gedenken*, 206. See also Hartley, *Leviticus*, 469.

144. Rendtorff, *Covenant Formula*, 18–19. See Appendix B for the covenant formula variants.

strand of interconnected covenantal formulas and themes that amount to an "indissoluble cohesion."[145] The nature of this continuity will prove helpful in delineating the postexilic understanding of the covenants, especially in relation to the psalmist's use of textual markers in his allusions to the Mosaic covenant.

---

145. Rendtorff, *Covenant Formula*, 21–22, see also 49–51.

8

An Analysis of the Covenant Intertextualities in Psalm 105

ALLUSIONS AND REFERENCES

IN TERMS OF THE allusion validation process, chapters 4 through 7 of this work address an analysis of the rhetorical argument of the referring text (Ps 105) and the stable meaning of the referents, the Abrahamic and Mosaic covenants. The final stage of this study entails the final three phases of validation and analysis: identifying the textual markers, discerning the rhetorical relationship between the referring text and the referents, and finally, the imported meaning and/or rhetorical impact of both covenants on the psalmist's composition.

Once the Abrahamic covenant references and the Mosaic covenant allusions have been analyzed, this study will delve into the way the psalmist has incorporated both covenants for rhetorical effect. The Abrahamic covenant references function within the psalmist's argument regarding the reliability of Yahweh as a covenant partner, both in his faithfulness and his sovereignty. The Mosaic covenant is incorporated into the psalmist's subtext in order to address Israel's past covenant failure and future path to covenant renewal. This intertextual analysis culminates in an examination of the inter-covenantal relationship in light of Ps 105.

INTERTEXTUAL MARKERS IN PSALM 105

In her seminal study of literary allusion, Ben-Porat points out that an allusive marker is usually textual but can also be a subtler signal exhibiting varying degrees of explicitness in accordance with the poetic function of the allusion.[1] The textual marker must be able to evoke an outside text or referent by linking recognizable elements from the referent with a corresponding element in the alluding text. Thus, it is possible for a subtle feature of an evoked text to be used as an allusive marker. The key is recognition by the reader, which is a function of relevance and context. Using principles derived from relevance theory, Klingler identifies two criteria that are essential traits of a valid allusive textual marker. First, the markers must be relevant, meaning, if the reader correctly follows the developing meaning of the alluding text, the markers should be comprehensible. Second, the marker should facilitate the reader's identification and comprehension of the marker with minimal processing effort.[2]

This section involves an examination of each textual marker and how these markers evoke a text or covenantal element that allows the reader to recognize the relevant aspect of the covenant in question. In the case of the Abrahamic covenant, the literary references are marked by explicit markers so the criteria used of allusive markers are not applicable. In the case of the allusive markers that link the Mosaic covenant to Ps 105, the formulaic nature of the self-declaration (הוא יהוה אלהינו) in v. 7, the *ḥesed-berit* expression "to a thousand generations" (לאלף דור) in v. 8b, and the torah synecdoche in v. 45 (ישמרו חקיו ותורתיו ינצרו) facilitate the validation of these allusive textual markers.

The Abrahamic Covenant Markers in Psalm 105

As noted, the Abrahamic covenant textual markers (vv. 8–11, 42) are literary references to the Abrahamic covenant with an emphasis on the promise of land made to Abraham and the patriarchs. A simple means of distinguishing an allusion from a reference is the removal of the referent from the evoking text. If the text is incomprehensible without the referent, it is a reference since the referent is rhetorically equivalent to the textual marker; however, if

---

1. An allusive marker can be subtle, like a metrical or syntactical feature. Ben-Porath, "Poetics of Allusion," 6.
2. Klingler, "Validity," 178–79.

the evoking text makes sense without the referent, it is an allusion since the referent adds imported meaning that transcends the textual marker.[3]

Thus, in the case of Ps 105:8–11, the referent is the Abrahamic covenant and the promise of land, which is clear since the textual marker consists of a litany of parallel expressions for the Abrahamic covenant (e.g., "eternal covenant," the "word of promise made to a thousand generations," "the oath sworn to Isaac," the "decree established with Jacob," and the "eternal covenant established with Israel") culminating in a statement of the land promise (vv. 8–11). If Ps 105:8–11 were read without the Abrahamic covenant as a referent, the passage would make no sense since the textual markers are rhetorically equivalent to the referent. The psalmist is simply referencing the Abrahamic covenant in an explicit manner, which means that there is no imported intertextual meaning.

The Mosaic Covenant Markers in Psalm 105

Applying this diagnostic test to Ps 105:7a, 8b, and 45 yields a positive result for the three references to the Mosaic covenant. When Ps 105:7 is read without the referent (the Mosaic covenant), the text still makes sense and has coherence within its immediate context. In Ps 105:7, the psalmist is transitioning from a hymnic opening call to worship into the main body of the psalm. The statement, "He is the LORD our God," concludes the hymnic call to worship while also transitioning into the section where the psalmist expounds on the Abrahamic covenant. This passage does not require the Mosaic covenant as a referent in order to be comprehensible.

In Ps 105:8, the psalmist has begun a series of affirmative propositions about the Abrahamic covenant (vv. 8–11) and in v. 8 the promise made to the patriarchs is characterized as enduring "to a thousand generations." This verse makes perfect sense without any knowledge of the Mosaic covenant and *ḥesed* as addressed in Deut 7:9/Exod 20:6. Again, this signals the presence of an allusive marker.

In Ps 105:45, the psalmist concludes by declaring that Yahweh has faithfully fulfilled his promise of land so that his people might "keep his statutes and his laws." Once again, the ending to the psalm can be read coherently without an explicit reference to the Mosaic covenant. Though this example is not as clear, the reader can read "statutes and laws" in a general reference to God's commands. In all three cases, there is an allusive textual marker pointing to the Mosaic covenant.

---

3. Machacek, "Allusion," 527.

The Self-Declaration Formula: "I am YHWH your God"

The allusive marker in v. 7 is the statement "He is the LORD our God" (הוא יהוה אלהינו). This statement is a third-person rendering of the so-called self-declaration formula "I am the LORD your God" (אני יהוה אלהיכם) in its extended form. The basic self-declaration (or self-introduction) formula "I am YHWH" (אני יהוה) occurs in several texts that have covenantal significance for the Abrahamic and Mosaic covenants (see Gen 15:7; 28:13; Exod 6:2, 6–8; 20:2; Lev 26:45; Deut 5:6).[4] The different variants of the self-declaration formula are used throughout Exodus, Leviticus, and Numbers in a variety of ways.[5] The most basic use is to identify Yahweh as the God of the patriarchs and Israel, which can include being used in combination with the so-called recognition formula (" . . . that they will know that I am Yahweh their God"). The use of the self-declaration formula as an identifier or in the recognition formula includes texts that are covenantally significant, such as, Exod 6:7; 16:12; 20:2, 5; Lev 11:44; 26:13; Deut 5:6; 29:6. The use of the recognition formula often relates to the validation of Yahweh before the people. Both variants are also used as a punctuator that emphasizes Yahweh's authority and sanction in important pronouncements and sections of legal material (e.g., Exod 6:2, 8; Lev 18:4, 30; 19:3–4, 10, 12, 14, 32, 34; 21:12; 22:3, 8, 30, 31, 33; 26:1; Num 3:45).

Though the self-declaration formula in Ps 105:7 can refer to numerous pentateuchal texts, Exod 6:2–8 is the seminal referent and this is where the formula is used twice as a punctuator (Exod 6:2 and 8) and in the recognition formula that addresses Yahweh's validation before the people (v. 7). As discussed earlier, Rendtorff views Exod 6 as a unique bridge text in that the patriarchal promises are connected to the exodus and the Sinai covenant.[6] The connection of the self-declaration formula with the covenant concept is valid. Schottroff also sees the remembrance formula as a concrete expression of the self-declaration formula since Yahweh is committing to preserve the covenant relationship, which is essentially distilled to the statement, "I

---

4. Since Deut 5:6 is a reiteration of Exod 20:2 in the context of the Decalogue in Deuteronomy, this study will focus on Exod 20:2, understanding Deut 5:6 as a parallel text.

5. Wenham posits that the use of the self-declaration formula may echo the preamble in Hittite treaty texts. He also views the formula as a condensed covenant formula (not to be confused with the covenant formula, "I will be your God and you will be my people"). Wenham further notes that it has its roots in the first revelation of the divine name to Moses in Exod 6 and connects to the patriarchal promises. This formula also evokes the command "Be holy for I am holy" (Lev 11:44) and serves as a motivation for following certain laws. Wenham, *Leviticus*, 250–51.

6. Rendtorff, *Covenant Formula*, 51, 69.

am Yahweh your God."[7] Per Wenham, "[the self-declaration formula] may also be described as the covenant formula. This has merit because this short phrase, only three words in Hebrew, encapsulates the fundamental truths about the Sinai Covenant."[8]

The usage of the self-declaration formula in Exodus, Leviticus, and Numbers, demonstrates that this simple yet profound formula is a key element in Mosaic covenant and Mosaic law texts. This formula also appears once in the context of the Abrahamic covenant (Gen 15:7) and identifies Yahweh as the covenant God of Abraham (Gen 17:1; 28:13). In fact, the parallel declaration formula using El Shaddai or Elohim functions similarly in the context of the patriarchal narratives (cf. Gen 17:1; 26:24; 28:13).[9]

In terms of Klingler's criteria for a valid marker, the literary context of Ps 105:7, which is in the midst of covenantal material (vv. 7–11) indicates that the referent is relevant to the author's developing argument. As for ease of recognition, the formulaic nature of the self-declaration statement in Ps 105:7 renders it highly recognizable to the psalmist's audience, requiring minimal processing effort for recognition.

The Mosaic Covenant and Ḥesed

The second Mosaic covenant allusion features the expression לאלף דור ("to a thousand generations"). In its immediate literary context, this expression is used to describe the Abrahamic promise of land in Ps 105:8b. This expression is only found verbatim in Deut 7:9 where Moses describes Yahweh as Israel's God who faithfully keeps covenant with those who love him and keep his commandments.[10] The exact correspondence between this expres-

---

7. Schottroff, *Gedenken*, 206.

8. Wenham, *Leviticus*, 251.

9. Rendtorff sees a contrastive relationship between the self-declaration "I am El Shaddai" of Gen 17:1 and the self-declaration "I am YHWH" in Exod 6:2. The self-declaration formula using "YHWH" is an advancement in understanding God's covenant identity. Rendtorff, *Covenant Formula*, 15.

10. The Hebrew expression in Deut 7:9 שמר הברית והחסד (lit. "keeps covenant and covenant loyalty") can also be read as a syndetic construction where חסד functions adverbially to express the manner in which Yahweh keeps his covenant. Tigay, *Deuteronomy*, 88. Craigie takes a more literal approach reading the phrase as a simple conjunctive construction where Yahweh keeps both covenant *and* covenant loyalty. Craigie, *Deuteronomy*, 176, 180. See also Christensen, *Deuteronomy 1:1—21:9*, 155. McConville reads the construction as a hendiadys where the two nouns explain one another, which he translates as, "who in faithful love keeps covenant." McConville, *Deuteronomy*, 148–49. Weinfeld also reads a hendiadys, but renders it "a gracious covenant." Weinfeld, *Deuteronomy 1–11*, 370.

sion in Ps 105:8 and in Deut 7:9 suggests that לאלף דור is a textual marker for a valid literary allusion.

Deuteronomy 7:7–13 is an important commentary on Yahweh's selection of Israel to be his chosen nation via the Mosaic covenant. This Mosaic discourse explains Israel's selection in terms of his covenant love (אהב) and covenant faithfulness (חסד), which is demonstrated by his fulfillment of the Abrahamic promises in the exodus and conquest (Deut 7:8). Sarna notes that Deut 7:9 corresponds to Exod 20:6 where a similar expression, "to thousands" (לאלפים), is used to describe the enduring nature of Yahweh's *ḥesed* to those who love him and keep the commandments stipulated in the Mosaic covenant.[11] In fact, Routledge takes the collocation of *berit* and *ḥesed*, which he renders "covenant of love," to be an identifier for the covenant at Sinai.[12]

Whereas *ḥesed* stands alone in Deut 5:9–10 and Exod 20:6, it is collocated with *berit* in Deut 7:9–10, which McConville understands as "covenant" and "faithful love" defining one another.[13] Thus, Deut 7:9 and Exod 20:6 address Yahweh's *ḥesed* in relation to the Mosaic covenant, yet Deut 7:8 also relates Yahweh's *ḥesed* to the Abrahamic promises by citing Yahweh's faithfulness to the patriarchs as the template for his pledged faithfulness to the Mosaic covenant.[14] The inter-covenantal dynamic in Deut 7 indicates that both covenants are based on Yahweh's covenant love (אהב) and faithfulness (חסד).

In a recent study of חסד in the Hebrew Bible, Britt makes the case that Deut 7:9–10 represents a "covenant" or "grace formula" that is an example of the "patterned" use of *ḥesed* in late biblical covenant traditions.[15] The formulaic use of Deut 7:9–10 and Exod 20:6 in later biblical writings and liturgical settings creates a tenable scenario in which these texts would have been familiar to the psalmist and his audience. Furthermore, the formulaic or liturgical use of such covenant texts increases the potential rhetorical impact of this allusion since the textual marker would be readily recognizable and the desired rhetorical effect could be elicited with minimal processing effort.

---

11. Though Exod 20:6 literally reads "to thousands" (לאלפים), Sarna affirms the JPS translation of "to a thousand generations" based on לאלף דור in Deut 7:9. Sarna, *Exodus*, 111.

12. Routledge, "Ḥesed as Obligation," 187.

13. McConville, *Deuteronomy*, 157.

14. McConville, *Deuteronomy*, 158.

15. Britt, "Unexpected Attachments," 295–96.

The Law and the Covenant

The final allusive marker in Ps 105:45 is fairly clear since the terms for the law (חקות and תורות) are a known means of referring to the Mosaic law.[16] Though both terms do have individual root meanings, when used in pairs or groups the standard Mosaic legal terms (e.g., קים, תורה, משפט, מצוה, עדות) are used synonymously in a hendiadys-like manner as a reference to the whole Mosaic law.[17] The combination of terms may be influenced by the individual meaning of the terms, but it may also be related to a given poetic, literary, or rhetorical context.

The issue is whether this is an allusive marker or a strict literary reference to the law itself. In this instance, the text can be read without the ostensible referent, the Mosaic covenant, and still make sense; however, if the referent is changed to the Mosaic law, then the marker is simply a literary reference. The key to resolving this issue is the formulaic use of synecdoche involving legal terms as a way of referring to the Mosaic covenant. Outside of the Pentateuch, the law often functions as the part that represents the whole (the Mosaic covenant). Eichrodt viewed the law as an essential part of the covenant and understood the law, not in strictly legal terms, but as the relational key to loyalty and covenant love in the divine-human relationship.[18]

In recent scholarship, some have raised questions concerning the precise relationship between covenant and law. Sperling posits that changes in the language of late writings demonstrate that the law had become a legal abstraction divorced from the concept of covenant.[19] On this question McCarthy offers helpful perspective by arguing that the changes in the covenantal and legal language of later OT books are the result of the new realities facing the postexilic community.[20] McCarthy concludes that the

---

16. "Statutes" (חקות) is often used together with תורה and can specifically refer to cultic regulations. Enns, "חק," 2:250–51. By the exilic/postexilic period, "law" (תורה) had become a standard term for the Mosaic legal material in the Pentateuch. It generally refers to a divine standard for conduct in cultic and civil spheres. Enns, "Law of God," 4:895.

17. McConville, *Deuteronomy*, 102–3.

18. Eichrodt sees Deut 6:4 (the Shema) as summary statement of God's intentions for the Mosaic covenant relationship. Eichrodt, "Covenant and Law," 309–14.

19. Sperling's study is based on the premise that in Israel's earlier history, bilateral covenants were necessarily used as a metaphor for monotheism. However, in the postexilic period, Jewish monotheism was established and such covenants were no longer necessary. Therefore, *torah* became an abstract set of rules, rather than laws defining covenantal loyalty. Sperling, "Rethinking Covenant," 51–53.

20. McCarthy, "Covenant and Law," 40–41.

essential relationship between covenant and law is still the same, which is that the law provides the community with a fundamental means of expressing loyalty to its covenant lord.[21] Rendtorff also observes that the required obedience to the law is a major covenantal theme related to the defining of Yahweh's chosen people.[22] In fact, the specific combination חקות and תורות ("statutes" and "laws") found in Ps 105:45 is used in the Prophets in reference to Mosaic covenant violation or renewal (see 2 Kgs 17:37; Amos 2:4; Mal 3:22 [MT]; Neh 9:13; 10:30 [MT]; 2 Chr 33:8).

One other factor commends the view that the textual marker in Ps 105:45 is an allusive marker that evokes the Mosaic covenant. In the development of the Mosaic covenant, a distinct and important theme emerges: the crucial nature of obedience to the law in relation to inhabiting the land. Clines notes that Leviticus features the land as the context in which the laws and ordinances are to be kept.[23] In Deuteronomy, Clines sees an emphasis on promise and fulfillment, but also an equal emphasis on the requirement of Israel's obedience, especially with regard to Israel's experience of blessings and curses.[24] Against this backdrop, the link between the fulfillment of the land promise and obedience to the law in Ps 105:44–45 takes on greater coherence. The implication is that there is now a context in which the Mosaic covenant would be relevant to the psalmist's readers. Given the ease of recognition, the inextricable link between law and covenant as well as the high degree of relevance to the context of Ps 105:44–45, it is likely that the psalmist's readers would have understood חקות and תורות as a metonymic allusion to the Mosaic covenant.

THE RHETORICAL FUNCTION OF THE ABRAHAMIC AND MOSAIC COVENANT IN PSALM 105

To this point, the alluding text, the evoked referents, and the textual markers have been discerned and examined. These elements lay the necessary groundwork for the final phase of this intertextual study. The remaining task is arguably the heart of this study as the rhetorical relationship between Ps 105 and the intertextual use of the Abrahamic and Mosaic covenants is examined in terms of rhetorical effect. As for the Abrahamic covenant

21. McCarthy, "Covenant and Law," 40–41.
22. Rendtorff, *Covenant Formula*, 49–55.
23. Clines, *Theme of the Pentateuch*, 56–57.
24. Clines, *Theme of the Pentateuch*, 98–99. Per Hossfeld, the link between Israel's obedience to the law and blessing in the land is a prominent theme of the Deuteronomist. Hossfeld, "Eine poetische Universalgeschichte," 303.

literary references, no further validation is necessary since they do not import meaning as allusions do. The primary emphasis for the remainder of this chapter is the rhetorical analysis of the three Mosaic covenant allusions in Ps 105:7, 8, and 45.

Intertextual rhetorical analysis entails a study of the rhetorical relationship between the alluded text (the Mosaic covenant) and the psalmist's developing argument as well as the imported meaning of each allusion and the resulting rhetorical effect. In other words, the referent is the Mosaic covenant in all three allusions, but the specific manner in which each allusion imports the covenant into the psalm differs. Determining the rhetorical significance of the three allusions helps elucidate the Mosaic covenant subtext that resolves a major problem in the psalm: how can the people experience covenant blessing having returned to the land by Yahweh's covenant faithfulness.

The Abrahamic Covenant

The Abrahamic covenant is featured in direct literary references therefore, the rhetorical significance of this covenant is not found in an evoked referent but in the immediate text. The Abrahamic covenant is the key to understanding the psalmist's rhetorical thought process and argument. In the postexilic setting, it is clear that the psalmist is concerned with the same overriding issue that is addressed in other postexilic writings, such as Ezra-Nehemiah, namely the question of the people's relationship to the land. In light of the exile, the psalmist uses his poetic medium to explore the question of whether there is a basis for hope regarding the possibility of prospering in the land.[25]

The canonical placement of Ps 105 does not bear directly on this study since this study's method is predicated on an author-centric analysis of the alluding text. However, it is worth looking at Ps 105's place in Book IV of the Psalter as a way of elucidating the significance of the Abrahamic covenant and the patriarchs in this canonical context. Assuming the editor(s)/compiler(s) read and understood the psalmist's intentions, a brief look at the canonical significance of Ps 105 can be a supplemental means of shedding light on the psalmist's understanding of the Abrahamic covenant.

Despite being back in the land, the postexilic community was far from settled. The temple and Jerusalem were being rebuilt, but the Davidic monarchy was no more, resulting in political instability from both internal

---

25. The exilic and postexilic elements in the psalm are discussed earlier in chapter 4 of this work in the section, "The Exile as the Key to Dating Ps 105."

and external threats. In light of this postexilic reconstruction, deClaissé-Walford concludes that the question of "What are we to do?" is the major theme of Books IV and V of the Psalter.[26] In Book IV the editors of the Psalter have compiled and arranged psalms so as to "remind the postexilic community that YHWH was their king long before the days of David and Solomon and tell the people that YHWH will continue to be their king with all the identity and stability that kingship entails."[27] The editorial activity is apparent since Book IV opens with Ps 90, an appropriate lament in light of the collapse of the Davidic dynasty and the national tragedy addressed in Ps 89. This lament gives way to hope by the end of Book IV, which is where Ps 105 is paired with Ps 106 as the conclusion to the book.

It is against this backdrop of postexilic uncertainty and national soul-searching over the future in the land that the striking appearance of Abraham as a prominent figure in Ps 105 makes sense. Since the promise of land was solemnized as an oath (Gen 22:15–18) and then confirmed to the patriarchs, it is logical that the psalmist would use the Abrahamic covenant as a fixed point in the rhetorical argument of the psalm. It is important to keep in mind that even the Mosaic covenant was fraught with uncertainty since the people were aware that it was their failure to keep that covenant that resulted in the exile. Thus, in the midst of Book IV where Moses has supplanted David, so to speak, the prominent appearance of Abraham and the patriarchs must be understood as a rhetorically and theologically significant moment in the Psalter.

The psalmist's rhetorical strategy makes use of the Abrahamic covenant and its sworn promise of land as the basis for his argument. In order to affirm the reliability of the divine promise, the psalmist uses historical narrative to validate his position. The curated historical narrative supports the psalmist's appeal to the Abrahamic covenant in two significant ways. First, the historical narrative validates the covenant faithfulness of Yahweh, and second, the narrative validates the sovereign ability of Yahweh. Therefore, if Yahweh is loyal to his sworn promise and if he is fully capable of keeping his promise, then Israel has a basis for hope. In terms of poetic and rhetorical structure, the references to the promise given (Ps 105:8–11) and the promise fulfilled (Ps 105:42) form an *inclusio* around the narrative. The rhetorical significance of the Abrahamic covenant and the psalmist's concerns in light of postexilic realities establishes the backdrop against which the allusions to the Mosaic covenant and the resulting subtext can be understood.

26. deClaissé-Walford, *Reading from the Beginning*, 82.
27. deClaissé-Walford, *Reading from the Beginning*, 82.

The Self-Declaration Formula in Psalm 105:7

The Referent: Exodus 6:2–8; 20:2 (Deuteronomy 5:6)

The use of the phrase, "He is the LORD our God" in v. 7 signals an allusion to the Mosaic covenant using a formulaic statement that uniquely identifies Yahweh as Israel's covenant partner. The self-declaration formula appears in the first person ("I am the LORD your God") in several pivotal places in the Mosaic covenant narrative. The most readily identifiable occurrence is Exod 20:2/Deut 5:6 where the self-declaration of the divine name opens the giving of the Decalogue, both at Sinai and on the plains of Moab. The other referent, Exod 6:2–8, is found in an important text that serves as the prelude to the Mosaic covenant narrative in Exodus. In fact, Noth observes that early traditions (pre-exilic) used the covenant formula "Yahweh the god of Israel, and Israel the people of Yahweh" as a way of indicating that Yahweh and Israel were joined in a covenant relationship that was first established at Sinai.[28] The self-declaration formula is also closely related to the covenant formula ("I will be your God and you will be my people"), both lexically and in terms of the relational dynamic.[29] The self-declaration formula identifies Yahweh with the reality of the covenant formula. In effect, "I will be your God" is realized in the self-declaration, "I am Yahweh your God."[30]

The self-declaration formula in Exod 20:2/Deut 5:6 functions like a title-line in ANE documents where the suzerain king customarily identifies himself to introduce royal proclamations, treaties, and law collections.[31] The prominence of the self-identification declaration at the opening of the Decalogue establishes Yahweh's authority and identity as Israel's covenant God. The declaration of Yahweh's name has covenantal significance, which makes this formula an effective referent that evokes the Mosaic covenant and Yahweh's unique covenant role. The rhetorical effect of this referent is fairly straightforward. The recognition of this self-declaration formula evokes the Decalogue, the Covenant Code, the covenant-making narrative from Sinai as well as the renewal on the plains of Moab. In essence, the

---

28. Noth, *Laws in the Pentateuch*, 37.

29. These formulas are not crystallized into specific lexical-syntactic forms, but rather express a fundamental idea using semantically related terms and equivalent constructions that are easily identifiable.

30. Schottroff makes a similar connection between the covenant formula and the self-declaration formula. Schottroff, *Gedenken*, 206.

31. Sarna, *Exodus*, 15. For examples of self-introductory declarations in ANE documents and inscriptions see Sarna, *Exodus*, 240n17.

recognition of this formula brings the whole of the Mosaic covenant into the rhetorical context of Ps 105.

The second referent may not be as obvious, but Exod 6:2–8 is a unique nexus where major covenant themes and formulas are linked to form an inter-covenantal bridge that spans the Abrahamic covenant (specifically Gen 17:1–8) and the Mosaic covenant. Therefore, this writer approaches Exod 6:2–8 as the key referent, while also allowing for other covenantal themes and concepts to be included in the constellation of relevant intertextual links located in Exod 6. In this sense, Exod 6:2–8 functions as a text that brings other covenant-related texts and concepts into the rhetorical context of Ps 105. While Exod 20:2/Deut 5:6 represent a straightforward referent, Exod 6:2–8 is rhetorically and intertextually more complex.

Before addressing the rhetorical significance of Exod 6:2–8 with respect to the entire psalm, it is necessary to examine the rhetorical relationship between Ps 105:7 and Exod 6:2–8 in this specific section (Ps 105:5–11). Since the psalmist is about to introduce the Abrahamic covenant and the promise to the patriarchs as the explicit focus of the developing argument (vv. 8–11), the placement of the Mosaic covenant allusion in v. 7 is significant. The self-declaration formula evokes Exod 6:2–8, which narrates the divine discourse in which Yahweh reveals his salvific and covenantal intentions. An allusion to this "bridge text" fits in the developing rhetorical context of Ps 105:5–11 because v. 7 also serves as a "bridge" between the hymnic introduction and the discourse on the Abrahamic covenant. Though vv. 8–11 seem to speak generally of the Abrahamic covenant, v. 11 narrows the focus to the land promise.

The promise of land also serves as a key intertextual link between Exod 6:2–8 and Gen 17:7–8. In one instance, the covenant formula is connected to the land promise and in the other instance, the self-declaration formula is connected to the land promise. The land is first promised by a unilateral covenant ceremony in Gen 15, but Gen 17:7–8 repeats the promise of land directly in conjunction with Variant A of the covenant formula ("I will be your God and the God of your descendants after you . . . I will be their God." Gen 17:7b, 8b). The key to this intertextual link is Gen 17:7–8 where the promise of land is framed by two occurrences of the covenant formula (Variant A).[32] In Exod 6:2–8, the self-declaration formula using the divine name occurs three times (vv. 2, 7, and 8). In Gen 17:1, God addresses himself to Abraham using an alternate version of the self-declaration formula, "I am El Shaddai" (אני־אל שדי).[33] This is an important intertextual clue because in

---

32. Rendtorff, *Covenant Formula*, 15. See also Appendix B.
33. Rendtorff, *Covenant Formula*, 15.

Exod 6:3, God tells Moses that he was known to the patriarchs as "El Shaddai" but not as Yahweh. The divine name is tied to God's covenant-making, and in Gen 17 and Exod 6 (see also Exod 20:2), there is an intertextual relationship between the Abrahamic land promise (Gen 17:7–8) and God's self-declaration by his covenant name, Yahweh.

The intertextual links between Exod 6:2–8 and Gen 17:7–8 are significant for not only is Gen 17 an important Abrahamic covenant text, it lays the groundwork for the continuity between the Abrahamic and Mosaic covenants. In Gen 17:7–8, Yahweh states:

> 7 I will establish my covenant as an everlasting covenant between me and you and your descendants after you for the generations to come, to be your God and the God of your descendants after you. 8 The whole land of Canaan, where you now reside as a foreigner, I will give as an everlasting possession to you and your descendants after you; and I will be their God." [NIV]

This is a rich text that speaks of the "everlasting covenant," ברית עולם, in such a way that the substance of the covenant is more than land, it is the covenant formula (variant A), which is repeated twice (" . . . to be God to you and to your offspring after you . . . I will be their God."). Rendtorff observes, " . . . it is especially significant that in this case the covenant formula stands right at the beginning of God's history with Israel, as an explication of what God's *berît* means for Abraham and his descendants."[34] This is rhetorically significant since the field of relevant references must include the promise of land and the covenant formula.

In addition to the promise of land and the Mosaic covenant, the covenant formula and self-declaration formula featured in Exod 6:2–8 are closely related to the concept of covenant election (בחיר, "chosen").[35] Rhetorically, this connection to covenant election in Ps 105:7 works in concert with the unusual appropriation of Mosaic and Davidic terms that are found in vv. 6, 15, and 43. The psalmist uses terms, such as "servant" (עבד), "chosen" (בחיר), and "anointed" (משיח), in reference to the people of Israel. In essence, the psalmist is saying that the God who "chose" Moses and "anointed" David, and called both of "his servants" is the same God who has elected Abraham and his descendants to be his people (the covenant formula). Rendtorff notes that בחר ("choose") is tied to the covenant formula

---

34. Rendtorff, *Covenant Formula*, 15.

35. Rendtorff traces the relationship between the covenant formula and election in the OT and notes that the covenant formula is an important link between *covenant* and *election*, two of the most fundamental terms for the divine-human relationship. Rendtorff, *Covenant Formula*, 39, see also 51–52.

in Deut 7:6 and 14:2 so that the use of בחר in a covenant context becomes an expression for election.³⁶ Interestingly, Abraham is never referred to as "chosen" in Genesis, but Yahweh *chooses* Abram (בחרת באברם, Neh 9:7) in Neh 9, which has several affinities to Ps 105.³⁷ Thus, Ps 105:6 can be understood as an affirmation of covenant election.

The link between the covenant formula and election (בחר) can also be demonstrated in relation to ANE marriage formulas. Sohn's study of the covenant formula suggests a novel means of connecting the covenant formula to the Mosaic covenant. As Sohn explores the origin of the OT covenant formula as an ANE marriage formula, he details both a proclamational and descriptive marriage formula in ANE contexts.³⁸ Sohn concludes that "the concept and formulas of covenant expressing the intimate relationship between Yahweh and Israel are essentially the same as those of marriage."³⁹ Sohn points out that the covenant formula and the election formula are distinct, but interrelated concepts in the OT.⁴⁰ He does note that there is no election without covenant, but if there is election, a covenant necessarily follows, which is why these formulas can be used interchangeably.⁴¹ So Sohn views the exodus and the covenant at Sinai as Yahweh and Israel entering "into a mutual relationship through election and into a legal bond through a covenant."⁴² The language used by Yahweh in Exod 29:45–46 resembles the imagery of marriage, for it depicts Yahweh dwelling with his chosen bride like a "newly wedded couple in their new home."⁴³

Sohn's research indicates that the self-declaration formula of Ps 105:7 may also evoke the election of Israel and the Mosaic covenant relationship via marriage imagery. When the psalmist opens the historical narrative section of the psalm by stating that "He is the LORD our God," he reminds the reader that Israel is related to Yahweh by an intimate, relational covenant bond. This establishing statement further reminds the audience that the nation is the covenantal possession and partner of Yahweh, which takes the audience back to Sinai. Rhetorically, the self-declaration formula is akin to the psalmist telling the postexilic community to remember that God is your covenant "husband" by dint of the covenant at Sinai.

36. Rendtorff, *Covenant Formula*, 3, 9, 39, 67–68.
37. Rendtorff, "Nehemiah 9," 112. See also Rendtorff, *Covenant Formula*, 3, 9.
38. Sohn, "I Will Be Your God," 355–72.
39. Sohn, "I Will Be Your God," 367.
40. Sohn, "I Will Be Your God," 367.
41. Sohn, "I Will Be Your God," 367.
42. Sohn, "I Will Be Your God," 367.
43. Sohn, "I Will Be Your God," 368.

From a rhetorical standpoint, a key to understanding this intertextual dynamic is the importance of *relevance* in allowing a reader to discern the rhetorical significance of the author's allusive act. Normally, it would be difficult to defend the notion that an allusive marker like the self-declaration formula and a single text, Exod 6:2–8, could evoke so many covenantal themes and ideas, but there is a particular phenomenon that favors just such an intertextual interplay. This key factor is the formulaic nature of certain OT texts. A formula greatly reduces the processing effort required of the reader to recognize relationships and correspondences. A formula is a mnemonic device that allows complex and expansive ideas to be learned and understood efficiently. Therefore, the self-declaration formula in Ps 105:7 not only evokes texts but also evokes the covenant formula and relevant corresponding ideas, such as the recognition formula, the exodus theme, the patriarchal promise of land, and the covenant at Sinai. These formulas and themes efficiently and effectively bring crucial covenantal concepts into the context of the psalmist's developing argument.

In terms of classical logical relationships, these dense covenantal texts create a *greater than* rhetorical relationship with the alluding text. The self-declaration formula signifies that Yahweh is not just Israel's God, but the God of the patriarchs who made the promise of land and remembers his covenant (Exod 6:2–5). The allusion also evokes the memory of Yahweh who delivered his people in the exodus (Exod 6:5–6), established a covenant with the nation that made Israel his treasured possession (election), and brought the people into the land as promised (Exod 6:8). Thus, Yahweh is not only the God of Abraham and the Abrahamic covenant (Ps 105:8–11), he is also the covenant lord of the Mosaic covenant, which established Israel as a nation in accordance with the promises made to Abraham. This same Mosaic covenant relationship is defined and upheld by obedience to the law, which sets the stage for the psalmist's developing rhetorical strategy. Having introduced the Mosaic covenant in conjunction with the Abrahamic, the psalmist has created a subtext that will address the bilateral aspect of the Mosaic covenant relationship (Ps 105:8b) and ultimately culminate in the concluding didactic prescription at the end of the psalm (vv. 42–45).

Imported Meaning and Rhetorical Significance

The final question is how this allusion to Exod 6:2–8; 20:2/Deut 5:6 and the Mosaic covenant imports relevant meaning into the psalmist's argument. As noted, the rhetorical relationship between Ps 105:7 and Exod 6:2–8; 20:2/ Deut 5:6 allows the psalmist to expand the covenantal identity of Yahweh.

Looking at the context of Ps 105:7 there is congruity between the covenant discourse of the psalmist, which bridges praise for Yahweh's mighty works (vv. 1–5) with the Abrahamic covenant (Ps 105:8–11), and the significance of Exod 6:2–8 as an inter-covenantal bridge text (see Gen 17:1–8).

The explicit discourse of Ps 105:8–11 establishes that Yahweh is the covenant God of the patriarchs who swore the land promise by divine oath. However, the allusion to Exod 6:2–8; 20:2/Deut 5:6 also imports Yahweh's identity as the covenant Lord of the Mosaic covenant, while further reaffirming the continuity between the patriarchal promises and the events of the exodus, Sinai, and the conquest. This reinforces Yahweh's instrumental role in the ensuing historical narration of Ps 105. This allusion serves the psalmist's rhetorical strategy by allowing the focus to narrow to the Abrahamic covenant, while also placing the Mosaic covenant in the context of the Abrahamic covenant promises. The obligatory aspects of the Mosaic covenant are now imported into the psalmist's subtext.

The Mosaic Covenant and *Hesed* in Psalm 105:8

The Referent: Deuteronomy 7:9 and Exodus 20:6 (Deuteronomy 5:10)

Deuteronomy 7:7–15 is a Mosaic discourse regarding Yahweh's exclusive selection of Israel as his chosen nation and covenant partner. While Deut 7:7–15 cites Yahweh's faithfulness to the Abrahamic covenant as the basis for his faithfulness to the Mosaic covenant, Exod 20:6 exclusively addresses the Mosaic covenant. Deuteronomy 7:9 uses the hendiadys הברית והחסד to speak of the enduring faithfulness that Yahweh demonstrates in keeping the Mosaic covenant. As noted above, scholars have interpreted this collocation of *hesed* and *berit* in various ways, but the essential point is that *hesed* emphasizes an enduring covenant faithfulness that characterizes the way Yahweh relates to all who keep covenant by loving Yahweh and obeying his law (Deut 7:9–10).[44] In the corresponding text of Exod 20:6, the term *berit* is not even used as only *hesed* is used to describe the Mosaic covenant relationship.

Though a thorough study of *hesed* is beyond the scope of this study, a brief discussion of the relationship between *hesed* and *berit* will help in discerning the significance of the psalmist's allusion to Deut 7:9/Exod 20:6. In his seminal work on *hesed*, Glueck observes that "the covenant concluded

---

44. See chapter 8, note 10 above for a brief survey of various approaches to the interpretation of הברית והחסד in Deut 7:9.

between Yahweh and the patriarchs, established through an oath, had *ḥesed* as a consequence. *Ḥesed, per se,* should also be the object of an oath."[45] Glueck's work helped demonstrate an essential connection between the concepts of *ḥesed* and *berit*. Routledge posits two basic types of relationships between *ḥesed* and *berit*: (1) *ḥesed* is the content of the *berit* where *ḥesed* is shown to Israel because of the covenant relationship (e.g., Ps 106:45), and (2) *ḥesed* is the basis for the covenant relationship where *ḥesed* actually precedes the *berit* and the covenant relationship affirms God's promises (e.g., Ps 89:28, 34–37).[46]

The organic link between *ḥesed* and *berit* in which one can be the result of or the basis for the other suggests that *ḥesed* is the basis for Yahweh's fulfillment of the Abrahamic promises (Deut 7:8). On the significance of covenant love and faithfulness in Deut 7:9–10, McConville observes: "His devotion to his chosen people cannot be compromised by anything in himself. And this now gives content to covenant, in a way that is consistent with the fulfillment of the ancient oath to Abraham that is recalled in the theology of election."[47]

Though the fulfillment of the Abrahamic covenant illustrates Yahweh's enduring covenantal faithfulness, Deut 7:9–10 limits Yahweh's *ḥesed* to those who keep covenant by loving him and obeying his commandments. This aspect of Yahweh's expression of *ḥesed* informs the way the obligatory aspect of the covenant relationship ought to be understood. In relation to the *ḥesed-berit* relationship, Routledge observes that righteousness (צדק) is also connected to this covenant pointing to the rightful demands placed upon God's people in the Mosaic covenant.[48] Routledge notes:

> Right behaviour for the people of God, within the context of the covenant, is behaviour that conforms to the demands of that relationship, which includes uprightness (Ps. 36:10; Is. 33:15), cleanness of hand and heart before God (2 Sa. 22:21, 25; Is. 64:6) and obedience to his Law.[49]

In addition to righteousness, Routledge observes that *ḥesed* is also related to grace in that *ḥesed* is understood as the basis for Yahweh's forgiveness in cases where the offender is guilty and has no claim to forgiveness

---

45. Glueck, *Ḥesed*, 73–74.
46. Routledge, "Ḥesed as Obligation," 187–88.
47. McConville, *Deuteronomy*, 158.
48. Routledge, "Ḥesed as Obligation," 188–91.
49. Routledge, "Ḥesed as Obligation," 190.

(e.g., Ps 51:3 [MT]).⁵⁰ This category of ḥesed is relevant to the idea of covenant renewal, especially when the people have violated the covenant and have no claim to forgiveness and renewal.⁵¹

Two studies by Britt and Dozeman, respectively, indicate that covenant formulas and expressions, especially those based on Exod 20:6, 34:6–7, and Deut 7:9–10, were formulaically and liturgically important in later covenant renewal settings. Britt notes that later biblical writings reflect a distinct "patterned usage" of ḥesed in association with covenant formulas and expressions that "represents a qualitatively and quantitatively significant feature of the biblical Canon."⁵² Dozeman posits that covenant formulas based on Exod 34:6–7, which is reflected in Deut 7:9–10, developed into a key component of covenant renewal texts.⁵³

The significance of Deut 7:9–10/Exod 20:6 in later covenant renewal contexts means that there is a tenable historical and liturgical setting in which these texts would have been easily recognized by the postexilic community of Ezra-Nehemiah. More importantly, the psalmist would have been aware of the importance of these ḥesed-berit texts in the context of covenant renewal. This writer posits that Ps 105 is written with the need for covenant renewal in mind, meaning, there is reasonable grounds for the psalmist to rhetorically use Deut 7:9/Exod 20:6 in his developing argument and subtext.⁵⁴

The Imported Meaning and Rhetorical Significance

A close reading of Ps 105:8–11 shows that the first explicit mention of the Abrahamic covenant is actually found in v. 9 where the relative clause clarifies that the covenant in v. 8 is actually the Abrahamic covenant. Thus, the reader who has just read v. 7, where the psalmist has allusively evoked the Mosaic covenant, could conceivably read v. 8 and see the Mosaic covenant. In v. 8 the description of Yahweh remembering his covenant, the one made

---

50. Routledge, "Ḥesed as Obligation," 191–92.
51. Routledge, "Ḥesed as Obligation," 192.
52. Britt, "Unexpected Attachments," 296.
53. Dozeman examines inner-biblical interpretation involving Jonah 4:2 and Joel 2:13ab-b and their use of the covenant renewal material in Exod 32–34. Dozeman views Exod 34:6–7 as axiomatic, which is why an appeal to Yahweh in the light of covenant violation includes a formulaic use of ḥesed. Dozeman, "Yahweh's Gracious and Compassionate Character," 218–23.

54. Weiser suggests that the complementary historical presentations in Pss 105 and 106 may be an indication that these psalms were part of the same covenantal liturgy. Weiser, *Psalms*, 680.

"to a thousand generations," reads like a description of the Mosaic covenant in light of Deut 7:9/Exod 20:6. It is not until v. 9 that the reader realizes that v. 8 is actually describing the Abrahamic covenant.

This poetic "twist" is an interesting feature of the allusion in v. 8b. The psalmist cleverly takes an expression, "to a thousand generations" (לְאֶלֶף דּוֹר), that is known to describe the enduring nature of Yahweh's *ḥesed* to Israel via the Mosaic covenant (Deut 7:9/Exod 20:6) and repurposes it to describe the enduring nature of the Abrahamic covenant (Ps 105:8). This clever reversal brings to mind the comforting thought of Yahweh's covenant faithfulness immediately followed by the realization that it is only shown to those who love him and obey his commandments. The realization that Yahweh's *ḥesed* is only for the faithful who keep the Mosaic covenant is at the heart of the imported meaning that irrupts into Ps 105:8. The allusion allows the psalmist to use the very affirmation of the Abrahamic covenant's enduring certainty to remind the reader of the harsh postexilic reality of Mosaic covenant failure.

The denial of Yahweh's *ḥesed* to those who have failed to love him and disobeyed his commandments coheres with the psalmist's understanding of why things are amiss in the postexilic period. In v. 7, the psalmist has just used another allusion to a familiar formulaic expression, "I am the LORD your God," to frame the Abrahamic covenant affirmations in light of the Mosaic covenant that defines nationhood for Abraham's descendants. The allusion to Deut 7:9/Exod 20:6 reminds the reader of the covenant failure that resulted in exile and explains why the return to the land has not been accompanied by unprecedented blessings. Furthermore, the likelihood that Deut 7:9 and Exod 20:6 were used liturgically and formulaically in postexilic covenant renewal settings adds another layer of relevance in relation to the psalmist's developing Mosaic covenant subtext.

In terms of the logical rhetorical relationship between the alluding text and the referent, this allusion is an example of an *ironic* allusion where the referent represents a failure or disjunction in relation to the alluding text. The alluding text affirms the reliability of Yahweh and the certainty of his covenant promise to Abraham and the patriarchs (Ps 105:8–11); however, the referent points to the reason for Israel's loss of covenant blessing in the postexilic period. The axiomatic description of Yahweh's covenantal loyalty in Deut 7:9/Exod 20:6 confirms an obligatory dimension to Israel's covenant relationship, and his *ḥesed* can only be experienced by those who keep the covenant. In light of this principle, the allusion highlights the failure of Israel in violating the Mosaic covenant. The psalmist uses the expression "to a thousand generations" to describe the enduring certainty of the Abrahamic promise but evokes a text that explains why Israel's violation of the Mosaic covenant ironically results in forfeiture of Yahweh's *ḥesed* "to a thousand generations."

The psalmist recognizes the significance of Yahweh's *ḥesed* as a source of hope for the postexilic remnant since covenant promises could still be counted as enduring and certain. However, the psalmist also sees the need for the remnant to recognize the violation of the Mosaic covenant, requiring repentance and covenant renewal. In a sense, these formulaic *ḥesed-berit* texts (Deut 7:9/Exod 20:6) possess a Janus-like quality that highlights both the promissory and obligatory aspects of Israel's covenant relationship. A Janus-allusion is a fitting intertextual feature to weave between a Mosaic covenant allusion in v. 7 and a series of Abrahamic covenant references in vv. 8–11. The psalmist demonstrates his poetic and rhetorical dexterity by evoking a referent that simultaneously affirms the enduring certainty of covenant promises while also calling attention to the need to fulfill ongoing obligations.

The Law and the Mosaic Covenant in Ps 105:45

The third allusion to the Mosaic covenant is found in Ps 105:45 where the psalmist concludes with a didactic purpose-statement regarding the necessity of obeying Yahweh's "statutes" and "laws." The rhetorical flow of the psalm indicates that obedience to the Mosaic law is the reason the people were brought into the land. In Ps 105:45, the allusion to the Mosaic covenant seems obvious, but there are some questions regarding the validity of this allusion since the Mosaic law is not necessarily a reference to the Mosaic covenant.[55] The metonymical use of the law as a reference to the Mosaic covenant exposes one other interesting dilemma. By definition, a literary allusion evokes another text. The Mosaic covenant is technically a concept entailing numerous texts. The Mosaic covenant texts also span four books of the Pentateuch (Exodus to Deuteronomy), which means that the Mosaic law in Ps 105:45 is an allusive marker that evokes a non-literary referent.

---

55. The final statement on the necessity of obeying the "statutes" and "laws" has elicited a range of views regarding the covenantal significance of v. 45. Some see the Mosaic covenant (Sinai) in v. 45, others do not. Goldingay notes that Sinai was conspicuously absent in the historical survey but becomes "all-important" in this final verse. Goldingay, *Psalms 90–150*, 216–17. Mays suggests that the psalmist was well aware of the nation's history of Mosaic covenant violations, leading to a focus on the Abrahamic promise. Mays, *Psalms*, 339. Hossfeld separates the law and the covenant, noting that the legal tradition of P and the Deuteronomic theme of obedience and the land is represented in v. 45 even though Sinai is not mentioned. Hossfeld and Zenger, *Psalms 3*, 74.

A Non-Literary Allusion

This issue can be resolved in a novel manner once the underlying concepts involved in the validation of a literary allusion are delineated. The key distinctive of an allusion, as opposed to a reference, is the rhetorical interaction between the alluding text and the referent. This rhetorical interaction requires that the referent (traditionally another text) has a stable meaning that can be imported into the alluding text, achieving the author's intended rhetorical effect.[56] Thus, even though the Mosaic covenant is not a proper text, it could still meet the criteria required of a valid allusion referent. The key is to determine if the covenant can be summarized, distilled, or reduced to a propositional or conceptual form that can function rhetorically in relation to the psalmist's argument. In this instance, can the Mosaic covenant be reduced or distilled in a way that carries rhetorical meaning?

Looking back at the rhetorically informed reading of Ps 105, the psalmist is composing his work of hymnic praise and historical review in order to validate two key ideas. The psalmist seeks to demonstrate that Yahweh is faithful to his promise and that Yahweh is sovereign. The implication of these two propositions is that the patriarchal promise of land is certain since Yahweh is faithful to his promise and he is able to fulfill his promise. However, there is one major issue of which the psalmist is aware, and that is the pall cast by the nation's failure to keep the Mosaic covenant resulting in exile.[57] In fact, the harsh truth is that it was faithful and sovereign Yahweh who brought final judgment upon his wayward people.

In this sense, the reality of the Mosaic covenant and the obligation to obey the law stand in tension with the irrevocable nature of the Abrahamic land promise. Thus, one of the psalmist's aims is to resolve this tension between the sworn patriarchal promise and the nation's covenant violation resulting in judgment. The psalmist does this by basing possession of the land upon Yahweh's promise to the patriarchs, while still exhorting the community to keep the law, which is the basis for prosperity and stability in the land. The psalmist has seen that the return to the land has not resulted in national stability, peace, or prosperity. The call for covenant renewal and obedience stands to reason in light of the existential questions facing the postexilic remnant.

---

56. Klingler, "Validity," 179–82.

57. "A basic postulate of faith is that God is faithful to his covenant commitment (cf. Neh 1:5), and that therefore the disasters of history must be due to human failure and not divine indifference." Blenkinsopp, *Ezra–Nehemiah*, 307.

The Relationship between Covenant and Law

As noted earlier, a source of difficulty in viewing the law as a synecdoche-based allusion to the Mosaic covenant comes from recent studies challenging the relationship between covenant and law in the exilic to postexilic period. The conspicuous absence of the Sinai events in Ps 105 raises a pertinent question regarding the relationship between the law and the Mosaic covenant. Is the absence of Sinai in the historical narration indicative of the fact that the Mosaic covenant is not a factor in the argument of Ps 105?

Like Ps 105, Neh 9:13–14 addresses Moses, who is the only figure explicitly mentioned other than Abraham. It is significant that this passage addresses the giving of the law but without mention of the covenant made there (Exod 19–24). The absence of an explicit mention of the Sinai covenant using the term ברית has been taken in various ways. Holmgren posits that the Mosaic law references in Neh 9:13–14 mean that the Sinai covenant and its laws are included under the Abrahamic covenant.[58] However, Fensham argues that the extensive reference to the law-giving at Sinai and the Sinai tradition mean that Neh 9:13 refers to the Sinai covenant.[59] Blenkinsopp posits that the absence of the Sinai covenant and focus on the Abrahamic covenant is an intentional way of focusing solely on the unconditional promise of land.[60] Fensham notes that the use of חקים has connotations regarding promise, as seen in Ps 105:10 where poetic parallelism links חקים with ברית עולם.[61]

Sperling takes a different tack in arguing that postexilic covenant theology had all but rendered the bilateral covenant obsolete, which explains the dearth of Mosaic/Sinaitic covenant references in late books.[62] Sperling's thesis is that the bilateral covenant was a monotheistic metaphor that was needed when Israel's early religious setting included the threat of other deities; however, in the postexilic setting where Judaism is now firmly monotheistic, the bilateral covenant form is obsolete and the emphasis is turned toward law and divine oaths or grant-type forms.[63] Sperling develops his argument by tracing the use of *berit* in Chronicles, Ezra-Nehemiah, Deutero-Isaiah, Daniel, Malachi, Haggai, Zechariah, and Ps 106, which leads to the observation that the use of Deuteronomic material often results in some

---

58. Holmgren, "Faithful Abraham," 252.
59. Fensham, "Neh. 9 and Pss. 105," 43.
60. Blenkinsopp, *Ezra–Nehemiah*, 304.
61. Fensham, *Books of Ezra and Nehemiah*, 230. For a link between חקק and promise, see Liedke, "חקק," 1:631.
62. Sperling, "Rethinking Covenant," 50–73.
63. Sperling, "Rethinking Covenant," 51–52, 60.

editorial changes where *berit* is replaced by the law so that the sin of Israel is breaking the law rather than covenant.[64] Sperling notes that in some cases the Sinai covenant tradition is bypassed in favor of the patriarchal covenant tradition with its unconditional promise.[65] He summarizes: " . . . in the exilic and post-exilic periods, unconditional covenants, by which Yahweh and Israel remained in permanent relation had triumphed over the notion of conditional covenant that might be broken."[66]

Linington challenges Sperling's thesis, especially within the context of Chronicles, Ezra, and Nehemiah.[67] Linington does not dismiss Sperling's views completely but points out that some of the emendations that Sperling cites do not prove that the bilateral covenant was forgotten.[68] For example, Sperling views Neh 10:1 [Eng. 9:38] and the avoidance of the word *berit* as an instance where there is an intentional avoidance of any reference to the Sinai covenant, since this would contradict the postexilic tendency to separate the law from covenant.[69] However, Linington notes that covenant is actually a legal concept so Sperling goes too far in seeing the law as being so distinct from covenant, especially since covenant is usually accompanied by stipulations and oaths.[70] Linington also notes that the triumph of monolatry in postexilic Judaism may be overstated since concerns over apostasy still influence the covenant renewal in Neh 8–10.[71]

In Neh 10:1 [Eng. 9:38], the term "agreement" (אמנה) is used where the term ברית is expected. A tenable explanation for this is explored in Holmgren's study of this covenant renewal pericope. Holmgren sees a lexical connection between the term אמנה and Abraham's "faithful" response, which was instrumental in God's covenant with Abraham (והאמן ביהוה ויחשבה לו צדקה, cf. Gen 15:6).[72] Holmgren sees the following logic in Neh 10:1 [Eng. 9:38]:

> Abraham's faithfulness was the basis of God's covenant with him which included the promise of the land. If the Exiles are

---

64. Sperling, "Rethinking Covenant," 53–72.
65. Sperling, "Rethinking Covenant," 53–72.
66. Sperling, "Rethinking Covenant," 72.
67. Linington, "Term *berît*," 671–93.
68. Linington, "Term *berît*," 675–76, 689–90.
69. Sperling, "Rethinking Covenant," 59.
70. Linington, "Term *berît*," 689–90.
71. Linington, "Term *berît*," 689.

72. Holmgren, "Faithful Abraham," 250–51. Duggan also takes a similar position on the relationship between ברית and אמנה in Neh 10:1. Duggan, *Covenant Renewal*, 286.

to recover fully Abraham's land, then there must be a return to Abraham-faithfulness—a sincere return to Abraham's God. The Exiles must live once again as Abraham did—must become, in reality, children of Abraham.⁷³

Linington notes that the covenant renewal ceremony, including the language of Neh 10:1 [Eng. 9:38], follows the general patterns of a suzerain-vassal treaty form so the use of an alternate term for covenant does not preclude the covenantal significance of the renewal ceremony.⁷⁴ Holmgren concludes that the use of the alternate term אמנה is about addressing the question of the exilic community's relationship to Abraham and the ownership of the land, which explains why an unexpected term is used to intentionally evoke the covenant made with Abraham (cf. Neh 9:8; Gen 15:6).⁷⁵ Holmgren's and Linington's analyses make sense since the Sinai covenant is associated with the Mosaic law, thus avoiding the term ברית ensures that the "faithful" promissory covenant with Abraham is not confused with the obligatory Sinai covenant.⁷⁶

McCarthy specifically addresses these same questions regarding the relationship between covenant and law and presents an alternate view that explains some of the issues Sperling raises. Per McCarthy's area of expertise, he delves into the specific covenant renewal narratives/texts in Chronicles and in Ezra-Nehemiah and finds strong commonalities with the Assyrian *adû* (loyalty oath), which he summarizes thusly:

> Both are presided over by royalty or its representatives. Each formulates a concern with fundamental loyalty. Rebellion . . . is the fundamental sin. Deference, prostration before the mighty lord . . . is the fundamental attitude of the subject in Israel and in Assyria. Finally, it is an oath which guarantees renewal of covenant and *adû*. In fact, 'loyalty oath' is the natural translation of the latter; *adû* means first of all 'oath.'⁷⁷

The actual question that McCarthy addresses is whether the Mosaic law had become divorced from covenant as a legal abstraction in the postexilic period.⁷⁸ By analyzing the differences between the covenant renewal

---

73. Holmgren, "Faithful Abraham," 253.
74. Linington, "Term *berît*," 689–90.
75. Holmgren, "Faithful Abraham," 253.
76. Linington, "Term *berît*," 690.
77. McCarthy, "Covenant and Law," 37.
78. McCarthy, "Covenant and Law," 26. The view that "covenant" and "law" had become separated in the exilic/postexilic period is featured in Noth's work on law in the Pentateuch. Per Noth, "the law" had become an "*absolute entity*, valid without respect

texts in Chronicles and contrasting them with the covenant renewal in Ezra-Nehemiah, McCarthy concludes that the apparent changes in the form and terminology of covenant renewal have more to do with the new realities and questions in postexilic Yehud than a fundamental change in the way law and covenant are understood.[79]

The essential relationship between covenant and law is still the same, which is that law provides the community with a means of expressing loyalty to their covenant lord.[80] In later OT writings, the law is still an expression of relationship between Yahweh and his chosen people, not a "self-existing" abstract idea that is used in a utilitarian manner to govern the community.[81] Though Noth famously viewed a significant "sundering" of the relationship between covenant and law in the exilic to postexilic period, he acknowledged that the earlier traditions (pre-exilic) viewed the Sinai covenant as the basis for the relationship between Yahweh and Israel, and that the law was inextricably tied into the concept of covenant.[82]

The main difference between Noth, Sperling, and McCarthy is whether there was a significant change in the relationship between covenant and law in the exilic to postexilic period. There is general agreement that there is an OT precedent for tying covenant and law together, which supports the view that legal terms can be legitimate metonymic references to the Sinai covenant. Linington notes that in Neh 9, ברית occurs twice (Neh 9:8, 32) and in the first case, it explicitly refers to the Abrahamic covenant, but in Neh 9:32, ברית seems to refer to the Abrahamic covenant in v. 8, but "also to the implied Sinai covenant whose stipulations have been outlined, but which has not been explicitly mentioned, in the remaining prayer."[83] It seems that

---

to precedent, time, or history; based on itself, binding simply because it existed as law, because it was of divine origin and authority." Noth, *Laws in the Pentateuch*, 86, 91–95.

79. McCarthy, "Covenant and Law," 40–41.

80. McCarthy, "Covenant and Law," 40–41.

81. McCarthy, "Covenant and Law," 41. This is where McCarthy's conclusion might contradict some of Sperling's positions on covenant in the postexilic period. Sperling contends that the term *berit* is redefined in later OT writings so that the bilateral concept of a suzerain-vassal relationship is obsolete in the postexilic period, specifically in Ezra-Nehemiah. Sperling sees "covenant" as being reduced to promissory concepts related to the patriarchal promises. Sperling, "Rethinking Covenant," 52–59, 72. Noth's view informs Sperling's analysis as he concludes that the late understanding of "covenant" (specifically in P) had lost significance as a figurative way of representing the relationship between Yahweh and Israel per the Sinai covenant. Noth, *Laws in the Pentateuch*, 93.

82. Noth, *Laws in the Pentateuch*, 37–41.

83. Linington, "Term *berît*," 688.

the legal terminology in Neh 9:13 is a metonymic reference to the Mosaic covenant.

The Postexilic Milieu and Covenant Renewal

Up to this point in the study, this writer has appealed to the importance of covenant renewal in the postexilic period as the backdrop for the psalmist's concerns. Thus, it is worth addressing the postexilic setting and the importance of covenant renewal in the psalmist's argument, subtext, and conclusion. In Ezra-Nehemiah, renewal of the Mosaic covenant informed the psalmist's understanding of the two covenants. In many respects, Neh 9 is analogous to Ps 105. The content and manner in which the historical material is presented in Neh 9 is uniquely similar to Ps 105.[84] Thus, Neh 9 is a valuable point of comparison for the historical narrative and covenant understanding of Ps 105.[85]

The penitential prayer in Neh 9 is found in the context of the postexilic community's renewal of the Mosaic covenant (Neh 8–10).[86] Nehemiah acknowledged that God had been faithful to the covenant, but it is the people who had failed to keep the Mosaic law (Neh 9:32–35; 10:29).[87] McConville surmises that the exilic and postexilic population was preoccupied with the question of the Mosaic covenant's status and how this covenant relationship would continue.[88] The question surrounding the Mosaic covenant is one reason the Abrahamic covenant is featured in Neh 9 and Ps 105.

Like Ps 105, Neh 9 emphasizes the foundational nature of the patriarchal promise of land (Neh 9:7–8). In addition, Neh 9 features the giving of the law at Sinai, including the use of every legal term associated with the covenant law given through Moses (Neh 9:13–14).[89] Like Ps 105, Neh

---

84. Duggan, *Covenant Renewal*, 226–28. See also Fensham, "Neh. 9 and Pss. 105," 40–45.

85. Rendtorff notes that Neh 9 represents a later text in which the major covenant traditions have been synthesized into a coherent covenant-theology. Rendtorff, *Covenant Formula*, 3, 9.

86. The prayer in Neh 9:6–10:1 [Eng. 9.38] takes place in the midst of covenant renewal, specifically as Ezra and the Levites lead the people in a day of mourning and repentance for both the sins of the people and their ancestors. Levering, *Ezra & Nehemiah*, 183–84. This follows the reading of Moses's teachings, which is the cause of the mourning (Neh 9:1–5a). Steinmann, *Ezra and Nehemiah*, 531–32.

87. Steinmann, *Ezra and Nehemiah*, 550.

88. McConville, *Deuteronomy*, 430–31.

89. Neh 9:13–14 features the terms, משפטים, תורות, חקים, and מצות, which represent much of the legal terminology associated with the Mosaic law. Fensham notes that the use of the "whole catalog" of legal terminology means the entire body of Mosaic law is

9 features the Abrahamic covenant prominently, especially the promise of land, which Duggan argues is presented as the focal point of history (not the exile) in the penitential component of the prayer (Neh 9:32–37).[90] Interestingly, Duggan notes that Neh 9:7 is the only place in the MT where God "chooses" (בחר) Abraham and in Ps 105 this same term is used conspicuously in reference to the selection of Abraham's offspring (Ps 105:6).[91]

Like Ps 105, Neh 9 features both the Abrahamic covenant and the Mosaic law in the context of a poetic recounting of Israel's history. Holmgren observes that the Sinai covenant is never explicitly mentioned and that the only *berit* mentioned in Neh 9 is the Abrahamic covenant with an emphasis on the promise of land.[92] Nehemiah 9:8 also stresses that Abraham was "faithful" and that this is balanced against Yahweh's righteousness.[93] In fact, Linington discerns a chiastic structure in Neh 9:8 that places the promise of land at the crux while also putting Abraham's faithfulness in parallel with Yahweh's righteousness, but the chiasm also parallels the making of covenant with the fulfillment of God's promise (דבר).[94] The ordering of the elements in Abraham's life also supports the rhetorical emphasis on the promise of land since the biographical information is out of sequence in relation to the Genesis narrative. Steinmann posits that the writer intentionally reordered the biographical elements so that the promise of land is in the climactic position.[95]

It is especially relevant that out of the historical psalms, only Ps 105 parallels Neh 9 and its focus on Abraham, the Abrahamic covenant, and the patriarchal promises.[96] Like Ps 105, Neh 9 and the focus on Abraham and the promise of land seems to be influenced by Deuteronomy (e.g., election of Israel's ancestors, see Deut 4:37; 10:15).[97] Duggan concludes with the notion that the prayer of Neh 9–10 is a hermeneutical key to Ezra-Nehemiah and based on this hermeneutical filter, Duggan sees an expansion of the historical horizon, which brings the Abrahamic covenant and the Mosaic law together in a defining way for the postexilic people who reaffirmed the

---

in view. Fensham, *Books of Ezra and Nehemiah*, 230.

90. Duggan, *Covenant Renewal*, 229.
91. Duggan, *Covenant Renewal*, 202.
92. Holmgren, "Faithful Abraham," 252.
93. Fensham, *Books of Ezra and Nehemiah*, 229.
94. Linington, "Term *berît*," 688.
95. Steinmann, *Ezra and Nehemiah*, 537.
96. Fensham, "Neh. 9 and Pss. 105," 41.
97. Blenkinsopp, *Ezra–Nehemiah*, 303–4. See also Williamson, *Ezra, Nehemiah*, 312–13.

covenant relationship with allegiance to the law.[98] This wedding of the Abrahamic covenant and Mosaic law is a significant contextual datum that makes sense of the relationship between the Abrahamic covenant and the Mosaic law in Ps 105.

The Law and the Mosaic Covenant in Ps 105:45

In light of the observations on the postexilic setting and Neh 9, it appears that postexilic writers, with the benefit of historical hindsight and a developed theological perspective, were able to relate the Abrahamic and Mosaic covenants to one another in a way that elegantly accounts for the perceived tension between promise and obligation. The Abrahamic covenant is not devoid of obligation since Abraham's obedience to Yahweh's torah characterized his part in the covenant-ratification process, and the Mosaic covenant is not devoid of promise since Yahweh assured the people that even after exile the people would be restored to unprecedented blessings by a "circumcision of the heart."

The psalmist's contribution is addressing this perceived tension in the context of the postexilic community's questions regarding life in the land after the exile. The relationship between the law and the Mosaic covenant in the context of Ps 105 is based on the issue of dwelling in the land under Yahweh's blessing. In the progression of the psalmist's argument, the Abrahamic covenant ensures possession of the land, but the psalmist still concludes with a didactic call to obey Yahweh's "statutes" and "laws" since this is the purpose of life in the land. The second allusion to Deut 7:9/Exod 20:6 strengthens the notion that keeping the Mosaic covenant is the only way to experience Yahweh's covenant faithfulness and love. The prominence of the land promise in Ps 105 is not unexpected when seen through the lens of the postexilic milieu. Despite returning to the land, the political and socio-cultural instability faced by the community elicited fair questions regarding the nature of national restoration (cf. Deut 30:1–10). It makes sense, then, that the promise of land was the psalmist's primary concern, but he also sought to resolve the question of complete national restoration, which brings the Mosaic covenant into the discussion.

The Torah (especially Deuteronomy) and Israel's history informed the psalmist that dwelling in the land under divine blessing was contingent on "keeping" the Mosaic law. Whether it is the product of historical perspective or the natural result of theological reflection, there is a heightened awareness of the continuity between the Abrahamic and Mosaic covenants in

98. Duggan, *Covenant Renewal*, 298.

the covenant theology of postexilic OT writings. Holmgren notes that the Mosaic law stands in continuity with the Abrahamic covenant, as demonstrated by the anachronistic description of Abraham's obedience to Yahweh's *torah* (וישמר משמרתי מצותי חקותי ותורתי; Gen 26:5), which is upheld as an example for his descendants (Gen 18:19).[99] Understanding Abraham's "faithfulness" as obedience to the law is suggested in Neh 9:8 where Yahweh makes the covenant only after he discerned Abraham's heart to be faithful (ומצאת את־לבבו נאמן לפניך). While some view Abraham's "faith" in Gen 15:6 as the background for Neh 9:8, Boda argues that "a faithful heart" in Neh 9:8 is better understood in terms of the Deuteronomic concept of the ideal covenant partner, which is characterized by obedience to the law.[100]

The postexilic community under the leadership of Ezra and Nehemiah moved to renew their commitment to the Mosaic covenant, while remembering the certainty of the patriarchal promise in the hopes of experiencing renewed blessing in the land. This provides a valuable understanding of the backdrop for the psalmist's message in Ps 105. Indeed, God is Yahweh, the covenant-making God who is faithful to his promises, but his covenantal faithfulness is only shown to those who love him and keep his commandments. The land has been promised by sworn oath so there is hope. However, the purpose of being a great nation and being blessed in the promised land was intended to shape Israel into a loyal people, obedient to their covenant lord and his righteous laws. McCarthy's observations about the centrality of loyalty and relationship in the covenant renewal of Ezra-Nehemiah bolsters the idea that the postexilic community understood the essential nature of keeping the law within the context of their covenant relationship with Yahweh.[101] Therefore, the psalmist's purpose statement exhorting obedience to Yahweh's "statutes" and "laws" is best understood in relation to the Mosaic covenant as a renewed commitment to covenant loyalty. The allusion to the Mosaic covenant in Ps 105:45 not only concludes the Mosaic covenant subtext, it also concludes the psalm's rhetorical argument by providing a reason for renewed obedience to the law as a means of renewing and maintaining the Mosaic covenant relationship.

Therefore, the Mosaic covenant, though it is not a proper literary text, has rhetorical significance based on its stable meaning. The Mosaic covenant defined the national relationship between Yahweh and his chosen people and stipulated that the proper expression of the people's covenant love was obedience to Yahweh's righteous laws. Since the gift of land, nationhood, and

---

99. Holmgren, "Faithful Abraham," 251–53.
100. Boda, *Praying the Tradition*, 104–5.
101. McCarthy, "Covenant and Law," 40–41.

blessing was intended to bless other nations, Israel was meant to become a torah-based community that exercised righteousness and justice. Naturally, this covenantal concept would develop into the Deuteronomic axiom that the people must be obedient to the law in order to dwell in the land under Yahweh's blessing. In terms of the rhetorical relationship between Ps 105:45 and the Mosaic covenant, this interplay can be characterized as an example of fulfillment—an "equal to" logical relationship—in which obedience to the law fulfills the Mosaic covenant and satisfies Yahweh's conditions for dwelling in the land under his blessing.[102]

The Imported Meaning of the Mosaic Covenant

The necessity of being loyal to the Mosaic covenant by obeying the law was the basis for the psalmist's use of the Mosaic covenant allusion in v. 45. The hymnic worship and the curated historical narrative argue that Yahweh's promises are trustworthy and that he is fully capable of fulfilling them. Therefore, the people could expect to be back in the land, especially since the Mosaic covenant itself allowed for just such a future restoration to the land (Deut 30:1–10). However, the people also had to remember that they were a nation because of the Mosaic covenant. Since they broke covenant resulting in the exile, they must now return to obedience in order to be restored to the Mosaic covenant relationship. Earlier in v. 8 the psalmist deftly used an allusion with a poetic twist in order to bring to mind that the Mosaic covenant needed to be renewed. The psalmist used this final allusion in v. 45 to drive home the point that the promise to Abraham had a purpose and that the people had to rediscover that purpose in the context of the Mosaic covenant relationship.

The imported meaning of the Mosaic covenant in this rhetorical setting has to do with the nation's postexilic life and restoration in the land. The rhetorical function of the Mosaic covenant as the referent of the allusion is to import the proposition that it is necessary to restore the covenant relationship so that they may experience Yahweh's covenant favor once again. The idea that blessing in the land is contingent on obedience to the covenant is a major theme in Deuteronomy and the historical recitation in Ps 105 is consonant with the contours of the Pentateuch's historical narrative. The idea that obeying the law is an essential expression of loyalty is consistent with the psalmist's rhetorical argument. In essence, the psalmist sought to

---

102. Under the B = A rhetorical relationship, Klingler includes validation ("this is that"), fulfillment, and implementation as key examples. See Table 5.6 in Klingler, "Validity," 183.

stress that the promise to the patriarchs was the basis for the people's hope, but they had to remember that the Abrahamic promises were given and sustained in the context of a national relationship, which began with election and was formalized by covenant at Sinai. Renewal of this covenant relationship could only be accomplished by returning to Yahweh and recommitting to covenant loyalty by keeping his law (see Deut 30:1–10).

In terms of rhetorical strategy, a direct mention of the covenant at Sinai would have introduced a disruptive tension into the rhetorical argument regarding the Abrahamic promise of land. However, by using the legal terms חקים and תורות as the allusive marker the psalmist was able to evoke the Mosaic covenant and use the marker to surgically connect the conclusion of the psalm to the covenant law that must be kept in order to fulfill Israel's obligations to Yahweh as his chosen covenant people. In addition, using an allusion to Sinai in the conclusion allows the psalmist to close his argument regarding the faithfulness and sovereignty of Yahweh and then seamlessly meld the irrevocable promise of land into a call to restore the Mosaic covenant relationship through covenant loyalty expressed in obedience to the law.

The Combined Rhetorical Effect of the Three Allusions

The three allusions to various Mosaic covenant texts and concepts import meaning into Ps 105's rhetorical context that enhances the development of the psalmist's argument in each individual section of the psalm. The rhetorical impact of these allusions is not limited to the individual sections in the psalm. In examining the overall rhetorical structure of the psalm, the three allusions complement one another in rhetorically and poetically supporting the psalmist's thesis. While the psalmist overtly develops his main argument by stating and validating two propositions about Yahweh's covenant faithfulness and Yahweh's sovereignty, he uses the Mosaic covenant subtext framed by the three allusions to poetically place the obligations of the Mosaic covenant relationship alongside the Abrahamic covenant's promise of land. The conclusion of the psalm ingeniously brings the argument and subtext together to a didactic, prescriptive solution that has been validated by the rhetoric of the psalm.

In addition to the interplay between the argument and the subtext, the psalmist also makes use of *inclusio* as a poetic means of bolstering his rhetorical structure. There is an obvious *inclusio* involving the Abrahamic promise of land (vv. 8–11) and the fulfillment of that promise (v. 42). This *inclusio* is marked by clear repeated terms as well as syntactical clues that signal the opening and closing of the psalm's main body. There is an additional, subtler *inclusio* formed by the repetition of the expression "chosen ones" (בחיר) in v. 6 and v. 43. This *inclusio* may also be an example of distant parallelism, but the net rhetorical effect is to affirm that the Abrahamic covenant, the Mosaic covenant, and Israel's salvation history are rooted in Yahweh's gracious election of the patriarchs and the nation comprised of their descendants.

The three Mosaic covenant-related allusions form a third *inclusio* featuring these allusive verses. In v. 7, the self-declaration formula and the allusion to Exod 6:2–8; 20:2 (Deut 5:6) connects the Mosaic covenant to the Abrahamic covenant. This allusion establishes that the people are not only Abraham's descendants but also Yahweh's chosen nation. The fulfillment of the Abrahamic promise of land is experienced by a nation that has been constituted by the Mosaic covenant.

The allusion to Deut 7:9/Exod 20:6 in v. 8 uses a clever poetic twist to open a section affirming the Abrahamic covenant's promises with a sharp reminder that Yahweh's *ḥesed* is only for those who keep the Mosaic covenant faithfully. This allusion also complements the allusion in v. 7 by reminding the reader that Yahweh is Israel's faithful covenant God, while v. 8 reminds the reader that Israel has not been Yahweh's faithful nation. This Janus-allusion to Yahweh's *ḥesed* also highlights both the promissory and obligatory aspects of the covenant relationship. This Janus-like quality works well as a hinge between the Mosaic covenant allusion in v. 7 and the Abrahamic covenant affirmations in vv. 8–11. Thus, the first two allusions address the question of where Israel stands in relation to the Mosaic covenant.

In v. 45 the closing allusion offers a solution by affirming the necessity of covenant renewal resulting in loyalty expressed as obedience to the law. When taken together, vv. 7, 8, and 45 form a subtext that functions like an *inclusio* that links the Abrahamic promise of land to the Mosaic covenant call to Torah-obedience and covenant love. Only when the people are restored to the Mosaic covenant relationship through obedience to the law will the promise of land reach fulfillment as the place where Yahweh's chosen nation dwells in righteousness.

9

Conclusion

Covenant Insights from a Song

THE RELATIONSHIP BETWEEN THE ABRAHAMIC AND MOSAIC COVENANTS IN LIGHT OF PSALM 105

When I began my research, little did I know that the search for a particular voice from Israel's past would result in an intertextual study of a postexilic song about covenants. This study of the Abrahamic and Mosaic covenants in Ps 105 represents my attempt to investigate these covenants via a biblical figure who was well acquainted with both traditions at a time when this covenant dynamic had great theological relevance. As a postexilic psalm, one must be mindful of factors that play into the interpretation of the work, such as genre, historical, literary, and socio-cultural contexts, as well as the author's rhetorical intent and design. Being aware that Ps 105 is not a theological discourse on postexilic covenant theology, it is still possible to develop a revealing snapshot of the Abrahamic and Mosaic covenants from the way an ancient singer remembered these covenants.

The Abrahamic Covenant

The Abrahamic covenant and its promise of land undergird the argument of Ps 105 and is the only promissory element that is explicitly mentioned. The exclusive focus on the land promise stands to reason in light of the psalmist's postexilic provenance where possession of the land was a pressing issue for those returning from exile. The accumulation of covenant language describing an eternal covenant and a sworn promise of land indicates that the psalmist viewed the Abrahamic covenant's land oath to be an irrevocable promise upheld unilaterally by Yahweh. In the Abraham narrative, the covenant promises are conditioned on Abraham's responses (Gen 17:1-2; 18:19; 26:5) until Yahweh swears a solemn oath that renders them irrevocable (Gen 22:15-18). In Ps 105, there is no explicit mention of conditional or bilateral elements in the Abrahamic covenant. This reflects the fact that the psalmist is writing at a time in history when the Abrahamic promises are already characterized as an irrevocable divine oath. In fact, the rhetorical use of the Abrahamic covenant indicates that the psalmist relies on the irrevocable nature of the land promise as the basis for his rhetorical strategy.

The Mosaic Covenant

There are three allusions to the Mosaic covenant, which the psalmist deploys in order to make the point that Yahweh's fulfillment of the land promise should result in obedience to the Mosaic law. In light of the postexilic setting, it is reasonable that the psalmist views obedience to the Mosaic law as an expression of covenant loyalty in conjunction with the renewal of the Mosaic covenant (see Ezra-Nehemiah).

The Mosaic covenant is not included in the narrative rehearsal in Ps 105 nor is Sinai explicitly mentioned in any of the narrative discourse of the psalm, but this is rhetorically effective since an explicit mention introduces a disruptive tension in relation to the irrevocable promise of land. However, it also stands to reason that the psalmist evokes the Mosaic covenant allusively to maximize poetic and rhetorical impact. The effective use of an allusion evokes texts that allow other voices and texts to speak into the alluding text in a way that leaves a deeper impression on the reader. In a broad sense, the three Mosaic covenant allusions form a subtext that functions as an *inclusio* around the narrative body of the psalm, which signifies that the fulfillment of the Abrahamic promise of land takes place within the framework of the national relationship defined by the Mosaic covenant.

The Inter-Covenantal Relationship in Light of Psalm 105

The rhetorical structure of Ps 105 and the allusive use of the Mosaic covenant in the psalmist's argument suggests significant continuity between the two covenants. The psalmist introduced the idea of inter-covenantal continuity into the developing rhetoric of the psalm by alluding to Exod 6:2–8, which is a rich bridge text between the Abrahamic and Mosaic covenants. The second allusion (Deut 7:9/Exod 20:6) also highlights an inter-covenantal dynamic since Deut 7:8 uses Yahweh's faithfulness to the Abrahamic promises as the template for the *ḥesed* he shows to those who keep the Mosaic covenant. The inter-covenantal continuity is even rhetorically highlighted by the placement of the first two allusions at the seam between the hymnic introduction and the discourse on the Abrahamic covenant.

The promissory elements of the Abrahamic covenant, such as becoming a great nation and mediating blessing to all nations, are later connected to the national relationship with Yahweh that is forged at Sinai. The concept of a "great nation," which is a fundamental promise of the Abrahamic covenant, comes into focus in the Mosaic covenant, especially through the concept of holiness and the Mosaic law. The telic nature of the Mosaic covenant leads Israel toward becoming a people separate from the other nations (holiness) and characterized by righteousness and justice (the Torah standard). Thus, it is holiness and Torah-obedience that defines Israel as a great nation.

The other seminal promise of mediating blessing to all nations is also shaped by the Mosaic covenant relationship. When a great nation takes its place among the other nations, a people characterized by holiness, righteousness, and justice should be a blessing to all surrounding nations. In relation to the promise of blessing to the nations, the Mosaic covenant functions as the constitution by which the descendants of Abraham are given the moral and ethical character to embody righteousness and exercise justice, not only within the community, but to all people.[1]

When these various promissory threads are traced through the Mosaic covenant it becomes apparent why the promise of land had such significance in relation to the other promises. A great nation and a people who will bless other nations must have land, for the land is an ANE hallmark of nationhood.[2] In tracing the various promise elements through the Pentateuch, Clines discerns a telling pattern:

> [T]he divine promises, while frequently alluded to in each of its forms throughout the Pentateuch, presents one or other of its elements more prominently in the successive books of the Pentateuch . . . in Genesis it is the promise of progeny that has predominated, in Exodus and Leviticus the promise of the

---

1. Alexander, *From Paradise*, 187–89.
2. Williamson, *Abraham, Israel, and the Nations*, 134.

relationship of Yahweh and Israel, and in Numbers and Deuteronomy the promise of the land.³

By the close of the Pentateuch, not only is the promise of land prominent, the necessity of obedience in relation to the land crystallizes as a central theme in Deuteronomy.⁴ The linking of the land promise to covenantal obedience and loyalty is reflected in the final didactic statement of Ps 105:45.⁵

In the body of the psalm (Ps 105:7–44), the psalmist affirms the trustworthiness of the land promise by validating two propositions about Yahweh: (1) he is loyal to his covenant promises (Ps 105:7–11, 42–44), and (2) he is sovereign (Ps 105:1–5, 7, 14, 16, 19, 24–25, 27–37, 39–41). The rhetorical shaping of the historical narrative emphasizes Yahweh's role in guiding history toward the fulfillment of the land promise. The concluding section includes a Deuteronomic description of the conquest (Ps 105:44; cf. Deut 19:1–2) culminating in a didactic statement regarding the necessity of keeping the Mosaic law (חקים and תורות).

This study has drawn together a rhetorically-informed reading of the psalm as well as an overview of the two covenants in order to discern the nature of the intertextual activity in the psalm. There are three allusions to the Mosaic covenant that create a rhetorical effect designed to connect the two covenants in a way that is theologically meaningful to the postexilic community. The postexilic historical situation presented a challenging dilemma for the descendants of Abraham. The promise of land, despite the existential threat of the exile, remained effective since resettlement was well underway. However, the failure of the Davidic monarchy, the presence of foreign oppressors, and questions regarding national identity created a dissonant situation that belied the Abrahamic promises and the national restoration predicted in Deut 30:1–10 (see also Lev 26:40–46).

The dilemma facing the psalmist was how to reconcile the return to the land with the present brokenness, especially in light of the patriarchal promises and Yahweh's covenant trustworthiness and sovereignty. His solution was found in a postexilic emphasis on covenant renewal (see Neh 8–10). Though there is no textual datum that connects Ps 105 to the events

---

3. Clines, *Theme of the Pentateuch*, 64–65.

4. Per Nelson, the land in Deuteronomy is a good gift to the ancestors, the place where the law is to be observed in order to build a righteous nation, and a place of security. Occupation of the land is conditioned on obedience. Nelson provides a list of passages in Deuteronomy that deal with the land. Nelson, *Deuteronomy*, 11.

5. See McKelvey's comment on the Deuteronomic theme of Torah-obedience and the land in Ps 105:45. McKelvey, *Moses, David*, 233–34. See also Williamson, *Sealed with an Oath*, 111–15.

of Ezra-Nehemiah, it is tenable that the composer of this psalm would have been aware of something as momentous as a national movement toward covenant renewal and the restoration of religious institutions. Being aware of covenant renewal, the psalmist was able to relate the Abrahamic promise to the Mosaic covenant in a theologically coherent manner.

The psalmist's thought process was an elegant way to address the dilemma facing the postexilic community. The psalmist drew a key distinction between being in the land and being under Yahweh's blessing. In the Pentateuch, the promise of land was fulfilled when the Moab generation enters Canaan, but their prosperity in the land is predicated on obedience to the Mosaic covenant's law, which was an expression of Israel's covenant love. In a similar way, the postexilic community was in the land, which fulfilled the promise of land, but they could only experience national blessing when they renew the Mosaic covenant and obey the law.

Thus, covenant renewal is the key to understanding Ps 105:45. The psalmist is not simply calling for obedience to an abstract moral-ethical code of conduct. He is calling the people to remember the covenant and be loyal by obeying Yahweh's law. As discussed above, the law is not divorced from covenant in the postexilic period, for it continues to be the means by which covenant loyalty is lived in practical terms.[6] Rhetorically, this is what the psalmist addresses by alluding to Exod 6:2–8 in v. 7, which evokes the inter-covenantal relationship between the promise of land in Gen 17 and the Sinai covenant. The second allusion to Deut 7:9/Exod 20:6 calls to mind that Yahweh's faithfulness to the Mosaic covenant is only for those who love Yahweh and obey his commandments. For the postexilic remnant, this is a stark reminder that they had failed to keep the Mosaic law. This allusion is complemented by the allusion to the Mosaic covenant in v. 45, which uses torah terminology to evoke the obligatory element of obedience to the law. The conclusion to the song leaves the community with hope based on the possibility of covenant restoration and a restoration of life under Yahweh's covenantal love and blessing.

In the covenant theology of Ps 105, the Abrahamic covenant is the seminal covenant consisting of the patriarchal promises that form the foundation for Israel as a people. Israel's aspirations for national significance, a large population, a meaningful relationship with the nations, and a homeland are all rooted in the divine programmatic promises made to Abraham and confirmed to the patriarchs. Though the Abraham narrative entails

---

6. See McCarthy, "Covenant and Law," 25–44; Linington, "Term *berît*," 671–93. McCarthy and Linington counter the view that the law had become divorced from covenant as an abstract code of conduct in the postexilic period. Sperling, "Rethinking Covenant," 50–73.

conditional elements in the development of the Abrahamic covenant, the psalmist views the promises as irrevocable based on Yahweh's divine oath and unimpeachable covenant loyalty.

As for the Mosaic covenant, it is the logical and complementary sequel to the Abrahamic promises. This view is consistent with the Mosaic covenant's constitutive function and the nation-defining nature of the Mosaic law. In the psalmist's song, this general understanding of the two covenants is elegantly applied to the perplexing question of the land promise in light of the postexilic setting. The psalmist understands that the patriarchal promise only guarantees land but does not constitute a "great nation." The manner in which the nation would inhabit the land is defined by the terms of the Mosaic covenant. Thus, the psalmist succeeds in coherently reconciling the certainty of the Abrahamic promise of land with the Mosaic covenant's promise of blessings in relation to Israel's covenant loyalty and obedience.

IMPLICATIONS FOR FURTHER STUDY

As with any study such as this, the scope did not allow for comprehensive or exhaustive discussion on related topics of interest. In other cases, the investigation surfaced new questions that point to promising areas of research. The following is a brief overview of issues and questions that would be worth further study.

This research has demonstrated that it is imprecise to characterize the Abrahamic covenant as an unconditional grant and the Mosaic covenant as a conditional treaty. There are obligatory elements that are at the heart of the covenant Yahweh institutes with Abraham, just as there are promissory elements that are a part of the Mosaic covenant. The psalmist's understanding of the two covenants indicates considerable continuity between the two covenants. The apparent tension between the irrevocable promise of land and the requirement of covenant loyalty and love expressed in obedience is not an irreconcilable one. It is fascinating that the psalmist was able to understand the difference between being in the land and being in the land under divine sanction and blessing. Despite the apparent effectiveness of the Abrahamic land promise, the postexilic milieu clearly fell short of the restored state anticipated in the Mosaic covenant (e.g., Deut 30:1–10; Lev 26:40–45) and even in the latter Prophets (e.g., Isa 40–66 Jer 29; Ezek 34).

Though the tension between the two covenants had traditionally been depicted as the incompatibility of unconditional and conditional covenants, this study suggests that this is an insufficient way of approaching the issue. The relationship between the covenants is complex and the simplistic categorization of a covenant as either wholly unconditional or conditional is not helpful. In this sense, Averbeck's approach to this issue is promising. Averbeck characterizes each major biblical covenant as having both obligatory and promissory aspects with each covenant expressing these aspects to varying degrees based on the covenant's form and function as well as historical and canonical context.[7] In other words, each biblical covenant entails "permanent promise and ongoing obligation."[8]

It is the hope of this writer that this work has demonstrated that the study of the biblical covenants continues to be relevant and fruitful. Further research in this area has the potential to help scholars who study the covenants through the lenses of systematic and biblical theology. The recent development of new theological approaches, such as Progressive Covenantalism shows that delineating the relationship between the Abrahamic and Mosaic covenants is still a relevant endeavor.

This study did not address Ps 106 due to the exigencies of scope and length. However, Ps 106 was paired with Ps 105 by the editor(s) of the Psalter for good reason. The two psalms function as "twin psalms" (*Zwillingspsalmen*) in that both are historical psalms that cover similar historical events. However, Ps 106 is the darker complement to the historical perspective of Ps 105. Psalm 105 focuses positively on Yahweh's role while conspicuously avoiding the failure of the people. Psalm 106, on the other hand, is negative in its depiction of the people and their repeated failures. Psalm 106 references an unnamed covenant (Ps 106:45) as the basis for Yahweh's restoration of the people in spite of a history of unfaithfulness. Further study on the identity of this covenant and the nature of the psalmist's rhetorical use of the covenant would provide additional insights into the postexilic covenant theology of the Jewish remnant.

In addition to intertextual literary devices, the psalmist makes use of theologically significant terms, such as "chosen," "anointed," and "servant," in innovative ways to accentuate continuities between Abraham's descendants and defining figures, such as Moses and David. In particular, the term "chosen" is used as a means of expressing election in a covenant context (e.g., Ps 105:6, 43).[9] An in-depth study of the relationship between covenantally significant terms, such as "chosen" and "servant," would be enlightening. A study that traces the significance of these terms over the course of the OT canon would provide valuable information for future inter-covenantal studies.

---

7. Averbeck, "Old Testament Treaties," 17–18.
8. Averbeck, "Old Testament Treaties," 18.
9. Rendtorff, *Covenant Formula*, 3, 9, 39, 67–68.

Since Neh 9–10 features a historical narrative that parallels the historical account in Ps 105, an intertextual study of the covenant references and their rhetorical function in Neh 9 would be an intriguing complement to this study. In fact, the notable parallels between Ps 105 and Neh 9 make an intertextual study of the relationship between these two texts a promising investigation in its own right.

From a broader perspective, it would be interesting to do a theological study of the new covenant as the ultimate answer to the dilemma facing the postexilic covenant community. As the replacement for the Mosaic covenant, the new covenant is the anticipated answer to the issues facing the psalmist and his postexilic community. The new covenant also represents the culmination of God's covenantal design in history. Delving into the inauguration of the new covenant in the NT, it would be fascinating to compare the Christian understanding of the covenants in the NT with the covenant theology expressed in Ps 105. Could a postexilic song about the Abrahamic and Mosaic covenants lead to fresh insights about the new covenant and the covenant theology of the NT writers?

CONCLUDING THOUGHTS

Hearing the psalmist sing of the covenants inspires fresh reflection on the relationship between divine promise and human obligation. The traditional understanding of unconditionality and conditionality in divine covenants does not do justice to the covenantal dynamics reflected in Ps 105. A more nuanced understanding of irrevocable promise and ongoing obligation can shed light on the relationship between grace and law as well as the law in relation to the Gospel. Since Jesus affirmed the goodness of the law and fulfilled it perfectly, what are the implications for God's new covenant people? On a related note, what is the significance of the law in the NT era?

On a practical level, such discussions can advance conversations about the nature of spiritual formation and sanctification in the NT era. Seeing the church in light of the postexilic congregation of the psalmist can be helpful in grasping the nature of God's saving grace and obedience to Jesus' commands. A reexamination of divine covenantal love and human obedience to the law can help in developing a better picture of a church that keeps the Great Commandment—a new covenant community that loves God, loves all neighbors, experiences divine blessing, and blesses the nations. Just as the psalmist used the past as prelude in calling the postexilic remnant to covenant renewal and obedience, perhaps the psalmist still speaks to God's people today. Given the challenges facing the church today, a renewed vision for keeping covenant is relevant and timely in considering anew what it means to be defined by grace, embody righteousness, and act justly in accordance with God's good law.

Appendix A
Author's Translation of Psalm 105 [MT]

THIS ENGLISH RENDERING GIVES the reader a sense of the Hebrew syntax, poetic shape, and the translation work that accompanies the exegetical and rhetorical analysis featured in this study. The general approach reflected here emphasizes a straightforward rendering of the Hebrew over a dynamic, aesthetically-refined reading. The use of italics in the translation reflects this writer's use of an English word or expression that smooths a Hebrew idiom or expression that might read awkwardly in English. The Hebrew text and text critical notes are from the BHS and its apparatus.[1]

---

1. *Biblia Hebraica Stuttgartensia,* edited by Karl Elliger and Wilhelm Rudolph, Fifth Revised Edition, edited by Adrian Schenker, © 1977 and 1997 Deutsche Bibelgesellschaft, Stuttgart. Used by permission.

105:1–6

1 Give thanks to the LORD! Call on his name! Make known his deeds among the nations.	1 הוֹדוּ לַיהוָה קִרְאוּ בִּשְׁמוֹ הוֹדִיעוּ בָעַמִּים עֲלִילוֹתָיו:
2 Sing to him! Play music to him! Speak of all his wonders!	2 שִׁירוּ־לוֹ זַמְּרוּ־לוֹ שִׂיחוּ בְּכָל־נִפְלְאוֹתָיו:
3 Praise his holy name! Let the hearts of those who seek the LORD rejoice!	3 הִתְהַלְלוּ בְּשֵׁם קָדְשׁוֹ יִשְׂמַח לֵב מְבַקְשֵׁי יְהוָה:
4 Seek the LORD and his strength.[2] Seek his face continually.	4 דִּרְשׁוּ יְהוָה וְעֻזּוֹ בַּקְּשׁוּ פָנָיו תָּמִיד:
5 Recall the wonders that he did, his miracles and the judgments he decreed.	5 זִכְרוּ נִפְלְאוֹתָיו אֲשֶׁר־עָשָׂה מֹפְתָיו וּמִשְׁפְּטֵי־פִיו:
6 Seed of Abraham[3], his servant[4], sons of Jacob, his chosen[5] ones.	6 זֶרַע אַבְרָהָם עַבְדּוֹ בְּנֵי יַעֲקֹב בְּחִירָיו:

    2. The LXX (and also Syriac) reads "be strengthened" (καὶ κραταιώθητε; 2p pl. aorist pass. imperative). The LXX is likely emending the noun + 3p sg. pronominal suffix, עֻזּוֹ, to an imperative verb since this is consistent with the surrounding imperative verb forms that characterize the hymnic exhortations in vv. 1–6. However, only the LXX and Syriac attest to this reading so the MSS evidence favors the MT reading. Allen reads "his might," which coheres with the depiction of Yahweh as sovereign and capable in this psalm. Allen, *Psalms 101–150*, 37n4. See also Hossfeld and Zenger, *Psalms 3*, 64.

    3. Several MSS, especially for 1 Chr 16:13, have "Israel" in place of "Abraham." Since Ps 105 features Abraham and the Abrahamic covenant in a rhetorically significant way, this is likely the psalmist's adaptation of an earlier hymnic passage for the given composition.

    4. 11QPsa and the LXX have the pl. (עבדיו), but v. 42 indicates the singular is preferred here. See Allen, *Psalms 101–150*, 37. The plural refers to descendants and is also parallel with "chosen ones." Ross, *Commentary*, 258n3.

    5. In addition to the two MSS in the apparatus, 11QPsa also attests to the sg here, used as a reference to Jacob. V. 43 supports the plural in the MT, as does the overall theme of Israel's election, which is rooted in the patriarchal promise of the land. Allen, *Psalms 101–150*, 37.

105:7-11

7 He[6] is the LORD our God, his judgments are in all the earth. 8 He always remembers his covenant, the word he commanded to a thousand generations, 9 which he made with Abraham[7], his sworn promise to Isaac,[8] 10 He confirmed it[9] to Jacob as a decree, an everlasting covenant for Israel;[10] 11 saying,[11] "To you[12] I will give the land[13] of Canaan, as the share of your inheritance.[14]"	7 הוּא יְהוָה אֱלֹהֵינוּ בְּכָל־הָאָרֶץ מִשְׁפָּטָיו׃ 8 זָכַר לְעוֹלָם בְּרִיתוֹ דָּבָר צִוָּה לְאֶלֶף דּוֹר׃ 9 אֲשֶׁר כָּרַת אֶת־אַבְרָהָם וּשְׁבוּעָתוֹ לְיִשְׂחָק׃ 10 וַיַּעֲמִידֶהָ לְיַעֲקֹב לְחֹק לְיִשְׂרָאֵל בְּרִית עוֹלָם׃ 11 לֵאמֹר לְךָ אֶתֵּן אֶת־אֶרֶץ־כְּנָעַן חֶבֶל נַחֲלַתְכֶם׃

6. The causal conjunction כי is found in 11QPsa frag. E. Dahood starts v. 7 with "For he . . . " Dahood, *Psalms III*, 53.

7. DSS (11QPsa frag. E) reads עם אברהם "people of Abraham" instead of את אברהם "to Abraham." The external evidence for the DSS reading is lacking. In light of the use of את in v. 42 and since the MT is the *lectio difficilior*, the MT is the preferred reading. Dahood, *Psalms III*, 54.

8. Some MSS, the Cairo Genizah, and 1 Chr 16:16 read ליצחק instead of לישחק. This is a variant spelling for Isaac, Abraham's son and patriarch. See Koehler et al., HALOT, 1:428, 442.

9. In v. 10 Harman notes that the verb form here is hapax legomenon. The psalmist uses the hiphil of עמד (lit. "to cause to stand"), not the expected קום (e.g., הקמתי את־בריתי; Gen 6:18). Harman, *Psalms*, 754n6.

10. The LXX (καὶ τῷ Ισραηλ) and some MSS read ולישראל ("and to Israel") instead of the MT's לישראל ("to Israel"). The syntax of the MT, however, carries the sense of an asyndetic sequence in which the conjunctive *waw* is unnecessary. It is likely that the LXX and some MSS reflect the use of the conjunction for clarification and to maintain a parallel with the preceding verse (v. 9) where *waw* is used between two verbal clauses. The MT remains the *lectio difficilior* and the preferred variant.

11. Several MSS omit לאמר "saying." Some posit that this may have been a later gloss added to emphasize the words of the original promise. See Kraus, *Psalms 60-150*, 307n11f and Anderson, *Psalms 73-150*, 729. The Greek translation also attests to לאמר with the use of λέγων. Ross, *Commentary*, 258n6.

12. The DSS 11QPsa frag. E reads לכם "to you (pl.)" instead of the MT's לך "to you (sg.)." This is likely a late emendation influenced by the 2p m. pl. suffix found on נַחֲלַתְכֶם ("your inheritance") at the end of the verse. The MT is the *lectio difficilior*. In addition, Dahood notes that biblical poets could use both singular and plural forms when referring collectively to a particular referent. Dahood, *Psalms III*, 54. This shift between singular and plural (cf. v. 6) also fits the theme of the psalm where the promise to Abraham and the patriarchs is extended to the people (corporate identification). Allen, *Psalms 101-150*, 37n11b. These factors, along with the paucity of external attestation for the variant reading, support the MT.

13. A few MSS and 1 Chr 16:18 omit the direct object marker את. However, external evidence favors maintaining the MT reading. Tov sees the omission of the direct object marker in 1 Chr 16:18 as a linguistic-stylistic change that may or may not have been done consciously. Tov, *Textual Criticism*, 258–60. Though omission or inclusion makes little difference, the MT is the likely original reading.

14. The Syr. Peshitta (codex Ambrosianus) reads a 3p pl. suffix on נחלה ("their inheritance"), instead of the MT's 2p pl. suffix נַחֲלַתְכֶם ("your [pl.] inheritance"). The context supports the MT reading since נַחֲלַתְכֶם occurs in a quotation directly addressing Abraham and the patriarchs. The Syriac may reflect an attempt to specify the patriarchs as the referent, hence "their inheritance." The context and the external evidence support the MT.

105:12–15

12 When they were few in number, just a few sojourners in it, 13 they wandered from nation to nation, from one kingdom to another. 14 He did not allow anyone to oppress them, he reproved kings for them. 15 "Do not touch my anointed ones and do not cause harm to my prophets."	12 בִּהְיוֹתָם מְתֵי מִסְפָּר כִּמְעַט וְגָרִים בָּהּ׃ 13 וַיִּתְהַלְּכוּ מִגּוֹי אֶל־גּוֹי מִמַּמְלָכָה אֶל־עַם אַחֵר׃ 14 לֹא־הִנִּיחַ אָדָם לְעָשְׁקָם וַיּוֹכַח עֲלֵיהֶם מְלָכִים׃ 15 אַל־תִּגְּעוּ בִמְשִׁיחָי וְלִנְבִיאַי אַל־תָּרֵעוּ׃

105:16-25

16 He called a famine upon the land, he wiped out all sources of food.[15] 17 He sent a man before them, Joseph was sold as a slave. 18 A fetter afflicted his feet[16], iron *surrounded* his neck[17]. 19 Until his word came *to pass*, the word of the LORD *validated* him[18]. 20 The king sent and released him, the ruler of nations *freed* him. 21 He set him as lord of his house, the ruler of all his possessions, 22 binding[19] princes at his pleasure,[20] and he taught his *advisors* wisdom. 23 Israel came to Egypt and Jacob sojourned in the land of Ham. 24 The *LORD*[21] caused his people to bear much fruit, he made them stronger than their enemies. 25 He turned[22] their hearts to hate his people, to *mistreat* his servants.	16 וַיִּקְרָא רָעָב עַל־הָאָרֶץ כָּל־מַטֵּה־לֶחֶם שָׁבָר: 17 שָׁלַח לִפְנֵיהֶם אִישׁ לְעֶבֶד נִמְכַּר יוֹסֵף: 18 עִנּוּ בַכֶּבֶל רַגְלָיו בַּרְזֶל בָּאָה נַפְשׁוֹ: 19 עַד־עֵת בֹּא־דְבָרוֹ אִמְרַת יְהוָה צְרָפָתְהוּ: 20 שָׁלַח מֶלֶךְ וַיַּתִּירֵהוּ מֹשֵׁל עַמִּים וַיְפַתְּחֵהוּ: 21 שָׂמוֹ אָדוֹן לְבֵיתוֹ וּמֹשֵׁל בְּכָל־קִנְיָנוֹ: 22 לֶאְסֹר שָׂרָיו בְּנַפְשׁוֹ וּזְקֵנָיו יְחַכֵּם: 23 וַיָּבֹא יִשְׂרָאֵל מִצְרָיִם וְיַעֲקֹב גָּר בְּאֶרֶץ־חָם: 24 וַיֶּפֶר אֶת־עַמּוֹ מְאֹד וַיַּעֲצִמֵהוּ מִצָּרָיו: 25 הָפַךְ לִבָּם לִשְׂנֹא עַמּוֹ לְהִתְנַכֵּל בַּעֲבָדָיו:

15. The expression, "staff of bread" (מַטֵּה־לֶחֶם), is likely a metaphor for food supply based on a literal staff of bread, which was a staff with bread rings hanging on it to keep bread away from pests (cf. Lev 26:26; Ezek 4:16; 5:16; 14:13). Koehler et al., HALOT, 1:573. See also Jacobson, "Psalm 105," 790.

16. The read form (Qere) is singular רַגְלוֹ while the written form (Ketiv) is plural רַגְלָיו. Though the singular is read (Q), it is more awkward when rendered in English. Goldingay's rendering, "They subjected his foot to the fetter," is a good English translation using the singular "foot." Goldingay, *Psalms 90–150*, 201.

17. The Targum may include the preposition ב- to parallel the use of the preposition with נפש in v. 22a, but this is an unnecessary gloss. Goldingay reads נפש in light of Isa 58 and renders it "his person." Goldingay, *Psalms 90–150*, 201. Hossfeld, Kraus, and Allen render נפש as "neck." Hossfeld and Zenger, *Psalms 3*, 63; Kraus, *Psalms 60–150*, 307n18h; Allen, *Psalms 101–150*, 38n18b. The parallelism of the feet and neck being bound supports the reading of נפש as "neck."

18. The Greek reads ἐπύρωδεν ("purified"), which is consistent with the MT's צְרָפָתְהוּ. Ross, *Psalms*, 259n10.

19. The form לְיַסֵּר ("to instruct"), which is based on the LXX's τοῦ παιδεῦσαι is often used instead of the MT's לֶאְסֹר since the MT form does not fit the parallelism here. Ross, *Commentary*, 259n12. Kidner chooses "to instruct" based on the parallelism. Kidner, *Psalms 73–150*, 409.

20. There is minimal attestation (2 MSS) for the variant reading using כנפשו. Allen notes that Ezek 16:27 supports the MT. Allen, *Psalms 101–150*, 38.

21. "The LORD" is used here to clarify the subject.

22. It is possible to translate הפך without an object which would read, "their heart turned to hate . . ." The marginal reading in the New JPS Tanakh Translation, "Their heart changed," reflects this reading. Though the Qal form normally takes an object, 2 Kgs 5:26 suggests a grammatical parallel where הפך occurs as an intransitive verb (כאשר הפך־איש, "when a man turned . . ."). Thanks to Robert Chisholm for his input on this matter.

105:26–36

English	Hebrew

26 He sent Moses, his servant,
   and Aaron, the one he chose.
27 They did[23] among them words of his signs
   and his miracles[24] in the land of Ham.
28 He sent darkness and made it dark,
   and they did not[25] rebel against his word[26].
29 He turned their waters to blood,
   and caused the fish to die.
30 Frogs swarmed[27] their land
   and *even* the king's chambers.
31 He spoke and flies came,
   gnats were throughout the land.
32 He *sent* rain on them *with* hail,
   and lightning on the land.
33 He killed vines and their fig trees,
   he shattered the trees within their borders.
34 He spoke and locusts came,
   grasshoppers without number.
35 They devoured all the grass of the ground,
   and devoured the fruit of the ground.
36 He killed all the firstborn in their land,
   the *source* of all their strength.
	26 שָׁלַח מֹשֶׁה עַבְדּוֹ אַהֲרֹן אֲשֶׁר בָּחַר־בּוֹ׃
	27 שָׂמוּ־בָם דִּבְרֵי אֹתוֹתָיו וּמֹפְתִים בְּאֶרֶץ חָם׃
	28 שָׁלַח חֹשֶׁךְ וַיַּחְשִׁךְ וְלֹא־מָרוּ אֶת־דְּבָרוֹ׃
	29 הָפַךְ אֶת־מֵימֵיהֶם לְדָם וַיָּמֶת אֶת־דְּגָתָם׃
	30 שָׁרַץ אַרְצָם צְפַרְדְּעִים בְּחַדְרֵי מַלְכֵיהֶם׃
	31 אָמַר וַיָּבֹא עָרֹב כִּנִּים בְּכָל־גְּבוּלָם׃
	32 נָתַן גִּשְׁמֵיהֶם בָּרָד אֵשׁ לֶהָבוֹת בְּאַרְצָם׃
	33 וַיַּךְ גַּפְנָם וּתְאֵנָתָם וַיְשַׁבֵּר עֵץ גְּבוּלָם׃
	34 אָמַר וַיָּבֹא אַרְבֶּה וְיֶלֶק וְאֵין מִסְפָּר׃
	35 וַיֹּאכַל כָּל־עֵשֶׂב בְּאַרְצָם וַיֹּאכַל פְּרִי אַדְמָתָם׃
	36 וַיַּךְ כָּל־בְּכוֹר בְּאַרְצָם רֵאשִׁית לְכָל־אוֹנָם׃

23. MT assumes Moses and Aaron as the subject while the LXX and Syriac imply Yahweh as the subject, which is consistent with God's providential role in this part of the narrative. However, the use of דברי אתותיו seems to put the stress on Moses and Aaron as the agents by which Yahweh acts. See Allen, *Psalms 101–150*, 38–39.

24. This use of the pronominal suffix is unnecessary since the earlier suffix in אתותיו carries over. Allen, *Psalms 101–150*, 39.

25. The LXX and the Syriac omit the negative, seeing this as a reference to Pharaoh's rebellious resistance to God. Allen, *Psalms 101–150*, 39. Kraus prefers the LXX and Syriac, seeing the omission as clearing up an "absurd text." Kraus, *Psalms 60–150*, 308n280. Hossfeld views the subject as the Egyptians, who did not resist Yahweh. Hossfeld and Zenger, *Psalms 3*, 65. In light of the MT of v. 27 where Moses and Aaron are the subjects, it is reasonable to view them as the subject in v. 28b, as well.

26. The singular, דְּבָרוֹ, (Qere) is well attested by many manuscripts, as well as the Leningrad Codex, the Targums, and the Syriac. There is no consensus regarding the use of the singular דברו or the plural דבריו when translating into English. It seems that there is no significant difference in the sense of the verse. The weight of the MSS evidence favors the read form (Q).

27. The verb form שרצה attested in the DSS 11QPsa text resolves the discrepancy in gender between the feminine noun ארץ and the masculine verb form שרץ used in the MT. Per Hossfeld, this is likely a secondary emendation in relation to the MT. Hossfeld and Zenger, *Psalms 3*, 65.

105:37–41

37 He brought them out with silver and gold[28]. Not one of his tribes stumbled.	37 וַיּוֹצִיאֵם בְּכֶסֶף וְזָהָב וְאֵין בִּשְׁבָטָיו כּוֹשֵׁל׃
38 Egypt rejoiced in their departure for the dread of them (the Israelites) fell upon them.	38 שָׂמַח מִצְרַיִם בְּצֵאתָם כִּי־נָפַל פַּחְדָּם עֲלֵיהֶם׃
39 He spread a cloud to cover and fire to provide light by night.	39 פָּרַשׂ עָנָן לְמָסָךְ וְאֵשׁ לְהָאִיר לָיְלָה׃
40 They asked[29] and he caused quail to come and he satisfied them (with) bread from the heavens.	40 שָׁאַל וַיָּבֵא שְׂלָו וְלֶחֶם שָׁמַיִם יַשְׂבִּיעֵם׃
41 He opened a rock and water flowed out. A river *flowed* in the desert.	41 פָּתַח צוּר וַיָּזוּבוּ מָיִם הָלְכוּ בַּצִּיּוֹת נָהָר׃

28. A few MSS, the Syriac, and the Targums add the preposition ב- to "gold" (זהב). This is likely a secondary emendation intended to parallel the use of the preposition with "silver." The MT is the original and preferred reading.

29. The singular in the MT is most likely due to haplography (loss of ו) and the plural form שאלו ought to be used of the people's request. Kraus reads the plural form here. Kraus, *Psalms 60–150*, 308. Hossfeld sees the singular form as consistent with the surrounding context and prefers the MT. Hossfeld and Zenger, *Psalms 3*, 65. Though the singular verbs can suggest that the verb in v. 40 should also be singular (which means it is Yahweh who commands the quail to come), the plural form with Israel as the subject better fits the narrative context.

105:42–45

42 For he remembered the sacred word he decreed[30] to Abraham his servant;	42 כִּי־זָכַר אֶת־דְּבַר קָדְשׁוֹ אֶת־אַבְרָהָם עַבְדּוֹ׃
43 When he brought his people out in joy, his chosen ones with a shout[31] of jubilation;	43 וַיּוֹצִא עַמּוֹ בְשָׂשׂוֹן בְּרִנָּה אֶת־בְּחִירָיו׃
44 He gave them the lands of the nations and the fruit of the peoples' labor they possessed;	44 וַיִּתֵּן לָהֶם אַרְצוֹת גּוֹיִם וַעֲמַל לְאֻמִּים יִירָשׁוּ׃
45 So that they might keep his decrees and observe his laws[32]. Praise the Lord![33]	45 בַּעֲבוּר ׀ יִשְׁמְרוּ חֻקָּיו וְתוֹרֹתָיו יִנְצֹרוּ הַלְלוּ־יָהּ׃

30. The "he decreed" is added for stylistic clarification based on v. 8 (דבר צוה).

31. The LXX (καὶ τοὺς ἐκλεκτοὺς αὐτοῦ ἐν εὐφροσύνῃ) and the Syriac place a conjunction before the second colon. The MT colon in v. 43 can be read asyndetically and does not require the conjunction before ברנה. The LXX and Syriac likely include the copulative conjunction for clarity. The MT is preferred based on external evidence and the principle of *lectio difficilior*.

32. The LXX (τὸν νόμον) reads a singular where the MT (תורתיו) has the plural of תורה. The external evidence for the plural attests to the MT as the preferred reading here.

33. The LXX and the Syriac omit the final call to praise (הללו־יה). The LXX includes this call to praise at the very beginning of Ps 105 [LXX 104], which is found at the end of Ps 104 in the MT. Dahood proposes that the call to praise found at the end of Ps 104 (v. 35b) should actually be included at the beginning of Ps 105 (like the LXX) forming an inclusio with the final הללו־יה in the MT. Dahood, *Psalms III*, 63. Per Allen, this call to praise at the end of Ps 104 does not belong in the structure of that psalm, thus providing additional support for shifting the הללו־יה in 104:35 to the beginning of Ps 105 and creating an inclusio, as Dahood suggests. Allen, *Psalms 101–150*, 28n35a.

Appendix B
Covenant-Related Formulas

These are the major covenant-related formulas and their respective variants as identified and developed by Rendtorff in his work, *The Covenant Formula*.[2]

THE COVENANT FORMULA

> Variant A: "I will be your God" (Gen 17:7–8; Exod 6:7)
>
> Variant B: "You shall be my people" (Deut 4:20; 7:6)
>
> Variant C: "You shall be my people and I will be your God" or "I will be your God and you shall be my people" (Lev 26:12)

THE RECOGNITION FORMULA

> Basic form: "You shall know that I am YHWH your God" (Exod 6:7)

THE REMEMBRANCE FORMULA

> Basic form: "I will remember covenant" or "I have remembered covenant" (Exod 6:5; Lev 26:40, 45)

---

2. Rendtorff, *Covenant Formula*, 13–17, 47–49.

THE SELF-DECLARATION (OR SELF-INTRODUCTORY) FORMULA

Basic form: "I am YHWH" (Exod 6:2, 8; Lev 26:45)

Full form: "I am YHWH your God" (Exod 6:7; Ps 105:7)

Bibliography

Aaron, David H. *Etched in Stone: The Emergence of the Decalogue*. New York: T. & T. Clark, 2006.

Alexander, T. Desmond. *From Paradise to the Promised Land: An Introduction to the Pentateuch*. Grand Rapids: Baker Academic, 1998.

Alfaro, María Jesús Martínez. "Intertextuality: Origins and Development of the Concept." *Atlantis* 18.1–2 (1996) 268–85.

Allen, Leslie C. *Psalms 101–150*. WBC 21. Waco, TX: Word, 1983.

Altman, Amnon. *The Historical Prologue of the Hittite Vassal Treaties: An Inquiry into the Concepts of Hittite Interstate Law* Bar-Ilan Studies in Near Eastern Languages and Culture. Ramat-Gan, Israel: Bar-Ilan University Press, 2004.

———. "How Many Treaty Traditions Existed in the Ancient Near East?" In *Pax Hethitica: Studies on the Hittites in Honour of Itamar Singer*, edited by Yoram Cohen, Amir Gilan, and Jared L. Miller, 17–36. Wiesbaden: Harrassowitz, 2010.

———. *Tracing the Earliest Recorded Concepts of International Law: The Ancient Near East (2500–330 B.C.E.)*. Legal History Library. Leiden: Martinus Nijhoff, 2012.

Anderson, A. A. *The Book of Psalms: Vol. II (73–150)*. 2 vols. New Century Bible Commentary. Grand Rapids: Eerdmans, 1981.

Anderson, Bernhard W. *Contours of Old Testament Theology*. Minneapolis: Fortress, 1999.

Averbeck, Richard E. "Israel, the Jewish People, and God's Covenants." In *Israel, the Church, and the Middle East: A Biblical Response to the Current Conflict*, edited by Darrell L. Bock and Mitch Glaser, 21–37. Grand Rapids: Kregel, 2018.

———. "Old Testament Treaties and Covenants in Their Ancient Near Eastern Setting." Deerfield, IL: Trinity Evangelical Divinity School, 2016.

———. "Psalms 103 and 104." In *Interpreting the Psalms for Teaching & Preaching*, edited by Herbert W. Bateman and D. Brent Sandy, 132–48. St. Louis: Chalice, 2010.

Baden, Joel S. "The Morpho-Syntax of Genesis 12:1–3: Translation and Interpretation." *CBQ* 72.2 (2010) 223–37.

Bakhtin, Mikhail. *Problems of Dostoevsky's Poetics*. Translated by Caryl Emerson. Theory and History of Literature. Minneapolis: University of Minnesota Press, 1984.

Baltzer, Klaus. *The Covenant Formulary in Old Testament, Jewish and Early Christian Writings*. Translated by David Green. Oxford: Blackwell, 1971.

Barr, James. "Some Semantic Notes on the Covenant." In *Beiträge zur alttestamentlichen Theologie: Festschrift für Walther Zimmerli zum 70 Geburtstag*, edited by Herbert Donner, Robert Hanhart, and Rudolf Smend, 23–28. Göttingen: Vandenhoeck & Ruprecht, 1977.

Barrick, William D. "The Mosaic Covenant." *MSJ* 10.2 (1999) 213–32.

Barthes, Roland. "The Death of the Author." In *Image, Music, Text*, 142–47. New York: Hill and Wang, 1977.

———. "From Work to Text." In *Image, Music, Text*, 155–64. New York: Hill and Wang, 1977.

———. *Mythologies*. Paris: Seuil, 1957.

———. *S/Z*. Translated by Richard Miller. New York: Hill and Wang, 1974.

Bautch, Richard J. "An Appraisal of Abraham's Role in Postexilic Covenants." *CBQ* 71.1 (2009) 42–63.

———. *Glory and Power, Ritual and Relationship: The Sinai Covenant in the Postexilic Period*. Library of Hebrew Bible/Old Testament Studies. New York: T. & T. Clark, 2009.

Bautch, Richard J., and Gary N. Knoppers, eds. *Covenant in the Persian Period: From Genesis to Chronicles*. Winona Lake, IN: Eisenbrauns, 2015.

Beale, G. K. *The Use of Daniel in Jewish Apocalyptic Literature and in the Revelation of St. John*. Lanham, MD: University Press of America, 1984.

Beckman, Gary M. *Hittite Diplomatic Texts*. 2nd ed. SBL: Writings from the Ancient World 7. Atlanta: Scholars Press, 1999.

Bellinger, W. H. Jr. "The Psalms, Covenant, and the Persian Period." In *Covenant in the Persian Period: From Genesis to Chronicles*, edited by Richard J. Bautch and Gary N. Knoppers, 309–23. Winona Lake, IN: Eisenbrauns, 2015.

Ben-Porat, Ziva. "The Poetics of Literary Allusion." *A Journal for Descriptive Poetics and Theory of Literature* 1 (1976) 105–28.

Ben-Porath, Ziva. "The Poetics of Allusion." PhD diss., University of California, Berkeley, 1973.

Blaising, Craig A. "A Critique of Gentry and Wellum's *Kingdom through Covenant*: A Hermeneutical-Theological Response." *MSJ* 26.1 (2015) 111–27.

Blaising, Craig A., and Darrell L. Bock. *Progressive Dispensationalism*. Wheaton, IL: BridgePoint, 1993.

Blenkinsopp, Joseph. *Ezra–Nehemiah: A Commentary*. OTL. Philadelphia: Westminster, 1988.

Bloom, Harold. *The Anxiety of Influence: A Theory of Poetry*. 2nd ed. New York: Oxford University Press, 1997.

———. *A Map of Misreading*. New York: Oxford University Press, 2003.

Bock, Darrell L. "A Critique of Gentry and Wellum's *Kingdom through Covenant*: A New Testament Perspective." *MSJ* 26.1 (2015) 139–45.

Boda, Mark J. *Praying the Tradition: The Origin and the Use of Tradition in Nehemiah 9*. Beihefte zur Zeitschrift für die Alttestamentliche Wissenschaft. Berlin: Walter de Gruyter, 1999.

Botterweck, G. Johannes, and Helmer Ringgren, eds. *Theological Dictionary of the Old Testament*. 14 vols. Translated by Geoffrey W. Bromiley et al. Grand Rapids: Eerdmans, 1974–2004.

Brack, Jonathan M., and Jared S. Oliphant. "Questioning the Progress in Progressive Covenantalism: A Review of Gentry and Wellum's *Kingdom through Covenant*." *WTJ* 76 (2014) 189–217.
Bright, John. *Covenant and Promise*. Philadelphia: Westminster, 1976.
Britt, Brian. "Unexpected Attachments A Literary Approach to the Term ḤSD in the Hebrew Bible." *JSOT* 27.3 (2003) 289–307.
Brooke, George J. "Psalms 105 and 106 at Qumran." *RevQ* 14.2 (1989) 267–92.
Brueggemann, Walter. *Abiding Astonishment: Psalms, Modernity, and the Making of History*. Literary Currents in Biblical Interpretation. Louisville, KY: Westminster/John Knox, 1991.
———. *Theology of the Old Testament: Testimony, Dispute, Advocacy*. Minneapolis: Fortress, 1997.
Brueggemann, Walter, and William H. Bellinger Jr. *Psalms*. NCBC. New York: Cambridge University Press, 2014.
Ceresko, Anthony R. "A Poetic Analysis of Ps 105 with Attention to Its Use of Irony." *Bib* 64.1 (1983) 20–46.
Chandler, James K. "Romantic Allusiveness." *Critical Inquiry* 8.3 (1982) 461–87.
Childs, Brevard S. "Biblical Interpretation in Ancient Israel." *JBL* 106.3 (1987) 511–13.
———. *Biblical Theology in Crisis*. Philadelphia: Westminster, 1970.
———. *Biblical Theology of the Old and New Testaments: Theological Reflection on the Christian Bible*. Minneapolis: Augsburg Fortress, 1992.
———. *The Book of Exodus: A Critical, Theological Commentary*. OTL. Philadelphia: Westminster, 1974.
———. *Old Testament Theology in a Canonical Context*. London: SCM, 1985.
Chisholm, Robert B., Jr. "Evidence from Genesis." In *A Case for Premillenialism: A New Consensus*, edited by Donald K. Campbell and Jeffrey L. Townsend, 35–54. Chicago: Moody, 1992.
———. "Unpacking Yahweh's Promise to Abram (Gensis 12:1–3): Some Linguistic Considerations." 1–22. Dallas: Unpublished Paper Delivered to the Southwest Regional Meeting of the Evangelical Theological Society, Spring 2014.
Choi, John H. *Traditions at Odds: The Reception of the Pentateuch in Biblical and Second Temple Period Literature*. Library of Hebrew Bible/Old Testament Studies. New York: T. & T. Clark, 2010.
Christensen, Duane L. *Deuteronomy 1:1—21:9*. Rev. ed. WBC 6a. Nashville: Thomas Nelson, 2001.
Clark, Herbert H., and Richard J. Gerrig. "Quotations as Demonstrations." *Language* 66.4 (1990) 764–805.
Clayton, Jay, and Eric Rothstein. "Figures in the Corpus." In *Influence and Intertextuality in Literary History*, edited by Jay Clayton and Eric Rothstein, 3–36. Madison: University of Wisconsin Press, 1991.
Clements, R. E. *Abraham and David: Genesis 15 and Its Meaning for Israelite Tradition* Studies in Biblical Theology, Second Series. Naperville, IL: A. R. Allenson, 1967.
———. *God's Chosen People: A Theological Interpretation of the Book of Deuteronomy*. London: SCM, 1968.
———. *Prophecy and Covenant*. Studies in Biblical Theology. London: SCM, 1965.
Clifford, Richard J. "Style and Purpose in Psalm 105." *Bib* 60 (1979) 420–27.
Clines, David J. A. "Nehemiah 10 as an Example of Early Jewish Biblical Exegesis." *JSOT* 21 (1981) 111–17.

———. *The Theme of the Pentateuch*. JSOTSup. Sheffield: Sheffield Academic Press, 2001.

Cohen, Elizabeth L. "Exploring Subtext Processing in Narrative Persuasion: The Role of Eudaimonic Entertainment-Use Motivation and a Supplemental Conclusion Scene." *Communication Quarterly* 64.3 (2016) 273–97.

Craigie, Peter C. *The Book of Deuteronomy*. NICOT. Grand Rapids: Eerdmans, 1976.

Cross, Frank Moore. "Kinship and Covenant in Ancient Israel." In *From Epic to Canon*, 3–21. Baltimore: Johns Hopkins University Press, 1998.

Culler, Jonathan. *The Pursuit of Signs: Semiotics, Literature, Deconstruction. An Augmented Edition*. Ithaca, NY: Cornell University Press, 2001.

Dahood, Mitchell. *Psalms III (101–150)*. 3 vols. AB 17a. Garden City, NY: Doubleday, 1966.

Danto, Arthur C. *Analytical Philosophy of History*. Cambridge: Cambridge University Press, 1965.

Davis, Dale Ralph. "Rebellion, Presence, and Covenant: A Study in Exodus 32–34." *WTJ* 44 (1982) 71–87.

deClaissé-Walford, Nancy L. *Reading from the Beginning: The Shaping of the Hebrew Psalter*. Macon, GA: Mercer University Press, 1997.

Derrida, Jacques. *Positions*. Translated by Alan Bass. Chicago: University of Chicago Press, 1981.

Dion, Paul-Eugène. "YHWH as Storm-god and Sun-god: The Double Legacy of Egypt and Canaan as Reflected in Psalm 104." *ZAW* 103.1 (1991) 43–71.

Dozeman, Thomas B. "Inner-biblical Interpretation of Yahweh's Gracious and Compassionate Character." *JBL* 108.2 (1989) 207–23.

Draisma, Sipke. *Intertextuality in Biblical Writings: Essays in Honour of Bas van Iersel*. Kampen: Uitgeversmaatschappij J.H. Kok, 1989.

Duggan, Michael W. *The Covenant Renewal in Ezra–Nehemiah (Neh 7:72b—10:40): An Exegetical, Literary, and Theological Study*. Dissertation series/SBL. Atlanta: Society of Biblical Literature, 2001.

Dumbrell, William J. *Covenant and Creation: A Theology of Old Testament Covenants*. Nashville: Thomas Nelson, 1984.

Eichrodt, Walther. "Covenant and Law." *Int* 20.3 (1966) 302–21.

———. *Theology of the Old Testament*. Vol. 1. Translated by John A. Baker. OTL. London: SCM, 1961.

Eisenstadt, S. N. "The Format of Jewish History: Some Reflections on Weber's Ancient Judaism: Transformations in the Second Temple Era and the Subsequent Course of Jewish History. Part II." *Modern Judaism* 1.2 (1981) 217–34.

Eising, Hermann. "זכר." In *TDOT* 4:64–82.

Elam, Helen R. "Textuality." In *The New Princeton Encyclopedia of Poetry and Poetics*, edited by Alex Preminger and T. V. F. Brogan, 1276–77. Princeton: Princeton University Press, 1993.

Emanuel, David. *From Bards to Biblical Exegetes: A Close Reading and Intertextual Analysis of Selected Exodus Psalms*. Eugene, OR: Pickwick, 2012.

Enns, Peter. "חק." In *NIDOTTE* 2:250–51.

———. "מצוה." In *NIDOTTE* 2:1070–71.

———. "משפט." In *NIDOTTE* 2:1142–44.

———. "עדות." In *NIDOTTE* 3:328–29.

———. "The Law of God." In *NIDOTTE* 4:893–900.

Eslinger, Lyle M. "Hosea 12:5a and Genesis 32:29: A Study in Inner Biblical Exegesis." *JSOT* 18 (1980) 91–99.

———. "Inner-Biblical Exegesis and Inner-biblical Allusion: the Question of Category." *VT* 42.1 (1992) 47–58.

Falk, Ze'ev W. "Hebrew Legal Terms." *JSS* 5.4 (1960) 350–54.

———. "Hebrew Legal Terms: II." *JSS* 12.2 (1967) 241–44.

———. "Hebrew Legal Terms: III." *JSS* 14.1 (1969) 39–44.

Fensham, F. Charles. *The Books of Ezra and Nehemiah*. NICOT. Grand Rapids: Eerdmans, 1982.

———. "Neh. 9 and Pss. 105, 106, 135 and 136: Post-exilic Historical Traditions in Poetic Form." *JNSL* 9 (1981) 35–51.

Ferda, Tucker S. "Reason to Weep: Isaiah 52 and the Subtext of Luke's Triumphal Entry." *JTS* 66.1 (2015) 28–60.

Fewell, Danna Nolan, ed. *Reading between Texts: Intertextuality and the Hebrew Bible*. Literary Currents in Biblical Interpretation. Louisville, KY: Westminster/John Knox, 1992.

Fishbane, Michael A. *Biblical Interpretation in Ancient Israel*. Oxford: Clarendon, 1985.

———. "Revelation and Tradition: Aspects of Inner-Biblical Exegesis." *JBL* 99.3 (1980) 343–61.

Fitzmyer, Joseph A. *The Aramaic Inscriptions of Sefire*. Rev. ed. Biblica et Orientalia. Rome: Istituto Biblico, 1995.

Freedman, David Noel. "Divine Commitment and Human Obligation: The Covenant Theme." *Int* 18.4 (1964) 419–31.

Freedman, David Noel, and David Miano. "People of the New Covenant." In *The Concept of the Covenant in the Second Temple Period*, edited by Stanley E. Porter and Jacqueline C. R. de Roo, 7–26. Boston: Brill, 2003.

Füglister, Notker. "Psalm 105 und die Väterheißung." In *Die Väter Israels: Beiträge zur Theologie der Patriarchenüberlieferungen im Alten Testament*, edited by Augustin Müller and Manfred Görg, 41–59. Stuttgart: Katholisches Bibelwerk, 1989.

Garr, W. Randall. "The Grammar and Interpretation of Exodus 6:3." *JBL* 111.3 (1992) 385–408.

Garrett, Duane A. *A Commentary on Exodus*. Kregel Exegetical Library. Grand Rapids: Kregel, 2014.

Gelston, Anthony. "Editorial Arrangement in Book IV of the Psalter." In *Genesis, Isaiah and Psalms*, edited by Katherine J. Dell et al., 165–76. Boston: Brill, 2010.

Gentry, Peter John, and Stephen J. Wellum. *Kingdom through Covenant: A Biblical-Theological Understanding of the Covenants*. Wheaton, IL: Crossway, 2012.

Gerstenberger, Erhard S. *Psalms, Part 2 and Lamentations*. FOTL. Grand Rapids: Eerdmans, 2001.

Gesenius, Wilhelm. *Gesenius' Hebrew Grammar*. Edited by E. Kautzsch. Translated by A. E. Cowley. 2nd ed. Oxford: Clarendon, 1910.

Glueck, Nelson. *Ḥesed in the Bible*. Cinncinnati: Hebrew Union College Press, 1967.

Golding, Peter. *Covenant Theology: The Key of Theology in Reformed Thought and Tradition*. Glasgow: Mentor, 2004.

Goldingay, John. *Psalms 90–150*. Vol. 3. BCOTWP. Grand Rapids: Baker, 2008.

Gosse, Bernard. "Abraham dans les Ps 105 et 47." *BZ* 54.1 (2010) 83–91.

———. "Le quatrième livre du Psautier, Psaumes 90–106, comme réponse à l'échec de la royauté Davidique." *BZ* 46.2 (2002) 239–52.

Green, Gene L. "Relevance Theory and Theological Interpretation: Thoughts on Metarepresentation." *Journal of Theological Interpretation* 4.1 (2010) 75–90.
Grogan, Geoffrey. *Psalms*. Two Horizons Old Testament Commentary. Grand Rapids: Eerdmans, 2008.
Gunkel, Hermann, and Joachim Begrich. *An Introduction to the Psalms: The Genres of the Religious Lyric of Israel*. Translated by James D. Nogalski. Mercer Library of Biblical Studies. Macon, GA: Mercer University Press, 1998.
Ha, John. *Genesis 15: A Theological Compendium of Pentateuchal History*. Berlin: Walter de Gruyter, 1989.
Hahn, Scott. *Kinship by Covenant: A Canonical Approach to the Fulfillment of God's Saving Promises*. AYBRL. New Haven, CT: Yale University Press, 2009.
Hamilton, Victor P. *The Book of Genesis: Chapters 1–17*. NICOT. Grand Rapids: Eerdmans, 1990.
———. *The Book of Genesis: Chapters 18–50*. NICOT. Grand Rapids: Eerdmans, 1995.
———. *Exodus: An Exegetical Commentary*. Grand Rapids: Baker Academic, 2011.
Haran, Menahem. "The *Berît* 'Covenant': Its Nature and Ceremonial Background." In *Tehillah le-Moshe: Biblical and Judaic Studies in Honor of Moshe Greenberg*, edited by Mordechai Cogan et al., 203–19. Winona Lake, IN: Eisenbrauns, 1997.
Harman, Allan M. *Commentary on the Psalms*. Vol. 2. Mentor Commentary. Fearn, Tain, Ross-shire, Great Britain: Mentor, 1998.
Hartley, John E. *Leviticus*. WBC 4. Dallas: Word, 1998.
Hauan, Michael James. "The Background and Meaning of Amos 5:17b." *HTR* 79 (1986) 337–48.
Hays, Richard B. *Echoes of Scripture in the Letters of Paul*. New Haven, CT: Yale University Press, 1989.
Hays, Richard B., et al., eds. *Reading the Bible Intertextually*. Waco, TX: Baylor University Press, 2009.
Hess, Richard S. "The Slaughter of the Animals in Genesis 15." In *He Swore an Oath: Biblical Themes from Genesis 12–50*, edited by Richard S. Hess, P. E. Satterthwaite, and Gordon J. Wenham, 55–65. Grand Rapids: Baker, 1994.
Hildebrandt, Theodore A. "A Song of our Father Abraham: Psalm 105." In *Perspectives on Our Father Abraham: Essays in Honor of Marvin R. Wilson*, edited by Steven A. Hunt, 44–67. Grand Rapids: Eerdmans, 2010.
Hillers, Delbert R. *Covenant: The History of a Biblical Idea*. Seminars in the History of Ideas. Baltimore: Johns Hopkins Press, 1969.
Hollander, John. *The Figure of Echo: A Mode of Allusion in Milton and After*. Berkeley, CA: University of California Press, 1981.
Holm-Nielsen, Svend. "The Exodus Traditions in Psalm 105." In *Festschrift Gillis Gerleman*, edited by Sten Hidal, Bo Johnson, Tryggve N. D. Mettinger and Stig Norin, 22–30. Leiden: Brill, 1978.
Holmgren, Fredrick Carlson. "Faithful Abraham and the 'amānâ Covenant Nehemiah 9,6—10,1." *ZAW* 104.2 (1992) 249–54.
Horton, Michael Scott. *God of Promise: Introducing Covenant Theology*. Grand Rapids: Baker, 2006.
Hossfeld, Frank-Lothar. "Eine poetische Universalgeschichte: Ps 105 im Kontext der Psalmentrias 104–106." In *Das Manna Fällt auch Heute Noch: Beiträge zur Geschichte und Theologie des Alten, Ersten Testaments*, 294–311. Freiburg: Herder, 2004.

Hossfeld, Frank-Lothar, and Erich Zenger. *Psalms 3: A Commentary on Psalms 101–150.* Translated by Linda M. Maloney. Hermeneia. Minneapolis: Fortress, 2011.

Hugenberger, Gordon P. *Marriage as a Covenant: A Study of Biblical Law and Ethics Governing Marriage, Developed from the Perspective of Malachi.* VTSup. Leiden: E. J. Brill, 1993.

Hurvitz, Avi. *A Linguistic Study of the Relationship between the Priestly Source and the Book of Ezekiel.* Paris: J Gabalda, 1982.

Irwin, William. "What Is an Allusion?" *Journal of Aesthetics and Art Criticism* 59.3 (2001) 287–97.

Jacobson, Rolf A. "Psalm 105: Chosen for God's Mission." In *The Book of Psalms,* edited by Nancy L. DeClaissé-Walford et al., 782–95. Grand Rapids: Eerdmans, 2014.

Janzen, J. Gerald. *At the Scent of Water: The Ground of Hope in the Book of Job.* Grand Rapids: Eerdmans, 2009.

Jenni, Ernst, and Claus Westermann, eds. *Theologisches Handwörterbuch zum Alten Testament.* 2 vols. Munich: Chr. Kaiser Verlag, Zürich: Theologischer Verlag, 1971–1976.

Jeppesen, Knud. "Promise and Blessing: Gen 12,1–3." *SJOT* 27.1 (2013) 32–42.

Kaiser, Walter C., Jr. "Inner Biblical Exegesis as a Model for Bridging the 'then' and 'now' Gap: Hos 12:1–6." *JETS* 28.1 (1985) 33–46.

———. *Toward an Old Testament Theology.* Grand Rapids: Zondervan, 1978.

Kalluveettil, Paul. *Declaration and Covenant: A Comprehensive Review of Covenant Formulae from the Old Testament and the Ancient Near East.* Analecta Biblica. Rome: Biblical Institute Press, 1982.

Kidner, Derek. *Psalms 73–150: A Commentary on Books III-V of the Psalms.* Vol. 2. TOTC. Downers Grove, IL: InterVarsity, 1973.

Kirkpatrick, A. F. *The Book of Psalms: Books IV and V, Psalms XC–CL.* CBSC. Cambridge: Cambridge University Press, 1901.

Kitchen, Kenneth A. "The Fall and Rise of Covenant, Law and Treaty." *TynBul* 40.1 (1989) 118–35.

———. *On the Reliability of the Old Testament.* Grand Rapids: Eerdmans, 2003.

Kitchen, Kenneth A., and Paul Lawrence. *Treaty, Law, and Covenant in the Ancient Near East.* 3 vols. Wiesbaden: Harrassowitz, 2012.

Kline, Meredith G. *The Structure of Biblical Authority.* Grand Rapids: Eerdmans, 1972.

———. *Treaty of the Great King: The Covenant Structure of Deuteronomy.* Grand Rapids: Eerdmans, 1963.

Klingler, David R. "Validity in the Identification and Interpretation of a Literary Allusion in the Hebrew Bible." PhD diss., Dallas Theological Seminary, 2010.

Knoppers, Gary N. "Ancient Near Eastern Royal Grants and the Davidic Covenant: A Parallel?" *JAOS* 116.4 (1996) 670–97.

Koehler, Ludwig, et al. *The Hebrew and Aramaic Lexicon of the Old Testament.* 2 vols. Translated by M. E. J. Richardson. Leiden: Brill, 2001.

Korošec, Viktor. *Hethitische Staatsverträge: Ein Beitrag zu ihrer juristischen Wertung* Leipziger rechtswissenschaftliche Studien. Leipzig: Theodor Weicher, 1931.

Kraus, Hans-Joachim. *Psalms 60–150: A Continental Commentary.* CC. Translated by Hilton C. Oswald. Minneapolis: Augsburg, 1989.

Kristeva, Julia. *Desire in Language: A Semiotic Approach to Literature and Art.* Translated by Thomas Gora, Alice Jardine, and Leon S. Roudiez. New York: Columbia University Press, 1980.

———. *La révolution du langage poétique; l'avant-garde à la fin du XIXe siècle, Lautréamont et Mallarmé*. Paris: Seuil, 1974.

———. "Le mot, le dialogue, et le roman." In *Semeiotikè: Recherches pour une Sémanalyse*. Paris: Éditions du Seuil, 1978.

———. "'Nous Deux' or a (Hi)story of Intertextuality." *Romantic Review* 93.1–2 (2002) 7–13.

———. *Semeiotikè: Recherches pour une Sémanalyse*. Paris: Seuil, 1978.

Kutsch, Ernst. *Verheissung und Gesetz*. Beihefte zur Zeitschrift für die alttestamentliche Wissenschaft. Berlin: de Gruyter, 1973.

Larsen, M. T. "The 'Babel/Bible' Controversy and Its Aftermath." In *Civilizations of the Ancient Near East*, edited by Jack M. Sasson, John Baines, Gary Beckman, and Karen Sydney Rubinson, 1, 95–106. New York: Charles Scribner's Sons, 1995.

Leddy, Michael. "Limits of Allusion." *British Journal of Aesthetics* 32.2 (1992) 110–22.

Lee, Archie C. C. "Genesis I and the Plagues Tradition in Psalm CV." *VT* 40 (1990) 257–63.

Leonard, Jeffery M. "Identifying Inner-Biblical Allusions: Psalm 78 as a Test Case." *JBL* 127.2 (2008) 241–65.

Levering, Matthew. *Ezra & Nehemiah*. BTCB. Grand Rapids: Brazos, 2007.

Lévi-Strauss, Claude. *The Savage Mind*. London: Weidenfeld and Nicolson, 1966.

Liedke, G. "חקק." In *THAT* 1:626–33.

Linington, Silvia. "The Term *berît* in the Old Testament. Part V, An Enquiry into the Meaning and Use of the Word in 1–2 Chronicles, Ezra and Nehemiah." *OTE* 19 (2006) 671–93.

Machacek, Gregory. "Allusion." *PMLA* 122.2 (2007) 522–36.

Malamat, Abraham. *Mari and the Bible*. Studies in the History and Culture of the Ancient Near East. Leiden: E. J. Brill, 1998.

Marttila, Marko. *Collective Reinterpretation in the Psalms: A Study of the Redaction History of the Psalter*. Forschungen zum Alten Testament 13. Tübingen: Mohr Siebeck, 2006.

Mascarenhas, Theodore. "Psalm 105: The Plagues: Darkness and Its Significance." In *Führe Mein Volk Heraus*, 79–93. Frankfurt am Main: P. Lang, 2004.

Mathews, K. A. *Genesis 11:27—50:26*. NAC. Nashville: Broadman & Holman, 2005.

Mays, James Luther. *Psalms*. Interpretation: A Bible Commentary for Teaching and Preaching. Louisville, KY: John Knox Press, 1994.

McCann, J. Clinton, Jr. "The Book of Psalms: Introduction, Commentary, and Reflections." In *NIB. Vol. IV: 1 & 2 Maccabees; Introduction to Hebrew Poetry; The Book of Job; The Book of Psalms*, edited by Leander E. Keck et al., 639–1280. Nashville: Abingdon, 1996.

McCarthy, Dennis J. "*Berit* in Old Testament History and Theology." *Bib* 53.1 (1972) 110–21.

———. "Covenant and Law in Chronicles-Nehemiah." *CBQ* 44.1 (1982) 25–44.

———. "Notes on the Love of God in Deuteronomy and the Father-Son Relationship between Yahweh and Israel." *CBQ* 27.2 (1965) 144–47.

———. *Treaty and Covenant: A Study in Form in the Ancient Oriental Documents and in the Old Testament*. Rev. ed. Analecta Biblica. Rome: Biblical Institute Press, 1978.

McConville, J. G. *Deuteronomy*. AOTC. Downers Grove, IL: InterVarsity, 2002.

McGowan, A. T. B. "In Defense of Headship Theology." In *The God of Covenant: Biblical, Theological and Contemporary Perspectives*, edited by Jamie A. Grant and Alistair I. Wilson, 178–99. Leicester: Apollos, 2005.

McKelvey, Michael G. *Moses, David and the High Kingship of Yahweh: A Canonical Study of Book IV of the Psalter*. Gorgias Dissertations. Piscataway, NJ: Gorgias, 2010.

Mendenhall, George E. "Covenant Forms in Israelite Tradition." *BA* 17.3 (1954) 50–76.

Merrill, Eugene H. *Deuteronomy*. NAC. Nashville: Broadman & Holman, 1994.

Meyers, Carol L. *Exodus*. NCBC. New York: Cambridge University Press, 2005.

Miller, Owen. "Intertextual Identity." In *Identity of the Literary Text*, edited by Mario J. Valdés and Owen J. Miller, 19–39. Toronto: University of Toronto Press, 1985.

Miller, Patrick D. "Syntax and Theology in Genesis 12:3a." *VT* 34.4 (1984) 472–76.

Moberly, R. W. L. *The Old Testament of the Old Testament: Patriarchal Narratives and Mosaic Yahwism*. Overtures to Biblical Theology. Minneapolis: Augsburg Fortress, 1992.

Moran, William L. "Ancient Near Eastern Background of the Love of God in Deuteronomy." *CBQ* 25.1 (1963) 77–87.

Morawski, Stefan. "The Basic Function of Quotation." In *Sign, Language, Culture*, edited by A. J. Greimas and Roman Jakobson, 690–705. The Hague: Mouton, 1970.

Morgan, Thaïs E. "Is There an Intertext in This Text?: Literary and Interdisciplinary Approaches to Intertextuality." *American Journal of Semiotics* 3.4 (1985) 1–40.

Mowinckel, Sigmund. "Psalms and Wisdom." In *Wisdom in Israel and in the Ancient Near East: Presented to Professor Harold Henry Rowley in Celebration of His Sixty-Fifth Birthday*, edited by Martin Noth and D. Winton Thomas, 205–24. Leiden: E. J. Brill, 1955.

———. *Psalm Studies*, Volume 2. Translated by Mark E. Biddle. History of Biblical Studies. Atlanta: SBL Press, 2014.

———. *Religion und Kultus*. Göttingen: Vandenhoeck & Ruprecht, 1953.

———. *Tetrateuch, Pentateuch, Hexateuch: Die Berichte über die Landnahme in den drei altisraelitischen Geschichtswerken*. Berlin: Alfred Töpelmann, 1964.

Naylor, Peter J. "The Language of Covenant: a Structural Analysis of the Semantic Field of *berit* in Biblical Hebrew, with Particular Reference to the Book of Genesis." PhD diss., St. Peter's College, Oxford University, 1980.

Nelson, Richard D. *Deuteronomy: A Commentary*. OTL. Louisville, KY: Westminster John Knox, 2002.

Nicholson, Ernest W. *God and His People: Covenant and Theology in the Old Testament*. Oxford: Clarendon, 1986.

Niehaus, Jeffrey Jay. "God's Covenant with Abraham." *JETS* 56.2 (2013) 249–71.

Noth, Martin. *Das System der zwölf Stämme Israels*. Darmstadt: Wissenschaftliche Buchgesellschaft, 1966.

———. *The Laws in the Pentateuch and Other Studies*. Translated by D. R. AP-Thomas. Philadelphia: Fortress, 1967.

Oden, Robert, Jr. "The Place of Covenant in the Religion of Israel." In *Ancient Israelite Religion: Essays in Honor of Frank Moore Cross*, edited by Patrick D. Miller, 429–47. Philadelphia: Fortress, 1987.

Olbricht, Thomas H. "The Rhetoric of Two Narrative Psalms 105 and 106." In *My Words Are Lovely: Studies in the Rhetoric of the Psalms*, edited by David M. Howard and Robert Louis Foster, 156–70. New York: T. & T. Clark, 2008.

Parpola, Simo, and Kazuko Watanabe. *Neo-Assyrian Treaties and Loyalty Oaths.* State Archives of Assyria 2. Helsinki: Helsinki University Press, 1988.

Passaro, Angelo. "Theological Hermeneutics and Historical Motifs in Pss 105–106." In *History and Identity*, 43–55. New York: Walter de Gruyter, 2006.

Paulien, Jon. "Criteria and the Assessment of Allusions to the Old Testament in the Book of Revelation." In *Studies in the Book of Revelation*, edited by Steve Moyise, 113–29. Edinburgh: T. & T. Clark, 2001.

———. *Decoding Revelation's Trumpets: Literary Allusions and interpretation of Revelation 8:7–12.* Berrien Springs, MI: Andrews University Press, 1988.

Perlitt, Lothar. *Bundestheologie im Alten Testament.* Neukirchen-Vluyn: Neukirchener, 1969.

Perri, Carmela. "On Alluding." *Poetics* 7.3 (1978) 289–307.

Polak, Frank H. "The Covenant at Mount Sinai in the Light of Texts from Mari." In *Sefer Moshe: The Moshe Weinfeld Jubilee Volume: Studies in the Bible and the Ancient Near East, Qumran, and Post-Biblical Judaism*, edited by Chaim Cohen, Avi Hurvitz, and Shalom M. Paul, 119–34. Winona Lake, IN: Eisenbrauns, 2004.

Rendtorff, Rolf. *The Covenant Formula: An Exegetical and Theological Investigation.* Translated by Margaret Khol. OTS. Edinburgh: T. & T. Clark, 1998.

———. "Nehemiah 9: An Important Witness of Theological Reflection." In *Tehillah le-Moshe: Biblical and Judaic Studies in Honor of Moshe Greenberg*, edited by Mordechai Cogan et al., 111–17. Winona Lake, IN: Eisenbrauns, 1997.

Rickett, Dan. "Rethinking the Place and Purpose of Genesis 13." *JSOT* 36.1 (2011) 31–53.

Riffaterre, Michael. "Interpretation and Undecidability." *New Literary History* 12.2 (1981) 227–42.

———. *Semiotics of Poetry.* Bloomington: Indiana University Press, 1978.

Robertson, O. Palmer. *The Flow of the Psalms: Discovering Their Structure and Theology.* Phillipsburg, NJ: P. & R., 2015.

Römer, Thomas. "Abraham Traditions in the Hebrew Bible Outside the Book of Genesis." In *The Book of Genesis*, 159–80. Leiden: Brill, 2012.

Ross, Allen P. *A Commentary on the Psalms.* Vol. 3. Kregel Exegetical Library. Grand Rapids: Kregel Academic & Professional, 2011.

Roudiez, Leon S. "Introduction." In *Revolution in Poetic Language.* New York: Columbia University Press, 1984.

Routledge, Robin L. "Ḥesed as Obligation: A Re-Examination." *TynBul* 46.1 (1995) 179–96.

Ruppert, Lothar. "Zur Neuinterpretation der Josefstradition in Ps 105." In *Studien zu Psalmen und Propheten*, edited by Carmen Diller, et al., 115–30. New York: Herder, 2010.

Ryrie, Charles C. *Dispensationalism Today.* Chicago: Moody, 1965.

Sarna, Nahum M. *Exodus: The Traditional Hebrew Text with the New JPS Translation.* The JPS Torah Commentary. Philadelphia: JPS, 1991.

———. *Genesis: The Traditional Hebrew Text with the New JPS Translation.* The JPS Torah Commentary. Philadelphia: JPS, 1989.

———. "Psalm 89: A Study in Inner Biblical Exegesis." In *Biblical and Other Studies*, edited by Alexander Altmann, 29–46. Cambridge, MA: Harvard University Press, 1963.

Schottroff, Willy. *Gedenken im alten Orient und im Alten Testament: Die Wurzel zākar im semitischen Sprachkreis.* Wissenschaftliche Monographien zum Alten und Neuen Testament. Neukirchen-Vluyn: Neukirchener, 1964.

Searle, John R. *Speech Acts: An Essay in the Philosophy of Language.* London: Cambridge University Press, 1969.

Seitz, Christopher. "The Call of Moses and the 'Revelation' of the Divine Name: Source-Critical Logic and Its Legacy." In *Theological Exegesis: Essays in Honor of Brevard S. Childs*, edited by Christopher R. Seitz and Kathryn Greene-McCreight, 145–61. Grand Rapids: Eerdmans, 1999.

Sohn, Seock-Tae. "'I Will Be Your God and You Will Be My People': The Origin and Background of the Covenant Formula." In *Ki Baruch Hu*, edited by Robert Chazan et al., 355–72. Winona Lake, IN: Eisenbrauns, 1999.

Sommer, Benjamin D. "Exegesis, Allusion and Intertextuality in the Hebrew Bible: A Response to Lyle Eslinger." *VT* 46.4 (1996) 479–89.

———. *A Prophet Reads Scripture: Allusion in Isaiah 40–66.* Contraversions. Palo Alto, CA: Stanford University Press, 1998.

Sperber, Dan, and Deirdre Wilson. *Relevance: Communication and Cognition.* 2nd ed. Cambridge, MA: Blackwell, 1995.

Sperling, S. David. "Rethinking Covenant in Late Biblical Books." *Bib* 70 (1989) 50–73.

Stanley, Christopher D. "The Rhetoric of Quotations: an Essay on Method." In *Early Christian interpretation of the Scriptures of Israel: Investigations and Proposals*, edited by James A. Sanders and Craig A. Evans, 44–58. Sheffield, England: Sheffield Academic Press, 1997.

Steinmann, Andrew. *Ezra and Nehemiah.* Concordia Commentary. Saint Louis: Concordia, 2010.

Sternberg, Meir. "Proteus in Quotation-Land: Mimesis and the Forms of Reported Discourse." *Poetics Today* 3.2 (1982) 107–56.

Stuart, Douglas K. *Exodus.* Vol. 2. NAC. Nashville: Broadman & Holman, 2006.

Tadmor, Hayim. "Treaty and Oath in the Ancient Near East: A Historian's Approach." In *Humanizing America's Iconic Book*, edited by Gene M. Tucker and Douglas A. Knight, 127–52. Chico, CA: Scholars Press, 1982.

Taggar-Cohen, Ada. "Biblical Covenant and Hittite *išḫiul* Reexamined." *VT* 61.3 (2011) 461–88.

Thompson, Michael. *Clothed with Christ: The Example and Teaching of Jesus in Romans 12:1—15:13.* Sheffield: JSOT, 1991.

Tigay, Jeffrey H. *Deuteronomy: The Traditional Hebrew Text with the New JPS Translation.* The JPS Torah Commentary. Philadelphia: JPS, 1996.

Tov, Emanuel. *Textual Criticism of the Hebrew Bible.* 2nd rev. ed. Minneapolis: Fortress, 2001.

Tucker, W. Dennis Jr. "Revisiting the Plagues in Psalm CV." *VT* 55.3 (2005) 401–11.

Van der Ploeg, J. P. M. "Studies in Hebrew Law (I)." *CBQ* 12.3 (1950) 248–59.

———. "Studies in Hebrew Law: Conclusions." *CBQ* 13.3 (1951) 296–307.

VanGemeren, Willem A., ed. *New International Dictionary of Old Testament Theology and Exegesis.* 5 vols. Grand Rapids: Zondervan, 1997.

Von Rad, Gerhard. "The Form Critical Problem of the Hexateuch." In *The Problem of the Hexateuch and Other Essays*, 1–78. New York: McGraw Hill, 1966.

———. *Old Testament Theology.* 2 vols. Translated by D. M. G. Salker. New York: Harper & Row, 1962–1965.

Wade, Elizabeth and Herbert H. Clark. "Reproduction and Demonstration in Quotations." *Journal of Memory and Language* 32.6 (1993) 805–19.
Wallace, Robert E. *The Narrative Effect of Book IV of the Hebrew Psalter*. Studies in Biblical Literature. New York: Peter Lang, 2007.
Waltke, Bruce K. "The Phenomenon of Conditionality within Unconditional Covenants." In *Israel's Apostasy and Restoration*, edited by Avraham Gileadi, 123–39. Grand Rapids: Baker, 1988.
———. "Superscripts, Postscripts, or Both." *JBL* 110 (1991) 583–96.
Waltke, Bruce K., and Cathi J. Fredricks. *Genesis: A Commentary*. Grand Rapids: Zondervan, 2001.
Walton, John H. *Ancient Israelite Literature in Its Cultural Context: A Survey of Parallels between Biblical and Ancient Near Eastern Texts*. Grand Rapids: Zondervan, 1989.
———. *Covenant: God's Purpose, God's Plan*. Grand Rapids: Zondervan, 1994.
Weber, Max. *Ancient Judaism*. Translated by Hans H. Gerth and Don Martindale. Glencoe, IL: Free Press, 1952.
Weeks, Noel. *Admonition and Curse: The Ancient Near Eastern Ttreaty/Covenant Form as a Problem in Inter-cultural Relationships*. JSOTSup. New York: T. & T. Clark, 2004.
Weinfeld, Moshe. "The Covenant of Grant in the Old Testament and in the Ancient Near East." *JAOS* 90.2 (1970) 184–203.
———. *Deuteronomy 1–11: A New Translation with Introduction and Commentary*. AB 5. New York: Doubleday, 1991.
———. *Deuteronomy and the Deuteronomic School*. Oxford: Clarendon, 1972.
Weiser, Artur. *The Psalms: A Commentary*. OTL. Translated by Herbert Hartwell. Philadelphia: Westminster, 1962.
Wellhausen, Julius. *Prolegomena to the History of Ancient Israel*. Translated by John S. Black and Allan Menzies. Eugene, OR: Wipf & Stock, 2003.
Wenham, Gordon J. *The Book of Leviticus*. NICOT. Grand Rapids: Eerdmans, 1979.
Westermann, Claus. *Genesis 12–36: A Continental Commentary*. CC. Translated by John J. Scullion. Minneapolis: Fortress, 1995.
———. *The Psalms: Structure, Content & Message*. Minneapolis: Augsburg Publishing House, 1980.
Whitley, Charles Francis. "Covenant and Commandment in Israel." *JNES* 22.1 (1963) 37–48.
Williamson, H. G. M. *Ezra, Nehemiah*. WBC 16. Waco, TX: Word, 1985.
Williamson, Paul R. *Abraham, Israel, and the Nations: The Patriarchal Promise and Its Covenantal Development in Genesis*. JSOTSup. Sheffield: Sheffield Academic Press, 2000.
———. "Covenant." In *Dictionary of the Old Testament: Pentateuch*, edited by David W. Baker and T. Desmond Alexander, 139–55. Downers Grove, IL: InterVarsity, 2003.
———. *Sealed with an Oath: Covenant in God's Unfolding Purpose* New Studies in Biblical Theology. Downers Grove, IL: InterVarsity, 2007.
Wilson, Deirdre. "Relevance Theory." In *The Pragmatics Encyclopedia*, edited by Louise Cummings. New York: Routledge, 2010.
Wilson, Deirdre, and Dan Sperber. *Meaning and Relevance*. New York: Cambridge University Press, 2012.
Wilson, Gerald Henry. *The Editing of the Hebrew Psalter*. Dissertation series, SBL. Chico, CA: Scholars Press, 1985.

Wimsatt, W. K., and M. C. Beardsley. "The Intentional Fallacy." *Sewanee Review* 54.3 (1946) 468–88.
Wiseman, D. J. *The Alalakh Tablets*. Occasional Publications of the British Institute of Archaeology at Ankara 2. London: British Institute of Archaeology at Ankara, 1953.
Worton, Michael, and Judith Still. *Intertextuality: Theories and Practice*. Manchester, England: Manchester University Press, 1990.
Wright, Christopher J. H. *Deuteronomy*. NICOT. Peabody, MA: Hendrickson, 1996.
Youngblood, Ronald F. "The Abrahamic Covenant: Conditional or Unconditional?" In *The Living and Active Word of God: Studies in Honor of Samuel J. Schultz*, edited by Morris Inch and Ronald Youngblood, 31–46. Winona Lake, IN: Eisenbrauns, 1983.
Zenger, Erich. "The God of Israel's Reign over the World (Psalms 90–106)." In *The God of Israel and the Nations: Studies in Isaiah and the Psalms*, edited by Norbert Lohfink and Erich Zenger, 161–90. Collegeville, MN: The Liturgical Press, 2000.
———. "Psalmenexegese und Psalterexegese: Eine Forschungsskizze." In *Composition*, 17–65. Walpole, MA: Peeters, 2010.
Zimmerli, Walther. "The History of Israelite Religion." In *Tradition and Interpretation: Essays by Members of the Society for Old Testament Study*, 351–84. Oxford: Clarendon, 1979.
———. "Zwillingspsalmen." In *Wort, Lied und Gottesspruch: Beiträge zu Psalmen und Propheten: Festschrift für Joseph Ziegler*, edited by Josef Schreiner and Joseph Ziegler, 105–13. Würzburg: Echter, 1972.

Scripture Index

OLD TESTAMENT/ HEBREW BIBLE

Genesis

1–3	15n93
1	116–17, 117n143, 155n9
1:29	116
6:18	229n9
12–22	145, 151
12	141n17, 142, 144
12:1–9	143, 146, 153
12:1–3	143, 143n23, 143n24, 144, 151, 163
12:2–3	143, 143n25, 144
12:7–8	110
12:1	143–44, 146, 147, 147n42, 167
12:2	144, 144n28
12:2a	144, 144n28
12:2c	144
12:7	143, 146
13	146
13:15	147n42
13:16	147n42
15	12, 17–18, 18n120, 23, 28, 29n199, 42, 139–40, 140n2, 140n8, 141, 141n11, 142–44, 144n28, 145, 145n31, 146, 146n36, 146n38, 147, 151, 164n55, 170, 171n85, 178, 197
15:1–6	140
15:7–21	140
15:9–17	147n42
15:9–10	146
15:13–21	122
15:18–21	106, 147, 164, 164n55
15:5	147n42
15:6	151, 208–9, 214
15:7	134, 163n54, 189–90
15:13	113
15:13a	181
15:13b	181
15:14	144n28, 181
15:17	147, 147n39
15:18	109, 109n95
17	13, 17–18, 18n120, 28, 29n199, 42- 43, 106, 139–40, 140n8, 141, 141n11, 142–45, 145n31, 146n36, 147, 148n45, 148n49, 149–51, 164, 178, 182, 182n135, 183–84, 198, 222
17:1–2	219
17:1–8	197, 201
17:4–8	147n43
17:5–6	148
17:6–8	144, 148n47
17:7–8	149, 163–64, 197–98, 235
17:10–14	148
17:19–21	148n47
17:1	141, 148, 151, 163n54, 171, 190, 190n9, 197
17:2	148
17:3	121n163
17:4	148, 148n46
17:6	110, 144n29
17:7	148–49, 164n56, 197
17:7b	197
17:8	106, 197

Genesis (continued)

17:8b	148, 197
17:9	148, 148n45
17:16	144n29, 148, 148n47
17:22	121n163
17:23	121n163
18:18–19	141, 143, 149
18:18	167
18:19	149, 149n53, 150–51, 171, 214, 219
18:25	106, 134n48
19:9—25	167
20:7	110
21:2	121n163
22	139, 140n8, 141, 141n11, 141n15, 141n17, 142–45, 146n36, 149, 149n53, 150–51
22:1–19	143
22:15–18	145, 150–51, 166, 195, 219
22:16–18	141
22:17–18	149
22:14	134
22:18	166
24:7	145n33
26	22
26:3–4	149–50
26:3–5	141n17, 143, 149
26:3	96, 145n33, 149
26:5	141, 150–51, 166, 171, 214, 219
26:24	163n54, 190
28:13	163n54, 189–90
31:45–54	169n76
35:11	148n47, 163n54
37	111
39–50	111
39:20	112
45:5–6	112
46:6–27	181
46:3	163n54
50:20	112
50:24	108–9, 145n33

Exodus

1–5	164n58
1:6–10	181
1:11–14	181
1:7	112, 114
1:11	113
1:12	181
2:23–25	181
2:24	106–9, 142, 163n54
3	153, 163, 168, 180
3:1–10	153, 163, 182
3:7–10	181
3:16–22	181
3:21–22	119
3:6	163
3:7	166n66
3:8	163–64, 164n55
3:10	166n66
4:10	103
4:22	156, 166n66
4:23	166n66
5:23	166n66
6	108, 153, 163–64, 168, 180, 182, 182n135, 182n136, 183, 189, 189n5, 197–98
6:2–8	105, 133, 153, 163–64, 181–82, 184, 189, 196–97, 200–201, 217, 220, 222
6:2–5	200
6:2–3	105, 164, 164n58, 165n62
6:3–8	109
6:3–7	134, 134n46
6:3–4	134, 163
6:5–7	164
6:5–6	200
6:6–8	163, 183, 189
6:2	164, 182, 189, 190n9, 197, 236
6:3	134n46, 164n58, 198
6:4	163–64, 164n56, 182
6:5	164, 183, 235
6:6	164, 164n56, 182
6:7	163–64, 164n56, 183–84, 189, 197, 235–36
6:8	105, 182, 189, 197, 200, 236
7:1–5	181
10:2	118

11:1–3	181
12:1–20	171n86
12:43–49	171n86
13:5	120
13:11	145n33
13:21	119
14:5	115
14:19	119
14:31	103
15	121
15:11–18	121
15:16	119
15:26	123, 137n53
16:4	119
16:12	189
16:13	119
19–24	23, 154–55, 207
19	148n45, 158, 165, 169n75
19:3–6	167
19:5–6	23, 166
19:5cd-6ab	167
19:9–25	167
19:12–13	155n6
19:21–23	168
19:3cd	167
19:4abc	167
19:5	23n158, 148n45, 166
19:5ab	167
19:6	111
19:6cd	167
19:8	169n75
19:9	168
19:12	168
19:18	155n6
20–24	142n18, 158n28
20–23	171
20	168, 171–72
20:1–17	171
20:1	161
20:2	105, 133, 133n45, 168, 189, 189n4, 196–98, 200
20:5	189
20:6	107, 107n89, 110, 135, 138, 174, 174n103, 177, 179n124, 188, 191, 191n11, 201, 203–5, 213, 217, 220, 222
20:19—23:33	154, 158
20:23—23:19	171n86
21–23	168
22:2–17	171n86
24	156, 158, 168, 169n79, 170, 170n81, 171, 176
24:1–3	168
24:4–8	169n79
24:4b-18	168
24:9–11	169n79
24:3	168–69
24:5	170n80
24:6	170
24:7	169, 170n80
24:8	170
24:11	170, 170n80
25—31:18	171
29:45–46	199
32–34	154, 157, 179n124, 203n53
32:9–10	154
32:13	104, 145n33
33–34	147n39
33:1	145n33
34	97, 154, 154n4, 155, 157–58, 171n85
34:1–6	155n6
34:6–7	174, 177, 179n124, 203, 203n53
34:11–26	171n86
34:10	155n9
37:9	119
40:34–38	119
40:19	119
40:21	119

Leviticus

1–7	171n86
11–15	171n86
11:44	189, 189n5
16–26	171n86
16	171n86
17–26	154, 158, 171, 178, 183
18:4	189
18:30	189
19:3–4	189
19:10	189
19:12	189
19:14	189

Leviticus (continued)

19:18	172
19:32	189
19:34	189
21:12	189
22:3	189
22:8	189
22:30	189
22:31	189
22:33	189
26	96, 171, 178, 182n135, 183–84, 184n141
26:27–39	178
26:29–33	178
26:33–39	178, 183
26:40–41	178
26:40–46	179, 183–84, 221
26:40–45	135, 223
26:42–45	178
26:42–44	178
26:44–45	184
26:1	189
26:9	96
26:12	184, 235
26:13	105, 168, 189
26:26	112n112, 231n15
26:40	235
26:42	97, 107, 142, 178, 183–84
26:43	183–84
26:45	107, 178, 178n122, 183, 183n140, 184, 189, 235–36
26:46	86

Numbers

3:45	189
5—10:10	154, 171
11:11	103
12:7	103
14:23	145n33
20:11	119
28–30	154, 171
28–29	171n86
32:11	108–9, 145n33

Deuteronomy

1	161
1:1–5	161
1:1	161
1:5	161
1:8	108, 145n33
1:34	145n33
3:18	122
4:1–2	150
4:37–38	173
4:2	176
4:8	86, 123, 137n53
4:20	235
4:37	212
4:40	123, 137n53
5	171
5:6–21	171n86, 172
5:9–10	191
5:6	105, 133, 168, 189, 189n4, 196–97, 200–201, 217
5:10	201
5:31	123n173
6:4–5	172
6:10–11	173
6:20–24	93n10
6:1	123n173, 150
6:4	105n77, 133n45, 172, 192n18
6:5	173–74
6:10	122, 145n33
6:18	145n33
6:23	145n33
7	191
7:7–8	109–10
7:7–15	174, 180, 201
7:7–13	174, 177, 179n124, 191
7:9–20	174n102
7:9–10	107, 110, 135, 138, 191, 201–203
7:12–13	174, 181
7:6	104, 199, 235
7:8	174, 181, 191, 202, 220
7:9	107, 107n89, 135, 174, 174n103, 188, 190, 190n10, 191, 191n11, 201, 201n44, 203–5, 213, 217, 220, 222
7:11	123, 123n173, 137n53
10:15	212

10:16	177n118
11:32	123, 137n53
12–26	154
12—26:15	171
14:2	104, 199
17:19	86, 123, 123n174, 137n53
19:1–2	122, 221
26	42
26:5–9	38, 110n101
26:5b-9	93n10
26:5	110
27—29:1	171
27:15–26	171n86
29	177–78
29:21–27	177
29:6	189
30	178
30:1–10	135, 177, 179, 183, 213, 215–16, 221, 223
30:1–3	177
30:2–3	177
30:2a-10a	177
30:4–5	177
30:6–10	177, 177n118
30:6	177
30:10	123, 137n53
31:20–21	145n33
32:9	109
33:9	123
34:4	145n33
34:5	103

Joshua

1:7	103
3–4	147n39
8:31	103
9:24	103
24	9, 9n54, 158n29, 159n33, 160, 160n34
24:2	110
24:2b	161
24:13	122
24:27	169n76

2 Samuel

1:1–16	111, 111n106
7:4–17	66
8	144n30
22:21	202
22:25	202
22:51	104n71

1 Kings

4:21	144n30
8:24–26	104n71
8:56	103
11:34	104n71
19:16	110

2 Kings

5:26	114n127, 232n22
8:19	104n71
13:23	142
17:37	86, 123n174, 193
18:12	103
19:34	104n71
22–23	xix

Isaiah

3:1	112n112
13:10	115
22:8	119
33:15	202
35:10	121n165
40–66	179, 223
40–55	95n22
45:7	115
47:5	115
51:11	121n165, 121n166
55:12	121, 121n165
58	231n17
61:1	111
64:6	202

Jeremiah

29	179, 223
29:17	112n112
31:31–34	177n118
32:39–40	177n118
33:21–22	104n71
33:26	97
34:18	146

Ezekiel

4:16	112n112, 231n15
5:16	112n112, 231n15
14:13	112n112, 231n15
16:27	231n20
34	179, 223
36:24–27	177n118
37:24	104n71

Joel

2:13ab-b	203n53

Amos

2:4	86, 123n174, 193
7:9	97
7:16	97
7:17	109

Jonah

4:2	203n53

Micah

6:8	85

Malachi

2:14	28
3:22 [MT]	86, 123n174, 193
4:4	103

Psalms

2:7–12	144n30
12:6	113n121
18	104n71
18:50	104n71
26:2	113n121
36	104n71
36:10	202
42:9	107n87
47:10 [MT]	103n69
51:3 [MT]	203
72:8–11	144n30
74:2	106
78	74n165, 99, 99n53
78:70	104n71
79:8	106
89	66, 101, 104, 105n75, 195
89:25–27	144n30
89:34–37	202
89:3	104n71
89:28	202
90	101, 195
93	101
95	101
96	101
97	101
99	101
101–106	101
104–106	98, 100n59
104	101n64, 116, 116n141, 117, 117n143, 118, 234n33
104:2–4	117
104:6–10	117
104:10–13	117
104:14–18	117
104:19–21	117
104:20–30	117
104:24–30	117
104:27–30	117
104:35	234n33

SCRIPTURE INDEX

104:35b	234n33
105–106	96, 127, 126, 126n8, 127n10, 203n54
105	43, 86–90, 91n3, 92, 92n5, 92n8, 93, 93n10, 94–95, 95n22, 96–97, 97n46, 98, 98n50, 99, 99n53, 99n55, 99n56, 100, 100n57, 100n58, 100n59, 101, 101n64, 102, 103n69, 104–5, 105n75, 106, 111, 111n110, 115–16, 116n137, 116n141, 117, 117n143, 120–32, 179, 187, 193–95, 197, 199, 203, 206–7, 211–16, 218–19, 221–22, 224–25, 228n3, 234n33
105:1–15	92, 92n8, 97–99
105:1–6	90, 102–3, 131–33, 228, 228n2
105:1–5	201, 221
105:1–2	103
105:2	103n66
105:3b	103
105:4	103
105:5–11	197
105:5	103
105:6	94, 97, 103, 110–11, 121, 130, 133, 137, 198–99, 212, 217, 224, 229n12
105:6a	97, 132
105:6b	97, 133
105:7–44	221
105:7–41	102
105:7–11	90, 102, 105, 109, 128, 131, 133–36, 142, 190, 221, 229
105:7	87, 106, 110, 111n109, 130, 134, 134n46, 135, 138, 153, 187–90, 194, 196–201, 203–5, 217, 221–22, 229n6, 236
105:7a	133, 135, 137–38, 188
105:7b	122, 135
105:8–10	108
105:8–11	87, 106, 138, 187–88, 195, 197, 200–201, 203–5, 216–17
105:8–44	137
105:8	87, 97, 103, 106–8, 120–21, 137, 153, 188, 191, 194, 201, 203–4, 215, 217, 233n30
105:8a	107–8
105:8b	107, 110, 135, 137–38, 187–88, 190, 200, 204
105:9–10	97, 108, 134
105:9	107–8, 108n90, 120, 121n163, 142, 203–4, 229n10
105:9b	107
105:10	96, 108, 108n91, 123, 207, 229n9
105:10b	108
105:11	108–9, 134, 136, 197
105:12–44	136, 138
105:12–41	131
105:12–18	90
105:12–15	102, 109, 230
105:12–13	110, 110n101
105:12	109–10
105:13	109, 121
105:14–15	110–11
105:14	110, 221
105:15	94, 97, 109–10, 198
105:16–25	102, 231
105:16	106n80, 111–12, 112n112, 221
105:16b	112n112
105:17	130, 133n42
105:18	95, 112, 114
105:18b	112n117
105:19–24	90
105:19	113, 221
105:20	111, 113
105:21–22	114
105:22	114
105:22a	231n17
105:23–38	106n80
105:23–25	114
105:23	111–12, 114, 114n126, 130, 130n31
105:24–25	221
105:24	108, 111–12, 114, 114n126
105:25–36	90
105:25–29	115, 129
105:25	114–115, 115n130, 133n42
105:26–36	102, 115, 232
105:26	115, 130, 133n42
105:27–37	221
105:27	115, 232n25
105:28	115, 117
105:28b	232n25

Psalms (continued)

105:29-30	118
105:29	111, 115, 117-18
105:30-31	117
105:30	118
105:31-40	130
105:31	116, 130
105:32-33	117
105:32	95, 116
105:33	95, 111
105:34-35	117
105:34	116, 130
105:35-37	111
105:36	115, 117
105:37-42	90
105:37-41	102, 118, 233
105:37-38	118
105:37	118-19
105:38	119
105:39-41	221
105:39	119
105:40-41	119
105:40	116, 116n136, 119, 130, 233n29
105:41	119-20
105:42-45	110, 120, 131, 200, 233
105:42-44	102, 137-38, 178, 221
105:42-43	133, 133n42, 137
105:42	87, 102, 106, 120-21, 128, 130, 137, 178, 183-84, 187, 195, 216, 228n4, 229n7
105:42a	103
105:42b	120
105:43-45	91
105:43	94, 121, 121n166, 183-84, 198, 217, 224, 228n5, 233n31
105:44-45	193
105:44	121-22, 136, 221
105:45	86-87, 91, 100, 102, 120, 122-24, 130, 135, 137-38, 153, 187-88, 192-94, 205, 205n55, 213-15, 217, 221, 221n5, 222
106	91, 97, 97n46, 99, 99n53, 100-101, 101n64, 195, 207, 224
106:32	97
106:45	202, 224
107:10	112
111:9	107n87
135	99, 99n53
136	99, 99n53
149:8	112

Proverbs

5:2	123

Daniel

9:11	103
11:14	96n36

Ezra

9:1	122
9:2	122
9:11	122

Nehemiah

1:5	206n57
1:7	103
8-10	100n58, 179, 208, 211, 221
9-10	212, 225
9:6—10:1 [Eng. 9:38]	211n86
9	86, 88, 99, 99n53, 104, 151, 199, 210-11, 211n85, 212-13, 225
9:1-5a	211n86
9:7-8	211
9:7	104, 199, 212
9:8	151, 209-10, 212, 214
9:13-14	207, 211, 211n89
9:13	86, 123n174, 141, 193, 207, 211
9:32-37	212

9:32–35	211
9:32	210
10:1 [MT]/[Eng. 9:38]	208, 208n72, 209
10:30 [MT]/[Eng.10:29]	86, 123n174, 193, 211

1 Chronicles

15–16	92–93, 100
16	92, 92n5, 92n8, 96–99, 100n57,
16:8–36	92
16:8–22	92, 97
16:13	228n3
16:13a	97
16:13b	97
16:15	97
16:16	142, 229n8
16:18	230n13
16:22	97
17:3–15	66
17:7	104n71
17:14	96n36

2 Chronicles

9:8	96n36
9:26	114
20:6	114
33:8	86, 123n174, 193

34–35	xix

NEW TESTAMENT

Matthew

22:34–39	172
22:35–40	86
27–28	142n18

Mark

12:28–34	86
12:28–31	172

Luke

10:25–28	172

Acts

3:25	142

Dead Sea Scrolls

11QPs[a] Frg. E	97, 121n163, 229n6, 229n7, 229n12
11QT[a] XXIX	97

www.ingramcontent.com/pod-product-compliance
Lightning Source LLC
Chambersburg PA
CBHW071244230426
43668CB00011B/1581